FRANCE 1848–1945
TASTE & CORRUPTION

FRANCE 1848–1945
TASTE & CORRUPTION

By
THEODORE ZELDIN

OXFORD NEW YORK TORONTO MELBOURNE
OXFORD UNIVERSITY PRESS
1980

Oxford University Press, Walton Street, Oxford OX2 6DP

OXFORD LONDON GLASGOW
NEW YORK TORONTO MELBOURNE WELLINGTON
KUALA LUMPUR SINGAPORE JAKARTA HONG KONG TOKYO
DELHI BOMBAY CALCUTTA MADRAS KARACHI
NAIROBI DAR ES SALAAM CAPE TOWN

© *Theodore Zeldin 1977, 1980*

First published in volume 2 of France 1848–1945 *by
the Clarendon Press 1977. First issued, with additional material, as an
Oxford University Press paperback, 1980*

British Library Cataloguing in Publication Data

Zeldin, Theodore
    France, 1848–1945.
    Taste and corruption
    1. France – Civilization – 1830–1900
    2. France – Civilization – 1901–
    I. Title
    944.07   DC33.6

ISBN 0-19-285100-4

*Reproduced, printed and bound in Great Britain by
Cox & Wyman Ltd, Reading*

CONTENTS

Cox & Wyman Ltd., Reading

1. Good and Bad Taste

'TASTE', said Littré in his dictionary, 'is a completely spontaneous faculty, which precedes reflection. Everybody possesses it, but it is different in everybody.' His definition raises several major puzzles. The first concerns the independence of the individual. Moralists have traditionally argued that man has the power to choose between the options facing him, between good and evil, between the beautiful and the ugly, and that the pressures around him do not ultimately determine his actions. In the course of this century, the individual was increasingly placed in an even more difficult position. On the one hand, he was assured that the rights of the individual were the Revolution's most sacred conquest and that he was therefore freer than ever; good and evil no longer had unchallenged sanctions behind them, they could no longer be easily recognised and the individual was required to think everything out for himself. On the other hand, he was assured that social and economic forces were more powerful than he was, or that he belonged inescapably to a class with identical interests, or that the effect of democracy was to level everybody down so that they became increasingly alike. Historians have usually preferred to discuss these problems as an ideological debate, instead of trying to investigate the realities alongside the beliefs. But whether people were in fact becoming more alike, whether there was now more or less room for whim and temperament, are uncertainties that need clarification.

This immediately comes up against the question of just how much history can or should explain. The popularity of biography comes in large measure from its implicit assertion that individuals have a uniqueness which transcends all the categorisations that can be made about them, and from its encouragement of the belief that individuals can make some impact on the course of events. Historians have moved increasingly away from this position and have preferred to write about causes, influences, forces and crises. There can be no doubt that, if they are viewed from a sufficient distance, all individuals can be made to fit into general patterns. But this leaves the reader with two sets of facts which are left unrelated and unreconciled. The history of the individual in the face of the forces that surround him has not been treated at a general level. Yet, after all the determinist influences had been at work, individuals did, equally certainly, behave eccentrically, make random choices, suffer accidents. There is on the one hand the world of the molecules, where combinations of atoms follow regular patterns, and the world of electrons, where apparent chaos rules. History can never produce the biography of every single individual, which would alone allow irrefutable generalisations. What it can try to do, however, is to study more carefully the relationship between the patterns and the chaos, between the universal and the particular.

Taste is a notion whose ambiguity makes it particularly suitable for this. Taste is the assertion of individuality but also the acceptance of standards. Popular taste has the appearance, as Littré claimed, of being instinctive or irrational and it can therefore be looked on as an instance of the resistance of the 'primitive' to what is imposed from above. Like love and anxiety, it is a spanner thrown into the works, which stops the machinery of society from functioning as its principles would have it, even if one can also show that society produces these spanners for its own destruction. Taste in literature and art is just one kind of taste; but it is a valuable starting-point because it is the most articulate kind. However, its significance can only be appreciated if it is placed in a wider context, among other prejudices, interests and amusements.

History is a sieve that picks up only a small portion of the debris of the past. What it salvages is, above all, books and manuscripts. But, as Goethe put it, 'of what has been done and said, only a tiny part has been written; and of what has been written, only a tiny part has been remembered'. What is honoured as literature is a 'fragment of fragments'. In this period there were perhaps thirty writers classified as being of the 'first importance', about whom it is possible to satisfy one's curiosity, and whose works have been minutely studied. There are a few hundred others who have been considered 'significant' and on whom more or less research has been undertaken. But these constitute a sort of ruling class, equivalent to the kings and parliaments of politics. The great mass of writers have been condemned to oblivion. The criteria by which they have been judged are literary; that is to say, 'taste' has decided. But exactly how some writers have become famous, how reputations have been created and broken, which writers were most read in their own day, how popularity has altered, what position writers had in society, how increasing circulation affected them, what influence critics exerted on attitudes to them: these are some of the questions that need to be answered before an adequate appreciation of historical sources is possible. However, it is not easy to supply the answers, because the history of publishing and bookselling is in its infancy, and the history of public opinion on non-political matters, of prejudice and of *idées reçues* is particularly difficult to write. There is a danger of setting up a vicious circle by arguing that literature 'reflects' society and that the answers to these problems can be found in literature itself. It is fashionable to hold that literature is not just beautiful, entertaining or revealing about human nature, but that it is the best form of history. 'Literature', one modern student of it has said, 'is the conscience of society. It expresses the social feelings of a period, at the same time as it analyses them and judges them. Like a seismograph, it registers and amplifies the shocks agitating society—currents of opinion, moods, confused aspirations, discontent, hope.'[1] It is indeed perfectly true that some novelists have left studies of society which are richer and livelier than what historians have written, but their testimony still needs to be subjected to scrutiny in the same way as all other testimony. Because historians have, until recently, avoided the intimate subjects on which novelists have concentrated, literature has been the major source of enlightenment on the deeper motivations, the ambitions, tastes and anxieties of ordinary people. One needs to look at its contribution, however, in the context of all the other material that is available. Authors inevitably express only their own opinions and their own vision: the historian finds their work most valuable as evidence of how one particular individual felt and interpreted the world around him. How 'influential' their

[1] Micheline Tison-Braun, *La Crise de l'humanisme* (1958), 1. ii. And for a more complex theory, Lucien Goldman, *Pour une sociologie du roman* (1964).

attitudes were is something that should not be judged too fast. The relation between author and reader is a complex one and cannot be unravelled in purely literary terms: the fact that literary schools—romantic, realist, symbolist and so on—succeeded each other does not mean that each generation can be given the same blanket label. The claim of novelists to speak for their generation can be dismissed almost out of hand, for one thing that is certain is that no generation spoke with a united voice. France was far too complicated a society to allow that. What needs investigation is the size of the audience the writer enjoyed, how far his ideas were accepted, but also what other ideas survived in his audience, side by side with his. Clear-cut, coherent attitudes were no more to be found in readers, than they were in writers, and every new study of a writer shows how the labels attached to him are exaggerated simplifications. What one must seek therefore is a way of understanding the incoherence and confusion of taste, which does not falsely diminish that confusion.

The first need is to look at all the books that were published, irrespective of the merits that have been attributed to them. The figures are:[1]

Number of Books Published (annual titles)

1815	3,357	1915	4,274
1830	6,739	1917	5,054
1847	5,530	1920	6,315
1848	7,234	1924	8,864
1855	8,253	1925	15,054
1860	11,905	1926	11,095
1869	12,269	1930	9,176
1870	8,831	1935	7,964
1875	14,195	1939	7,505
1880	12,414	1945	7,291
1885	12,342	1948	16,020
1890	13,643	1950	11,849
1900	13,362	1955	11,793
1910	12,615	1960	11,827
1913	14,460	1970	22,935

[1] Estivals, *La Statistique bibliographique de la France sous la monarchie au 18ᵉ siècle* (1965), 415.

Two facts are immediately striking. Books multiplied before the advent of mass literacy. The most rapid increase in book production took place in the eighteenth century, when it rose fivefold. In the nineteenth century, there were indeed more books than ever before, but the great novelty was the newspaper rather than the book, and it was to the newspaper that the newly educated masses turned. Books cannot be regarded in a simple way either as the immediate expression of democratic public opinion, or as the major influence on people's ideas. Secondly, France does not appear to be as much of a literary nation as its reputation suggests. The exceptional brilliance of French literature and the fame that the country's great writers enjoyed have given the impression that literature mattered more in France. That, paradoxically, may be due to fewer books being published there than in other countries: writers seemed less important when there were more of them. When comparative statistics were collected, France came fairly low on the list of book producers:

Number of books (titles) published

	1950	1970
France	11,849	22,935
Japan	13,009	31,249
German F.R.	14,094	45,369
U.K.	17,072	33,441

Book production took a new turn after 1950. What characterises the century before that is a relative stability. This seems to have applied to the kinds of books published as well as to their total numbers, at least from 1900, when comparable figures become available:[1]

	General	Religion	Philosophy	Science	Medicine	Applied Science
1900	40	793	192	286	1,347	890
1910	40	891	168	350	1,229	842
1920	39	422	108	178	392	1,041
1930	80	402	217	781	791	706
1938	353	558	238	424	501	1,044

[1] Brigitte Levrier, 'Sources bibliographiques et statistiques concernant la production intellectuelle en France et l'exportation 1900–1951', Mémoire présenté à l'Institut National des Techniques de la Documentation, Conservatoire National des Arts-et-Métiers (1952 typescript) (B.N. Q.4666), 9–18.

	Social Science	History & Geography	Fine Arts	Literature
1900	2,516	1,568	190	2,185
1910	1,985	1,894	516	2,397
1920	867	1,205	172	1,383
1930	735	1,765	289	3,414
1938	1,140	1,170	411	2,297

'Literature'—which includes all fiction—represented less than a quarter of the total, but it was the largest single category, and there is no doubt that this was the age of the novel. Literature's lead has been maintained since 1950; for although social science titles had quadrupled by 1970, those of literature had doubled and still remained ahead. What, unfortunately, is not clear, is how many copies of these books were sold, as opposed to how many titles were published. It is only recently that figures have been collected to show that in 1970 literature accounted for roughly half the total copies sold; school books and books for children accounted for nearly a third; scientific books for only about 5 per cent, the social sciences for perhaps 3 per cent, only a little more than religion; art for just over 1 per cent and history and geography for under 0·3 per cent.

Just how many readers of books there were is uncertain. Voltaire claimed that there were 3,000 people in the court and in the city of Paris who determined taste and decided what other people read. What Paris liked was not as decisive as all that. It has been estimated that in 1660 France had about 150,000 readers of books and in 1820 perhaps one million. There are no statistics until the opinion polls got to work. In 1960 they revealed that half the country never read a book, which came as a great shock to the intellectuals. The figures would have been worse but for the enormous growth of education: only 18 per cent of adolescents did not read books, whereas 53 per cent of adults were abstainers. The peasants and workers read least (but some workers, though poor, were avid readers), and reading was far more frequent in large cities than in rural areas and small towns. Another, fuller, survey in 1974 showed that 70 per cent of those interviewed had read at least one book in the course of the year; 8·9 per cent claimed to have read between twenty-five and fifty books and 12·6 per cent over fifty books. These high figures must be related to the doubling of the productivity of the French publishing industry since the last war, and the spread of secondary and higher education. Even so, 27 per cent of homes had no books in them.[1] The position today is that out of the thirty-eight million people aged over fifteen, who may be assumed to be capable of reading books, about five million buy and read books in sufficient quantities to make them true citizens of the republic of letters. Before 1945 half that figure would probably be over-generous.

The failure of the reading public to grow faster was due in part to the high cost of books. At the beginning of the nineteenth century, English octavo books cost 12 or 14 shillings, and duo-decimo novels as much as 5 or 6 shillings; but Sir Walter Scott published his *Lady of the Lake* at 42 shillings and sold 20,000 copies all the same. Dickens's *Pickwick* (1837) was cheap at 21 shillings. At the same time in France books were normally published at 7 fr. 50, which was the equivalent of about 6 shillings; but novels were issued in several sparsely printed volumes (fifteen to eighteen lines a page): Alexandre Dumas issued his *Les Mohicans de Paris* (1854) in nineteen volumes, so that the total cost was 142 fr. 50 (nearly £6). This system was encouraged by the *cabinets de lecture*, or public reading-rooms, which was where most people read these novels, and where many volumes meant the book could be more easily shared out. *Cabinets de lecture* began to develop during the Restoration. There were 23 of them in Paris in 1819, 198 in 1845, 183 in 1860, 146 in 1870 and 118 in 1883; and there were probably many more obscure ones omitted in this count. For a subscription of 5 francs a month one had access to a library of between 2,000 and 10,000 volumes. The largest of these *cabinets* in Paris, that of Madame Cardinal, had 160,000 volumes in 1888 (bought by Louvain after 1918 to replace their own library, destroyed by the Germans). For an extra 10 or 20 centimes per volume, a reader could take his book home. Otherwise he read in what was often a congenial social meeting-place, provided also with newspapers and journals.[2] French lending libraries were far less successful, nevertheless, than English ones. Mudie's in New Oxford Street, already in the 1850s had a stock of

[1] *Pratiques culturelles des Français* (Dec. 1974).
[2] Claude Pichois, 'Les Cabinets de lecture à Paris pendant la première moitié du XIXe siècle', *Annales* (1959), 521-34.

960,000 books (only half of them novels); it bought 2,400 copies of the third and fourth volumes of Macaulay's *History of England* and 2,000 of *The Mill on the Floss*. In France the average novel was printed in only a thousand copies.

Books became cheaper owing to two new developments. First, pirated editions appeared in large quantities, printed in Belgium, and selling at low prices. Their success was such (they sold books at about a tenth of their normal price) that the production of pirated books is said to have increased tenfold in the decade 1834–45. Balzac calculated that half a million pirated copies of his works were printed in Belgium, depriving him of as many francs in royalties. Novels began to be serialised in the newspapers from the 1840s, so that they could be read by a far wider public. The *Constitutionel* in 1844–5 increased its readership from 3,000 to 40,000 by serialising Eugène Sue's *Juif errant*. So, in 1838, Gervais Charpentier, then aged thirty-three, replied to this challenge by publishing books at 3 fr. 50, half the normal price, complete in one volume. Michel Lévy went further during the Second Empire and reduced his price to 2 francs; his rival Jacottet went down to 1 franc (about 10*d*.). In 1904 Arthème Fayard published new and illustrated novels at 95 centimes and in 1913 classics at 10 centimes. Nevertheless France failed to bring its prices down as fast as England did, for the sixpenny novel had arrived there by the 1860s. The French, accordingly, were unable to rival the English publishers' mass sales, and there is no record of anything comparable in France to the million-copy edition of Kingsley which Macmillan brought out in 1889.[1]

Regional variations in book reading remained enormous, despite the unification of the country by the railways and despite the fact that by 1882 Hachette had bookstalls at 750 stations. A survey published in 1945 revealed that many departments still spent less than 10 francs per annum per inhabitant on books, and this did not refer simply to the poor provinces of the west and centre. The highest expenditure was in the Seine and Rhône but also Haute-Garonne, Allier, Haute-Savoie and Alpes-Maritimes. Large towns on the whole did not

[1] R. D. Altick, *The English Common Reader. A Social History of the Mass Reading Public 1800–1900* (Chicago, 1957). There is no French equivalent of this book, either.

read much (Bordeaux is the main exception). These variations seem to be due to historical causes, rather than to differences in industrial or other modern developments. There exists a survey of bookshops made in 1764, which shows a geographical distribution remarkably similar to that of 1945. Book buying was to a considerable extent a traditional habit.[1] Tobacco caught on much more easily, and even today Frenchmen spend more on smoking than on books. Per head of population they spend on books only two-thirds of what the Germans and the Dutch do.

Public libraries provided negligible opportunities for reading novels or modern works. Most public libraries were taken over from bishops, parlements, monasteries or émigrés and enriched by the chance bequest of some local scholar. They were run by erudite products of the École des Chartes, biased towards medieval studies; their hours of opening suited only those with plenty of leisure. In 1968 there were still only 700 municipal libraries in France, that is to say most towns with over 15,000 inhabitants had one. Only in 1945 did the state order the creation of libraries for small communes, for which it offered an 80 per cent subsidy, but by 1960 only twenty-three departments had established them and in 1968 only forty-four. Half the rural population thus had no public library. The number of books borrowed by Frenchmen from their libraries in 1960 was still extremely small.

	France	U.S.A.	G.B.
Number of loans per inhabitant per annum	0·74	5·4	9·4

France's public library position then was thus inferior to that of England in 1900.[2]

The tastes of French readers must be guessed at, first of all, from the fragmentary evidence of sales of individual works. What is at once clear is that many of the works now regarded as among the most important gems of literature were barely noticed in their time. Baudelaire's *Fleurs du mal* (1857) sold a

[1] François de Dainville, 'La Géographie du livre en France de 1764 à 1945', *Le Courrier géographique* (Jan.–Feb. 1951), 43–52.
[2] *La Lecture publique en France. Notes et études documentaires*, No. 3459, 1 Feb. 1968; C. de Serres de Mesplès, *Les Bibliothèques publiques françaises* (Montpellier, 1933); J. Hassendorfer, *Les Bibliothèques publiques en France* (1957).

mere 1,300 copies; Verlaine's *Poètes maudits* (1884), 253. The *Nouvelle Revue française*, which printed works later greatly admired or successful, started at 120 copies an issue, reaching about 2,000 by 1914, and Gide's *Nourritures terrestres* (1897) sold only 500 copies in its first edition. In the early nineteenth century, a sale of 2,500 copies made a book exceptional, and only Paul de Kock and Victor Hugo normally reached this figure. Authors like Eugène Sue, Soulié and Janin sold about 1,500 and Alfred de Musset only 600–900. Constant's *Adolphe* (1816) sold 2,000 copies. Lamartine was the first person to break this pattern: his *Méditations* (1820) sold 20,000 in three years; but Lamennais made the standard for best-sellers wholly different when his *Paroles d'un croyant* (1834) sold 100,000 copies in a year. Renan's *Life of Jesus* (1863), after having sold 60,000 copies in five months at 7 fr. 50, reached 130,000 copies in four years, plus 100,000 copies of an abridged edition.[1]

In 1961 publishers were asked to name the best-sellers of the century from their records. The *Petit Larousse* came top with 25,000,000 copies sold since 1906. There were only a dozen books published in this century which had sold over 1,000,000. These included Saint-Exupéry's *Vol de nuit* (1931), Alain Fournier's *Le Grand Meaulnes* (1913), Marie-Anne Desmarets's *Torrents* (1951), Paul Geraldy's poems *Toi et Moi* (1921), a pious biography of Guy de Fontgalland, published by the Catholic Bonne Presse, the *Diary of Major Thompson* (1955), Irwin Shaw's *Le Bal des maudits*, F. G. Slaughter's *That None Should Die* (1942), the comic strip *Tin Tin*, the *Book of Hymns and Psalms* and Xavier de Montépin's 1,000-page sentimental novel (published in 1895) *La Porteuse de pain*. Two of Saint-Exupéry's other books had very nearly reached a million. Other great successes were *Le Maître des forges* by Georges Ohnet (1848–1918), *Cyrano de Bergerac* (1898) by Edmond Rostand and Closterman's war book, *Le Grand Cirque* (1951) (all over 900,000 copies); Hector Malot's *Sans famille* (1879), Jules Verne's *Voyage au centre de la terre* (1864), Ginette Mathiot's *Je sais cuisiner* (1932), Françoise Sagan's *Bonjour Tristesse* (1957) and Margaret Mitchell's *Gone with the Wind* (1936) (all over 800,000). Camus's most successful book *La Peste* (1947), Malraux's *La Condition humaine* (1933) and Vercors's *Silence*

[1] J. A. Neret, *Histoire illustrée de la librairie et du livre français* (1953).

de la mer (1943), had sold about the same as the comtesse de
Ségur's best-seller, *Les Malheurs de Sophie* (1859), Henry
Bordeaux's *La Neige sur les pas* (1911) and G. Acremant's *Ces
dames aux chapeaux verts* (1934) (over 700,000 copies). Another
of the comtesse de Ségur's children's books, *Les Mémoires d'un
âne* (1860), the New Testament, D. H. Lawrence's *Lady
Chatterley's Lover* (1928), Pierre Benoit's *L'Atlantide* (1919),
Bernanos's *Journal d'un curé de campagne* (1936), Victor Mar-
gueritte's *La Garçonne* (1922), Louis Hémon's *Maria Chapdelaine* (1916) and Gilbert Cesbron's *Les Saints vont en enfer* (1952)
were equal at over 600,000. Gide's most successful work was
La Symphonie pastorale (1919) (594,000 copies) which was
roughly what Zola's *Nana* (1871) and *L'Assommoir* (1876) had
each sold, as well as Jacques Prévert's *Paroles* (1947), Barbusse's
Le Feu (1916) and Armand Carrel's *L'Homme cet inconnu* (1935).
Proust's *Du côté de chez Swann* (1913) had reached 449,000,
about the same as General de Gaulle's *Memoirs* (1954-9),
Radiguet's *Le Diable au corps* (1923), Pagnol's *Marius* (1931)
and Maurice Thorez's autobiography *Fils du peuple* (1937).
Zola over three-quarters of a century had got half a dozen
books at three or four hundred thousand, but Delly and H.
Ardel had done as well with several of their books for women.[1]
It is unlikely that these names constitute a comprehensive list:
it is unlikely such a list could ever be produced, given the disappearance of so many publishers' archives. The success of the
different classics of previous centuries has yet to be studied.
But this list is useful as showing the wide variety of books that
have been popular, and that the accolade of literary merit is
only sometimes reflected in popular esteem; on the other hand
it should not be assumed that a book was 'influential' simply
because many people bought it.

The public's idea of a great writer was largely determined by
what they had read as children. When conscripts were asked
in 1966 to name five authors, Victor Hugo was mentioned
most frequently, followed by La Fontaine, Alexandre Dumas,
Molière, Alphonse Daudet, Voltaire, Saint-Exupéry, Racine
and Lamartine. Over half the authors mentioned were nineteenth-century ones. The answers of the graduates of secondary

[1] 'Les Bestsellers du siècle', *Bulletin du livre*, 15 Oct. 1961 and 15 June 1962
(nos. 65 and 81).

schools, however, were very different, and showed how general
taste lagged about fifty years behind that of the intellectual
élite. They talked instead of Descartes, Stendhal, Flaubert (who
came very low down in the popular list, perhaps because his
books had not yet been made into films), Dostoevsky, Bergson,
Proust, Péguy, Kafka and Bernanos.[1] It will be noticed that
nearly all these names were French. It is indeed only recently
that foreign books have been translated into French in any
numbers. In 1913, only 127 translations of foreign books were
published (half of them from English). Between the wars, under
the influence of such men as Gabriel Marcel, foreign books for
the first time appeared in significant quantities: 430 translations
in 1929, 834 in 1935 and over 1,000 in 1938, that is reaching
13 per cent of all books (a proportion which has been equalled,
but not exceeded since). Only the Spaniards translated more;
the French translated several times more books than the English.[2]
Translations increased the reading of Shakespeare, but also of
Charles Morgan, Enid Blyton and Rex Stout.

The 1966 survey of the reading habits of conscripts showed
that the classics interested 40 per cent of teachers and students
but only 23 per cent of clerks, 8·6 per cent of workers and 5 per
cent of peasants. Teachers and students read novels more than
other classes, but detective stories were read most by clerks
(57 per cent), workers (52 per cent) and peasants (37 per cent),
all of whom however declared (unlike the more educated
classes) that they preferred the cinema to books. The proposi-
tion that no novel was good unless it had a love story in it was
approved by 49 per cent of peasants, 41 per cent of workers,
26 per cent of clerks, 15 per cent of students and 11 per cent of
teachers; peasants and workers demanded a happy ending too.
Science fiction interested all classes except peasants and teachers.[3]

In 1934 a sixth-form master in one of Paris's best schools
analysed the books read by his pupils. Twenty-two per cent

[1] R. Escarpit, *Le Livre et le conscrit* (1966), 85–7.
[2] Julien Cain, *Le Livre français* (1972), 263–79—a mine of statistics and information. Foreign interest in French books is revealed by export statistics for 1971:
Canada and Switzerland were by far the most important buyers of them (29 m.
francs' worth each). Italy came next (12 m.), and the U.S. after it, but far behind
(7 m.). The U.K. imported less (3 m.) than the Netherlands (3·5 m.), Spain (3·7
m.) or Germany (4 m.)—*Bibliographie de la France* (1971), 680–2.
[3] Escarpit, op. cit. 48, 79.

were contemporary novels (the most popular being André Maurois, Claude Farrère, Pierre Benoit and François Mauriac; only one pupil had read Proust). Eight per cent were novels of the previous generation (particularly Alphonse Daudet, Pierre Loti, Anatole France, Émile Zola and Maupassant). Eighteen per cent were romantic works (Hugo—by far the most widely read—Vigny, Dumas, Chateaubriand, Flaubert, Sand). Four per cent were detective stories, especially Conan Doyle. Eleven per cent were adventure books (Jules Verne, Jack London, H. G. Wells, Kipling). French classics not studied at school accounted for nearly 9 per cent; contemporary English novels 4 per cent, poetry 3 per cent, the theatre 5 per cent, politics and social books 1 per cent, war books 4 per cent, history, literature and music 7 per cent, erotica 1 per cent.[1] Too many conclusions should not be drawn from this one example, but it illustrates again the divergence between popular taste and the judgement of critics and of posterity. The romantics were not necessarily read most during the romantic age. The popularity of the classics survived strongly into periods which supposedly rebelled against them: it would be worth studying the changing fortunes of different authors. At the *Comédie-Française*, Molière remained the most popular playwright—one-seventh of all performances there between 1680 and 1920 being of his plays. That made him three times more popular than Racine. Hugo's *Hernani* was performed only 102 times in its first twenty years 1830–49, but six times as often in the supposedly anti-romantic years 1867–1920. The popularity of men like Scribe and Augier during the Second Empire and Pailleron in the 1870s and 1880s deserves to be remembered.[2]

What the national statistics do not show is that there was more reading at certain periods than at others. The sales figures of one firm suggest that though the total number of titles published may have been fairly constant, the number of copies printed and sold went up in periods of prosperity and that the high point may have been reached in the years 1895–1925. The First World War gave publishing a great stimulus.

---

[1] Philippe Van Tieghem, professeur de première au lycée St. Louis, 'Ce que lisent nos élèves', *Revue universitaire* (Dec. 1934), 408–15.

[2] A. Joannidès, *La Comédie-Française de 1680 à 1920. Tableau des représentations par auteurs et par pièces* (1921).

The success of books about the war revealed that there was a large market that had still not been exploited. But there was then a crisis, brought about partly by too many publishers trying to take advantage of this, and sales dropped drastically during the 1930s. Fayard, who used to publish novels in the first decade of the twentieth century with first printings of up to 82,000, reduced them to 35,000 in 1924, 20,000 in 1934, 16,500 in 1937 and 12,000 in the 1950s. The overproduction was not disastrous, however, because in the Second World War the demand for books rose to unprecedented levels; almost any book could be sold, if paper could be found to print it, and publishers were able to get rid of all their old, hitherto unsaleable stocks.[1]

A large number of books were published at the expense of their authors. By the middle of the century the cost of both paper and printing had fallen considerably and it was not difficult even for relatively modest people to pay a few hundred francs, as for example Camille Flammarion did in 1862, when he was an unknown boy of nineteen anxious to publicise his views on life in other planets. His book was printed in 500 copies and costs were covered by charging 2 francs a copy.[2] Printing costs were even lower in the provinces, and that explains the proliferation of erudite monographs which in some cases were printed only in 100 or 500 copies.[3] When Proust had difficulty in finding a publisher who would take his book as it stood, he preferred to have it printed at his own expense. Huysmans, Gide and Mauriac also made their débuts in this way. Until 1870, the number of printers was limited by the state, but after that anyone could become one, so their numbers decupled and competition forced prices down to unprecedented levels. It was as a result of ruthless bargaining with printers that publishers like Fayard were able to sell their books so cheaply.

[1] Archives of Librairie Arthème Fayard, registers of sales figures. For the history of publishing in the Second World War, see Comité d'Organisation des Industries, Arts et Commerce du Livre, 'Séances de la commission consultative centrale' (stencilled minutes in B.N. 4° Fw 106 etc.).

[2] C. Flammarion, *Mémoires biographiques et philosophiques d'un astronome* (1911), 214.

[3] For a 300-page book in 18mo the cost of paper, printing and binding was 725 francs for 500 copies and 900 francs for 1,000 copies, in Paris. In the Aube, a book of 156 pages in 12mo cost 340 francs for 500 copies—G. Tillié, *Éditeurs contre auteurs* (n.d. about 1910), 53–4.

The problem of distribution was however more difficult. Much publishing had originally been done by booksellers, who either acted as agents for the authors and printers, charging a commission which was at first only 5 per cent, or sometimes took the financial risks themselves. By 1815 they were charging 33 per cent commission and soon after, when they became just retailers, they demanded 40 per cent. They gained the privilege, moreover, of being simply depositaries for the publishers, able to return unsold copies and obtain a complete refund on them. The result was that the cost of distributing books eventually rose to 51 per cent of the published price.[1] Competition between booksellers led to vigorous price cutting—21 per cent discounts, post free, used to be advertised around 1900; but somehow booksellers managed to survive and in 1974 there were still 1,300 who did nothing but sell books. Because they did not have to pay for their books until about three months after they received them, booksellers were willing to display new books in their windows, and then send them back if no one bought them. This meant that books came in fashion for brief moments and then vanished to be replaced by the next batch; stocks were kept low and getting a book that had been published a year before usually meant writing to the publisher. There was a custom in the early nineteenth century for booksellers to form little committees of clients to decide which books to order from Paris, both for sale and for the *cabinets de lecture* which were often an adjunct to the shop. This was local taste judging Parisian fashion; booksellers then formed a personal opinion on everything they sold; but with the great increase in titles this became more difficult.[2] Booksellers, however, had rivals in door-to-door salesmen. It was in 1875 that Abel Pilon began to sell books on credit and by 1922 twelve firms had followed him, so that there were then 'thousands of salesmen on the roads', using elaborately worked out techniques: a 300-page book, showing them exactly what to do and say, served as their guide.[3] It was largely by this method that Larousse sold 150,000 copies of his

[1] Robert Laffont, *Éditeur* (1974), 140, says a book of 320 pages, in 8,000 copies, selling for 23 francs, involves 51·39% in distribution costs, 17% for its manufacturer, 3% for advertising, 6·5% in state taxes, 10% author's royalty, 12·78% for the publisher.   [2] Alfred Humblot, *L'Édition littéraire au 19e siècle* (1911).
[3] Schwartz, *Guide du courtier en librairie. Conseils pratiques pour la vente et la diffusion du livre* (1922).

many-volumed New Encyclopedia (1928) at 200 francs each, an operation that brought in 30,000,000 francs.[1] The problems of the bookseller were aggravated by the growing practice of remaindering, which was already active in 1840. Firms used to buy up unsaleable books, bind them in gold and sell them, at a 200 per cent profit, but still at only a quarter of the price they originally cost, to schools to be used as prizes. Newspapers bought them up to give away as free gifts to readers who took out long subscriptions. Many readers held back from buying books in the expectation that they could get them as remainders in due course. There were therefore constant complaints about chaos and crisis in the bookselling business.

Nevertheless, there was still plenty of room left for second-hand bookshops. These seem generally to have sold books at five-sevenths of their published price, but one could also (in 1886) buy a forty-seven-volume edition of Voltaire's complete works, bound in calf, for only 30 francs, and five volumes of Montesquieu's works, unbound, for 5 francs.[2] Book collecting was a widespread mania, of the same kind as art collecting but far more active. The *quais* of the Seine in Paris provided a busy hunting-ground for collectors, and revealed the existence of an enormous variety of specialities. The dispersion of monastic and aristocratic libraries fed the market with masses of old works. During the Second Empire one could buy books by weight, for 20 or 30 centimes a kilogramme, at Père Joux's shop on the Quai Conti. Just how far collecting could go was shown by A. M. H. Boulard, a notary who gave up his profession to devote himself to his hobby; when he died in 1825 he left over half a million books, which he had acquired for their appearance rather than their content. Eugène La Senne, by contrast, bought up every book about Paris and its history he could find, and his invaluable collection is now in the Bibliothèque Nationale. After the First World War, many provincials descended on Paris to find replacements for books lost during the war and it was significant that they often tried to reconstitute their libraries exactly as they had been before the Germans destroyed them.[3] These book collectors formed a sort

---

[1] Henri Baillère, *La Crise du livre* (1904), 82.
[2] J. Espagno, *Ouvrages d'occasion, Catalogue* (75 rue Madame, 1886–7).
[3] Charles Dodeman, *Le Journal d'un bouquiniste* (1922).

of loose fraternity; they knew who owned what and where one could find certain kinds of books; the distinction between collector and bookseller was vague, for the specialist booksellers were often erudite experts. On the whole, however, it seems that the lovers of old books despised new books. There were also collectors with a passion for books that completely ignored content, appreciating them only for their extraordinary bindings, luxurious paper, original illustrations and rare first editions. Around 1917 the collecting of modern first editions arrived as a new speciality, and publishers profited from it by printing 'first edition' on their title-pages, and producing some copies of every work on beautiful paper just to satisfy this new market. One wrote in 1929, 'There is such emulation in the world of the bibliophiles, such an appetite for the acquisition of all that is rare, that if a writer enjoying esteem in our day took it into his head to publish his laundry bills in sixty copies on Madagascar paper, I am certain that even if he sold them at 200 francs a copy, he would find they would be over-subscribed twenty times over.'[1]

The public chose from among the mass of works offered to it in this way according to principles which a few perceptive publishers vaguely intuited but which no one fully understood. An opinion poll in 1967 found that roughly one-tenth of books were bought as a result of reading reviews and one-tenth from seeing advertisements.[2] Advertising in newspapers, as will be seen,[3] only sometimes involved payment and more often required good relations with the editors and staff. The publisher Aubanel, for example, kept a list of 500 newspaper book reviewers: 'some are happy that we should prompt the article we would like from them, others will feel offended that we should appear to want to dictate their opinions'.[4] The known venality of the press was perhaps one reason why reviews carried such little weight. They probably mattered more to authors than to buyers, for they were essentially a system for the distribution of mutual esteem among authors. The weakness of advertising, however, led to the increasing reliance on literary prizes as a method of stimulating sales. These were originally

[1] Bernard Grasset, *La Chose littéraire* (1929), 172; Baillère, op. cit. 58.
[2] Cain, op. cit. 214–15.   [3] See chapter 11.
[4] Édouard Théodore-Aubanel, *Comment on lance un nouveau livre* (1937).

designed to encourage the publication of certain kinds of book,
in the tradition established by the Academies (the Prix Mon-
tyon for the book most useful to the improvement of morals,
the Prix en l'honneur de la Vierge, for a book or poem on the
Virgin Mary, the Prix J.-J. Weiss for the book 'in the purest
classical style', the Prix des Français d'Asie for the book that
spread love of Asia and the civilising mission of France in
Asia, the Prix Jules Favre for a non-fiction book by a woman,
the Prix Lucien Graux for a work by an author living in the
provinces in praise of the provinces).[1] In 1939 there were
at least sixty major literary prizes. The one which probably
became most influential, as far as fiction was concerned, was
the Prix Goncourt. The judges, however, were inevitably
authors themselves; and between the wars, most of the judges of
literary prizes were published by either Gallimard or Grasset.
One stood little chance of winning the prize unless one's book
was published by one of these firms, for a powerful *esprit de
corps* developed between authors and their publishers. This
prize thus became essentially a subtle method of advertising
the works of these major firms. After the Second World War,
Gallimard won ten out of the fourteen Goncourt prizes awarded
between 1949 and 1962; it and Hachette (which absorbed
Grasset) between them carried off 85 per cent of the major
literary prizes in the 1960s.[2]

The influence of publishers on taste, exercised in the course
of selecting what they brought out and in deciding how large
the printing of each book should be, was clearly important, but
very little is known about either the personality or policy of
these men. The first general characteristic about them was that
they were on the whole highly specialised, in the same way that
the retail food trade was split up into people who sold only eggs
and cheese, or cakes, or smoked meats. In the Second Empire,
medical books were published above all by Masson, law books
by Hingray, Cotillon and Durand, theatrical plays by Tresse,
religious books by Lecoffre and Gaume, books in foreign
languages by Klincksieck and Galignani. J. B. M. Baillère
(1797–1885), who had started as a specialist in medical publish-

1 E. Théodore-Aubanel, *Cueillons des lauriers. Promenade à travers le jardin des prix
littéraires* (1937).
2 R. Laffont, op. cit.

ing in 1819, expanded into general scientific publishing. But
the leading scientific publishers were Baudry (originally established in Belgium, but moving their main office to Paris in
1863); in 1884 Charles Bérenger, a graduate of the Polytechnic
and the École des Mines, invested in the firm and in 1899
bought it up; by 1925 its catalogue was more than 300 pages
long.[1] The classics became a major specialisation of the Garnier
brothers who had originally started, in 1833, as publishers of
light literature and political books. Some of their pamphlets,
like *La Vérité aux ouvriers, aux paysans et aux soldats* (1848–9),
sold in unprecedented numbers—over half a million copies; they
also acquired fame as the publishers of Proudhon's *La Justice
dans la Révolution* (1858), for which they were sent to prison. It
was then that they moved to the safer realms of the eighteenth-
century classics and also produced a vast collection of Latin
authors in translation, which has remained the steadfast crib for
schoolboys ever since. One of the brothers emigrated to Brazil,
which became their main export market.[2] Armand Colin (b.
1842), the son of a provincial bookseller, set up in 1871 as a
publisher of textbooks for primary education, and made his
fortune out of the best-sellers for the school market like Niel's
reading books, Lavisse's histories, Larive and Fleury's grammar,
Paul Bert's science books, Leyssenne's *Arithmetic*, etc.; he became a leading populariser of knowledge with his Collection
Armand Colin (started in 1921 by Paul Montel). The firm of
Calmann-Lévy was founded during the July Monarchy by
Michel Lévy and his brother Calmann originally to publish
theatrical plays; and it then spread into periodicals (*l'Univers
illustré, le Journal de dimanche*, etc.). Their bookshop stayed open
till ten o'clock at night and became a kind of literary *salon*,
where many of the famous writers of the day met, and the
firm indeed published an extraordinarily large proportion of
the great names of contemporary literature, from Guizot and
Tocqueville to Anatole France, as well as Edgar Poe, Macaulay and Dickens. It is unfortunate that these and other entre-
preneurs of literature and learning should have been so neglected
by historians, for, quite apart from their own interesting careers,
they played an important part in winning an audience for

[1] J. Makowsky, *Histoire de l'industrie et du commerce en France* (1926), 3. 194.
[2] Vapereau, *Dictionnaire des contemporains* (6th edition, 1893).

writers. It would be worth investigating to what extent their skill made it possible to publish so many philosophy books for example (a speciality of Felix Alcan), or whether it was the educational system which created the demand for such publications. The precise process by which taste of this kind developed is still very much clouded in obscurity.[1]

There was one section of the community which, to a certain extent, lived its own independent life in the matter of book reading, largely isolated from the literary currents of the time, or rather absorbing only the conservative elements in them. The Catholics had their own bookshops, libraries and publishers. The clergy were, despite their poverty, always passionately interested in books and convinced also that the right kind of book, given to innocent minds, could make a great difference to the development of the ideas of successive generations. They encouraged and disseminated a special kind of literature, the history of which has not been written. They had parish libraries, which may well have been much more numerous than those set up by the state. What those libraries bought can be seen from the catalogues of a bookseller of Arras who has long specialised in supplying them. The books he still offers are extremely cheap, and are very largely by authors totally neglected by literary historians, but they are what generations of pious girls have been brought up on. Much of what the world had judged to be best in the literature of France was, in this period, on the Catholic Church's Index of Prohibited Books. Abbé Louis Bethléem produced a guide to tell the faithful what books they could safely read and what they ought to avoid.[2] This showed that in 1932 most of the 'love stories' if not the complete works of Balzac, Dumas, Flaubert, Stendhal, Zola, E. Sue, Maeterlinck and Anatole France were on the Index, as well as Montesquieu, Rousseau, Bentham, Darwin, Kant and even Taine's *History of English Literature*. The books which were recommended were those of Dickens, Conan Doyle, George Eliot, René Bazin, Henri

---

[1] For other publishers, see A. Parménie and C. Bonnier de la Chapelle, *Histoire d'un éditeur et de ses auteurs: P. J. Hetzel* (1953); J. Mistler, *Le Librairie Hachette de 1826 à nos jours* (1964); J. Debu-Bridel, *Les Éditions de Minuit* (1945); D. Montel and G. Rageot, *Rapport sur l'organisation de la lecture publique, du commerce du livre etc.* (1937); A. Dinar, *Fortune des livres* (1938); A. Rétif, *Pierre Larousse* (1975).

[2] Abbé Louis Bethléem, *Romans à lire et romans à prescrire: essai de classification au point de vue moral des principaux romans et romanciers 1500–1932* (11th edition, 1932).

Bordeaux and above all a host of obscure writers who clearly sold very well because they had this Catholic accolade. The best example of these is probably Paul Féval (1817–87), who was already the author of some 200 books when in 1876 he was converted to Catholicism 'as a result of a reversal of fortune and under the influence of his wife'. He bought his works back from his publishers and corrected them to make them acceptable to Catholics. They were placed by Bethléem 'in the first rank of Christian novels' and forty-five of them were particularly recommended. One reprint of his *Le Chevalier de Lagardère* sold a quarter of a million copies simply between 1900 and 1923.[1] Another example was Zenaïde Fleuriot (1829–90) whose eighty-three books were said to be 'still much read' in 1932, especially by girls, even though 'a certain number of them contain descriptions of worldly parties, whose size and brilliance might disturb country-folk and persons with little education'. Edgar Wallace, though 'morally irreproachable' was considered unsuitable for 'excessively young imaginations'. Catholic readers were thus protected from the disturbance of changes in morals and their taste was preserved as if clocks were kept running at different times in different groups. Catholics, of course, did not ignore what non-believers published, if only because they were keen to refute and attack their enemies, and they could also make good use of the trends in literature that pleased them. Thus Huysmans, who is now remembered chiefly as the author of the immoral *A Rebours*, was nowhere near as successful with that work as with the novels which recounted his conversion to religion. *A Rebours* sold 14,000 copies in his lifetime and another 50,000 copies between 1910 and 1960. But *La Cathédrale* sold 20,000 copies in 1898 and another 169,000 by 1960, and *En route* has sold 90,000 copies.[2] In 1951 there were about 120 Catholic publishers, or at any rate publishers whose activity was mainly directed to satisfying the Catholic market. Bloud et Gay (founded in 1875) were responsible for the series 'Science and Religion' (started in 1897) which had 700 titles by 1950. Desclée de Brouwer (1877) by the same date was publishing nearly a million volumes a year; Mame (established as printers in 1767 and as publishers

[1] Fayard archives.
[2] M. Issacharoff, *J.-K. Huysmans devant la critique en France 1874–1960* (1970), 15.

in 1796) employed about a thousand workers. One should not forget, however, those firms which published Catholic authors in the company of others of a different persuasion, in the way that Fayard published Daniel Rops and Flammarion published Mauriac. The Éditions du Seuil (1936), originally a Catholic house, revived after the war as a much more eclectic one, but one which gave Catholics a new integrated status in the literary world.[1]

Why some books were more successful than others was to a certain extent a mystery.[2] It might be argued that literature involved a constant lottery, in which 99 per cent of manuscripts were rejected and never even drew a ticket. Why some authors became famous and others not was, however, not simply a question of chance. Enough work has not yet been done on the process by which books were selected for publication, launched and sold for it to be possible to generalise about the origins of literary reputations, but a few examples can show some of the forces involved in making reputations. Marcel Proust's career provides evidence of one form of pressure. When he started offering the manuscript of his novel to publishers in 1911, it was 1,500 pages long, and barely legible in places, for he did not have it typed. He did not dare send it to the large respectable firms, for fear that it would be considered too improper. He hoped that the *Nouvelle Revue française*, which was run by authors, would take it, but he had a reputation as a dandy, an amateur, a journalist; people talked about his eccentricities but few knew how hard he had worked on his book. André Gide, for the *N.R.F.*, leafed through the manuscript, and was at once put off by a few phrases which seemed incomprehensible or obscure. It was assumed that the subject of the book was simply the smart society which these puritan authors despised and so they rejected it. The *Mercure de France* rejected it because it was too long. Fasquelle, the publishers of Flaubert and Zola, rejected it because, as they said, 'it was too different from what the public is accustomed to read'. Ollendorff could make no sense of it: 'I may be dense,' he said, 'but

[1] A Luchini, *La Production, la distribution et la consommation du livre religieux en France* (1964); *Catholicisme (encyclopédie)* (1952), 3. 1358.

[2] G. Rageot, *Le Succès: auteurs et public* (1906); F. Baldensperger, *La Littérature: création, succès, durée* (1913).

I cannot understand how a man can use up thirty pages to describe the way he turns over and moves about in bed before falling asleep. It makes me want to scream.' So Proust published the novel at his own expense. He was not unhappy about this because it meant at least that he did not have to cut his manuscript. His only sacrifice was that he limited the first instalment to 500 printed pages. After this difficult start, Proust had no further trouble in having the rest of his novel published in the normal commercial way. His experience does not prove that only the well-to-do could get into print. A few years before, an ordinary, almost penniless peasant, Émile Guillaumin, had succeeded in having his autobiography published, after several rejections, on a shared-profits basis. But it does show that an author seeking to get into print came up against the desire of publishers to produce books which accorded with what they considered to be contemporary taste. It does not follow that publishers made taste when they tried to be conformist in this way, for the competition between them, and their own eccentricities, made it impossible for them to agree on what taste was or should be. They were moreover advised by authors who spoke with many different voices. The publisher Grasset claimed that it was the second-rate authors who made most decisions about which novels were published, because they acted as publishers' readers. These men conscientiously and indulgently acted as 'the advocates of acceptable mediocrity': there were so many authors in the republic of letters that mediocrity was inevitably in the majority. The readers judged that a manuscript was no worse than any other. They were inevitably moved by the spirit of camaraderie. This limited their openness but it also allowed beginners with influence to get published, however unusual their ideas or their style. Grasset considered publishers, or at least himself, as the enemy of these mediocre readers, who were too confident that they knew 'what pleases the public'. There were always enough such publishers to enable at least some unorthodox authors to break through.

There were two kinds of author: those who fought hard to get their books noticed and those who waited for their contemporaries, or more usually for posterity, to judge them. Proust was definitely in the first category, a category which could be joined only if one had a lot of friends. Proust was very keen to have his book noticed. So first of all he had it put on sale at one-third of the price needed to make it commercially viable. He then pestered his friends to make the press draw attention to the book. He very ingeniously had one favourable review reproduced not directly, but by writing an article in praise of his reviewer and quoting the review as an illustration of the reviewer's talent in recognising important new works. He got the *Figaro* to reprint this article by adding a headline that *Swann's Way* was dedicated to the *Figaro*'s editor. On one occasion, when he received a notice of his book on page two of a newspaper, he considered this inadequate and made such a fuss that the paper reprinted the notice the next day, word for word, on the front page. He used a female friend to persuade *Le Temps* to publish an extract from the novel, a very unusual thing for such a serious political paper to do. He knew many of the leading writers of the day; his first book of essays had been launched with a preface by Anatole France, partly because Proust was a close friend of the son of France's mistress. *Swann's Way* was accordingly reviewed by his friends who compared him to Shakespeare, Goethe and Dostoevsky. But when he entered the book for the Prix Goncourt, it was not even discussed: his influence did not extend that far. However, in 1919 he did win the prize, largely thanks to hard work on the part of Léon Daudet, father of another of Proust's close friends. This is usually considered the event which made him famous. The controversy it aroused was however probably more important than the prize itself: there was a lot of hostile comment. Proust, in fact, was for long famous only to a relatively small group of people. His association with right-wing and aristocratic circles made him distasteful to many; his work seemed irrelevant in the 1930s when political commitment and guidance were sought from authors. By 1960 the book which Proust had narrowly defeated for the Goncourt prize by six votes to four, Dorgelès's war novel *The Wooden Crosses*, had sold almost 50 per cent more copies than *Swann's Way*. Proust did not enjoy a mass market until after the Second World War, when his book was put into paperback and into the Pléiade edition (1954). In 1956 it had still not made the list of books that sold over 10,000 copies in that year, when Françoise Sagan sold 450,000 copies, Camus 84,000,

Dorgelès 63,000, Sartre 12,000 and Conan Doyle (translated) 20,000. *Swann's Way* seems to have sold about seven times more copies than the other volumes: it is not clear that many people have read the whole work, or that his message has penetrated very far.

What success Proust did have was paradoxically not due to his originality, or to his innovations in literary technique and in analysis of character. The reviewers were much troubled by his unusual style. Souday, who was a famous reviewer of the time, complained that the book was chaotic, terribly boring in parts and loaded with useless digressions which served only to increase its obscurity. What was more significant was that many of those who were favourable were so because they were able to fit him into traditions they could understand: they did not value him for the qualities for which he is now admired. Jacques Rivière, though interested in the psychological side of the book, praised it on the ground that it analysed the emotions in a positivist way, such as Claude Bernard and Auguste Comte would have approved. He said the book was revolutionary, because it knocked down the supremacy of the will, but he insisted that it represented a classical revolution, a reply to the woolliness of romanticism and a triumph for the mind, the logical French intelligence. Rivière did not accept Proust's iconoclastic attitude towards love. Indeed, Proust was interpreted by some so as to appear almost a bastion of moral order. There was one reviewer who praised Proust for showing respect for the family, filial love and understanding of provincial life: he said Proust had written a moral book. Lamartine had suffered the same fate. The poems most appreciated by his admirers in his lifetime are those now considered least original. To say, therefore, that Proust expressed the attitudes of his period is quite unjustifiable. At first Proust was in fact less popular in France than he was abroad, but there too he owed his fame to the adulation of a small clique. In England, his book sold roughly 1,250 copies a year in translation between 1922 and 1959, when Painter's biography publicised his eccentricities and had an immense effect in widening his reputation. Till then, he was read on personal recommendation by a clique of aesthetes. (Proust's greater popularity abroad may have had something to do with the fact that France was the country which was least favourable to Freud's ideas.[1]) Originally a clique could more easily confer *succès d'estime* on an author than large sales, but its power has grown more recently. Thus Proust's admirers have grown into something of a minor industry thanks to the expansion of education. In the 1940s no less than 108 books were published about him. In 1955 he had more books written about him than any other modern French writer. In 1971 alone, another seventeen books and at least seventy-four articles appeared, but by then he was no longer the largest literary industry: Camus, Gide and Teilhard de Chardin each had twenty-three books about them, Beckett and Sartre twenty-two, Claudel nineteen. Proust came sixth after them. Zola still managed to produce twelve, which shows that this academic interest can breed on itself. There are over 2,000 members of the Society of the Friends of Proust (founded 1947), who perpetuate the cult. A large variety of commercial, social, literary and personal factors have thus contributed to making the reputation of this author, a reputation moreover which is constantly changing.

The influence of publishers on what people read was exerted, at its most elementary level, by the number of copies they printed of a book. Balzac and Alexandre Dumas had their books printed and reprinted in the second half of the nineteenth century in roughly equal numbers, as far as the number of titles was concerned, but Balzac's works tended to be produced in small editions of between 500 and 1,000 copies, while Dumas's were considerably larger.[2] A publisher who was very determined could make many people read a certain book. This can be illustrated from the way the publisher Grasset made a bestseller out of a novel written by a boy of seventeen, Raymond Radiguet (1903–23). Radiguet was to begin with a protégé of Cocteau, who liked beautiful boys. Grasset had set up a new literary prize, the Prix Balzac, ostensibly to encourage young authors, but designed no less to attract them to his firm, which kept the right to publish the winning entry and which benefited from the publicity. When he heard about Cocteau's friend, and saw the manuscript, he was convinced he had discovered a genius. He took it upon himself to make sure that Radiguet was

---

1 See my *Anxiety and Hypocrisy* (1981), ch 3.
2 Information from Dr. Bellos, who is doing a computerised study of the *Bibliographie de la France*.

recognised as such and that the firm of Grasset should be associated with his fame. He signed a contract by which Radiguet would allow Grasset to publish all his works written within the next ten years, in return for a monthly allowance of 1,500 francs, payable for two years. Before publishing the book, he sent the proofs to forty-one leading critics, asking their opinion, but informing them that his was that nothing like it had been seen since Rimbaud had published his first poems at the same precocious age. This association of Radiguet with Rimbaud became Grasset's slogan, which he repeated endlessly. He, Cocteau and Radiguet together composed a striking blurb which dominated all that the critics wrote about the book. The thirty-odd reviews that appeared in the first month after publication all quoted this blurb either to agree or to refute it. A film was distributed showing Radiguet 'the youngest novelist in France' signing his contract with the great publisher who uncovered the talent of the age. Radiguet was awarded not only the Prix Balzac, on the jury of which Grasset's friends had a majority, but also the Prix du Nouveau Monde, on which Cocteau sat. The book sold 40,000 copies in its first year. This was a remarkable figure for a first novel. It was nothing much compared to what Grasset had achieved with *Maria Chapdelaine* which had sold 160,000 in its first year, but for that he had spent over 100,000 francs on advertising and had distributed over 10,000 free copies to journalists and writers. Grasset argued that the success of a book was decided before it was published. His methods, however, were considered improper and many critics joined in a campaign to condemn the introduction of vulgar processes of common trading into the world of letters. Grasset unrepentantly replied that he could see no reason why 'we should do less for art and faith than Cadum does for its soap'. He prepared an even greater campaign to launch Radiguet's second novel, and got his author deferment of military service, through the influence of a friend on the President of the Republic's staff, to enable Radiguet to correct the proofs. But it is significant that one of Grasset's editors, Daniel Halévy, refused to include this novel in the series which he ran: the independence of literary men was almost automatically reasserted when too much pressure was put on it. A publisher could not repeat such successes too often. Rivals immediately made similar discoveries of boy geniuses, the public grew tired of young authors, and the young authors for their part tried to monopolise the market as they established themselves and won a following.[1]

Why people had the tastes they professed was therefore no simple matter. It does not follow that they always read the books they did because they were able to identify with the characters in them, or because they found in them an exposition of the dilemmas of their time: there were other pressures at work. It is uncertain how exactly authors influenced their public. The most influential books were probably those which could be understood in different ways at different times (the most famous of these is perhaps Rousseau's), so the influence has not always been what the author intended: authors have probably been as much misunderstood as influential. Occasionally, an author wins a following while he is still young, and his admirers, as they become influential, turn him into a hero, but by then he is often dead. The process by which the tiny minority of heroes were selected in literature involved a large element of accident: perhaps that was why increasing numbers bought lottery tickets to fame by becoming authors. In the seventeenth century, it is estimated, there were only 300 or 400 authors in France; in 1876 about 4,000 people declared themselves to be 'men of letters' to the census.[2] In 1960, only 3,500 considered themselves to be professional enough to be members of the Society of Men of Letters, though about 40,000 were writers of some sort.[3] The average annual earnings of those who lived off writing were then only 4,000 francs.[4] The consolation prizes, even for the successful, were small. Victor Hugo sold *Les Misérables* for 240,000 francs, Lamartine got 2 million francs for his complete works, and Louis Blanc half a million francs for his history of the Revolution, but it should not be forgotten that Sainte-Beuve sold his best-selling *Causeries de lundi* for only 2,000 francs a volume (an outright sale of copyright), that Flaubert got only 400 francs for *Madame Bovary*, that George

[1] Gabriel Boillat, *Un Maître de 17 ans: Raymond Radiguet* (Neuchâtel, 1973).

[2] Statistique de la France, *Résultats généraux du dénombrement de 1876* (1878), 198–203.

[3] R. Escarpit, *Le Littéraire et le social* (1970), 140, 145, 155.

[4] M. Mansuy, *Positions et oppositions sur le roman contemporain* (1971), 35.

Sand received the same amount for her first novel. It was estimated in 1899 that the average successful author could not hope, after ten years of success, to earn more than 10,000 francs a year (i.e. £400), which was roughly the same as an obscure member of parliament. At this time most novels made their authors between 500 and 1,000 francs.[1] But authors were compensated, at least so far as their vanity was concerned, by the increasing critical attention they received, from the ever-growing periodical press and university system. The constant debate about merit and significance was, it is true, largely an internal one, within the republic of letters itself, but its growth meant that the republic could be self-sufficient. One should not criticise the critics for awarding the medals to authors whom subsequent generations discarded. Literature was not for most people synonymous with revolution and originality, but with taste, which meant that it had to be acceptable and meaningful to the average intelligent man, who was, moreover, nurtured on the classics. René Doumic, the editor of the *Revue des Deux Mondes*, was called the 'prefect of police of Parisian literature', because he was slow to accept novelty, at least until people got used to it, but he illustrated the inevitable difficulty that change and originality, by their very nature, had to encounter. Every generation criticises its predecessor for its blindness; and every generation also has its own reasons for turning forgotten writers into masters.[2]

Popular Literature

There was another sort of book that the critics ignored or barely noticed. There was a separate literary world, of books condemned as 'trash', or as 'popular'. To like them could never show good taste; and yet they sold in far larger numbers than books with higher pretensions. They were produced entirely for

---

[1] Camille Mauclair, 'La Condition matérielle et morale de l'écrivain à Paris', *Nouvelle Revue* (Sept.–Oct. 1899), vol. 120, 26–52; Anon., 'Ce que gagnent les écrivains', *Revue encyclopédique* (1897), 957–8; Bernard Leuilliot, *Victor Hugo publie Les Misérables* (1970), 24–32; A. Bellesort, 'L'Écrivain français d'aujourd'hui', *Revue hebdomadaire* (1926), vol. 2, 147–68.

[2] F. Baldensperger, *La Critique et l'histoire littéraires en France au 19e et au début du 20e siècles* (New York, 1945); cf. Henri Peyre, *Les Générations littéraires* (1948); L. L. Schücking, *The Sociology of Literary Taste* (1944); G. Lanson, 'L'Histoire littéraire et la sociologie', *Revue de métaphysique et de morale* (1904), 621–42.

commercial reasons, not to influence; but the question may be asked whether they reflected interests which the masses already had. There was a long tradition behind 'popular literature'. It never got into libraries or bookshops, and was sold principally by pedlars. The Bibliothèque bleue de Troyes, one of the popular series of this kind that had a wide sale in the eighteenth century, contained, among its 450 titles, about 120 works of piety, about 80 novels, stories and plays, about 40 history books and 50 practical manuals about games etc. This perhaps gives some indication of the interests of the 'popular' audience at this time. There were very few books in this series about science, but many more on the occult; calendars with astrological information were eagerly bought: readers wanted to know what the future held and how to deal with the practical problems that faced them; they needed arithmetical and meteorological tables and medical prescriptions. They bought few books about how to practise trades, because this was learnt orally, not through books. What they turned to books for, rather, was magical formulae. They were centuries out of date compared to what the élite was thinking in Paris. Their books contained much that was copied out of sixteenth-century aristocratic, religious and chivalric works; the travel they read about was not that of the latest geographical discoveries but itineraries for pilgrims and merchants. The history in these books was about Charlemagne, the lives of the nobility and the Crusades, but never about the suffering of the poor, the conflict of bourgeoisie and aristocracy or excessive taxation. The educational works were above all manuals of etiquette, how to write polite letters, and behave as well-brought-up men should; there were no complaints about social discrimination. The Jansenist controversies were completely ignored in the religious books, and Christianity was always presented in an elementary way, with liberal additions of magic. The songs were frequently about saints, about how the good were rewarded; but the majority (60 per cent) were about love and a quarter about the virtues of drink. The stories showed the world divided into three categories, the ruling class, the common people and the outlaws. The masses were usually presented as contemptible while the nobles were praised. There were some anti-conformist heroes, who went around redressing wrongs, and there was an interest in outlaws, but there were no social implications behind this: their misadventures were designed to evoke laughter; the most popular were those full of slang and swear words, puns and burlesque. The adventure story and the romantic hero had not yet arrived. Love-stories were about how to make a conquest of women, how to choose a wife, but they were seldom optimistic: they painted marriage as destructive of passion, women as inconstant and naughty. Crime attracted great interest, being presented as the result of passion men could not control. Death appeared as terrifying, though it was also used to prove that all were ultimately equal, and the clergy were criticised for trying to make money out of men's fears.[1]

This was the basis from which nineteenth-century popular literature developed. In 1852 a government commission was established to examine it, and recommended that two-thirds of it should be prohibited as immoral; what was left should be censored and subject to the prefects' authorisation.[2] There were at this time about 3,000 pedlars who toured the country selling these books, together with pictures, wallets, spectacles, diaries and stationery; they were mainly peasants from the poor regions of the Pyrenees and Gascony, but behind them were several hundred specialist publishers. Altogether they distributed between 10 and 40 million volumes a year. In 1868 the 37 million items they sold consisted of about 10,000,000 almanacs, 1,400,000 books, 6,000,000 pamphlets and 20,000,000 'prospectuses and miscellaneous opuscules'. These enormous figures should not be compared with the figures of book production, even if the latter were available: the earliest statistics of the total number of copies of books printed are for 1959, when 145 million copies appeared; in 1970, 322 million copies were published.[3] One should rather see this mass literature as in some ways a primitive version of the daily and weekly newspapers, whose growth was one of the main causes of its eclipse (much more than censorship); it is in this perspective that one should understand both the rise of the periodical press and also the direction in which most of it went.

[1] Robert Mandrou, *De la culture populaire aux 17e et 18e siècles* (1964).

[2] Charles Nisard, *Histoire des livres populaires ou de la littérature de colportage* (1864, 2nd edition).

[3] J. Dumazedier and J. Hassendorfer, *Éléments pour une sociologie comparée de la production, de la diffusion et de l'utilisation du livre* (1962), 17–20; Cain, op. cit. 113.

Already by 1852 novels of the kind which the newspapers were to serialise with such success constituted the largest single category of book; photographs were beginning to compete with the engravings; songs remained numerous. *The Art of Not Getting Bored*, *The Key to Dreams*, *The Catechism of Lovers or the Art of Making Love* and the *Historic Account of the Glories of the French Armies* were typical titles that were and remained popular, though, for example, Charlemagne was replaced by Napoleon as the historical hero. The almanacs, with their hints on health, their Bonapartist propaganda, sermons, funeral orations, model marriage contracts, reports of criminal trials, lives of famous men, models of business letters and novelettes, were carried over almost wholesale into the newspapers. Novels based on medieval stories were still sold in this period, but they were increasingly replaced by a new set, written in the late eighteenth or early nineteenth century, like the works of Madame Daubenton (*Zélie dans le désert*, first published in 1786, and reprinted at least twenty-one times by 1861). The masses were only slowly given new reading matter: story-telling was still to a certain extent a repetitive ritual. But specialists in popular novels had already emerged, the most successful (who can be regarded as the ancestor of the newspaper serial writers) being F. G. Ducray-Duminil (1761–1819), who, imitating Mrs. Radcliffe, specialised in terror stories, and took good care to write in a way that could appeal to children at the same time. It is tempting to argue that the masses, even if they welcomed the useful and edifying books the schools gave them, were already addicted to a very different intellectual diet: they wanted to know about the world, but, quite as much or even more, they seemed to want to escape from it, to identify with criminal heroes who broke all the rules they themselves had to obey in real life, to use literature as an instrument of wish fulfilment, day-dreaming and vicarious emotionalism. The establishment of compulsory education was to some extent an attempt to tear the masses away from what was considered pernicious and demoralising reading. The *instituteurs* were supposed to replace the *colporteurs* (pedlars) and to distribute a new, more wholesome, diet. They were not altogether successful.[1]

However, when one looks in greater detail at the popular

[1] J. J. Darmon, *Le Colportage de librairie en France sous le second empire* (1972).

literature, one becomes less certain that it expressed popular taste against the taste of the educated. Popular literature should not be confused with folklore, though it incorporated elements of it. It was still literature of sorts. The authors who produced the popular books were bourgeois; they were very often journalists who had not made the grade for 'literary' achievement. The masses were thus offered several alternatives by bourgeois writers, and most chose the alternative with the least pretension or which approximated nearest to their own inclinations. The popular novels were as subtly graded in quality as they were in price, according to the audience they were intended for. The 'masses' were not a homogeneous category, and the same novelists did not appeal equally to primary and secondary school graduates. The rise of the detective novel was indeed an acknowledgement that a new audience was developing, which, though it still wanted escapism, also demanded exercise for its intelligence.

Popular novels thus passed through several stages. In the traditional story, the reader often knew how things would end before he had begun: suspense was a new device to compensate for the diminished role of supernatural mystery. In the 1830s, the first popular novels written for newspaper serialisation had (to the extent of about 50 per cent) historical subjects. The crime story was an extension of the eighteenth-century tales about great bandits, but it was given a new twist by the rise of the detective. Crime and violence had always been fascinating. The detective added a new kind of game, which Gaboriau (1835–73) the inventor of Monsieur Lecoq (1868) defined as a battle of wits between author and reader. One year before the first Sherlock Holmes story was published, Henri Cauvain (1847–99) invented a similar hero called *Maximilien Heller* (1886), who was, like Holmes, a drug addict, who had a faithful doctor accompanying him, and who in addition was involved with a character called Dr. Wickson. Increasingly the English detective story was the model on which the French based themselves and indeed a large proportion of the detective stories published were translations from English. Maurice Leblanc (1864–1941) created Arsène Lupin as a French alternative to Holmes, though there was, it was true, a difference: Lupin was a French kind of hero, a weak 'small man'

who proved to himself and to his readers that he could overcome his weaknesses: he knew how to resist authority and how
to be theatrical about it. Maurice Leblanc was however himself the son of a well-to-do Rouen shipowner. Gaston Leroux
(1867–1927), the creator of Rouletabille (an infant-prodigy
newspaper reporter detective) and of Cheri-Bibi, became a
writer only after gambling away the million francs he inherited.
The pioneer of the endless adventure story, Ponson du Terrail
(1829–71), creator of Rocambole, had called himself a viscount.
These writers made their heroes mildly anti-social, but they were
not aiming to challenge the established order. The fascination
with scientific techniques diverted attention from social problems.

But the traditional hero of the popular novels had been a
redresser of wrongs, an outlaw who could be admired despite
his crimes. Fantômas carried this tradition further, by abandoning the convention that good should triumph over evil. Fantômas was so rebellious, indeed, that in Russia he has been
officially condemned as an enemy of society. The first volume
in the Fantômas series (1909) had sold nearly 2,500,000 copies
by 1967: between 1909 and 1914, thirty-one more volumes of
his adventures were published, and the series continued to be
churned out until 1962. Its main author, Marcel Allain (1885–
1969) wrote 197 books in all. He used to write a book in ten
days (until 1914 in collaboration with Pierre Souvestre: they
took it in turns to write alternate chapters). In the five years
1909–14, Allain and Souvestre also produced thirty-five
volumes of Naz-en-lait and twelve of Titi-le-Moblot; in addition
Allain worked as a journalist on Comoedia, and Souvestre on
L'Auto; together they also produced a specialised motoring
periodical, La Poids lourd. They were mass producers of literature. They aimed to give readers what readers wanted. Marcel
Allain said that if he did put in philosophical ideas of his own,
his readers did not notice, whereas if he made a small mistake
about some detail, for example about how a steam-engine was
brought to a halt, he would receive 200 letters from train
drivers complaining that he had got it wrong. Eugène Sue had
also had this communication with his readers.[1] There was far
more of it now. The message Marcel Allain got was that his
readers did not want complicated psychological explanations,

[1] J. L. Borel, Eugène Sue (1962).

and they were not interested in the unconscious. They did accept novels which were essentially irrational, but at the same time they valued accurate documentation of real life. Marcel Allain obtained his material from *faits divers* newspaper stories, which he cut out and collected for use whenever he needed a new twist.[1] Above all, he was a story-teller.

Simenon (1903–   ) appealed to a slightly higher social class. He was the son of a Liège insurance clerk and he wrote mainly about the poor people among whom he had grown up; but his theme was more universal, for he saw life as the problem of being true to one's nature. This involved escaping from the hypocrisy on which respectability was built, freeing oneself from the pressures of family and work which shut one in, but then also coping with a world which was harsh and unfriendly. Simenon's favourite uncle had been a tramp and the tramp was always a hero for him. But he wanted to bring order into this confusing world: in the course of his life he refurbished no less than thirty farms or châteaux to express this side of himself. Simenon believed that every man has a shady part, of which he is more or less ashamed: his books were designed to show the reader that he was not alone, that others suffered the same internal torments, and that one could be lovable, even successful, despite them. Simenon identified with the criminal, seeking to restore his self-respect, arguing that no humiliation was more intolerable than that of feeling one was rejected by one's community. His detective was therefore not a policeman but a 'mender of destinies'. His solutions were male ones; he thought paternal love was stronger than maternal love and that many women indeed did not know what maternal love was: he usually showed women as adversaries; he said he preferred to call them 'females'. He was an infinitely careful observer of the humbler sections of society, but also one who tried to explain their behaviour. Before the Maigret series, he had already published over 200 popular novels and over 1,000 short stories, having started at the age of seventeen; between 1932 and 1970 he published another 230 novels; and by 1970 over fifty million copies of his books had been sold, in twenty-seven languages, so that it was estimated that 450 million people had read him.

[1] See Marcel Allain's 'Confessions' in Noel Arnaud, *Entretiens sur la para-littérature* (1970), 79–96.

He was the only French-language crime writer to win international popularity, in Russia as well as the U.S.A.[1]

One may wonder whether the effect of success of this kind was to subject ever larger parts of the nation to the same addiction, on the assumption that popular literature had previously been more regionalised. Certainly during the Second Empire, there was still much popular literature being produced in the provinces, for local consumption. Aix, Lyon, Toulouse were important centres of such publishing. The books of Lille have been studied more particularly: the public library of that city, though rich in theology, history, science and the arts, had practically no books of 'general utility', only one work by Jules Simon, only one by Quinet; it ceased to lend books from 1836 to 1872 and visitors in 'blouses or sabots were much disapproved of'. However, a local publisher produced cheap books at 50 centimes (1859) and these seem to have provided the inhabitants of Lille with much of their reading matter. Three thousand copies was the normal size of an edition and some were reprinted more than ten times. This one publisher, Lefort, between 1827 and 1866, produced 692 titles, and he was only one (though the largest) of many others in Lille. He wrote many of the books himself, but he had a large panel of equally obscure authors to help him—pious ladies, retired gentlemen and industrious priests. One of his authors was Madame Josephine de Gaulle, grandmother of the general. Many of his books appeared anonymously. They all preached standard Christian morality: there was little that was local about them except their place of publication. They had such titles as *Jules, ou la vertu dans l'indigence*, which pointed out that starving workers would attain bliss eventually in the next world.[2] The market for this kind of book did not disappear. Women and girls always had their own separate intellectual and emotional diet. What happened was therefore not the imposition of a uniform national novel, in place of regional variations, but the continuous discovery of special interests, so that an ever richer variety of alternatives was placed before readers.

[1] 'Le Roman Feuilleton', special issue of *Europe* (June 1974), with a good bibliography; J. J. Tourteau, *D'Arsène Lupin à San-Antonio. Le roman policier français* (1970); Regis Messac, *Le Detective Novel et l'influence de la pensée scientifique* (1929).

[2] Pierre Pierrard, *La Vie ouvrière à Lille sous le second empire* (1965), 268–76.

Children's literature was one example. This was a genre that was already well established at the beginning of the nineteenth century: 80 titles for children were published in 1811, and 275 in 1836. Production continued at almost exactly this annual figure for a whole century and it was only after 1945 that it suddenly doubled, reaching 650 titles in 1958.[1] One must, however, beware of attributing too much influence to these books. Madame de Ségur (1799–1874) was one of the most successful of authors for children, but it is doubtful whether this authoritarian Russian-born lady had much effect with her recommendations to sobriety, to acceptance of hierarchy and duty, which have led modern interpreters to accuse her of sado-masochism.[2] Children had an ability to use the stories given to them for their own purposes. Parents, for their part, transformed the significance of works they turned into children's classics. Thus Perrault's Mother Goose stories originally represented a seventeenth-century reaction against classical mythology, which schools had made boring, and a precocious return to folklore: they were not intended for children, but were adopted as such when their mythological significance was forgotten. Grimm's Tales, originally published weighed down with learned footnotes as a contribution to the creation of a German national consciousness, were taken over none the less by French parents, because they seemed to create a separate, fantastic world for their children. La Fontaine's Fables were written as an ironic study of the *ancien régime* and as a general satire on man: Rousseau and Lamartine both condemned them as preaching a hard and cold philosophy; they were made into children's books irrespective of their message.[3]

Taste, good and bad, seems to be the work of time. It can be deflected by fashion, and express itself in the cult of novelty, but this novelty must not be too new. Most best-sellers were books that successive generations got into the habit of reading. This

---

[1] Odile Limousin, 'Essais statistiques sur l'évolution de l'édition du livre pour enfants et l'évolution de la scolarisation de 1800 à 1966', *Bibliographie de la France* (1971), chronique, 699–711.

[2] P. Guérande, *Le Petit Monde de la comtesse de Ségur* (1964).

[3] Marc Soriano, *Guide de la littérature enfantine* (1959); Anne Pellowski, *The World of Children's Literature* (1968); Paul Hazard, *Les Livres, les enfants et les hommes* (1949 edition); M. T. Latzarus, *La Littérature enfantine en France dans la seconde moitié du 19e siècle* (1923).

was particularly the case with children's books, which came to form part of the ritual of growing up. But one can see this also in novels. It usually took time for authors to build up their following; once established they could go on producing virtually the same sort of book over and over again; finally they were raised to the status of masters and adopted as set books by the schools. Before the war Simenon's books were published in relatively small editions; he produced so many titles they added up to large totals; but even so it was only after the Second World War that the really large printings became a regular practice, as his cult spread. Gide, now regarded as the most important novelist of the inter-war period, reached his peak again only after the Second World War.[1] *Le Grand Meaulnes* (1913) sells roughly three times as many copies per year today as it did in all its first twenty years put together, substantial though those early sales were.[2] The popular books which did not establish themselves as literature took a long time to die, just as the medieval romances had. Thus *La Porteuse de pain* (1885) by Xavier de Montépin (1823–1902) still sold 320,000 copies between 1907 and 1923, but sold almost twice that amount again between 1923 and 1956. Paul Féval (1816–87) was still popular enough for him to be reprinted after the Second World War in editions as large as Gide's. But publishers seem to have suddenly tired of reprinting old books, as the dramatic revision of publishers' catalogues in the late Second Empire, and again in the 1950s, indicates. The significance of these breaches has still to be investigated.

Though the normal run of history books sold few copies, history was nevertheless one of the most popular subjects in this period when it was written in a suitable way. The growth of the market can be seen if one remembers that the first volume of Michelet's *History of the Revolution* (1847) was printed in 6,000 copies and that six years later 3,500 copies still remained

[1] *La Porte étroite* was published in 1934 in an edition of 26,400. There were four reprints 1935–41, of between 8,250 and 13,200 copies each. But in 1947 it was reprinted in 33,000 copies, and again in 1950 in 44,000 copies. Fayard Archives.

[2] Sales 1913–31 were 59,523; before 1950 it used to sell about 12,000 a year; in the 1970s it has been selling between 160,000 and 200,000 copies a year. G.H., 'Recherches bibliographiques sur Le Grand Meaulnes', *Le Livre et l'estampe* (Brussels, 1972), 9–16.

unsold.[1] Jacques Bainville's *History of France* (1924), printed in 22,000 copies, sold out at once and was reprinted five times in that same year, selling in all 77,000; it continued to be reprinted every year, with particularly large prints in 1941 (40,000) and 1946 (30,000), so that by 1969 it had sold altogether 303,000 copies. Bainville's *Napoléon* (1931) sold 55,000 in its first year and by 1968 had reached 197,700 copies; his *Troisième République* (1935) sold 64,000 by 1941 and 100,000 by 1960. André Maurois's *History of England* (1937) was reprinted seven times in its first year, selling 84,000; by 1940 it had sold 108,000 and by 1951 146,000. Louis Bertrand's *Louis XIV* (1923) sold 75,000 by 1949. Funck Brentano's *Ancien Régime* (1926) printed in 1,100 copies, sold out within three months, was reprinted twice in the same year and had sold 42,000 by 1942. Hitler's *Mein Kampf*, translated in 1938, sold 33,000 in its first year, but altogether only 41,825 by 1942. This was less than Pierre Gaxotte's *Frédéric II* (1938) which sold 44,000 by 1941. Perhaps that was because Gaxotte was considered a better writer; his *French Revolution* (1928) had sold 40,000 in its first year and had reached 124,000 by 1970. Or perhaps the French were more interested in their own history, rather than in foreigners. Maurois showed that England, in the hands of a fluent writer, was a subject of wide appeal, but Firmin Roz's *History of the United States* (1930) had sold only about 25,000 by 1943 and only 41,000 by 1956; Louis Bertrand's *History of Spain* (1932) sold 36,000 by the same date. That was just about what a biography of the Empress Eugénie sold and half of one of the King of Rome and another St. Augustine. Of course, one way of encouraging people to buy books was to pretend that everybody else was buying them. It was customary to put the number of copies sold on the front cover, for example, 50th thousand. It was generally known in the book trade that this should not be taken literally. Fayard's practice was to give exactly double the real figure, but many firms gave four times the real one, so that 1,000 meant 250. Thus Gustave Lanson's *L'Art de la prose* (1921) was printed in 1,650 copies; by 1936 it

---

[1] However, Michelet's *La Femme* (1859) sold nearly 13,000 copies in its first year and his *Amour* (1858) sold 5,700 in its first year. Information kindly supplied by M. Paul Viallaneix from the unpublished correspondence of Michelet with his publishers.

had sold less than 6,000 but was described as 26th thousand. This gives a useful contrast, to show that learned and literary works, even by famous authors, often appeared in very small editions. The complete theatre of Capus (1921), a popular dramatist in his day, appeared in seven volumes but only 2,200 copies were printed and there was no call for a reprint. Donnay's *Molière* (1922) was published in 1,650 copies and one reprint of the same number was issued four years later.[1]

The Cinema

What is now remembered of the history of cinema is likewise not what the majority of Frenchmen were aware of at the time. The same clash of artistic and popular taste manifested itself, but in a more serious way, because films were so very much more expensive to produce than books and needed audiences so very much larger to pay for them. When Lumière put on the world's first public film show in the basement of the Grand Café, in the boulevard des Capucines, on 28 December 1895, the films he offered, which lasted only one or two minutes each, were the beginnings of what came to be known as newsreels, though they were then little more than animated picture postcards; but within three weeks he was making a profit of 2,000 francs a day. The cinema was originally popularised by travelling showmen, and it fitted in with the traditional entertainment they offered. Comic films were the most popular and France's first international film star was Max Linder (1883–1925), whom Chaplin was to acknowledge as his master, and who, having made his fortune in France, went on to make another in the U.S.A., before committing suicide, in a classic case of comic's depression. Georges Méliès (1861–1938) was an amateur magician who used the fortune he inherited from his father, a shoe manufacturer, to buy the Théâtre Robert-Houdini; he saw in trick photography a new way of making the magician's art more marvellous still. He also specialised in newsreels and in films reconstituting contemporary events, like the Dreyfus Affair. He produced nearly 500 films before the First World War, but by then his skills had been overtaken by new forms of competition: he ended up selling toys at the Gare Montparnasse.

[1] Figures from Fayard Archives.

In 1908 the action film arrived with the *Adventures of Nick Carter*, followed by the filming of Fantômas (1913) and of an interminable series of popular detective novels. In 1912 Charles Pathé, a butcher's son who had started life as a travelling showman with a gramophone, and who came to be France's leading film magnate, produced *La Femme fatale*, which was to inaugurate an inextinguishable genre. Religious films were highly popular at this time, and several were made of the life of Jesus, until the Pope forbade the cinema to use biblical themes. War films made their appearance in 1914 but were not generally successful: audiences seemed to wish to get away from real life. Cinema receipts in France were now 16,000,000 francs a year, and, a newspaper claimed, films had become the third largest commodity in international trade, after wheat and coal.[1]

For a time, while the novelty of the new art continued to excite wonder, there was little problem about distinguishing between the taste of different kinds of audience. Intellectuals delighted in the cinema's absurdities, its gaffes and its naïveté. The poet Louis Aragon, replying to an inquiry by a newspaper, said 'I like straightforward films where people kill each other and make love. I like films where the actors are beautiful, with magnificent skins that you can see close up . . . films which have neither philosophy nor poetry.'[2] American films, which began invading France in 1915, quickly came to provide the basic fare of the French cinema-goer, partly because they fulfilled these conditions, partly because they were produced in such large numbers, partly because the French film industry failed to organise itself—its magnates found there was more money to be made distributing American films than making French ones. In 1927 Charles Pathé sold his company (in part) to Eastman-Kodak; his main French rival, Léon Gaumont, retired in the following year; and in 1929 Paramount established its European studios in Paris, to turn out versions of its American films in the major European languages.

[1] Jacques Deslandes, *Histoire comparée du cinéma*, vol. 1: 1826–96 (1966), vol. 2: 1896–1906 (1968); Maurice Bardèche and Robert Brasillach, *Histoire du cinéma* (1935); Jean Mitry, *Histoire du cinéma: art et industrie*, 3 vols., up to 1925 (1963–73).

[2] René Clair, *Réflexion faite. Notes pour servir à l'histoire de l'art cinématographique de 1920 à 1950* (1951), 26; and Paul Reboux in 'Histoire du cinéma', *Le Crapouillot*, special issue (Nov. 1932), 11.

However, the lowering of standards, which René Clair was
already lamenting in 1925, saying that 'cinema as an art is
dying, devoured by its double, the cinema industry', was not an
obstacle to inventiveness and originality. The French were the
first to treat the cinema as an independent art; in 1920 they
established the 'Friends of the Seventh Art' and specialised
small cinemas were opened in Paris and elsewhere to allow
low-cost films to be shown. There was enough competition
among financiers—precisely because there was an element of
gambling in film making and the rewards could be high—for
backers to be available even for obscure beginners. The film
industry was probably the most cosmopolitan of any, in its
actors, directors, technical staff and backers; and the extreme
right was able to denounce it as an international Jewish conspiracy.[1] René Clair's early talkies, for example, were financed
by the German firm Tobis, before he emigrated to England and
the U.S.A. That did not prevent the French from developing a
very distinctive genre of their own. Clair himself insisted that
the general public could not be expected to applaud innovation and experiment until this was already outdated. He saw
the cinema as a kind of drug, which opened the mind to new
experiences; what mattered was not the script, but the picture;
and the spectator should treat it like a dreamer, allowing himself to be carried away by its suggestive powers.[2] Louis Delluc
(1890–1924), who was also a novelist, poet and playwright,
made films which did not attempt to tell a story, but only to
create a mood, and to play on the theme of memory and dream.
Marcel Pagnol (1895–1974), by contrast, thought the text was
all-important; he loved speech and eloquence; but his films
probably owed their power more to the atmosphere they
created, even if the Provençal villages he portrayed were studio
reconstructions. Jean Epstein (1897–1953) (of Polish origin,
but educated in Lyon) tried to use the film as a means of discovering aspects of the world the naked eye did not notice.
Abel Gance (b. 1889) carried the absorption in the technical
possibilities of the camera to its limits, trying to produce overwhelming effects, as in his *Napoléon* (1927) which was three
films in one, simultaneously projected on three contiguous

[1] Lucien Rebatet [François Vinneuil], *Les Tribus du cinéma et du théâtre* (1941).
[2] Clair, op. cit. 111–12.

screens. It was a German firm that originally put up the money
for this. It was a Polish industrialist who enabled Jean Vigo
(1905–34), son of the anarchist Almereyda, to enter film-
making as a powerful social satirist and it was a Jewish businessman who financed his masterpiece *Zéro de conduite* (1933), in
which children were shown as oppressed by adults in the same
way as the masses were exploited by the bourgeoisie. The Catholic papers called this film 'the work of an obsessive maniac who
expresses his deranged thoughts without art': its showing was
prohibited by the censors until after 1945.[1] Originality was not
rewarded, but it was not altogether stifled. Jean Renoir
(b. 1894), the son of the painter, was able to enter film-making
because he inherited 3 million francs, plus a share of the paintings. That was not enough to last very long. Of his twenty-
five films some did make money, like *On purge Bébé* (1930),
based on Feydeau, which he filmed in four days, the script
being written in a week and the editing being completed in
another week; it brought in over a million francs for an outlay
of one-fifth of that amount. But those of his films which are
now considered his best work were flops, and *La Règle du jeu*
(1935) was also banned. Renoir had no esoteric aims, but even
though he cultivated simplicity, he clearly put too much into
his films. He was absorbed by the problem of class differences,
by the complexity of human motivation, by the fact that
'everyone has his reasons . . . and convincing reasons'. He was
fascinated by physical appearance, by everyday sights, and
used film to study 'French gestures', helped by the similar
study his father and other painters had also made. He tried to
'look at the world and tell what he saw' but with 'naked eyes',
putting aside the coloured lenses with which habit screened
reality. But this 'demystification', as he called it, was not
generally appreciated, at least until after the war. 'Ingenuous-
ness', he said, 'is absolutely essential to creation.' That was to
offer something too raw. It required the gap of a generation for
Frenchmen to be able to look at themselves through his mirror.[2]

[1] P. E. Salès Gomès, *Jean Vigo* (1957), one of the few film biographies based on
private papers.
[2] Pierre Leprohon, *Renoir* (1967), 121, 127; François Poulle, *Renoir 1938* (1969);
Charles W. Brooks, 'Jean Renoir's The Rules of the Game', *French Historical
Studies* (Fall, 1971), 264–83, and his forthcoming work on the French cinema in the
thirties.

In 1954 a survey of the public's declared preferences in films showed that the most popular kind were historical ones. This probably meant that adventure in exotic surroundings and beautiful costumes, with the large dose of brutality that often appeared in this sort of film, was the kind of mixture that was considered a balanced diet. The order of priorities of what constituted a good film was:

> history 13%, murder mysteries 10%, sentimental comedies 9%, documentaries 9%, comedies with music 7%, operettas 7%, dramatic comedies 6%, adventure films 6%, light comedies 6%, social problems 5%, cartoons 4%, dramas 4%, cloak and dagger 4%, British humour 3%, military comedies 2%, Westerns 2%, war 2%, hellzapoppin 1%, science fiction 1%, horror 1%.[1]

It is uncertain when Westerns first became as unpopular as they were at this period. More people said they hated Westerns than any other kind (22 per cent), immoral films coming next (13 per cent) and war films third (12 per cent). But the artistic merit of films did not seem to be of much concern: though the middle classes read reviews, a sizeable proportion of poorer people declared that they went to the cinema irrespective of what was showing. But the cinema had not captured the public taste as much as it did in other European countries. The average Frenchman saw only nine films a year, compared to the West German who saw twelve, the Italian who saw fifteen and the Englishman who saw twenty-five. The average Frenchman spent ten times more on drink than on films.[2]

The history of book publishing, reading and cinema-going shows some of the difficulties that generalisation about taste encounters. Taste can only be understood if it is seen as the expression of choice made among many conflicting pressures. Its chronology remains imprecise. So one must isolate the different factors at work and examine them in turn.

---

[1] Dourdin Institute, *A Survey for the French National Cinema Center*, adapted by Jane Palmer White (Sept. 1954).

[2] Ibid. 34. Cf. Thorold Dickinson, *A Discovery of Cinema* (1971); André Malraux, *Esquisse d'une psychologie du cinéma* (1946); Pierre Leprohon, *Cinquante ans de cinéma français 1895–1945* (1954); G. Charensol, *Quarante ans de cinéma 1895–1935* (1935).

2. Conformity and Superstition

THE conflict between conformity and individualism must be, to a certain extent, the theme of every modern history, in every country. In France, however, the conflict has involved a great deal of polemic and it has been obscured by value-judgements. The political divisions of the country have dominated discussion of the subject, so that the conflict has been seen in terms of reaction against revolution. This simplification, based on the belief that all divergences can be explained in concordant ways, conceals the fact that there are several meanings to conformity. There is conformity to traditional attitudes and values, but also to fashionable new ideas; there is the conformity that shows the cohesiveness of a society and that which results from insecurity in competitive situations; and there is a great deal of difference between conformity in public, under the pressure of group influences, and conformity in private, in ways of thinking and feeling. This book has, at various stages, shown the powerful efforts made by governments to impose a uniform language, a uniform education, uniform ways of thinking, a centralised government and an egalitarian political system on the country. It has analysed the loyalties and patterns of behaviour that grew up within classes and professions; and it has studied the conventional roles men, women and children played as members of the family. The argument throughout has been that none of these pressures towards conformity were totally successful, that the ideals of the moralists, educationists and politicians were far from being implemented in practice, and that the different affiliations of Frenchmen cut across each other in an infinite variety of permutations.

However, in the middle of the nineteenth century, an outstanding political thinker, Alexis de Tocqueville (1805–59), claimed that Frenchmen were in fact becoming more and more alike, under the influence of two forces which he considered to be almost irresistible: the centralisation of government and the spread of democracy. The United States showed, in his view, how democracy could lead to the tyranny of the majority, which, living 'in perpetual adoration of itself' is hurt by the least reproach, the least criticism. As a result, independence of mind and liberty of discussion are shackled, mediocrity is preferred to genius, peaceful habits are more esteemed than heroic virtues, vice is more tolerated than crime and material prosperity becomes the universal goal. In the United States, there were various obstacles to the majority being omnipotent, but France had far fewer, because centralised government gave the state unlimited power and destroyed the barriers that local initiative, private societies and religious sects could raise against it. If Tocqueville was right, then a history of the century covered by this book should be a description of the social consequences of democracy, in terms of the gradual triumph of conformity. That, however, did not happen, first because the democracy that France adopted did not involve as total a breach with aristocracy as Tocqueville feared, and secondly because centralised government proved less effective against regional variety than it had hoped. One of Tocqueville's most important arguments was that institutions had 'only a secondary influence over men's destiny', that political action and legislation had only limited results and that the character of societies was determined more by 'the notions and sentiments dominant in a people', 'their habits of thought', 'their *mores*'. But he did not fully integrate these beliefs into his major writings. He was ultimately more a politician than a moralist, a failed politician, who had never quite liberated himself from his legitimist heritage. His theory of the tyranny of the majority was the protest of an aristocrat against tendencies he did not like, but which he did not study in sufficient detail; he attributed great importance to intellectuals in influencing public opinion, but he did not go very deeply into the mechanisms of their influence.[1]

Tocqueville's statement that the *mores* and habits of thought of a country are more influential than its institutions needs to be pursued further if the pressures on individuals and the nature of

[1] A. de Tocqueville, *De la démocratie en Amérique* (1951 edition), 1. 256, 265–6, 2. 145; id., *L'Ancien Régime et la Révolution* (1856), Book 2 and chapters 1 and 2 of Book 3; id., *Souvenirs* (1893); A. Redier, *Comme disait Monsieur de Tocqueville* (1925); G. W. Pierson, *Tocqueville and Beaumont in America* (New York, 1938); J. Lively, *The Social and Political Thought of Alexis de Tocqueville* (Oxford, 1962).

conformity are to be properly understood. Rather than study conformity, therefore, as a growing menace, in confrontation with individualism; rather than see these as opposing alternatives, it is best to examine, one by one, the different attitudes to life that were practised or preached. It is common to divide these chronologically, as a series of 'ages' which succeeded and replaced each other. Thus the romantic age lasted until roughly 1848, to be followed by a positivist age until around 1890 when anti-intellectualism followed; finally disillusion and extremism dominated the period between the two world wars. This simplifies the truth too much. No one way of thought was ever supreme at any one time. It only seems to be so when the ideas of a few outstanding writers are allowed to eclipse the great mass of obscure and muddled men. Even if the leading men of letters are accepted as representative of the age in which they lived, they are usually far more complicated than the labels attached to them suggest; to identify them with a certain idea is usually to leave out a great portion of their personality. Historians of ideas and of literature naturally try to extract the originality and unique features of the authors they deal with, but if one is trying to understand behaviour as well as ideas, and to treat the total man and the total society, one needs to see the ideas as a succession of layers, superimposed on each other and continuing to be influential long after they were fashionable. For ideas took time to be accepted and absorbed: they were usually incorporated into a different set of ideas, with more or less superficial reconciliation, and did not totally replace old beliefs. People picked up ideas from many different sources, which were themselves far from coherent. Fashionable people who adopted the vocabulary of new ideas were thus often doubly conformist, in that they also superimposed this verbiage on traditional ways of thinking.

The first layer of conformity that needs to be examined, therefore, is what may be alternatively termed traditional, irrational, pre-literate, or superstitious. Because, by the end of the nineteenth century, France had become a literate country, little mention is made of the civilisation of the spoken word, which existed side by side with that of science, literature and government. Though disdained by these, the spoken word preserved traditions and attitudes which remained influential.

To call this civilisation simply one of the spoken word would, however, be misleading, because much that mattered in it was assumed rather than uttered, and the spoken word, besides, took on new functions when society became literate. Literacy paradoxically made spoken fluency and certain accents a source of power and prestige. But it is important to appreciate the forces that resisted science and rationality.[1]

The contrast between civilisations which are literate and those which are not was first studied by Lucien Lévy-Bruhl (1857–1939), who was a professor of the history of modern philosophy at the Sorbonne, and the author of a whole series of books on the subject of 'primitive' man. Lévy-Bruhl's dramatic suggestion was that mankind was not, intellectually, of one kind and that there was a clear distinction between what he called the primitive mentality and the mentality of modern societies. Basing himself on the discoveries of anthropologists, he argued that the inhabitants of primitive societies had a different logic, or rather were not ruled only by logic: they did not worry about contradictions and they had a different view of causation, because they saw the supernatural active everywhere. Its manifestation inspired fear, and the world, for them, was emotional and mystical, rather than open to cognitive understanding. Whereas modern man kept mysticism and reason in more or less separate compartments, confining the former to religion and children's fairy-tales, primitive people did not even distinguish between dream and reality, or symbols and what they symbolised; they did not draw a clear line between the individual and the collective, between body and soul, regarding their clothes and their footprints, for example, as parts of themselves. In the course of time, Lévy-Bruhl modified these views, and abandoned his original idea of a primitive mentality existing only in primitive societies: in his journal, which was published after his death, he admitted that he had exaggerated the mystical side of primitive life, as well as the rational character of modern thought, and suggested that there were degrees of mysticism, or pre-logical thinking, to be found in both.

These problems attracted the attention of folklorists, whose numbers increased greatly in the 1880s, just as the old illiterate

[1] Cf. Marcel Cohen, *L'Écriture et la psychologie des peuples* (1963).

society was disappearing. The folklorists were, until the last decade, virtually excluded from the universities and almost from respectability. But their work throws much light on the outlook of those whom science and technology failed to dominate. Science, it will be seen, was influential on certain aspects of life only and there was hardly anyone whose views were completely formed by it. The simple distinction between science and superstition, moreover, is a survival of nineteenth-century polemic and is not adequate to describe the dimensions of the conflicts which were set up. Recent research on illiterates entering a literate world has claimed, for example, that a major change is the passage from the world of sound to that of sight; the eye takes on new functions. Time too takes on another meaning, and the nature of freedom alters. The illiterate who used to express his feelings in an extrovert and emotional way, while also accepting subordination of his personal wishes to the interests of his family, is launched on the path of individual ambition, which opens more horizons but requires conscious self-control. The conflict of reason and passion, which the Greeks invented, and which classical Frenchmen continued to believe in, over-simplified human behaviour into a schizophrenic model, which the cult of moderation and the golden mean was supposed to overcome. This dichotomy was a way of keeping society in order, by relegating large portions of activity to inferior status. The precise nature of these inferior activities, however, needs closer study.[1]

One set of beliefs that survived throughout this period was superstition and, in particular, faith in astrology. Unusually precise information about the hopes of those who consulted astrologers is available thanks to some ingenious work by a medical student, L. H. Couderc, in the 1930s. He was training

[1] Cf. H. J. Martin, *Le Livre et la société écrite* (1968); Lucien Lévy-Bruhl, *Les Fonctions mentales dans les sociétés inférieures* (1910); id., *La Mentalité primitive* (1922); id., *L'Âme primitive* (1927); id., *Le Surnaturel et la nature dans la mentalité primitive* (1931); id., *La Mythologie primitive* (1935); id., *L'Expérience mystique et les symboles chez les primitives* (1938); id., *Carnets* (1949); Jean Cazeneuve, *Lévy-Bruhl* (1961), and id., *La Mentalité archaïque* (1961). On the folklorists, cf. Robert J. Theodoratus, *Europe: a selected ethnographic bibliography* (New Haven, 1969); the works of P. Y. Seignolle; Robert Jalby, *Le Folklore du Languedoc* (1971) and other volumes in this series published by Maisonneuve; and Van Gennep, *Bibliography* (1964); J. and C. Fraysse, *Mon Village* (1965). For a comparative study of transition to literacy, M. E. Morgaut, *Cinq années de psychologies africaines* (1962).

to be a psychiatrist and, noting that a very large number of patients in his mental hospital had consulted astrologers, card-readers and clairvoyants, he decided to write his thesis about these. His investigations showed that the popularity of the occult profession was far greater than any scientist, locked up in his own private world, could even imagine; it was far from being the case that only the feeble-minded consulted the astrologers. Science undoubtedly had more prestige than astro-logy; though some astrologers gave themselves fancy oriental names, many called themselves professors, of imaginary insti-tutes they had created themselves, or entitled themselves *voyante diplômée* or *médium agréé*. Their advertisements were to be found in nearly every newspaper, as well as in literary, scientific and pornographic periodicals, in far greater numbers than those of procurers proposing 'relationships', midwives offering abortions or quacks promising to cure cancer or syphilis by correspondence. What the astrologers held out was 'happiness and success', with the emphasis on love and money. They catered for every class of society, some charging only 5 francs and some 500; the luxury ones had receptionists and waiting-rooms full of respectable-looking people, as serious as any to be found in ministerial antechambers. Couderc answered a large number of the advertisements, of every kind, but received strangely uniform replies, virtually all of them not personal but stencilled and couched in more or less identical terms, almost as though the astrologers all belonged to a trade union. They stated that their fee was 200 francs, or 80 francs, but that they would offer him a special discount price of 40 or 50 francs. If their letter was ignored, they sent others, increasingly threatening but also lowering their fee; they promised to return the fee if the client was dissatisfied, though they seldom carried out their promise. But there was a considerable difference in the kind of function these astrologers performed, despite the uni-formity of their epistolary and divining methods. Those who worked by correspondence were interested simply in making money. The card-readers, however, often became confessors and moral guides to their clients. Some 'fakirs' catered for erotic needs: one was convicted for undressing and 'massaging' his clients. Having learnt their skills, Couderc put his own advertisement in the papers, offering his services, and sent out stencilled letters in exactly the same way. He received a vast number of replies, and he was thus able to show what the clients were seeking. Very few of them, he said, were mentally defective: most were of average intelligence and educated, some even highly intelligent; what they had in common most of all was anxiety about the future, difficulty in coping with daily problems, loneliness or exasperation. 'I wish to know', wrote one man, 'how a young girl I love, but with whom I am on bad terms, spends her Sundays, whether she has any flirtatious relationships with anyone else and if so, who; and whether she is chaste.' A woman of sixty wrote: 'I have had many troubles in the course of my life; and these have not been my fault, for I have always been hard-working, thrifty and straightforward, as I think you will see from my handwriting. Now tell me if I ought to get married again. A young man has asked my hand in marriage: should I accept? Is he sincere or acting from self-interest? Please study my handwriting carefully.' Couderc wrote back assuring her that she was a courageous and intelligent woman, so she asked for further guidance: should she buy a certain piece of land? Another of the clients who approached him was a graduate army officer who wrote: 'Could you rid me of a woman obsessed by the idea of marriage; she has a hold on me only because I fear scandal; I cannot escape her. My social situation does not allow me to marry her because she has neither my education nor my culture.' It turned out in further correspondence that she was an Annamite girl he had kept while serving in the Far East and who had followed him back to France. He asked that Couderc should use 'hypnotic suggestion' to get her to leave him alone; but when he discovered that Couderc was in fact a doctor, he broke off the correspondence. The value of the occultists was that they were outsiders to the normal world. One tradesman wrote: 'Can you destroy a business which is competing with mine by annihilating the two women who run it and who are my greatest enemies?' Another correspondent begged for a 'serious car accident' to be arranged for 'a person who does me nothing but harm'. Other frequent requests were for a win on the national lottery, or guidance on how to find a husband. The penal code forbade 'divination, prognostication and the explanation of dreams' (article 479), and in 1896 the Prefect of Police issued an injunction repeating the prohibition, on pain of severe penalties; but the courts held that there was no fraud involved, in that the astrologers sold advice, and their clients knew what they were getting when they bought it.[1]

It was in medicine that superstition survived most noticeably as an alternative to rationality. The choice between scientific and superstitious cures was not always obvious in the nineteenth century: Balzac, for example, showed the qualified doctor Bénassis prescribing snail soup as a cure for tuberculosis; the textbook nursing nuns and amateur healers relied on right up to the Second World War was Dr. Cazin's old *Treatise on Medicinal Plants*;[2] midwives, even if they practised their art in the way the medical experts prescribed, still preserved, into the 1920s, the custom of keeping the dried umbilical cord until the child's seventh birthday; and in 1961 doctors in the Saumurois were still being asked to cut the tongues of new-born babies, 'to facilitate speech'. Non-scientific medicine was by no means all magical. Though bone-setters used hot sweetened wine, or butter, as their disinfectants, charms were not necessarily involved. One particularly skilful amateur doctor, the Auvergnat Pierre Brioude (1831–1905), was originally a cheesemaker but his success both with animals and humans was such that around 1890 he was being visited by twenty-five or thirty patients daily, some coming long distances, and a few even from the Auvergnat community in the U.S.A. He made so much money that his son-in-law was able to start a hotel, which lodged these sick visitors. After his death a statue of him was put up at Nasbinals, paid for mainly by the Auvergnats of Paris. This man was probably an osteopath before his time, but he was also a fervent Catholic, who was considered to have special powers of healing. His kind need to be distinguished on the one hand from sorcerers and on the other from miracle workers.

Sorcerers, said an author of a book on them published in 1910, were to be found in almost every canton of France. In the previous year, their power had been publicised by the arrest of a married couple living in Blois, on the charge of extorting from peasants sums of between 3,000 and 30,000 francs for freeing

---

[1] Louis-Henri Couderc, *Astrologues, voyantes, cartomanciennes et leur clientèle. Enquête médico-psychologique sur la pratique commerciale de l'occultisme* (Paris medical thesis, 1934).

[2] F. J. Cazin, *Traité des plantes médicinales* (1847, 5th edition, 1886).

them from spells: their services were in such demand that they were rich enough to visit their clients by car and to own three houses. Sorcerers were sometimes people with some physical deformity; nine-tenths of them were said to be shepherds, who lived lonely lives and who were held in suspicion and awe. Blacksmiths, considered to have a special relationship with the devil, tailors and cobblers, held to have a particular influence on women, ambitious children who had unsuccessfully tried to become priests and who had acquired a little learning, midwives and women who prepared the dead for burial, were also among those who dabbled in this field. Often they inherited their secrets from their parents, as others inherited a grocery or a notary's practice; and there was a widespread feeling, at least until 1914, that every village needed a sorcerer.[1]

That diseases could be cured by the miraculous intervention of the saints was a belief which survived independently of other forms of religious practice. This has been strikingly shown by surveys of the cult of 'healing saints' carried out in the 1960s. A questionnaire distributed in the *arrondissement* of Villefranche (Aveyron) revealed that 59 per cent of men and 78 per cent of women had appealed to these saints at some time; only 20 per cent of men and 12 per cent of women had not (the rest were vague). There was no appreciable difference in these proportions as between areas with high and low levels of church attendance, or between rural and industrial regions; indeed the workers of the mining town of Decazeville were very assiduous pilgrims to these saints' shrines, even though only 5 per cent of them attended church. The great majority of rural families in this *arrondissement* went on two or three pilgrimages a year, simply to ensure that the saints would protect their animals against disease; specific illnesses would produce additional visits. The workers of Decazeville were, however, constantly searching for new saints to help them, and they sometimes visited two or three each Sunday, even though they were incapable of reciting a Christian prayer: they demanded to be told, at each shrine, what gestures they had to perform, and were uncomprehending if they were required to show a wider religious faith. Though the old appealed to these saints more often, that was rather because they were more frequently ill, and

[1] Charles Lancelin, *La Sorcellerie des campagnes* (1910).

there were several saints who attracted the appeals of the young, like Saint Blaise, popular among young motor-cyclists with colds.[1] People very seldom appealed to their local village saint for help: physical hardship in getting to a shrine was considered desirable; but villages often created new cults to commemorate local heroes. Thus in the 1960s about 2,000 people a year still visited the grave of the *curé* Guy of Malleville (1758–1840) who had in his lifetime suffered from rheumatism and who has ever since been regarded as offering a cure for that disease. At Orlhonac, between 150 and 200 masses were still being said each year to invoke the intervention of the *curé* Boscredon, a sufferer from diseases of the throat who died in 1857 and who has been valued particularly for curing whooping cough.[2] Parish records reveal that the cult of these saints has remained remarkably constant. In Saint-Privat (Lozère), for example, about 15,000 pilgrims visited the shrine in June 1906, about 20,000 in June 1939, and 15,000 again in June 1958.[3] Some cults fell into decay, but new ones were constantly being invented to replace them. Those that decayed had often specialised in diseases that had vanished. The demand in the 1960s was above all for the treatment of animals' and children's diseases, pains of undefined character, skin diseases and burns, nervous troubles, toothache and indigestion. Saints, of course, could perform other services. Until 1962 the statue of Saint Gondon was kept in the village of Thoureil, for example, for girls to stick nails into, so as to obtain his help in finding them husbands. In the 1939–45 war, the help of religion, more vaguely, was sought at Fontenay-le-Comte, when the threshing-machine stopped working: a visiting teacher was horrified to see that when all efforts to restart it had failed, the mechanic sent for a bottle of holy water and sprinkled it on it. In a national opinion poll in 1965 49 per cent of Frenchmen admitted that if conventional medicine failed to cure them, they would turn to the healers. This was a continuation of the attitude of

[1] 73 per cent of those over 65 who were questioned admitted to having appealed to healing saints, 68 per cent of those between 45 and 65 and 59 per cent of those between 35 and 45.

[2] Monique Bornes, épouse Vernet, 'Les Saints guérisseurs en Bas Rouergue' (Montpellier sociology thesis, troisième cycle, unpublished, 1969).

[3] Frédéric Uhmann, 'Le Culte des saints en Lozère' (Montpellier ethnology thesis, troisième cycle, unpublished, 1969), 156.

peasants who, when science failed them, turned to 'those who had not been spoiled by the primary school'.[1]

The desire to predict the future kept astrology alive also, though a vigorous battle was fought over it. The *Almanach liégeois* or *Almanach Laensberg*, which was one of the best-sellers of the seventeenth and eighteenth centuries, continued to sell in the nineteenth in large numbers. The Catholic Church had not attempted to destroy the beliefs for which it catered, at least not wholly. It combated that part of astrology which claimed that the stars influenced human destiny, but it allowed that they could influence the climate, and so agriculture. Scientists, however, were more determined: in 1800 Lamarck produced an *Annuaire météorologique* to put the facts straight, but it was of course too learned to have any popular effect. A publisher, Veuve Lepetit, issued an almanac entitled *L'Astrologie parisien ou le nouveau Mathieu Laensberg* which argued that the moon had no influence on the weather and still less on health; but it is significant that she kept Laensberg in her title, as too did another publisher, Pagnerre, with his *Le Petit Liégeois* (1837). Faith in the old almanacs survived; and when they began to die out, astrological horoscopes were saved by the new popular press.[2] These in fact became the townsmen's alternative for the more complex beliefs of the peasants. An inquiry in 1963 revealed that 53 per cent of the population regularly read their horoscopes in the press. Another inquiry, in 1968, showed that clerks were the most fervent addicts (68 per cent read the horoscopes in the press regularly or occasionally) with employers and workers not far behind (62 to 63 per cent), but only 44 per cent of peasants were interested. It was claimed in 1954 that France had 30,000 professional fortune tellers, and in 1971 it was calculated that Parisians alone spent 60 million new francs annually to discover their future.[3]

Interest in the occult was often propagated by educated people, who were rebels against the limitations and disappointments

---

[1] Marcelle Bouteiller, *Médecine populaire d'hier et d'aujourd'hui* (1966) with an excellent bibliography. The author was head of the Department of Beliefs at the Musée des Arts et Traditions Populaires. Cf. Pierre Neuville, *Les Meilleurs Guérisseurs de France* (1951).

[2] P. Saintyves, *L'Astrologie populaire étudiée spécialement dans les doctrines et les traditions relatives à l'influence de la lune* (1937).

[3] M. Gauquelin and J. Sadoul, *L'Astrologie hier et aujourd'hui* (1972), 53, 55.

of science. Large tomes, of confused mysticism and erudition, were published to interpret the discoveries of science in an occult sense. Louis Lucas (1816–63) tried to produce a synthesis of alchemy and the new medicine.[1] Dr. Philippe Encausse, finding the teaching of positivism 'too dry for the heart' and the theory of evolution 'comforting only to the successful', founded the 'independent group for esoteric studies', and the 'School of Hermetic Sciences', which attracted quite a few second-rate writers and artists. He sought to keep his approach compatible with Christianity; that is why he resigned from the Theosophical Society, which was interested in eastern mysticism. Interest in the occult has left its mark on several important novelists and poets; it is something that deserves further study in a wider context.

Arnold van Gennep (1873–1957) was the most remarkable and the most original of the many scholars who tried to record and explain the various beliefs and customs which were lumped together as folklore. He had the complicated family background that was almost a model for a certain type of anthropologist: of mixed national origin, his parents divorced when he was six, and his mother remarried twice after that. His stepfather, a doctor, wanted him to follow in that profession, but Van Gennep went off to study sociology, ethnology and languages in Paris; he married a wife without a dowry, so his stepfather cut him off and he was forced to earn his living as a tutor in Russian Poland. He wrote theses on Taboo in Madagascar and Myths in Australia, but he could never get a proper university job: Durkheim, who was the king of French sociology, execrated him. After his return to France in 1901, Van Gennep lived at Bourg-la-Reine, just outside Paris (apart from a six-month experiment raising chickens in the south), keeping himself as a translator, first in the ministry of agriculture and later at the Pelman Institute: he knew most European languages. In his spare time, working regularly till the early hours of the morning, he wrote his *Manual of Contemporary French Folklore* (1943–58) and edited several journals on the same subject. It was only after 1945 that he at last obtained a grant from the C.N.R.S.

[1] Louis Lucas, *La Chimie nouvelle* (1854); id., *La Médecine nouvelle* (1862); P. Encausse, *Sciences occultes ou 25 années d'occultisme occidental. Papus, sa vie, son œuvre* (1949).

to complete his masterpiece. He attempted to show that the study of folklore should not be considered as simply the collection of quaint customs for the amusement of antiquarians, nor as a branch of theology concerned with devil worship and heresy. He defined it as the study of 'the popular' and the 'collective beliefs of the masses', contrasting its subject-matter with that of literature, which was concerned with the creation of individuals, and which was usually addressed to an élite audience. He urged that folklore should not confine itself to legends and songs but look also at all ceremonies, games, devices, cults, domestic utensils, all 'institutions and ways of feeling and expressing oneself which differentiated the popular from the superior'. The nineteenth-century folklorists, he said, had been essentially historians or antiquaries; and he thought that sociologists had taken over the historical method: 'The whole of sociology needs to be redone.' He felt more akin with linguists, who understood that language was constantly changing: he called his own method 'biological', meaning that he based himself on observation of the present, but linked this with the evolving lives of his subjects. He respected peasant culture as it was and was scathing of the attempts by scholars to produce erudite theoretical explanations of it. He resisted the definition of folklore as excluding all that is transmitted by writing, because writing sometimes played an important part in the transmission of songs, for example. He appreciated that the distinction between collective and individual creation was a weak one; he was as interested in the folklore of the forces that overthrew old beliefs as he was in these. He urged the study of the folklore of schoolchildren, conscripts and convicts.

The study of folklore, Van Gennep argued, revealed that peasants lived mentally in two worlds, one of which had rules which were officially and formally taught, while the other was governed by custom. They did not make any clear distinction between these, but managed their lives as if each was binding or true; this implied no exclusive commitment to either. Van Gennep collected a vast array of facts to illustrate the survival of customary habits at every stage from birth to death and he made a particular study of rites of passage from one stage to another, which continued side by side with the examination system and the state's official classification. He showed the recurring themes of birth, rebirth and seasonal change in these rites of passage; he sought therefore to study man not in terms of individual psychology, which he considered inadequate, but as part of nature, of biology. He produced elaborate documentation of superstitious behaviour in pregnancy (the fear of envies), in infancy (rites to encourage growth, like not cutting the hair, or leaving fleas in it, and judging health by the abundance of vermin), in marriage and in death. He showed how the official education system had done little to destroy the solidarity of children in face of the school on the one hand and other generations on the other, how children had kept their own codes of violence and property, their own language, but also had strong internal divisions amongst themselves, with cliques and peer groups. He was one of the first to study adolescent gangs, to record the depredation they caused and the battles and brutalities that kept them together. He showed how when the pharmacy students of Paris marched through the streets in 1939, burning their overalls behind giant effigies of a devil and of Julius Caesar, they were unwittingly reproducing almost exactly the symbolism of their predecessors in the middle ages. Despite his isolation from the university, Van Gennep had able disciples and collaborators, some of whom carried out remarkable studies on the lines he laid down; the Seignolle brothers, for example, analysed the relationship of urban and rural cultures in the villages just outside Paris, tracing both the decay and the survival of folkloric beliefs. At Orly in 1937, parents marrying-off their last daughter still carried her through the village in a chair, to a bonfire in the square, where the chair was ritually burnt, to show they had no daughters left to marry. Orly airport had been opened (as a military base) at the end of the First World War.[1]

The Classical Spirit

Respect for the past was not the crucial element in these kinds of conformity. Conformity based on historical grounds was much

[1] *Bibliographie des œuvres d'Arnold van Gennep*, ed. K. van Gennep (Épernay, 1964); A. van Gennep, *Le Folklore: croyances et coutumes populaires françaises* (1941); id., *Manuel de folklore français contemporain* (1943–58); C. and J. Seignolle, *Le Folklore de Hurepoix (Seine, Seine-et-Oise, Seine-et-Marne)* (1937), 83. Cf. *Niveaux de culture et groupes sociaux* (1967), proceedings of a conference held at the École Normale Supérieure.

more the result of education, which, as has been seen, was not as revolutionary as it was often believed to be. The chapters on education have shown how the schools cultivated an approach to life that took past attitudes as the starting-point of its reasoning. Successive generations of rebels had to fight what could be called the classical spirit, and they had to do this repeatedly because it survived so indestructibly. The minister of education of 1877–9 publicly declared that the ideal that all teachers ought to hold before them was 'the *honnête homme* as the seventeenth century understood him'.[1] The men of the Renaissance and the ancient Greeks continued to be models of conduct in this period. Educated people could probably recite an ode of Horace more easily than verses from the Bible, and Livy and Marcus Aurelius provided them with ideals of virtue as much as the Church. That the revolution of 1789 should have strengthened the cult of antiquity was no temporary aberration, for that cult became even more widespread with the growth of schooling, and with the development of classical erudition, in archaeology, comparative philology and ancient religions. Théophile Gautier (1811–72) read the *Iliad* some thirty times in the original Greek.[2] The Parnassian poets found in antiquity the majesty, grandeur and ideal beauty they could not see in their own day. The classics were admired not only as the source of French civilisation, as containing models of wisdom and simplicity, but also as an escape from the present. Flaubert, that arch-critic of both the romantic and bourgeois minds, read a great deal of Greek. Leconte de Lisle's translation of Homer won many to hellenism. The politicians Herriot and Clemenceau wrote in praise of Greece, the latter regarding Demosthenes as his hero. Barrès's *Voyage de Sparte* (1906), Thibaudet's *Images de Grèce* (1926) show the constant return to the past. Gide records in his Journal how the mere name of Agamemnon in the theatre sufficed to cause tears to flow down his cheeks and how terribly he suffered seeing Sophocles' *Antigone* profaned by the over-clever Cocteau. He, like Cocteau and Giraudoux used Greek themes freely. Giraudoux in 1929 claimed, as a

[1] Agénor Bardoux, in Anon., *L'Église de France et les réformes nécessaires* (1880), 32.

[2] Daniel Mornet, *Histoire de la clarté française* (1929); Pierre Moreau, *Le Classicisme des romantiques* (1932); Harold T. Parker, *The Cult of Antiquity and the French Revolution* (Chicago, 1937).

matter of pride, 'I believe no writer of my age is as impregnated by antiquity as I am'. Claudel in turn has been called 'The most Latin Frenchman since Bossuet': he regarded Virgil as the greatest genius humanity had ever produced.[1] The taste for originality, though a marked feature of the century covered by this book, was combined with a respect for the classical past. Total originality met with considerable resistance among the reading public. The poems of popular authors which were most admired by their contemporaries were those now considered least original.[2]

In 1891 J.-J. Weiss, an acute literary critic, wrote, 'The classical spirit is dead . . . so is classical culture. Around 1869 still, there was hardly any conversation between educated men (*honnêtes gens*)—whether serious or frivolous, learned or worldly—which was not strewn and spangled with Greek or Latin quotations, bits of the Bible, mythological references, aphorisms from ancient history. All these things became with time so usual, so common and so banal that no one bothered asking how they had come into modern conversation. People understood each other in this way with references which summed up a whole series of ideas, sensations and arguments—abbreviations as clear and quick, more substantial and concise than those of stenography. Today these references would sound like Sanskrit. A quarter of a century has sufficed to alter French vocabulary in this way and to modify so considerably the atmosphere in which familiar conversation was made.' J.-J. Weiss was probably accurate about conversation, but the classics, respect for the past, pleasure in identifying oneself with antique models, survived for several generations longer. The widespread fondness for quotations was only a superficial indication of this. What this attitude implied was the assertion of the respectability of the ordinary man, who did as other sensible men before him had done, and who did not claim to greater wisdom than previous generations.

The philosophic doctrine for this attitude had been provided

[1] Henri Peyre, *L'Influence des littératures antiques sur la littérature française moderne* (New Haven, 1941). This book has useful suggestions for further research. Cf. Charly Clerc, *Le Génie du paganisme. Essais sur l'inspiration antique dans la littérature française contemporaine* (1926).

[2] Henri Peyre, *Writers and their Critics. A Study of Misunderstanding* (New York, 1944), 92–3.

by Victor Cousin (1792–1867). His book, *Du Vrai, du Beau et du Bien* (1837), was an official textbook not only during the July Monarchy, when he personally dominated the university, but for much of the nineteenth century, when schoolboys studied it on a par with Plato and Descartes. It enjoyed its vogue because it was a true epitome and justification of middle-class common sense. Known as *eclecticism*, Cousin's doctrine sought to combine all that was best in the philosophies of the past. It sought to apply the Orleanist idea of the *juste milieu* to philosophy, to abandon the revolutionary method by which all previous French philosophies had condemned their predecessors, and to practise instead the spirit of conciliation with a view to ending the clash of ideas. It was directed against scepticism, but it also avoided dogmatism. It claimed to be based on experience, but it rejected empiricism. It called its method psychological, by which it meant that it studied human nature, but it took as its guide common-sense beliefs. Instead of showing up the philosophical difficulties which these entail, it accepted them as necessary truths and combined them into a complete moral and aesthetic system. It began with the principle that the great need of the time was for absolute truths. It rapidly established these, refuting the objections of men like Locke and Kant. Since truth was impossible without God, therefore God existed. He necessarily had to be good and the established order was his work. Reason was man's faculty for understanding this and it led directly to truth. Cousin's conclusions soon sounded banal, but he was at first a great innovator himself. He reintroduced into French philosophy Plato—whose works he had translated by an army of pupils, under his own name—and Descartes, discredited by the *philosophes* of the eighteenth century. He travelled in Germany and brought back Kant's morals of duty, which placed the primitive study of ethics in France on an entirely new basis. He made friends with Hegel, and brought back his dialectic; he introduced the philosophical term *Absolute* into France. These influences were to have an important effect on French thought in the future. They gave Cousin himself an enormous prestige in his youth and made him appear the creator of a new morality, 'We have tried too long', he proclaimed, 'to be free with the ethical code of slaves. It is time to inaugurate a philosophy which is, as Plato says, the philosophy of free men.' 'It is difficult to realise', wrote Jules Favre, 'what his lectures meant to the young. They gave men hope, confidence, pride.'[1]

Cousin's great achievement was to abolish doubt. He told men exactly what they must do and gave the blessing of philosophy to traditional behaviour which waning religious faith could no longer justify. The most important duty, he said, was self-discipline, to maintain the rule of reason. Men should show prudence and moderation in all things, they should improve their intelligence by education, cultivate their sensibilities, feel affection for their family, donate to charity, respect property, justice and the rights of others, and support governments which guaranteed liberty, which could be none other than the Orleanist constitutional monarchy. They should love art, because that stimulated an admiration for the ideal, and so for God—art purified and perfected the soul. The best art was not the purely representational, nor the religious kind which sought to be moral by direct means; it was rather that which satisfied reason, taste, imagination, and sentiment all at once.

His doctrine, which owes much to Plato, came very near pantheism. The Church attacked Cousin and he, anxious to please everybody, consequently modified his teachings very considerably. In later editions, he cut out large sections of the metaphysical part of his book—precisely those which had won him his philosophical reputation—and made it largely a work on morals and aesthetics. He rebaptised his doctrine 'spiritualism'. He abandoned one of his most important achievements, the setting-up of philosophy as a study totally independent of theology; and instead increasingly stressed the need for religion; and it is significant that he did this at the very time when many were beginning to fear the results of free-thinking and going back to Catholicism. But by allying with the Church just when it was losing prestige among a new generation of intellectuals, he invited attack from them. In the same way, by concentrating on the philosophical syllabus, he neglected the study of science, just when this was becoming popular.

Under the July Monarchy it had not been easy to attack Cousin, for he established an extraordinary ascendancy. He appointed all the teachers of philosophy in the country, who

[1] Paul Janet, *Victor Cousin et son œuvre* (1885), 158.

were known as his regiment. He used them as the mouthpiece of his doctrine and, in the vacation, they came to pay court to him in his apartment at the Sorbonne. He was a self-made man, the son, like Rousseau, of a watchmaker (some say of a jeweller); his mother had been a washerwoman. His eloquence, which made him more of a preacher than a professor, won him acclaim when he was still in his early twenties. He had a prodigious memory, which as much as anything was the basis of his power. After thirty years he could still recall word for word every reply a man had made in his university examination. He seldom flattered, he never yielded, he was a master of raillery and contempt; he was hardest on those he liked best; he obtained from his pupils terror and admiration; he never forgot their faults or their virtues, he devoted endless trouble to their promotions and transfers, and he kept them intellectually alive by allocating philosophical tasks, translations or commentaries to each one. He convinced men that he was master of every imaginable subject, for he could talk brilliantly about anything. In time, however, the lack of coherence, rigour and precision in his theories became too evident. His disciples modified their doctrines too. But woolly-headed men long continued to think as he did.

Cousin represented the conformity that tried to avoid arguments and to allow some truth to every point of view, without lapsing into scepticism. Respect for the past was encouraged in another form by the leading conservative literary critic during the July Monarchy and the Second Empire, Désiré Nisard (1806–88), who was as important as Cousin, in that he dominated the teaching of literature in almost the same way as Cousin dominated philosophy. Nisard was head of the Division of Science and Letters at the ministry of education and Member of Parliament under Louis-Philippe, professor of Latin eloquence at the Collège de France and then of French eloquence at the Sorbonne; he was elected Member of the French Academy in 1850, against Alfred de Musset; he was inspector-general of higher education under Napoleon III, and Director of the École Normale Supérieure, 1857–67, where he was able to influence a whole generation of schoolmasters. Nisard had made his name as a young man with a *Manifeste contre la littérature facile* (1833), attacking the novel, on the ground that the sole

respectable form of literature was that which could be understood only after study, application and criticism. His doctrine
was formulated in his *Histoire de la littérature française* (1844–61)
in which he asserted that the aim of literature, and the criterion for judging it, was not originality. 'The man of genius
in France is he who says what everybody knows. He is only the
intelligent echo of the crowd. Instead of astonishing us by his
private opinions, he makes us see the inside of ourselves, as
Montaigne says, and he gets us to know ourselves.' Nisard's
view implied that there was no more knowledge to be discovered
about humans; all that was needed was to express that knowledge: that was the function of art. 'Art is the expression of
general truths in perfect language.' Perfect language was
recognisable because it was 'at once clear and intelligible to the
nation (which spoke it) and to the cultivated minds of all
nations'. The truths expressed by art, and the terms it used, were
not liable to change. In this history of French literature, he
sought to study not change—because what changed was
ephemeral—but what was 'constant, essential and immutable
in the French spirit'. French literature was not a reflection of
changing ideas and social conditions: Nisard's view was firmly
anti-sociological. French literature, he confidently asserted,
reached maturity and perfection in the seventeenth century;
the eighteenth century was the beginning of decadence. The
seventeenth century alone gave proper expression to the French
genius—which was for clarity, discipline and practicality. It
differed from that of ancient Greece in that Greece gave too
much time to 'vain curiosity and idle speculations', favouring
liberty, 'which is full of perils and aberrations, rather than
discipline which gives strength'. The best in French literature
was the study of the ideal of life, in all countries and in all
times, but with a practical intention. 'It gives little attention
to pure curiosity and to speculations which do not lead to some
truth which can be put into practice. It removes the gross and
superfluous from reality, to render knowledge of it at once
useful and innocent. . . . In France all that is not knowledge
interesting to the majority and a rule of conduct for men of
goodwill is in grave danger of being irrelevant and inadequate.'
France believed in the supremacy of reason, clarity, simplicity,
precision. Reason should be applied to practical purposes—

art's function was to teach morals, to purge the passions. What it advocated must be plausible, and conforming to common educated opinion.[1]

The complex results of basing oneself on the classical tradition can be seen in the life of Anatole France (1844–1924). He shows that classicism survived so long because it did not frontally oppose the forces which challenged it, but sought to absorb them. As a result, it degenerated into a colourless scepticism. In the case of Anatole France, it produced brilliant wit and fluent style, but this was only a false veneer concealing a profound despair. He shows how wrong it is to equate conformity with complacency, or to assume that conformity is necessarily static. He was undoubtedly one of the most popular authors in the country in the twenty years before 1914. A pamphlet was published entitled *Three Thinkers: Anatole France, Jesus, Pascal*. He was admired both by the cultured élite and by the masses.[2] He was considered the equal of Rabelais, Montaigne and Voltaire. His death was heralded as the end of an epoch and was greeted by an offensive on his memory comparable in violence only to that launched against Victor Hugo on his death.[3] He was one of those authors whose enormous popularity during his lifetime is paid for by almost total oblivion afterwards. Valéry, his successor in the Academy, ridiculed his superficiality. Everybody agreed he had no influence on literature and that he left no school: but he remains important because he reveals many of the problems that conformity created.

Anatole France was an unhappy man: his classicism was not based on contentment. His contemporaries knew very little about him and assumed that he was a gentle, wise old pedant, disabused of illusions but remaining sensitive and kind. It was only after his death, with the publication of more intimate

---

[1] D. Nisard, *Histoire de la littérature française* (4 vols., 1844–61) and *Précis de l'histoire de la littérature française* (1878), *Études de critique littéraire* (1858); obituary in *Modern Language Notes* (1888), 294; E. des Essarts, 'Désiré Nisard', in *La Nouvelle Revue* (1888), vol. 51, 929–36; René Bray, *La Formation de la doctrine classique en France* (1927).

[2] Paul Gisell, 'Sur la popularité d'Anatole France', *Revue mondiale* (1 Nov. 1924), 22–9.

[3] Gaston Picard, 'L'Influence littéraire et sociale d'Anatole France. Enquête', *Revue mondiale* (1 and 15 Dec. 1924), 227–56, 339–66.

reminiscences by his friends, that he was shown up as a tragic and melancholy figure, wounded by life, torn by doubt and appallingly alone; sparkling with intelligence, often smiling but never gay. The explanation was partly personal. He was a self made man (the son of a bookseller), but one whom success could not satisfy. The only passion of his life, he said, was his adoration for his mother; he did not love his wife, whom he soon divorced; he broke off relations with his daughter when she contracted a marriage of which he disapproved. For twenty years he conducted a celebrated liaison with Mme Arman de Caillavet, of whose salon he was the principal ornament; but she was in some ways a substitute-mother, who kept him working hard, to the extent that he had to indulge in ludicrous subterfuges to be able to read light novels. He left her, too, in the end, and spent his final years living with her maid. Anatole France could never escape his childhood and he wrote four autobiographies. His heroes in his books were nearly always orphans, and like himself, unfulfilled ones. He was tormented by his inability to find satisfaction in love, arguing that love is necessarily jealous, seeking an impossible unity and never giving men what they want. So he tried to confine himself to being an observer of life. He said he was in this way typical of the curious, idle, ingenuous Parisians, who were basically still children, whom everything amused. He wrote books though he disliked writing, finding it painful, like a task imposed on a child as a punishment.

'Why are we unhappy?' was the title of one of his articles. The answer went beyond the failure of family life. Anatole France represented disillusionment with knowledge and progress, despair at the discoveries of science—which showed man his insignificance—loneliness after the loss of religious faith, horror at the prospect of society being dominated by 'engineers and electricians', awareness of the mediocrity of life. He was too clever to believe in any ideal. His solution was to seek to embellish life, to render it tolerable by superficial gaiety, humour and beauty. He gave up his youthful enthusiasm for knowledge and change. What men needed, he decided, was imagination and 'enchantment', 'to forget the sad truth', to escape from themselves; he no longer wanted to discover reality but to reorganise it in fantasy, to make it amusing, to conceal its unpleasant aspects. Beyond truth, it was even more important to find hope and consolation; without lies, he said, humanity 'would perish of despair and boredom'. He therefore placed supreme importance on art, but not as a means of innovation. Originality was not necessary to beauty and the function of the artist was not to advance into the unknown. He wrote only 'to give brief amusement to delicate and curious minds'. He addressed himself to 'delicate' people, to the educated public; he could be understood by them only, he said, and his wide popularity was accidental, due to incomprehension. *Délicatesse* was his password. Delicate people must not be disturbed, but their jaded nerves needed refined and sophisticated entertainment. It was in this way that he was a classic. He emulated the clarity and simplicity of seventeenth century prose and the balance and polish of the eighteenth; he was hailed as the final flowering of the classicism of Greece and Rome as well as of that of France; his books were full of Greek myth. He said of himself that he had no pretence to originality: 'All my art is to scribble in the margins of books'. He was genuinely modest, and that was how Gide defined classicism, as opposed to the pride of romanticism.

His humour, and his political tergiversations, were both the result of this. His humour was above all ironic, and irony he himself defined as 'the last phase of disillusion'. One of his most famous fictional characters, Monsieur Bergeret, is told by his wife: 'You laugh at what is not laughable and one never knows if you are joking or if you are serious.' Anatole France spared nothing and no one; but it was not from arrogance: 'Though I have been a mocker in all stages of my life', he wrote, 'I have never made fun of anyone so cruelly as of myself, nor with such delight.' This did not mean that he was incapable of idealism. He supported almost every progressive idea of his day, constantly keeping up with his times. He was a liberal republican under Napoleon III; he was terrified by the Commune, but then became one of the principal supporters of Dreyfus, moved on to socialism and finally ended up, at least in name, a communist. While remaining convinced of the vanity of all human action, he became one of the country's most popular political orators. He wrote his sceptical books in the morning and talked hopefully of a new world at socialist banquets in the evening. He was not insincere: 'our contradictions', he said, 'are not the least true part of ourselves'. It is this complexity that makes him illuminating about conformity. Conformity did not necessarily involve faith. The classicism with which Anatole France was identified was supposed to signify repose and ·harmony, but this was what he sought, not what he achieved.[1]

Conformity was one of the principal problems that the new subject of sociology tried to study. In France, under the leadership of Émile Durkheim sociology concentrated on the relationship of the individual and the group. It took as the starting-point the view that society was threatened with collapse and needed to be restored by a new discipline and new moral bonds.[2] Durkheim argued that the growth of nations did not increase conformity, but on the contrary stimulated individual diversity: the larger the social group, the more it had to be adaptable to the multiplicity of situations it encountered, and the less it was able to resist individual variations. As a result 'everyone increasingly follows his own path', and the country was 'gradually proceeding to a state of affairs, now almost attained, in which the members of a single social group will no longer have anything in common other than their humanity'. There was nothing stable to 'love and honour in common, apart from man himself'.[3] This should not be taken as an accurate description of French society at the turn of the century, for Durkheim owes his fame not to his powers of observation of the situation around him, but for developing an analytical approach to the study of social phenomena. Durkheim's laments—for that is what they were—represented a longing for closer ties between humans, and for an expansion of the individualism of the eighteenth century, which had essentially

[1] H. M. Chevalier, *The Ironic Temperament. Anatole France and his time* (N.Y. 1932); J. Levaillant, *Les Aventures du scepticisme. Essai sur l'évolution intellectuelle d'Anatole France* (1965); L. B. Walton, *Anatole France and the Greek World* (Durham, North Carolina, 1950).

[2] Raymond Aron, *La Sociologie allemande contemporaine* (1935), 170. Cf. C. Bouglé, *Bilan de la sociologie française* (1935).

[3] E. Durkheim, 'L'Individualisme et les intellectuels', *Revue bleue* (1898), 4th series, vol. 10, 7–13; English translation published by Steven Lukes. Cf. Joan Rowland, 'Durkheim's social theory with special reference to the position of the individual in society' (M.A. London, unpublished thesis, 1948).

been a rebellion against political constraints. Durkheim was the secretary-general of the Bordeaux section of the League of the Rights of Man, a founder of the *Jeunesse laïque* association in that city and a sympathiser of the socialist party. He had inherited the individualist principles of the Revolution. But he was also a philosopher who was uncomfortable with these principles. The supporters of the Revolution hoped, as another philosopher, Charles Renouvier put it, to convert the superstitious, sensual and immoral individuals, who were thus liberated, into rational beings, with the ability and the will to lead moral lives. Philosophers looked on the rabble as barbarians, who needed to be tamed, and on the educated élite who were emerging from them as lost souls, who could not be left simply to their own devices. Durkheim, the son and grandson of rabbis, and trained as a philosopher, was above all a moralist. He was a sociologist because he believed that the functions once performed by common ideas and sentiments were now determined by new social institutions and relationships; and this had transformed the nature of morality. He attacked traditional moralists for regarding the individual as an autonomous entity, depending only on himself, irrespective of the social context in which he found himself. He wished to place the study of morality on a scientific footing. He called himself a rationalist. He was the disciple both of Kant and of Comte. He believed that individual appetites are 'by nature boundless and insatiable: if there is nothing to control them they will not be able to control themselves'. Morality was therefore concerned with imposing social discipline. It was not a means to individual happiness, but to the prevention of anarchy, both in society and within the individual himself. Durkheim, his biographer records, could never experience happiness himself without a feeling of remorse. He believed a free man was one who was victorious over his instincts: self-discipline was a good in itself. Children were like primitive peoples, who needed to be civilised. That is why he devoted so much of his efforts to the study of education, and why the book he wanted to write more than any, but which he never got round to, was on the sociology of morality. His ideal was rational uniformity, in which men would be free, but would nevertheless recognise their duties and act altruistically. But he also saw that sacrifice and disinterestedness could not be understood in purely intellectual terms and he was increasingly interested by religion.[1]

Durkheim shows the problem of conformity growing ever larger, as its social dimensions were revealed. His school, at the same time, illustrates another aspect of conformity, in that it itself represented at once a rebellion, an orthodoxy and a catalyst. Sociology as he developed it was a breakaway from philosophy. His disciples, in the first generation, were like himself, philosophers who opted for a heresy. This was shown in the way they were not particularly attracted by fieldwork, but specialised in general methodology, in defining what constitutes scientific fact and in distinguishing between different kinds of truth. Like the school of Cousin, they obtained much of their impetus from the introduction of foreign ideas. Forty per cent of the books reviewed in Durkheim's periodical, *L'Année sociologique*, were German ones, 21 per cent were English, 12 per cent Italian, and only 26 per cent were French. Just how far Durkheim was absorbed by morals and religion may be seen from the fact that 47 per cent of the references in this periodical were to books concerned with religion, 15 per cent were on law and only 20 per cent on economics.[2] Durkheim was raised to his pre-eminence in French sociology by the admiration of philosophers, particularly those in the École Normale Supérieure. It was the *Revue de métaphysique et morale*, the *Revue philosophique* and the *Revue de synthèse historique* which wrote in praise of the *Année*, and it was educators and moralists like Gustave Belot, and the logician Goblot, who backed Durkheim. Durkheim's sociology was vigorously attacked by that of others who had rival schools, like Worms (who inclined more to law and economics) and the disciples of Le Play (who specialised in empirical monographs and who were politically more right wing). Durkheim gradually established his brand of sociology as the dominant one in the universities of France, so

[1] The indispensable source is Steven Lukes, *Émile Durkheim: his life and work* (1973), which also contains the best bibliography. Cf. in particular, E. Durkheim, *L'Éducation morale* (1938). Also Claude Lévi-Strauss, 'La Sociologie française' in G. Gurvitch and W. E. Moore, *La Sociologie au 20ᵉ siècle* (1947), 513-45.

[2] Yash Nandan, 'Le Maître, les doctrines et le magnum opus: une étude critique et analytique de l'école durkheimienne et de l'Année sociologique' (unpublished thèse de troisième cycle, Paris V, 1974), 129.

that his approach—though much modified by his followers—produced almost a new way of talking.[1]

This was due, in part, to the marriages sociology entered into with other heretics from other subjects. The *Annales* school of history was, to some extent, an offspring of one of these marriages, though Lucien Febvre, in his rebellion against the political historians, found inspiration not only in Durkheim—or rather in his son-in-law Mauss—but also in Vidal de la Blache the geographer, the economist Simiand, and not negligibly, in Michelet also. History was immeasurably broadened as a result, but, as Lucien Febvre said, he felt he was better understood by people in other disciplines than by other historians. The sociological approach (though Febvre's ideas had more to them than this label would suggest) represented an alliance of a generation (or rather of part of one, for traditional history, like traditional philosophy, continued to flourish).[2] What held these rebels together was a common temperament and a similar kind of curiosity, that transcended the apparent divisions of their subjects. Their alliance could be called a new kind of conformity. The study of conformities reduces one to recognising a whole variety of conformities, and conformity emerges as much more than static resistance.[3]

[1] For the rival theory of conformity by imitation, see the works of Gabriel Tarde, especially *Les Lois de l'imitation* (1890) and Jean Milet, *Gabriel Tarde et la philosophie de l'histoire* (1970); A. Matagrin, *La Psychologie sociale de G. Tarde* (1910).

[2] H. D. Mann, *Lucien Febvre* (1971).

[3] T. N. Clark, *Prophets and Patrons: The French University and the Emergence of the Social Sciences* (Cambridge, Mass., 1973). For the psychological problems, e.g. the relationships of detachment, radicalism and introversion, see M. Brewster Smith, J. S. Brunner and R. W. White, *Opinions and Personality* (1956), full of interesting ideas for the historian.

3. Fashion and Beauty

Furniture

FURNITURE is a particularly valuable indicator of national taste. Everybody needs furniture and everybody in theory has to declare his preferences when buying it. The history of furniture reveals aesthetic ideals in their social context, subject to a whole variety of pressures, of fashion, technical change, snobbishness, economy and practical needs. It is a great misfortune that its development is, nevertheless,. one of the most neglected branches of art history, and indeed of every kind of history: there is still an enormous amount to be discovered about the economic history of the industry which played a major part in satisfying the mass demand for comfort and well-being, about the social history of the changes in behaviour which new kinds of homes both produced and reflected, and about the political history of the furniture makers, who had an extraordinary record of revolutionary agitation. The fragments of information at present available make possible only the most tentative generalisations.[1]

Much more has been written about the furniture of the eighteenth century, because pieces of outstandingly skilful craftsmanship were produced then. Many of these are now preserved in museums, and they are readily available for study. The nineteenth century never had the same pride in its taste, perhaps because it made its taste serve other more powerful ideals. The *ancien régime* is generally associated with expensive, elaborate furniture made for kings and aristocrats; the nineteenth century is usually seen as an age of cheap production and banal copying of old styles for a mass market. The contrast is, however, false, and the nineteenth century's achievements have been underestimated because its aims have been misunderstood. To use the same criteria on it as on the *ancien régime* is misleading. It is

---

[1] Jacqueline Viaux, 'Bibliographie du meuble' (unpublished, stencilled, 1966), is the indispensable starting-point—by the librarian of the Musée Forney, which specialises in industrial art.

wrong to assume that all eighteenth-century furniture was as fine, as elegant or as well made as the museum pieces. No one was more scathing of the furniture-making of this period than its most revered craftsman Roubo (1739–91), who lamented even then that there were very few artisans capable of making beautiful furniture. Specialisation was already so advanced in his day that nearly all the people in the trade made only a single part; 'their skill', said Roubo, 'consisted only in a more or less successful routine'. There were few enlightened patrons either: most buyers were 'without taste and without knowledge and, what is worse, without the money to pay for good work; they take what is offered to them, indiscriminately, provided it is cheap, which is the reason for the large amount produced and its poor quality'.[1] Good furniture was very expensive, and all the more so because intermediaries took their cut. It is true that artisans went to the houses of buyers, to receive orders and detailed instructions, and it has been argued that this system was the basis of the high standards and individual design of the age; but professional 'decorators' also played an important role in determining what was produced, and the artisans resented their interference and profiteering as much as they later resented the department stores. The pressure to produce cheaply was always present, except in rare cases. Mercier, writing in 1788, said that three-quarters of the furniture produced in Paris went to buyers from the country, who were given the worst and shoddiest goods. Fraud was rampant; the decorators sold on credit, demanding down payments of 30 per cent—which was the cost of the furniture to them—and pocketing the rest as profit; much furniture was held together by glue and quickly fell apart. The decorator was able to dominate the market, because buyers wanted to furnish whole rooms with complete sets which he put together: the alternative to his shoddy goods was to buy older, more solid furniture, which had stood the test of time, but that was hard to find. The great cabinet-makers flourished thanks to the idea adopted by some sections of the aristocracy and the rich that furniture should be changed almost as frequently as one's clothes. The cult of fashion and novelty provided a great stimulus to the best artisans, as also did the mania for collecting fine objects, which were beautiful even if

[1] J. A. Roubo, *L'Art du menuisier* (1769–72), 2. 366.

they were useless. There were thus two kinds of chairs—those
made to sit on, and those which simply decorated a room; and
in the best houses, people also had chairs made to measure, to
suit their individual dimensions. But though the cult of originality predominated (resulting in the introduction of embellish-
ments based, for example, on Chinese models), buyers were
already divided between those who favoured the exotic and the
new, and those who were attached to antiques. In 1777 the
comte d'Artois himself purchased a reproduction of a piece of
furniture by Boulle.[1]

Furniture-making in the nineteenth century continued trends
which were already well established. Thus the production of fine
pieces, not unworthy of comparison with the more celebrated
ones of the eighteenth century, continued in the Second Empire.
Second Empire furniture has for long been dismissed as ugly and
unoriginal, but it is the cheap copies of the best work which have
given the period its bad reputation. Henri Fourdinois († 1887),
Napoleon III's principal cabinet-maker, was a craftsman of
great ingenuity and skill; thirty-two manuscript order books,
with illustrations of every piece he made, survive to show the
ingenuity with which he combined borrowing from past designs
with original creation. He made furniture not only for the
imperial yacht and for the grandees of the regime like Achille
Fould, but for many middle-class clients who simply wanted
'armchairs in rose and violet silk'.[2] Napoleon III's chief cabinet-
maker, Jean Becker, who was permanently employed to look
after the imperial furniture, received a salary of 1,500 francs a
month, as much as senior officers. Enough information is beginning to emerge about these artisans to show that there was no
uniform fashion, slavishly copied—that is the impression given
by the second-rate imitations which followed twenty years later.
One of the leading arbiters of Second Empire taste, Aimé
Chenavard (b. 1798), had a wild imagination which led him to
mix Gothic, Renaissance and Oriental styles; another, M. J. N.
Lienard (1810–70), however, was an advocate of greater simplicity. The upholsterers now became rivals of the cabinet-
makers, adding skirts to chairs and urging the elaborate use of
rich cloths; but the most accepted rule was that each room

1 Pierre Verlet, *La Maison du 18ᵉ siècle en France: Société, décoration, mobilier* (1966).
2 Fourdinois MSS. (Forney Library).

should be in a different style: the dining-room Renaissance, the drawing-room eighteenth century, the boudoir and library Empire. A whole variety of new tables, for every kind of purpose, were introduced. There was thus a great deal of inventiveness in this period, and too many rich men to allow the drab monotony which is normally attributed to it.[1]

In selecting from this vast and increasing range of styles the young couple setting up home had to declare their taste almost in the way they had to admit their political opinions. They could follow the conservative programme set out by Charles Blanc, France's director of Fine Arts in 1848 and again in 1870–3. Paradoxically and significantly this gentle brother of the socialist Louis Blanc was, for all his sympathy with the working class, an admirer of the classical tradition in art; Raphael and Ingres were his heroes even if he preached that art should be carried to the masses; he illustrates well how limited the revolutionary elements in republicanism were, and how men with aspirations to modernity and justice retained (as has been shown in the political chapters of this book) many of the values of the *ancien régime*. Charles Blanc's *Grammar of the Decorative Arts* argued that nature, on its own, was not beautiful, because it lacked order, proportion and unity. These were the three qualities one should seek to create in one's home. Order, in particular, was 'the sovereign law of the decorative arts'. The furniture of Louis XVI, he thought, captured the dignity, grace and elegance one should aim for, better than any other. He advocated symmetry, harmony, discretion: decency was an inseparable element of beauty; and taste was 'the delicate appreciation of the relationships between men and things'. One should not seek to follow fashions slavishly, therefore, but rather to reflect one's moral worth in one's surroundings. The love of domestic luxury was a good thing because it encouraged the love of family life. One did not have to be rich to have a graceful home, for grace 'had no need of more than the appearance of richness'. There was nothing wrong with fakes or imitation. That was one reason why wallpaper was such a great invention: it gave if not the equivalent of luxury, at least the mirage of it. All the resources of modern technology should be used freely,

[1] J. Viaux, 'Le mobilier Napoleon III', *Revue de l'ameublement* (Mar. 1965), 191–7, (Apr. 1965), 175–81, (May 1965), 123–9.

because they showed the superiority of art over matter and enabled the humblest material to be given artistic shape. Charles Blanc showed that there were very good reasons why ordinary people should find merit in the banal copying of classical tàste, and also why they should have a sense of achievement in doing so successfully. His advice was the counterpart of that of the professors who taught the men of the Third Republic to express their humanitarian principles according to the rules of traditional rhetoric.[1] But Blanc represented only one approach. An alternative was that of the individualistic school, of which an inspector of Fine Arts of the next generation, Henry Havard, was a particularly influential example. His *Grammar of Furnishing* (1884) said that just as it would be ridiculous to wear eighteenth-century clothes, so it was absurd to surround oneself with eighteenth-century furniture. Outside the home, men should respect dominant taste, but inside it they should follow their own and concentrate on pleasing themselves. There were no fixed rules, particularly in the bedroom, where one could do as one liked, and seek comfort above all else. The dining-room should not distract attention away from the main function of eating; it should not be filled with old furniture or decorated excessively, but made light and gay. Old people should sit in Louis XIV chairs if they wished to give expression to the authority they incarnated, and the middle-aged in Louis XVI chairs, but eclecticism in styles was a good rule, and modern furniture was quite in place in intimate sitting-rooms. However, eclecticism should not be exaggerated: the heaping of bibelot upon bibelot was not enough: that was where *taste* came in. It was better to have a single masterpiece than a mass of furniture of doubtful value. 'If people judge our fortune by quantity, it is by our choice that they judge our taste.' Havard shows that ultimately taste was the one thing that no book could teach.[2]

That was one reason why the third alternative, which was the school of modernity, had a certain appeal. In reaction against copying the past and the chaotic mixing of styles, a movement arose to make furniture original in a fuller sense and to give the applied arts in general a higher status. The leaders—Gallé,

[1] Charles Blanc, *Grammaire des arts décoratifs. Décoration intérieur de la maison* (2nd edition, 1882), 10, 22, 135, 146, 337–9.

[2] H. Havard, *L'Art dans la maison. Grammaire de l'ameublement* (1884), 356, 431.

Majorelle, Prouvé, Émile Ruhlmann—were influenced by William Morris. Living mainly in Nancy, they were conscious of trends in German art. They produced unusual jewellery, ceramics, book illustrations, but they met most resistance in furniture, even though they obtained the patronage of Corbin, the young heir of the Magasins Réunis of Nancy. It was only after 1921, when one of their group, Dufrène, became artistic director of the Galeries Lafayette in Paris and another, Francis Jourdain, abandoned painting for business, that their furniture became widely available to the public. The decorative pieces they designed were just as bastardised in mass production as fine pieces of the eighteenth century were in reproduction. The escape from the banal was not easy.[1]

The kind of furniture people bought was ultimately determined as much by the development of the furniture-making industry as by that elusive gift of taste. This industry has almost always been in a state of crisis: furniture is something people can always do without in hard times, and undercutting, by the use of cheaper materials, is a constant temptation and problem. In the depression of 1848, many cabinet-makers emigrated to England in search of work; the war of 1870 and the Commune were again disastrous, 'like an Edict of Nantes', because several thousand German furniture workers left France. The surviving artisans sought refuge not in innovation, but in reducing costs, by dispensing with the services of designers. Duchesne's collection of some 12,000 models of the sixteenth to eighteenth centuries made it unnecessary for manufacturers to find new ones for almost half a century. There was money to be made in reproduction furniture, because the boundary between copying and forging was so uncertain. The ambition of the best artisans was to emulate the great cabinet-makers of the past, to produce work indistinguishable from theirs, to have their pieces exhibited in museums as originals. In the twentieth century there were perhaps only eighty or a hundred top-class cabinet-makers of this kind, and they could make a very good living. André Mailfert, a highly skilled polisher who could fool the experts, set up a veritable forging industry at Annemasse in 1923; it was very

---

[1] Pierre Olmer, *La Renaissance du mobilier français 1890–1910* (1927); id., *Le Mobilier français d'aujourd'hui 1910–1925* (1926); Francis Jourdain, *Né en 76* (1951), 175–6; Madeleine Prouvé, *Victor Prouvé 1858–1943* (n.d.), 13.

successful; he sold one of his commodes for 1,200,000 francs; and he has unashamedly written about the gullibility and greed of his customers.[1] There was indeed always a certain mystery about reproduction furniture. It was not generally known—and the furniture makers of the Faubourg Saint-Antoine took care to keep the fact quiet—that chairs sold as the product of Parisian artisan skill were manufactured in Liffol-le-Grand (Meuse), a small town of barely 2,000 inhabitants, virtually all of whom made 'antique' chair frames; Paris artisans then polished these to make them more or less indistinguishable from genuine antiques. This industry had been set up in Liffol in 1864 and prospered continuously since then. The Parisian workshops did their best to maintain public interest in antique furniture by organising 'retrospective exhibitions', devoted to whatever period they had particularly large unsold stocks of at the time. The Union Centrale des Arts décoratives, which claimed to be a dis-interested body devoted to the applied arts, was for a time controlled by the forgers and the copyists. The export of pseudo-antiques mounted steadily, to reach a peak in 1927-9. The U.S.A. was France's best customer. The U.S.A. played an indispensable part in the history of modern French furniture-making, as it did in that of French painting, replacing the patronage of the old aristocracy. It was possible to sell to it at as much as four times the cost of manufacture; and the Americans were attracted by poor quality furniture also, provided it was skilfully advertised: clever merchants describing themselves as the leading manufacturers and artisans of France made hand-some profits from the shoddy goods they unloaded on the other side of the Atlantic. The essential feature of this trade was that the customer never quite knew what he was buying. The invest-ment value of antiques made the buying of old or pseudo-old furniture attractive, whatever one thought of its appearance: prices roughly doubled between 1865 and 1913, though between 1914 and 1939 they rose only 12 per cent. But by 1929 good modern furniture began to appreciate with age (rising by 27 per cent in the next decade). The more the value of money fell, the more did speculation in objects become widespread.[2]

[1] A. Mailfert, *Au pays des antiquaires: Confidences d'un maquilleur professionnel* (new edition, 1959).

[2] Janine Capronnier, *Le Prix des meubles d'époque 1860-1956* (1966), 75, 83.

The paradox about the art that went into making this furniture was that the artist accepted an inferior role. The furniture makers, with few exceptions, were content to remain nameless, and their individual skill—unlike that of painters—was never recognised outside trade circles. This was because the industry was dominated by merchants and intermediaries, who profited from the extreme specialisation and division of labour. In 1938 nearly 90 per cent of furniture makers worked in units of between one and five workers: each process, from that performed by the sawyer, to the finishing by the mirror maker, lacquerer, polisher and *patineur*, was a separate, independent activity. It took a long time for all these specialists to do their little bit on any particular item and they were therefore always short of cash. Merchants hovered around them, buying up their products cheaply, particularly on Fridays and Saturdays when they had to pay their wages and needed ready money; and these merchants usually resold at 40 or even 100 per cent profit. The great department stores carried this even further, by making regular contracts for very low prices, and insisting that their own names be affixed to the furniture. The contact between the artisan and the public, which, as one cabinet-maker said, had given them 'a constant communion of taste, ideas and initiative', was thus destroyed; 'personal originality and professional conscience' vanished when the sole aim was the largest possible turnover. Factories grew up to meet the demands of the *nouveaux riches*, each specialising in a definite type. Caned chairs from the 1880s onwards were made very largely in Halluin (Nord), Neuville-Coppegueule and the Bresle region; plain wooden chairs in Orthez; hotel furniture in washable beech in Montbéliard and modern furniture in Limoges, in a large factory founded in 1890 originally to produce Henri II styles from local walnut. Provincial styles (folkloric, rustic, chests and four-posters) which became popular after the First World War (like regional cooking), thanks to the development of tourism, were produced mainly in Auray (where fifteen factories with over 100 workers each were established) and in Bourg-en-Bresse (which switched from Louis XV to meet the new demands of the antique trade). The most decisive change in production was, however, due not to changed demand, but to the invention of plywood, the first patent for which was taken out in London in 1884 (though a machine to saw wood very thinly had been invented in 1834). Plywood could not be sculpted; it required large square surfaces; and that is what the customer increasingly got; but it was only after 1945 that new habits, the desire to reduce housework, and limitations of space, made people accept simple furniture of this kind with pleasure. Then for the first time furniture ceased to be a major sign of wealth and became just a collection of useful objects.[1]

The intervention of the department stores meant that one could buy cheap reproductions for not much more than plain furniture. Thus in 1878 at the Bon Marché a straightforward 'Victorian' armchair cost 75 francs, or even 59 francs, but one could buy a 'Pompadour' for 95 francs, a 'fauteuil anglais' or a 'polonais' for 85; and a carved Louis XII was only 125 francs.[2] At the Galeries Nancéiennes in 1898 reproduction chairs were often exactly the same price as modern ones: Louis XIII and caned bamboo both cost 12 fr. 75; the cheaper bentwood chair was 6 fr. 50, but the 'old oak François I' chair was only double that. An ordinary, plain 'modern' sideboard was 225 francs, whereas an elaborately carved 'Renaissance' one in 'old oak' was 600 francs, but one could get a variation of this massive piece, with slightly modified decoration, in 'Breton' style, for only 300 francs. Nevertheless the best buy was the 'Henri II' sideboard for only 180 francs.[3] The furniture shops that sprang up in provincial cities in the late nineteenth century ensured that what traces there were of local originality vanished. Louis XIII and above all Louis XV styles had already transformed the general appearance of country furniture by then; the influence of Paris had become all-powerful, even if functional peasant furniture—as opposed to furniture designed for ostentation—continued to be made up to the 1880s by local craftsmen.[4] Bordeaux, which in 1827 had 1,700 furniture makers, came to be dominated by the grand new stores, which relied increasingly on small country artisans producing to firm specifications. Every clerk getting married, it was said here, demanded a full set of Henri II or Louis XV furniture, at rock-bottom prices;

[1] Paule Garenc, *L'Industrie du meuble en France* (1957).
[2] Maison Aristide Boucicault: Au Bon Marché, *Album de l'ameublement* (1878).
[3] Aux Galeries Nancéiennes, *Album de l'ameublement* (1898).
[4] Suzanne Tardieu, *Meubles régionaux datés* (1950). Cf. J. Gauthier, *Le Mobilier des vieilles provinces de France* (1933).

the twenty-five antique shops of the city increasingly commissioned fakes of the styles they were asked for; and that was
what the artisans had to produce. The president of the trade
union of wood sculptors said in 1884 that his members were 'as
skilful today as at any other period, but we are not now allowed
to be original; we are asked for Renaissance, Louis XIV, Louis
XV and Louis XVI; we are being turned into machines by
being forced to copy'. Objects produced for a few hundred
francs—including enamel miniatures, jewellery, porcelain—
were covered in dirt, distributed among foreign antique shops
and resold there for ten times their original cost.[1] The trouble
was that foreigners became just as skilful at faking and they
could do it more cheaply, because they paid lower wages. Old
regional centres like Lyon stopped producing their own designs,
modelling themselves on Parisian styles, because snobbery preferred these.[2] One author put the blame for the decay of quality
on architects, competition among whom led to fierce price-
cutting. Between 1877 and 1897 the number of architects in
Bordeaux, for example, rose from 8 to 121. The obsession with
economy, among patrons who could not quite afford to satisfy
their ambitions, and among public authorities with rising costs,
led to the adoption of contracts by tender, so that frequently the
shoddiest workman got the job. A massive trade developed in
bits of old châteaux, which were pulled apart for use in new
houses: the craftsmen complained that commissions for interesting and original work became even rarer.

The simplification of wallpapers as they became increasingly
popular illustrates this tendency. In the middle of the nineteenth
century, papers were produced which were enormous murals,
often involving thirty different scenes, like 'The Lyon–Saint-
Étienne Railway' (1854) by Paillard (the wallpaper manufacturer who was mayor of Saint-Denis) which still survived in a
café in the 1930s; or, on an even grander scale, Délicourt's
'Hunting in the Forest' (1851) involving 4,000 engravings.
Already in the eighteenth century the poor used to buy small
bits of these and paste them up like pictures; but the introduction of steam machines (1858) turned wallpaper into an

[1] Marius Vachon, *La Crise industrielle et artistique en France et en Europe* (n.d.)
[c. 1886].
[2] Marius Vachon, *Les Industries d'art* (Nancy, 1897).

enormous industry—there were over 200 firms producing it by
1889. Much ingenuity was used to imitate silk and other signs of
luxury; and some very remarkable papers were printed for the
rich, but cheap, elementary repetitive patterns, bearing little
resemblance to these sophisticated products, soon drowned the
market.[1]

What the people of this period liked in their furniture was
thus first of all a symbol of status. The poor had virtually no
furniture; even the middle classes took a long time to collect
more than bare essentials—a bed, a table and cheap chairs. It
was natural that the taste of an age of increasing prosperity,
obsessed by social climbing, should have expressed itself in the
collection of objects and bric-à-brac, simply to indulge its
pleasure in the ownership of property, and that it should have
favoured in particular furniture that was solid, impressive and
that gave evidence of the hard work and money that had gone
into it. Since furniture was above all property, people wanted
theirs to look as much like the furniture of the rich as possible.
There were alternative ways of gaining status, but when it came
to exhibiting one's wealth, it was hard to fool one's neighbours.
The people of this period tried hard, nevertheless, to do so; they
tried to make their homes—or at least their sitting-rooms—into
miniature versions of châteaux. But they favoured the old and
the fake-old also because it had the essential quality of property,
permanence and investment value. They preferred the styles of
Paris, which had as it were received the consecration of the state,
to the eccentricities of what local craftsmen had escaped the
attractions of the city; and it was only when Paris set the fashion,
after 1919, for regional styles that the regions set up industries
to produce these. Since competitiveness played such an important role in the exhibition of taste, each class, each profession,
each set of people developed minor variations in the way it
collected and displayed domestic equipment, but the overriding
general uniformity between them testified to the fact that taste,
like education, had purposes other than its own satisfaction.

The counterpart of the concern with ostentation was the con-
straint of economy. This was probably the most important
influence on the changing appearance and construction of furni-

[1] H. Clouzot and C. Follot, *Histoire du papier peint en France* (1935); M. Vachon,
Les Arts et les industries du papier 1871–1894 (1894), 205–17.

ture; and one should not judge people's taste too simply on the basis of what they bought. A survey carried out in Britain some years ago revealed that there were almost three times as many people who disliked the furniture they owned as those who were pleased with their purchases. One should not imagine that the furniture produced reflected the taste either of the manufacturers or the artisans who made it; both had to make a living, to cut their costs to the minimum; and the buyer had to buy what he could afford. If there was an increasing preoccupation, it was not with beauty, but with comfort, which was a more easily attainable alternative. The variations in people's idea of beauty have still to be studied, taking into account all these distorting factors. But the sale prices of furniture have hitherto barely been used with the precision that economic historians have learnt to apply to other consumer goods.

Fashions in Clothes

Taste in clothes seems, at first sight, to have followed very different trends. Whereas in furniture most people continued to admire antique and unchanging styles, in their personal appearance they seemed to demand constant, almost annual, changes. Paris became established as the capital of fashion. This contrast is, however, deceptive. The cult of status dominated clothes exactly as it determined the choice of furniture, though men, it is true, pursued this goal more obviously and openly than women.[1]

The revolution that took place in men's clothes in this period brought about a most unusual and perhaps unique change in the landscape and in human relationships. Virtually all males took to wearing black or dark suits, without decoration, and with differences of cut and cloth so slight as to be barely distinguishable. Men had previously dressed to show their rank, their profession, their pride. Now discretion, modesty and, on the surface, acceptance of equality were what they paraded instead. In 1848 men wore their hair in every conceivable style, and in every length; fifty years later, long hair had virtually vanished and the skill of the male barber was reduced to the handling of clippers that left room for only minute variations.

[1] René Colas, *Bibliographie générale du costume et de la mode* (2 vols., 1933).

The differing speed at which this happened in different parts
of the country suggests that this increasing uniformity reflected
the gradual triumph of the Parisian principles of fraternity and
equality (though perhaps not of liberty). It was only in the
period 1880–1900 that the Breton peasants adopted what they
called the 'French style'. Previously they had worn distinctive
jackets and waistcoats—the *chupen manchek* and the *jilet*—which
were decorated and embroidered in a whole variety of ways, so
that one could at a glance tell what village, or group of villages,
the wearer came from. This was a uniform, but each uniform
was shared by only a few hundred people, and the specimens of
them that survive—with their elaborate and colourful needle-
work patterns—suggest a sense of pride in belonging to the local
community, almost as though it was a military regiment.[1] A
Breton doctor writing in 1904 said that one could still see these
varied costumes at fairs and markets, but one could also recognise the inhabitants of more modernised towns, like those from
the canton of Pont-l'Abbé who had in the last fifteen years taken
to buttoning up their jackets at the front 'the French way', concealing their embroidered waistcoats, dropping the decoration
though keeping a coloured lining, moving steadily, as he put
it, towards the monotony and platitude of 'the European-
American' style.[2] This style was in fact originally the style of
the English country gentleman, which the French aristocratic
dandies had imported in the early nineteenth century as a mark
of distinction and originality.[3] The theory behind it—developed
by Beau Brummell—was that men should seek to impress not
by decoration, strong colour or rich materials, but by the perfect
fit of their clothes, which should follow the natural line of the
body. The arrangement of their neckcloth was the only way
they could henceforth allow themselves some scope for fantasy,
and the cleanliness of their linen should be the measure of their
respectability. It is excessively simple to explain the triumph of
this fashion in terms of the progressive democratisation of the
western world, for it was first adopted by the most aristocratic
of nations. The gentlemen of England wore the same clothes,

---

[1] See the large display in the municipal museum of Rennes.
[2] Dr. C. A. Picquenard, *De l'evolution moderne du chupen et du jilet dans le costume masculin aux environs de Kemper* (Vannes, 1904).
[3] J. Boulenger, *Les Dandys* (1907).

originally, as a kind of caste uniform. To ape them was to pretend that one belonged to this exalted group. The universal black suit denoted not the triumph of democracy, so much as a new form of the search for social distinction.

The remarkable speed with which other classes succeeded in looking like gentlemen was due to the transformation of the tailoring trade by new commercial practices. The French Revolution had not produced an immediate simplification of male clothing: elegant people in 1803 wore three or four waistcoats one on top of the other; in the Restoration 'Polish' trousers, 'Turkish' boots, 'Cossack' waistcoats, short 'English' coats and a profusion of gold buttons were at various stages fashionable. But around 1825 ready-made tailoring shops appeared in Paris and by the end of the Second Empire they had completely altered men's habits in dress. At first these shops simply sold unclaimed bespoke clothes. The poor had always worn the cast-off clothing of the rich: differences in appearance between the classes had been mitigated by this, but the poor perforce mixed the different styles they picked up, so that variety was even greater. But in 1830 the firm of Coutard was founded in the rue Croix des Petits Champs to sell ready-made and bespoke suits at the same price, for cash only, but at a great saving on what ordinary tailors—who always gave long credit—charged. By 1867 this firm employed forty cutters; it dressed the bourgeoisie of every rank, and it exported 3 million francs' worth of suits a year, mainly to South America and Egypt.[1] The Paris department stores, with their mailed catalogues, soon extended this system to the provinces. La Belle Jardinière, founded in 1827 to produce ready-made clothes, moved into a palatial new building on the Pont Neuf in 1866.[2] Charles Blanc in 1875 was still laying it down that clothes should give expression to a man's functions in life, but they were on the contrary increasingly doing just the opposite. Blanc noted that clothes were now being made of materials that would not last long; that was the mark of the new mobile society. He urged that men should cultivate gravity in their appearance, because clothes were a 'moral indication'.[3]

[1] Charles Eck, *Histoire chronologique du vêtement (homme) jadis et aujourd'hui, suivie de l'art de se vêtir au 19ᵉ siècle* (1867).

[2] By 1913 it was employing 10,000 workers. For other men's wear firms see H. Detrois, *Industries de la confection et de la couture* (1913).

[3] Charles Blanc, *L'Art dans la parure et dans le vêtement* (1875), 239, 366.

The appearance of respectability could now be bought very cheaply. Appearances were, of course, deceptive. The president of the Syndicate of Men's Underwear Manufacturers reported in 1908 that 'there are quite a large number of men who demand fancy linen (*linge de fantaisie*) and bring much coquetry into their undergarments'; though the white shirt was most popular, printed coloured ones had recently been increasingly asked for.[1] But these were cravings which men were not allowed to publicise. It could be claimed that the age of the black suit coincided more exactly with the age of sexual inhibitions than with that of democracy. Men had to abandon sartorial provocativeness at the same time as they had to start concealing their marital infidelities. The black suit was what one wore, in particular, to church on Sundays. Men's clothes showed the limitations on eccentricity that were generally accepted; a general conformity was required and obtained; individual whim could manifest itself only in trivial details, and it was nearly always inspired by snobbishness or by wealth.

But why, if the capital of men's fashion was London, was the capital of women's fashion Paris? It had not yet become so in 1850. It is true that at the end of the *ancien régime* Mademoiselle Bertin, dressmaker to Marie-Antoinette, included many foreigners (and particularly Russians, but also the Duchess of Devonshire) among her clients, but fashion had not yet taken on its modern characteristics: she specialised above all in hats and in the garnishing of dresses with ingenious accoutrements.[2] Women's fashions used to move very slowly, partly because making women's clothes, with all their lace and embroidery, took so long that they could not be worn until many months after they were ordered. There was enormous variation in the nature and juxtaposition of colours and ornaments but the basic forms were relatively limited, a single model being made up in different cloths. Dressmakers were frequently given an old dress to copy in a new cloth. It was only in 1850 that the first shop appeared in Paris which both sold cloth and undertook to make it into clothes, but its owner, Madame Roger (of the rue

[1] Georges Dehesdin, *Exposition internationale de Milan, 1906. Section française, groupe 42* (1908), 599.

[2] Pierre de Nouvion and Émile Liez, *Un Ministre des modes sous Louis XVI: Mademoiselle Bertin, marchande de modes de la reine 1747–1813* (1911).

Nationale Saint-Martin), had only one model. Worth, who had arrived in Paris at the age of 20 four years before, noting her success, persuaded his employers, the drapers Gagelin, to follow her lead, but now he gave each cloth a different model and ingeniously invented a whole range of variations that could be added. His originality was much criticised, but by perseverance, and also by making his clothes more comfortable, more in accord with the human shape, he persuaded an increasing number of clients that they should abandon following the standard patterns and seek instead to have a unique dress, suited to their individual personality. These clients were at first largely foreigners: Englishwomen in particular came to Paris to be dressed by this Englishman. Worth's success came from his confidence and powers of persuasion. He introduced new forms of decoration which people disliked, but by persuading enough rich women to wear them, he made them fashionable and then popular. He got the silk manufacturers of Lyon to produce new types and new colours; and he persuaded his most famous customer, the Empress Eugénie, who vigorously resisted all the innovations he recommended, that in wearing these novelties, she was performing a national duty by stimulating the textile trade. The number of silk looms in Lyon did indeed double during the Second Empire. Worth also transformed widows' weeds by introducing alternative types of crêpe, violet and jade. In 1872 he started making clothes out of sculpted and beaten velvet, one of the oldest of Lyon furnishing fabrics: after some years of resistance by his clients who objected to being dressed like furniture, this material became so popular that a vast new industry developed to mass produce it, except that this was done in cotton instead of silk, and velvet dresses thus became a popular fashion. Worth's adoption of new materials and new ornaments did an enormous amount to stimulate business, to develop mechanical lace-making and a gigantic flowers and feathers industry (Paris came to have 800 firms specialising in this). Fashion, as Worth established it, aimed at individuality in clothes; far from meeting a demand for novelty from women, it had to fight against their conservatism. It was only when rich, eccentric women or actresses showed off new styles—and the theatre played an essential role in the popularisation of female fashions—that women imagined that they could become as pretty as them, if only they wore similar clothes. Fashion, as the masses came to understand it, meant imitation, the opposite of individuality.[1] Fashion now had to change constantly, because with the development of a large dressmaking industry, new styles were imitated so quickly that the rich demanded yet further innovation to keep one step ahead; and the poor were offered such parodies of the original styles, in cheap materials, with the grace missing both from cut and colour, that their admiration for the original innovation rapidly flagged. The industry became so competitive with the almost infinite multi-plication of cloths, that it was impossible to be sure any longer who took the lead, as between manufacturers and couturiers, in inventing new cloths. A silk manufacturer who accumulated excessive stocks, say, of moiré would be glad to sell it off at a low price to a famous couturier, who would use it to line his coats. This would make moiré 'fashionable' and the factories would start churning it out for all sorts of other purposes. The unpredictability of the market made it difficult to make money in this business, but because there was an element of gambling and indefinable ingenuity involved, it attracted increasing re-cruits. In 1850 the *Bottin* listed 158 couturiers in Paris; by 1872 there were 684, by 1895 1,636; and these excluded small inde-pendent dressmakers. In 1895 six of these firms employed between 400 and 600 workers each, and fifty others around 100 each. France as a whole then had 400,000 workers exclusively employed in making women's clothes.

There was an enormous difference between the sort of gar-ments which were produced at either end of this business. 'Haute couture' meant the production of individual items for particular customers, which cost (at the turn of the century) from 800 to 1,500 francs. Only 37 per cent of its purchasers were French. French inventiveness in clothes design was largely sustained by foreign admiration (as art in general was): it was admired because it was well made, but also because it was foreign. The cost to the couturier in wages for one of these expensive dresses was usually only about 150 francs; but he had to spend a great deal of money on the paraphernalia of luxury, on elegant show-rooms in the most expensive parts of Paris, and on well-advertised high living. At this time, the average working dressmaker made

[1] Gaston Worth, *La Couture et la confection des vêtements de femme* (1895).

only 2 francs a day: it was this kind of person who produced the mass of clothes for the French market.[1] But the Germans were more efficient at mass production and imports played an increasing role. The notion that Frenchwomen were universally well dressed or elegant is a myth that cannot be sustained by what is known about price-cutting and savings on quality perpetrated by the producers. For the age in which women still made their own clothes, or had them individually made, was on the point of disappearing by the end of the nineteenth century. There were then still no firms manufacturing women's underwear—that was still hand-made—but the corset industry had become very largely mechanised. In 1848 about 10,000 workers were employed in making corsets; by 1889 that number had doubled; the money spent on corsets rose from 11,000,000 to 55,000,000 francs between 1878 and 1889, which was the period when mechanisation transformed the industry: only a quarter of this sum now went on made-to-measure corsets. In the 1830s a corset cost between 8 and 15 francs (depending on whether it had whalebone in it or not); in the 1850s they were being imported from England at 60 centimes each. In 1839 they were considered dangerous and banned from the Paris Industrial Exhibition, even though 'safe', 'painless' and rubber ones had been invented. But that made no difference and in 1902 the ministry of education vainly forbade schoolgirls to wear them.[2] The mountains of feathers, flowers and fruit—largely manufactured in Paris—that women wore increased enormously as the masses abandoned bonnets and kerchiefs and took to parading in hats. The importance of hats as status symbols became such that neither men nor women dared show themselves in the street without one, and of a kind appropriate to the rank to which they aspired (this was one of the ambivalent contributions of the early Third Republic to visible equality). In the Second Empire the *Code de la mode* said that fashion consisted in 'imprinting the cachet of one's personal fantasy' on the clothes one wore: the problem was to find or make individual ornaments, and to avoid the ruses of manufacturers who produced cloth stiffened

[1] Cf. Henriette Vanier, *La Mode et ses métiers. Frivolités et luttes de classes 1830–70* (1960).

[2] See *Les Dessous élégants* (founded 1901), the organ of the Union of Corset Manufacturers; Dehesdin, op. cit. 525–36.

with glue and made to shine with sugar, which disintegrated in the rain.[1] Women took to wearing ready-made dresses roughly fifty years later than men adopted ready-made suits. By 1930 most Frenchwomen bought their clothes ready made, because these were now available not just in department stores but from a whole host of small shops; manufacturers no longer produced thousands of copies of the same style but limited themselves to a few, and besides they created new styles every week; improvements in dyeing techniques after the First World War made it possible for the colours of expensive cloths to be reproduced for the masses.[2]

It was these technical improvements that made possible the acceleration of fashion, with a new style every season. The new styles were of course very slight amendments, but only a united effort by manufacturers selling something different each year could force women to change their appearance. The top couturiers at first fought against this tendency, before exploiting it. The next great innovator in fashion after Worth, Paul Poiret, reiterated Worth's injunction that women should wear what suited them: he was horrified by the question he was increasingly asked, 'What would next year's fashion be?'. He rose to fame in the employment of Worth's two sons, but they took him on to produce a simple range of clothes. Jean Worth loved making dresses out of rich materials, held together with jewels; his brother Gaston, who looked after the commercial side of the business, argued that with the coming of the twentieth century even princesses sometimes travelled by bus, and they needed appropriate clothes. 'We find ourselves', he said, 'in the situation of a great restaurant, which would prefer to serve only truffles. But we need to create a bar producing fried potatoes.' Poiret, who soon set up on his own to pursue this revolution in his own way, won fame with his kimono-coat, which introduced the Oriental influence into ordinary clothes. In 1903 he declared the abolition of petticoats, then of corsets, then of false hair, then of hats with leaves, flowers, ribbons, fruits and plumes, each decree sounding the death knell of an industry and producing protests and delegations from them. Poiret was not trying to

[1] H. Despaigne, *Le Code de la mode* (1866), 14, 30.
[2] Germaine Deschamps, *La Crise dans les industries du vêtement et de la mode à Paris pendant la période de 1930 à 1937* (1938), 1–20.

'liberate' women: though he revealed their natural shapes more, he put them into sheath dresses in which they could not walk, and he bared their backs so that they froze. He declared that fashion was a 'provocation to good sense'; its function was essentially sexual, and Paris was the leading city in fashion because it allowed the freest development of 'the sensual and voluptuous life'. But he did not expect women to follow his models slavishly: his designs were only 'suggestions' which each woman should adapt to her own personality. Certain of his suggestions were rejected: he insisted (before 1914) that the culotte would inevitably become a dominant fashion, because the scope for varying the skirt had been exhausted; he tried to make women wear really bright colours, but they resisted this. He was the first couturier to tour America, which had always played an essential part in the prosperity of his trade; he was hailed there as the King of Fashion; but he was soon dethroned by the capitalist forces which were transforming the clothes business. He chided American women for lacking imagination and individuality; he deplored their readiness to buy a model exactly as he made it, whereas Frenchwomen would demand it altered and made up in a different colour and cloth. American women, he said, kept their schoolgirl mentality all their lives, so that they looked like a giant orphanage in uniform. Their manufacturers took advantage of this, bought last year's success from Paris and reproduced it *ad nauseam*. Fashion was thus reduced to simple annual changes. The French couturiers saw their creations plagiarised and mutilated; they were reduced to selling their names to be stuck on stockings and handbags and even clothes, in the manufacture of which they had no hand. Poiret's bankruptcy, and his subordination to a group of financiers who knew nothing about fashion, made public the constraints that shackled individual genius. The great depression completed the massacre of the couturiers. After the war, when new alliances between manufacturers and designers developed, the former were in the saddle: Christian Dior was financed by the textile manufacturer Boussac. Dior showed that a single Frenchman could still make women all over the world throw away their old clothes, but this involved the co-operation and self-interest of a vast industry. French supremacy in female fashion was partly a legend, fostered by the women's magazines. Only a small proportion of the designers' fashions penetrated to the masses, and that was through the mediation of capitalists, whose history is still unwritten.[1]

The relationship between ideas of female beauty, fashion and the desire for comfortable clothes also needs careful investigation. It is very difficult to know whether there was an ideal woman in popular taste, or how this evolved, because virtually all evidence about this comes from writers, whose taste is not representative. The courtiers of the eighteenth century seem to have admired majestic women, but the intellectuals found merit in less classical forms, in irregular and rebellious features that hinted at sarcasm and wit. Under the Revolution, grace, innocence, Olympian dignity were all praised with confusing variety. The romantics did not always fall for thin, pale, worried and tubercular women; and it is too simple to say that the mother or matron, mistress of the household, was the type of the rest of the century: it was just that there were far more portraits, in paint and in photography, to unbalance all comparisons. Novelists were surprisingly imprecise in saying what exactly made their heroines beautiful. The two main changes were probably the triumph of the thin over the fat woman, of which the healthy, sporty type of the twentieth century was only one variation, and the prolongation of the years of a woman's life during which she might be considered attractive. Men used to say that woman was God's finest creation, but, like a flower, she was beautiful only for a brief moment (which was when a man married her). They implied, and also wrote, that most women were ugly.[2] Women clearly believed this. At the same time as the masses became obsessed by Paris fashions in clothes, they also began to make increasing use of cosmetics. The playwright Feydeau's father wrote in 1873 that if you took a walk in the Bois de Boulogne, or the Champs Élysées, or even on the Boulevards, you would find that at least half the young women were heavily made up.[3] It was fashionable then to dye your hair

[1] Paul Poiret, *En habillant l'époque* (1930); Lucien François [pseud. of Lucien t'Serstevens], *Comment un nom devient une griffe* (1961); Bernard Roscho, *The Rag Race. How New York and Paris run the breakneck business of dressing American women* (New York, 1963).

[2] Marcel Brunschvig, *La Femme et la beauté* (1929).

[3] Ernest Feydeau, *L'Art de plaire. Études d'hygiène, de goût et de toilettes, dédiées aux jolies femmes de tous les pays du monde* (1873), 113.

colours known as 'egg yolk' and 'cow's tail'. The aristocrats of the eighteenth century wore wigs; the masses at the beginning of the twentieth century built up their heads with false hair similarly, though with less show of artificiality: imports of hair into France were rising at such a speed that they doubled between 1902 and 1906, reaching about a third of a million kilogrammes. 'Institutes of Beauty' now sprang up which undertook to rejuvenate women who feared they were losing their charms.[1] Women, in short, expended more and more effort in trying to be different from what they were, so that the ideal of feminine beauty, far from being an inspiration, was, at least for women, a source of constant anxiety.[2] Their main worry, according to a doctor who ran an advisory service for a women's magazine in the 1880s, was the size of their bust (40 per cent of the letters he received were about this), how best to make themselves up (25 per cent) and how to deal with hair in the wrong place (10 per cent). In this period women were willing to spend large sums at the hairdresser's: 5 francs was the price of an 'ordinary' styling, 15–20 francs for arranging the hair for a ball, with flowers and feathers, 20–30 francs for a *coiffure poudrée*, 30–40 francs for a 'historic' style and 40–50 for a *coiffure de genre pour travestissement*.[3]

The great attraction of fashion was that it diverted attention from the insoluble problems of beauty and provided an easy way —which money could buy—of at any rate approximating outwardly to a simply stated, easily reproduced, ideal of beauty, however temporary that ideal. That was why women bore with the tyrants of fashion, even when they maligned them. Beside the severe prescriptions of traditional dress, these tyrants almost represented freedom. The women who protested, and those who objected to the main burden of fashion being placed upon their sex, had little success. This was partly because the battle was not a straightforward one between comfort or equality and the fashion industry. The great designers were liberators also, in their own way. Even the crinoline represented a liberation when it was invented, because it dispensed with the heavy petticoats,

[1] Alfred Capus, *L'Institut de Beauté* (1913).

[2] Henri Lavent, *Le Peuple et la beauté* (1902); Eugène Montfort, *La Beauté moderne* (1902); Émile Bayard, *L'Art de reconnaître la beauté du corps humain* (1926).

[3] A. Coffignon, *Les Coulisses de la mode* (1888), 19, 30.

whose number had progressively increased. Many of the decrees
of fashion appeared, at the time, to be improvements and clever
ideas. Efforts by women to wear the same clothes as men were
repeatedly repressed. The prefect of police, in an ordinance of
the Year IX, 'informed that many women dress as men', laid
it down that they must get an individual authorisation from him
to do so, which would be given only for reasons of health. In
1848, a women's club was formed demanding that the skirt
should be replaced by breeches (and that men should do housework at least three times a week). No one in France, however,
followed the American Bloomerists, and it was ultimately sport
that enabled women to abandon skirts. But by then trousers had
already, after a long struggle, been accepted as a form of female
underclothing. They were worn at balls (as the *Moniteur de la
mode* reported in 1852) 'to guard against the indiscretions of the
waltz and the polka'; the *Conseiller des dames* published a pattern
in 1853 for 'ladies who travel'; and *La Lingerie parisienne* (1854)
'at the request of many of our readers' produced a pattern also,
defining the *pantalon* as 'a garment women must never be without, especially in winter'. The crinoline finally made trousers
essential, because when getting through confined spaces, it had
to be partially dismantled. *La France élégante* complained in 1857
'Our clothes are becoming like men's: we wear round hats,
turned-down collars, musketeer's cuffs; nothing is missing, not
even trousers for many of us.' But on this occasion the fashion
did not last: the peasants and workers could not afford this fancy
style; a doctor said he recognised them by their dirty knees.

One should not too easily associate this fashion with sexual
equality, any more than one should assume that short hair
'liberated' women. The first occasion on which women cut their
hair short, wearing it *à la Titus*, was during the First Empire;
the Eton crop (1927) compelled women to use the services of
hairdressers far more often.[1] More important perhaps was the
revolution of Coco Chanel (1883–1971) who during the First
World War invented a new elegance for the masses by ennobling
cheap materials and producing fashionable, unornamented
comfortable clothes, originally out of jersey, which no one
wanted and which she picked up for a song. In 1921 she naturalised

---

[1] Laure-Paul Flobert, *La Femme et le costume masculin* (Lille, 1911); Pierre Dufay,
Le Pantalon féminin (1906).

the Russian peasant's blouse (the *roubaschka*), in 1926–31 she pushed English fashions with a 'resolutely masculine cut'. But she was something of an outsider—an illegitimate daughter of a pedlar, who began as a maid servant until picked up by the garrison officers of Moulins. She then had a series of foreign lovers, all of whom were orphans like herself—Arthur Capel, an Englishman said to be an illegitimate son of Pereire, the second duke of Westminster, the Grand Duke Dmitri and German aristocrats under Vichy. It was only in the 1950s that her styles really caught on, and above all in America. The new fashion of dressing down was thus invented by women and followed later by men.[1] That shows fashion coming full circle—begun as part of the rat race produced by the ending of barriers to social climbing, and taking on a new direction when social climbing ceased to be a major preoccupation.[2] How far people liked what they wore is a different matter.

Painting

The painting of this period is, in popular belief, distinguished by the much publicised divorce that took place between public taste and artistic genius. The painters who had the most successful careers, like Bouguereau and Meissonier, are now remembered only by art historians, while those who are now considered to be among the greatest artists of all time, like Manet and Cézanne, had much trouble selling their works. From Impressionism to Cubism, every new school was greeted with almost universal hostility. To be a painter seemed, in most cases, to involve a rebellion against 'bourgeois' society and a condemnation of its sentimentality, hypocrisy and materialism. The whole question of the relationship of art and society seems to require consideration in new terms.

However, this contrast of the modern with the good old times is superficial. In the first place, the breach between the artists

[1] Edmonde Charles-Roux, *L'Irregulière, ou mon itinéraire Chanel* (1974).

[2] For an attempt at a statistical analysis of fashion, see Jane Richardson and A. L. Kroeber, *Three Centuries of Women's Dress Fashions. A Quantitative Analysis* (U.C. Berkeley and L.A. 1940). Cf. Raoul de La Grasserie, *Du rôle psychologique et sociologique du monde et de la mode* (Bologna, 1902, by a judge of Rennes). The standard general history is still James Laver, *Taste and Fashion from the French Revolution to the Present Day* (1937, new edition 1945). Cf. Giselle d'Assailly, *Les 15 révolutions de la mode* (1968).

of this period and their contemporaries appears to be pro-
founder than it was, because of the intervention of a new factor
quite extraneous to art, but which became a most important
influence on attitudes towards art, namely the newspaper. Art
now received more attention than ever before. To this extent,
art—in all its forms—attracted more interest, even if some manifestations of it pleased only a small circle of initiates. The newspapers introduced far greater polemic into the discussion of art
than had ever been seen—as they did into every sphere of
activity; but they should not be taken as accurate reflections of
public opinion.[1] The division of artists into conflicting schools
was to a certain extent a journalistic simplification, and partly
a mystification by artists adopting literary and political techniques. It will be some time before the history of art in this
period can finally be seen in terms which are less clear cut, and
the dramatic battles, into which journalists and critics have tried
to condense it, can be appreciated as only one side and one part
of the story.

The role of art had become more complex in any case, if only
because more people were involved in it. The Salons (the official
annual art exhibitions) of the eighteenth century had generally
exhibited only three or four hundred paintings a year; but
during the first half of the nineteenth century they expanded to
include over 2,000 paintings, and by 1864 they had reached
3,478 a year. The first open Salon, in 1791, at which anybody
who wished could exhibit, without approval from official judges,
showed 794 works; the second one, in 1848, showed 5,180. The
latter figure constituted the production of 1,900 painters. During
the next century, numbers increased still further, though the
break-up of the Salon system makes it difficult to say by how
much. In 1885, 3,851 artists submitted their work to the Salon.[2]
In 1954 (and again in 1962) about 11,500 people declared themselves to the census to be artists;[3] and the Salons (fragmented

[1] See chapter 4.

[2] 1,243 of these artists were successful in having their works exhibited; but note
that 389 of these were foreigners, Americans being most numerous (98), then
Belgians (47), English (34), Germans (31).

[3] 1954: 7,600 painters (2,260 of them women); 2,220 teachers of painting
(equally men and women) and 1,700 sculptors and engravers (of whom 260 were
women). In 1962 only 2,595 of the artists said they earned more than half their
income from art.

into over thirty different ones) now exhibited the work of roughly 4,500 painters. The expansion of painting as a profession occurred about a century later than that of literature (the number of books published, as has been seen, quadrupled in the eighteenth century, trebled in the early nineteenth and then remained roughly steady). Painting therefore grew under the scrutiny of a sister or rival art, which, with unceasing comments and criticisms, made its existence infinitely more complicated.

The audience for painting moreover did not evolve in simple correlation with this expansion. The Salons had quickly become a much-enjoyed popular entertainment, in which all classes partook. In 1884 238,000 people visited the Salon, in 1887 as many as 562,000 in the course of the fifty-five days which Salons usually lasted. The Salons were free on Sundays and roughly half the visitors entered in this way. In 1887, however, there were 8,612 people who paid 5 francs to gain admission on special days (instead of the 1 or 2 francs normally charged) and who might have been the core of the connoisseurs, or the snobs. Such figures should not mislead into conclusions about the popularity of art. Art exhibitions were decidedly less popular than other exhibitions, as was revealed already in 1855: the Paris International Exposition of that year was so arranged that those wishing to see the fine arts in it had to go to a separate building: whereas 4,180,000 visited the industrial sections, only 982,000 visited the fine arts exhibition.[1] These are impressive numbers, but they already show over three-quarters of the visitors refusing to look at the paintings. Moreover, art did not enjoy the same popularity in the provinces as it did in Paris. Not even the largest provincial cities managed to get over 10,000 visitors into any of their art exhibitions in 1887, when—in a single day—the Paris Salon of that year drew in about 50,000. The Moulins Art Exhibition (held in conjunction with the *Concours agricole*) in 1885, included 275 'proprietors' among its subscribers, but also 164 small shop keepers and artisans and 24 clerks. However, when provincial art exhibitions were organised on their own and not as part of some such regional show, they always got a low attendance and were almost exclusively middle-class affairs. After 1918, and more noticeably after 1945, two new

[1] *Exposition universelle de 1867 à Paris: rapports du Jury internationale publiés sous la direction de M. Michel Chevalier* (1868), introduction to vol. 1.

developments altered this situation. The great increase in travel
put museums and historical monuments on the holiday itinerary
and a new class of person—the idle tourist—came to look at
pictures, even though he was very often a person who never set
foot in his own local museum. The number of small exhibitions
increased, but they came to rely on a restricted, predominantly
middle-class clientele, with a strong contingent of leisured housewives. But despite all the increase in leisure, only 4·4 per cent
of French people, questioned in 1974, claimed to paint or sculpt
as a hobby—a figure which needs to be compared with the 15·4
per cent who said they played a musical instrument and the
49·4 per cent of men who said photography was a hobby. Art
lovers tended to look at pictures much more than actually to
paint themselves, whereas music lovers entertained themselves
more than they went to concerts. In this survey, 18·6 per cent
said they had been to at least one art exhibition that year, but
70 per cent said they had read at least one book, and 51 per cent
had been to the cinema, on average thirteen times. Despite their
new affluence, almost half the French population, according to
this survey, had no pictures or reproductions with pretensions
of any kind to art in their homes; about 20 per cent had reproductions; about 26 per cent had original paintings by amateurs,
which shows a wide distribution of the production of the hobby-
ists, 23·5 per cent had posters and 8 per cent had paintings by
contemporary professional artists (but this last category were
to be found four times more frequently in Paris than in the
provinces).[1] Those interested in art were always a minority, and
the arrival of unorthodox and 'incomprehensible' art probably
did not make all that much difference to the size of this minority:
academic art had often demanded erudition and imagination
for the deciphering of its allegories and significance. The important point is that the growth of education did not dramatically
increase the audience for art. On the contrary, the effect of mass
schooling was that art became part of that rather indefinable
'culture' which the schools did not really impart to their pupils,
but for the appreciation of which a great deal of schooling
seemed to be required. Culture, and therefore art, was what
highly educated people alone knew how to enjoy. Museums

    [1] Secrétariat d'État à la Culture, *Pratiques culturelles des Français* (Dec. 1974),
41, 100–13.

(which of course had never been particularly popular) remained the preserve of the highly educated classes. Thus in the 1960s, only 1 per cent of visitors to museums in France were peasants, only 4 per cent workers and 5 per cent artisans and shopkeepers, but 45 per cent were 'upper class'. Forty per cent of those who went to museums had studied Latin, a third had the *baccalauréat*, a quarter had university degrees.[1]

There may at first sight appear to be a contradiction between this monopolisation of art by the most literate classes (whose training was essentially verbal) and the alienation of the masses, who were distinguished precisely by their preference for the pictorial over the literary, but who confined themselves to the illustrated magazines and newspapers. This is a question of definitions. Popular illustrations were not classified as art, any more than popular novels were accepted as literature. Taste implied contempt; refined taste could not, by definition, be shared by the masses. Exclusiveness became an essential feature in the appreciation of art; and no serious effort was made to interest the masses in art, to accompany the compulsory spread of literacy. The attitude of schools towards art went through four different stages. Until 1853 they ignored it. Art was then introduced for the first time into the syllabus of secondary education, under the influence of the philosopher Ravaisson. Basing himself, as he believed, on the doctrines of Leonardo da Vinci, Ravaisson insisted that the schools should not teach rough drawing and should not adopt any hasty methods. The aim of art education was to 'train the eye', to develop taste, to show people how to recognise the ideal in ordinary objects. Children were therefore required to draw the human face, so as to study the different emotions. On the principle that they should move from the simple to the complex, they were asked to draw parts of the face first, like the nose or ear, and only when they had learnt to do these could they proceed to drawing a complete face. They were first given prints and photographs from which to copy their drawings, then bits of antique sculpture, and only when they were well advanced were they allowed to draw the human face directly from nature. This method not surprisingly created too many difficulties, and there were few teachers

[1] Pierre Bourdieu and Alain Darbel, *L'Amour de l'art. Les musées d'art européens et leur public* (2nd edition, 1969), 36.

available in any case to implement it.[1] In 1878 it was therefore
replaced by a totally different system, known as the 'geometrical
method', as opposed to Ravaisson's 'intuitive' one. The inspiration behind the reform was Eugène Guillaume—a painter this
time rather than a philosopher—but a painter conscious that he
was living in the age of science.[2] He saw drawing as above all a
science; the purpose of teaching it was not to stimulate the personality but to enable children to reproduce their models accurately; and it was the mathematics teachers who were required
to teach drawing. Nature and landscapes were to be the very
last things pupils would be allowed to draw: first they had to
learn to draw in two dimensions, then to produce drawings of
cones and cubes. Quite often, the pupils were not even allowed
to copy real-life cubes, but only photographs or drawings of
cubes; but little geometrical objects, made of paper, plaster or
wire, were sometimes distributed as the principal equipment for
art lessons. Primary schools never got beyond this stage, but
more senior children were then allowed to graduate to copying
vases and bits of architecture, usually antique. In theory, the
drawing of the human head and of animals was to come next,
the study of the human figure after that, and landscapes last.
There was a mixture therefore of the antique—for most models
were plasters of old statues—and of science. The inspectors who
implemented this programme said there was a need to develop
'the feeling for art and the ability to experience the emotions
that the sensations of sight can procure' but the ability to
measure was more important, for science was the basis of modern
civilisation. Traditional literary methods were applied to art:
the 'dictated drawing' was the equivalent of dictated prose: the
teacher drew on the blackboard and the pupil copied. The
intuitive method was condemned as anarchic because children
had had their exercises corrected individually. Now 'collective
teaching' meant everybody in the class did the same thing and
marks were given immediately after the class.[3] But geometric art

[1] F. Ravaisson, *De l'enseignement du dessin dans les lycées* (1854).

[2] Eugène Guillaume (1822–1905) won the prix de Rome in 1845 with his 'Thésée
retrouvant l'épée de son père sur un rocher'. He became a member of the Academy
of Fine Arts in 1862, and was appointed Director of Fine Arts by Jules Ferry in 1879.

[3] Eugène Guillaume and Jules Pillet, *L'Enseignement du dessin* (1889); J. J.
Pillet and P. Steck, *L'Enseignement du dessin en France dans les établissements universi-
taires* (Berne and Paris, 1904).

was soon attacked, first by industrialists who complained that it did not produce good draughtsmen—its purely practical aims were not fulfilled—and secondly by educationists, in the name of the teachings of child psychology. The fourth stage, which got going with the reform of 1909, was that of the 'active' method, inspired this time by Gaston Quénioux, professor at the School of Decorative Arts in Paris. He argued that the aim of art education should not be the teaching of technical skill but rather the development of personal impressions: the teacher should give higher marks for sincerity than for exact execution; the child's art must be creative in its own terms; it must be an expression of its joy in life. Quénioux protested against the precedence that French education gave to writing over drawing, saying that drawing came naturally to children, and they should, until the age of nine, be allowed to draw as they pleased. They should not be given antique busts to copy, but should be allowed to draw what they liked. Later, they might be helped to observe, and at the age of fifteen perhaps be allowed to copy great paintings; but art lessons should be not the inculcation of a skill so much as a contribution to the general increase of happiness.[1] One should not imagine that the schools in fact switched from one style of teaching to another, as the official instructions did. There were never enough art teachers; the training programmes for them were rudimentary. One of the men associated with Quénioux in his reform, Pottier, who was a keeper at the Louvre museum, said that he himself had never had any art lessons of any kind at school. Many teachers did not like first the mono-polisation of art by the mathematicians, and then the idea that children should be allowed to do what they pleased, in contra-diction with the schools' general emphasis on discipline. More investigation is needed, however, of the effects of this teaching, not simply on the receptivity of people at large, but also on painters; for hitherto, only the training of the art schools has attracted the attention of historians.[2]

Art in ordinary schools had two faces. On the one hand, until

[1] L. Guébin, *L'Enseignement du dessin* (1908), article by Quénioux 63–89; P. Buisson, *Nouveau dictionnaire de pédagogie et d'instruction primaire* (1911), article by Quénioux under 'Dessin'; Marcel Braunschvig, *L'Art et l'enfant. Essai sur l'éducation esthétique* (1907).

[2] For a link, see Horace Lecoq de Boisbaudran (who was Rodin's teacher), *Coup d'œil sur l'enseignement des Beaux-Arts* (1782).

well into the twentieth century, it was taught in an abstract technical way which may, in a few cases, have prepared pupils for a certain kind of artistic appreciation; but it was perhaps only when freedom was allowed to children in their art lessons that they could begin to approve an art which stressed personal expression before all else. But on the other hand the decoration of schools evolved in a totally separate way and with a different chronology. In the first half of the nineteenth century, there were very few pictures on the walls of schools beyond portraits of the kings of France, 'Amusing Arithmetic' and geographical maps. In the early infant schools, the pictures were kept in a folder and brought out only for the appropriate lessons; they were usually too small for the whole class to see. The break comes with the Paris Exhibition of 1867, which had a remarkable section of teaching materials. The invention of lithography, and the new catchphrase *la leçon des choses*, stimulated publishers to produce a new range of posters for schools. E. Deyrolle began (1871) publishing a successful series on Animals and Industry, trying to represent aspects of nature and of the world, with the stress on accuracy, in colour, and as far as possible in life-size. He argued that children loved to learn about natural science but had difficulty in finding suitable pictures; they must be given colourful pictures which appealed to them and did not tire them. In 1879 Hachette followed with Pictures for Schools, producing six years later a series of a hundred pictures illustrating the history of France, for only 11 fr. 40. Delagrave in 1888 published his *Modern Languages Taught in Pictures*. A government commission was established to organise the artistic decoration of schools, to develop the taste and aesthetic curiosity of children. But a special children's art developed which became too concerned with instilling moral lessons. The first works distributed by the government were *L'Hiver* by Henri Rivière, *Little Red Riding Hood* by Willette and *Alsace* by Moreau-Nélaton. Mademoiselle Dufau then produced a series with titles such as *Love Your Parents*, *Courage is Better than Force*, *Co-operation*, etc. Visual taste always came low in the priorities of the schools, long behind didactic morals. The art teacher was too humble to contribute to the appearance of the classroom. The art lesson was completely divorced from the rest of the school's activities.[1]

[1] J. Pichard, 'Les Images éducatives et leur utilisation dans l'enseignement au

Museums, where people could freely look at works of art, were
an essentially modern phenomenon; and in this period they
were an inadequate intermediary between art and the public.
Until 1789 there were virtually no public museums outside
Paris. It was the Revolution which made public the royal collection in the Louvre, and it was Napoleon who in 1801 created
the provincial museums, to show works of art for which the
Louvre had no room. The state undertook a regular programme
of buying both old and new art, to build up these new institutions, which already numbered over 100 in the 1880s and over
700 by 1945. Benefactions and bequests from collectors became
an established custom. The state and the municipalities became
by far the largest owners of works of art. But the museums were
not inspired by any proselytising zeal; they saw their role more
as one of conservation than exhibition, and indeed they could
exhibit only a small proportion of what they accumulated.
Provincial collections grew up on a rather haphazard basis,
though two principles influenced them: that the works of
painters born in the region, and of representatives, as far as
possible, of every school and period, should be included, even
if only by a single minor work. The untutored eye would be
more likely to be confused rather than inspired by the fragmentary nature of most museums. The salaries offered to the
staff were small, so most curators were amateurs, often part-
time. It is not surprising that the provincial museums were
called, at the turn of the century, 'prisons of art'. There were
then museum curators who thought that Meissonier and Brascassat were still alive, and who recorded the dates of Eugène
Boudin as 'unknown'. The museum of Vaucouleurs (Meuse),
founded in 1893, clothed its replicas of ancient statues in paper
underpants. The museum of Besançon was occasionally used as
a market-place. Comparatively few people studied the painting
exhibited with very great care: in the first decade of the twentieth century, the museum of Dijon sold only forty copies of its
catalogue a year, which was perhaps because this was incomplete and out of date, but Grenoble, which also had excellent
collections, sold only 125. However, entrance fees varied, rang-
ing from one franc to nothing, to make it possible for large

19e siècle' (unpublished, Centre Audio-Visuel, 1961); Bibliothèque Nationale,
Cabinet des Estampes, files of old pictures used in schools.

numbers to visit museums.[1] The choice available broadened far
beyond traditional painting. In 1818 a Museum of Living
Artists was founded in the Palais du Luxembourg (which moved
to the Orangerie in 1886 and which became the Museum of
Modern Art in 1937).[2] In 1879 Ferry established the Museum
of French Monuments, which came to illustrate the whole
history of sculpture. The Lyonnais industrialist, Émile Guimet,
founded the museum bearing his name, as a centre for the study
of oriental religions, ten years later; and in 1896 Henri Cer-
nuschi, a friend of Gambetta, of Maltese origin, bequeathed
his collection of Chinese art to the nation. The duchesse de
Galliera's collections formed the nucleus of the Museum of
Decorative Arts (1877), and the Museum of Popular Arts and
Traditions (1937) preserved the masterpieces of peasant craftsmanship.[3] How much was spent on museums has not been
properly calculated, though it has been claimed that the Third
Republic's expenditure on acquisitions was roughly one-third
that of London's National Gallery.[4]

It was probably through reproductions that most people discovered painting, and the masses had a well-developed taste for
prints, which went a long way back, but it was a taste for
traditional, well-known and well-liked subjects. In the nineteenth century, print makers were still selling barely modernised
versions of seventeenth-century drawings. *Crédit est mort* which
many cafés still exhibited in 1914 was a print that had hardly
altered since it first appeared in 1720. J. C. Pellerin (1756–1836)
created a highly successful children's print business at Épinal,
which turned out about seventeen million prints during the
Second Empire, many of them making use of traditional
material. The print pedlar, who toured the countryside with
his pictures fastened to a string by clothes-pegs, was an important source of entertainment.[5] But in the second half of the

---

[1] Ministère de l'instruction publique, *Rapport de la commission chargée d'étudier . . .
l'organisation des musées de province* (25 Oct. 1907), by Henry Lapauze (1908).

[2] This exhibited 149 paintings in 1849, 240 in 1875.

[3] *Arts, musées et curiosité en France* (1946) for a list of museums with descriptions;
J. Comyns Carr, *L'Art en France* (1887), a review of museums, by a correspondent
of the *Manchester Guardian*.

[4] Jeanne Laurent, *La République et les Beaux-Arts* (1955), 29.

[5] Musée National des Arts et Traditions Populaires, *Cinq siècles d'imagerie française*
(1973); J. Mistler, *Épinal et l'imagerie populaire* (1961); for comic strips, see F. F.
Empaytaz and J. Peignot, *Les Copains de votre enfance* (1963).

century, the original print came increasingly to be classified as a rare work of art,[1] and the masses turned to the newspapers and to photographic reproductions. A pioneer in the popularisation of these was Adolphe Braun (1811–77), who for long had the exclusive right to reproduce the paintings in the Louvre. He had set up as a photographer in Mulhouse in 1848 and had won a reputation with the photographs of flowers that he published in six albums, originally intending them as models for textile printing; but he then turned to photographing paintings in museums all over Europe, using plates a yard square or more in size. By 1867 he was employing 100 workers. His catalogue of 1896 contained about 20,000 different reproductions, which he sold for 15 francs each (40 × 50 cm). Every year he added a couple of hundred pictures from the Salon, so that in 1907 he was able to offer nearly 9,000 modern works painted over the previous thirty years by over a thousand different artists. His catalogues are probably more representative of what pictures the masses were conscious of, than the catalogues of museums. He offered about 800 different reproductions of Raphael, nearly 400 each of Leonardo, Rubens and Rembrandt, about 300 each of Michelangelo and Holbein, 250 of Dürer and Van Dyck, 200 of Titian. Among the moderns, Corot and Millet were the favourites, with about 150 each, Puvis had 40 paintings and 150 drawings, Paul Baudry about 100, Charles Chaplin (1825–91) about 80, Ingres, David, Bouguereau and Chenavard about 60, Meissonier, Rosa Bonheur and Delacroix about 50, Degas 5, Monet 2, Manet 1. It was the Germans who were the pioneers in the reproduction of the Impressionists: the first illustrated books about them were published in Germany from 1903 onwards, with photographs by the Frenchman Édouard Druet. The popularisation of the Impressionists in France began only in 1926 when *Les Albums d'art Druet* started coming out (the first was on Cézanne), but this was still in black and white. The firm of Braun—now in its fourth generation, but employing Georges Besson, a friend of many *avant-garde* painters—began publishing collections of Impressionist pictures between the world wars, but it was only after 1945 that they got round to volumes on Monet and Manet. The public in general were thus not exposed to the

[1] Jean Laran, *Inventaire du fonds français après 1800, Cabinet des Estampes* (1930 ff.) lists the half-million nineteenth-century prints in the Bibliothèque Nationale.

Impressionists until about half a century after they had died.[1] To what extent these painters appeared on postcards (which were first produced in the early 1870s) is uncertain. The whole history of reproduction remains obscure, partly because the sources are not easily accessible.[2] But it would be worth investigating what painters were most frequently reproduced in the press. In *L'Illustration*, for example, Cézanne did not appear till 1905; Manet was not mentioned by it before 1883 and it was only in 1929 that he was given a major article. Bouguereau, by contrast, was written about in this journal twenty-eight times between 1853 and 1905, but has had only one mention since then. Puvis, Rodin, Roll and Paul Thomas were regular names, but the journal had not, in 1932, yet heard of Seurat or Signac.[3]

Buying reproductions has become an activity, predominantly, of the educated. A survey, published in 1973, reported that 58 per cent of buyers possessed the *baccalauréat*, and only 7 per cent of them had got no further than primary school. The Impressionists are now the most popular painters: when asked to name ten painters, Renoir and Van Gogh are the two most frequently mentioned, followed by Monet and Picasso. Three-quarters of the sample could recognise a painting by Renoir and Van Gogh, but only a third could recognise Rubens, El Greco or Corot, and only a tenth Poussin or Klee. People, however, have their own reasons for buying one reproduction rather than another: colour counts most, and the subject-matter next; great weight is always placed on harmonisation with furniture, curtains and walls; some bring cuttings of wallpaper with them. It is only the highly educated who ignore these considerations, and it is only they who choose abstract paintings. Nudes are bought for bedrooms and still lifes for dining-rooms. Relatively uneducated and older people like landscapes and flowers, and it is for that reason that they like the Dutch painters and some Impressionists equally.

[1] Éts. Braun et Cⁱᵉ, *Un Siècle de technique* [1948]; Ad. Braun et Cⁱᵉ, *Catalogue général des reproductions inaltérables au charbon* (1896); id., *Galerie contemporaine* (1905 and 1907). Julius Meier-Graefe, *Manet* (Berlin, 1903), *Cézanne* (Munich, 1910); Les Albums d'art Druet, *Cézanne* (1926); Éditions Rieder, *Maîtres de l'art moderne* (1925): 1. Toulouse-Lautrec, 2. William Blake, 3. William Turner.

[2] For the difficulties see Marcel Neveux, *Le Dépôt légal des productions des arts graphiques* (Paris law thesis, 1934); 'Centenaire de la carte postale 1871–1970', *Le Vieux Papier* (Nov. 1970), fasc. 238; Jules Adeline, *Les Arts de reproduction vulgarisés* (n.d.); L. Tarible, *Les Industries graphiques* (5th edition, 1952).

[3] *L'Illustration*, Index 1843–1932.

Middle-aged people with a secondary education, or university graduates who are children of uneducated parents, tend to like the old masters, some moderns such as Utrillo and Vlaminck, but only Buffet among the contemporaries. It is above all the young, highly educated people from cultured backgrounds who like 'modern' painting—beginning with the Post-Impressionists. The decisive factor seems to be not education as such, nor wealth, but the tastes acquired in childhood, and here the influence of mothers has been shown to be noticeably greater than that of fathers. It is the cultured mother who passes on taste for *avant-garde* art.[1] Another psychologist, investigating the taste of French and American children, found no significant difference according to the social origins of parents; children as a whole preferred realistic painting, but American children, who received a free kind of art education, were noticeably less inclined than French ones to reject abstract painting as they grew older. The French working class, it is true, continued to value realism in painting in adult life, as well as technique and colour; whereas educated people gave purely subjective replies, which merely affirmed that they liked or disliked a painting, they preferred to talk about expressiveness and atmosphere rather than about subject-matter.[2] It is obvious therefore that it is quite impossible to talk about the taste of a period, without explaining whether one is referring to the taste of *avant-garde*, traditional or Sunday painters, to a particular generation, class or group, to a particular region, to museum visitors or the readers of the popular newspapers. Attempts to make Impressionism, for example, a reflection of economic or social changes, or, even more boldly, of contemporaneous philosophical trends, are completely misleading and simplistic.[3]

The popular visual art of the nineteenth century was photography, just as that of the twentieth was to be the cinema. This had a profound effect on attitudes towards painting, as well as on the character of painting itself. In the first place, the increase in the output of paintings was nothing compared with the proliferation of photographs. It was said that in 1849, in Paris alone, 100,000 daguerreotype portraits were taken; another

[1] Yvonne Bernard, *Psycho-sociologie du goût en matière de peinture* (1973).
[2] Robert Francès, *Psychologie de l'esthétique* (1968), 87, 127.
[3] A. Hauser, *A Social History of Art* (1951) is an appalling example.

source claims that in 1847 half a million photographic plates
were sold there. In 1850 Marseille had four or five miniature
painters, two of whom had some reputation for artistry, and
they did roughly fifty portraits a year each. A few years later
the city had nearly fifty photographers, each of whom produced
on average about a thousand portraits. The miniaturists had
barely kept themselves alive with their work. The photographers
made a handsome income; and soon every sizeable town boasted
one or more photographers. A photographic portrait in the
1840s cost about 15 francs, and sometimes as much as 100 francs;
but in the 1850s the invention of a new method and a new
format (the 'visiting-card' portrait, 6×9 cm) brought the price
down to 20 francs for a set of twelve portraits; in the 1860s every
worker could afford the 2 francs that was asked. The leader in
the popularisation of the photograph, Disderi, quickly made an
enormous fortune, though the competition he stimulated eventually ruined him and he died as poor as he had begun, a beach
photographer at Nice. Disderi's motto was: 'One must seek the
greatest beauty that the subject is capable of.' His idea of beauty
was distinctly banal, but it was for that reason popular. Nadar,
the exotic journalist and balloonist whom poverty diverted into
photography, showed that portraits of high artistic quality were
possible, and these early photographs remain unsurpassed, partly
because many of the first photographers were often also painters.[1]
The first victim of the camera was the miniaturist painter, who
virtually disappeared between 1850 and 1890, when a reaction
against the vulgarity of the photograph gave him a new lease
of life. Many miniaturists became photographers, or they
coloured photographs or painted portraits over photographs.
The invention of the camera did not mean that the demand for
painting was reduced, but rather that most people demanded
that painting should be as accurate as photography. The quasi-
photographic paintings of the second half of the nineteenth
century are the result. Some painters even prided themselves on
producing works which were almost indistinguishable from
photographs. Portrait painting was revolutionised, because

[1] Gisèle Freund, *La Photographie en France au 19ᵉ siècle* (1936); Félix Tournachon
Nadar, *Quand j'étais photographe* (1900); Disderi, *Esthétique de la photographie* (1862);
Secrétan, *Prix courants de tous les articles de photographie* (May 1859), shows camera
prices then starting at 200 francs, going up to 2,000; daguerreotypes cost 195–480
francs.

many painters made increasing use of photographs, instead of relying on sketches. No less a master than Ingres took the lead in this new technique. In the 1860s methods were invented to enable photographs to be projected directly on to canvas, so that the artist could paint over them. Manet relied on photographs for the figures in the *Execution of the Emperor Maximilian*, which is therefore an accurate historical document, whatever symbolism or significance may be read into it. Photography thus for a time accentuated the traditional character of painting, in encouraging it to be even more erudite and accurate; but it also produced new kinds of painting. Corot in 1848 suddenly adopted a blurred style which seems to have been associated with his discovery of coated-glass photography, which created the same effect. Impressionism coincided with the advent of the snapshot, which had already produced the same sort of hazy images, and the same kind of composition, with randomly distributed figures, cut by the frame. The development of the fast shutter, allowing objects in motion to be captured as they never had been before, 'proved the painters wrong' by showing, for example, that a horse at the gallop had all four legs off the ground. No one had painted it like that before. The painter Meissonier, who was a maniac for accuracy, held a party in honour of the photographer who made this discovery; and Degas translated the new knowledge of motion into painting, inspired probably more by photography than by Japanese prints. It is true there were artists like Rodin who said that galloping horses seem to be motionless in photographs and that only painters, even if they were anatomically wrong, could make them look as though they were galloping. Painters resented the pretensions of photographers to the status of artists, and they generally concealed their use of photography. With the Post-Impressionists, a reaction set in against photography, and all painting that resembled it, and painting turned, in a more radical way than ever before, from the simple representation or imitation of nature. But 1888 was the year of the appearance of the Kodak camera; and in 1900 it was estimated that 17 per cent of the people admitted to the Paris Universal Exhibition carried portable cameras. That could mean as many as 50,000 people carrying cameras in Paris in a single day. So, though superficially it might seem that a break now occurred between everyman's photographic art, which was essentially representative, and the art of the painter, who concerned himself with images as such, for their own sake, one could see both developments as showing the same concern with individual creativity. The distinction is rather between those who liked to make their own pictures and the vast majority for whom pictures were simply a source of information.

It is customary to be scathing about the enormous industry of pornographic photography that arose as early as the 1840s, but anyone wishing to understand the emotional and imaginative responses to higher art cannot ignore the appeal of the non-intellectual, visual experiences this afforded. Photography and painting were not as much rivals as they might at first appear to have been. 'What we see, and how we see it, depends on the arts that have influenced us', said Oscar Wilde. The relationship between these two visual forms brings out the very important changes that took place in what people did see.[1] Photography showed people things they had never seen before. Indeed the development of optical science in general should be regarded as an important instrument of greater equality between men. About 15 to 20 per cent of Europeans are short-sighted and about 50 per cent long-sighted. Until efficient spectacles were generally worn by these, the world looked very different. Just how different can be judged from the work of numerous painters whose visual defects are known about. Impressionism has been called 'the triumphant exploitation of myopic vision', a condition which of course affects perception of colour as well as outline. Cézanne, Monet, Renoir, Pissarro, Degas can all be shown to owe some of their eccentricities to myopia, or cataract, or corneal ulcers. A recent survey of masters and pupils at the School of Fine Arts in Paris revealed that 48 per cent of them were myopic, which is almost three times more than the national average.[2]

The diversity and richness of French art in this period was stimulated by the existence of patrons with many different motives and tastes. The seventeenth-century diarist John Evelyn

---

[1] Aaron Scharf, *Art and Photography* (1968) is a highly intelligent guide to this problem.

[2] Patrick Trevor-Roper, *The World through Blunted Sight. An Enquiry into the Influence of Defective Vision on Art and Character* (1970).

was struck by the fact that in the Holland of his time perfectly ordinary farmers bought paintings for two or three hundred pounds. In nineteenth-century France, the buyers of pictures had long ceased to be simply kings, aristocrats and very wealthy men. Paintings had become an essential decoration for every home with pretensions. 'Every rich family', wrote a connoisseur describing the collections of Bordeaux in 1893, 'is necessarily obliged to possess a gallery of pictures, and this for two compelling reasons: first, from a natural taste for modern luxury, and, secondly, because *fortune oblige*.'[1] Snobbishness was certainly important, as well as the desire to make a sound investment. The royal and aristocratic collections were copied by the millionaires, Rothschild leading the way. The department store owner Cognacq-Jay seems to have bought pictures without any particular love of art, and painters offering him their works were normally sent away to speak to an assistant he employed for the purpose. Some people were collectors by inheritance, preserving and building up bequests from relatives and ancestors, in the same way as they looked after all their other property. An inquiry carried out in the 1960s among French collectors found all these extraneous motives still surviving: some saw in collecting simply a pastime, some found in pictures a substitute for friends and a cure for loneliness; some saw in it a way of purchasing prestige, especially when the source of their wealth was not a subject of particular pride. Those with a taste for erudition, or with a desire to lead fashion, preferred obscure or unpopular artists; those who sought the approval of conformist circles, and who simply wanted to decorate their homes with a painting of whose value they could be sure, chose from the artists who won prizes at the official Salons. Local loyalties played their part: in Flanders it was said painters were supported by patrons with the same zeal as the football clubs were by not very different kinds of benefactors; provincial painters who made good in Paris could usually count on buyers in their native regions. But it was rare for anyone to admit that financial or social considerations were predominant; and many indeed developed a collector's mania and an obsession with art which defied any explanation in terms of self-interest. Some were able to describe

[1] Georges de Sonneville, *Collections et collectionneurs bordelais* (Bordeaux, 1893), 1–7.

their love of art only with the language of romantic passion; their zeal was stimulated precisely because the search for good pictures was as hard as that for the perfectly beautiful woman.

Just how much people were willing to invest in painting can be seen from the collection of Secrétan, an industrialist who, within the space of fifteen years, built up the most important private collection in France, as it was described in 1879 when he went bankrupt and it was sold by auction, for 6 million francs. Over half of this sum was paid for French paintings. Secrétan was a great admirer of the Salon's favourite, Meissonier, and had twenty-three of his works; he also had seven paintings by Troyon, five by Diaz, four by Corot, one by Courbet, Millet's *Angélus*, as well as four Rembrandts, two Rubens, one Velasquez, four Frans Hals and many other Dutch and Flemish works.[1] The art sales of this period show, among the owners of important collections, some solid well-to-do middle-class men, like Armand Bertin, the editor of the *Journal des Débats*, or Jules Claye, a printer who favoured Troyon, Géricault and Français. There were also people who had had a chance to pick up masterpieces cheaply, like Collot, director of the Paris Mint, who returned from Bonaparte's 1799 campaign in Italy laden with a Leonardo and various other old masters.[2] In the 1860s, it was said that there were sometimes up to three art auctions a day in Paris; leading industrialists and politicians attended the important ones; there was constant movement in these treasures.[3] Provincial art collectors were a distinct group in their communities. They were not rivals of the great Paris collectors, for they could not afford Paris prices. A favourite practice of theirs was to form local art societies (there were 368 of these in 1885) and organise local exhibitions, at which they would run lotteries. Sometimes the lottery tickets would cost only 25 centimes and in such cases 15,000 might be sold (at Agen in 1886) or even 60,000 (as in Cherbourg in the same year); more usually they were 10 francs —one-tenth of what they cost in Paris. For its exhibition of 1885, the Society of Arts of Bordeaux bought forty-two of the entries, which it resold by lottery in this way; private individuals bought

---

[1] *Catalogue de tableaux anciens et modernes . . . formant la célèbre collection de M. E. Secrétan* (1889); prices realised in *Larousse du XIXe siècle*, second supplement (1890), 1. 830.

[2] Charles Blanc, *Le Trésor de la curiosité* (1857), a major source for art prices.

[3] Ivan Golovine, *Manuel du marchand de tableaux* (1862), 124.

a further seventy-one; on average prices were between 500 and 650 francs. Only occasionally were really high prices paid, and this by rich foreigners, as in the Nice exhibitions of that year, where two Bouguereaus went for 25,000 francs each.[1]

Bordeaux in 1893 had about thirty private collections of paintings sizeable enough to attract public attention. Dr. Azam, for example, had about 200 mainly Dutch and Flemish paintings, which his uncle, who had been a merchant trading with Holland, had collected since the 1830s. Fourestier had inherited a collection of old masters, again mainly Dutch and Flemish, from his uncle, a senior tax official, but had added modern works by Salon painters like Armand Leleux and Jean-Paul Laurens. Bourges, a member of the chamber of commerce, had thirty paintings by Eugène Boudin, many more by Bordeaux painters and others by Swedish and Norwegian artists, acquired in the course of his business dealings in Scandinavia. There were collectors infatuated with the work of a single artist. Thus Degas found a passionate admirer in Friedmann, who bought virtually nothing else; Auguste Pellerin bought seventeen Manets and then over a hundred Cézannes. Renand at one time had forty Corots.[2] Friendship was sometimes the basis of their patronage: the marine engineer Gustave Caillebotte, whom Monet met boating on the Seine, whom he taught to paint and with whom he became very close, bought large numbers of Impressionist paintings, which he subsequently bequeathed to the state, from admiration, but also from a desire to help painters he liked personally.[3] Painters were among the most important collectors of paintings, as too were those who came most into contact with them—auctioneers, colour merchants, and dealers. Writers who backed artistic movements with sympathetic criticism helped to create little cliques of admirers who gave material encouragement. The publisher Georges Charpentier, for example (whose father Gervais, founder of the firm, had been a supporter,

[1] Raymonde Moulin, 'Les Expositions des Beaux-Arts en province 1885-7' (unpublished thesis Paris, 1967, in the Sorbonne library), 246.

[2] Jean Dauberville, La Bataille de l'impressionisme, suivi de En encadrant le siècle, par Jean Dauberville (1967), 516. Cf. La Collection Oscar Schmitz (1936), describing the patronage of the Impressionists by the Swiss cotton merchant of Le Havre (1861–1933).

[3] Cf. Maurice Rheims, Art on the Market: Thirty-five Centuries of Collecting and Collectors from Midas to Paul Getty (1961).

of the romantics), was a Maecenas to the Impressionists, as Renoir's paintings of his family commemorate.[1] In 1956, still, the marquis de Chasseloup-Laubat had a painter installed in his château as a permanent guest, almost as blind as Degas and working in a similar style, with his studio in the stables. This was continuing the tradition of hospitality to art that had enabled the animal painter Brascassat (1804–67) to establish himself, supported by the civil servant-engineer-painter Théodore Richard, who was president of the Society of Fine Arts of Bordeaux. Brascassat, when he became famous, used to go round the country staying with aristocrats, painting portraits of their prize cattle.[2] Bouguereau got his start in life decorating the walls of houses bought by rising financiers like Bartholoni and Pereire. But these kinds of domestic commissions became increasingly rare.

As in seventeenth-century Italy, the patrons of contemporary art were often people outside the traditional ruling class, with tastes unshackled by the prevalent conventions.[3] Thus the Fauves sold their paintings to odd men like King Milan of Serbia and the restaurant owner Bauchy (whose Café des Variétés was decorated also with the still cheap works of Cézanne and Van Gogh). But they relied ultimately on a handful of faithful admirers. The socialist deputy Marcel Sembat (whose wife had studied painting with Gustave Moreau) was one of their regular buyers: he bequeathed his collection of their works to the state, which refused it—as it had once refused Caillebotte's bequest of Impressionists. (It was the socialist curator of the museum of Grenoble who rescued Sembat's collection, so that Grenoble was the first French Museum to exhibit the Fauves.) The Americans Leo and Gertrude Stein and Dr. Barnes, the inventor of the antiseptic Argyrol, were important patrons not only to the Fauves, but to many of their contemporaries. Barnes finally accumulated about 120 Cézannes, 200 Renoirs, 95 Picassos and 100 Matisses. Two Russian merchants, Morozov and Shchukin, similarly bought in large quantities and the vast collections of modern French paintings in the Soviet Union are

[1] Michel Robida, *Le Salon Charpentier et les Impressionistes* (1958).

[2] C. Marionneau, *Brascassat, sa vie et son œuvre* (1872).

[3] F. Haskell, *Patrons and Painters. A Study in the Relations between Italian Art and Society in the Age of the Baroque* (1963) is full of stimulating ideas; id., *Rediscoveries in Art* (1976), published since this book went to press, is indispensable.

the results of their enthusiasm and generosity in Paris.[1] The owners of Cézanne paintings just before the First World War included writers like Octave Mirbeau and Zola, dealers like Bernheim and Vollard, but also many foreigners, in Berlin, Hamburg, Budapest, Moscow and the U.S.A.[2] One of the reasons why French art acquired an international reputation and influence was perhaps because an important section of it was rather neglected in France itself, picked up by foreigners.

In 1938 Britain was the largest importer of French paintings, followed by the U.S.A., as these figures show:[3]

Britain	317
U.S.A.	270
Netherlands	82
Belgium and Luxembourg	51
Sweden	49
Other countries	88

By 1953 the U.S.A. had overtaken Britain and by 1963 Switzerland had also. The export of French paintings to England still awaits proper investigation, but a certain amount is known about exports to the U.S.A. The great American collectors enthusiastically patronised the most successful contemporary French painters. Bouguereau, Gérome, Meissonier, Troyon and Rosa Bonheur were to be found in almost every collection by the middle of the nineteenth century; scenes from domestic life and landscapes with interesting figures were preferred to grand historical themes. In 1849 Goupil and Vibert founded the International Art Union in New York to stimulate this taste and for the rest of the century the 'academic' painters continued to please the Americans. Collectors in Boston and New England, however, repeatedly took the lead in introducing more controversial artists. From 1850 Quincy Adams Shaw began buying the Barbizon school and by 1870 he had twenty-five Millets. The French dealer De Vose established himself in Providence (Rhode Island), and in 1852 organised the first exhibition in the U.S.A. of Corot, who failed to make much headway in England, but who became such a success in America that a vast number

---

[1] J. P. Crespelle, *The Fauves* (c. 1962), 344–7.
[2] J. Meier-Graefe, *Paul Cézanne* (Munich, 1913).
[3] Figures of exports in thousands New Francs.

of forgeries of his paintings, as well as pastiches by his pupils amiably signed by him, were profitably exported there. The French, of course, had to compete with the Düsseldorf school and the modern Dutch school, and American taste extended very broadly, to all periods and over all kinds of artistic objects. But the French had special advocates in the American painters who came to study in France and who spread the fame of the younger generation; and there were some American collectors with special links with France, like Henry Walters of the Atlantic Coast Line Co. Durand-Ruel's exhibition of the Impressionists in New York in 1885 attracted sympathetic interest; by the 1890s every picture Monet could produce was readily sold in America for 4–6,000 francs; in 1922 the Chicago Art Institute received a large bequest of Impressionists and in 1929 the Havemeyer donation added 36 Degas, 20 Courbets, 9 Corots, 8 Manets, 8 Monets and 5 Cézannes to the collections of the Metropolitan Art Museum. The Impressionists became museum masters in the U.S.A. well before they reached that status in France. (In England sales of the Impressionists were slower: of the two main collectors, Sir Hugh Lane started buying in 1905 and Samuel Courtauld in 1922. In Russia, Shchukin had begun his collection in the 1890s.) Cézanne, the Fauves and the Cubists owed their introduction into the U.S.A. above all to the Armory Show organised by American painters in 1913. But there were individual collectors, like Adolph Lewisohn, who bought modern paintings ahead even of these fashions, with great independence and sureness of taste.[1]

There were 104 picture dealers in Paris in 1861; in 1958 there were 275 (and another 70 in the rest of the country). These figures, however, represent only a proportion of the many middlemen, painters' widows, unemployed artists, women of leisure, and crooks who lived on the fringes of the art world, profiting from the passions of collectors, the poverty of painters and each other's gambling instincts. Art was a merchandise but one clothed in secrecy and mystery, because its price was so difficult to fix, and because its relationship with commerce was so ambivalent. Art had long been an international merchandise, whose value was usually increased by export; and dealers had

[1] René Brimo, L'Évolution du goût aux États-Unis d'après l'histoire des collections (1938).

become essential already in the seventeenth century. But because of the increase in the number of pictures and because the vast majority of them were no longer commissioned, dealers now had a larger role as bankers, stockists and promoters. Rembrandt had sold his paintings to a dealer for what was virtually a salary. This system was now much developed by Durand-Ruel (1831–1922), who introduced a new element by seeking a monopoly of the production of the artists he patronised, building up large stocks first of the Barbizon school and then of the Impressionists. In 1866 he bought seventy paintings by Théodore Rousseau; in 1872 he visited Manet and bought all the paintings he had —twenty-three of them, for 35,000 francs. He worked hard to spread his taste among collectors, by holding exhibitions, starting art journals and opening a branch office in New York (1886). Behind Durand-Ruel was the banker Feder, of the Catholic Union nationale, but it crashed in 1882, and Durand-Ruel was at times on the verge of bankruptcy himself. He had too many rivals for him to be able to profit fully from his efforts.[1] The American dealer Sueton, who had collected 120 Monets, was only one of the army of middlemen who were combing Europe for rare objects to sell in the United States, exports to which had become very considerable since the 1840s. It was Kahnweiler (b. 1884), the Cubists' art dealer, who perfected Durand-Ruel's monopoly methods: he undertook to buy all the paintings of Juan Gris and also of Picasso at a fixed price according to size; but he had a contempt for art criticism and for mass opinion, and never spent a penny on advertising. The ultimate factor in a dealer's success was how long he could afford to wait. The one who probably waited longest was Nathan Wildenstein (1851–1934) whose motto was *Savoir Attendre*. Wildenstein was originally an Alsatian textile merchant; he turned to picture dealing by chance, and came to specialise in old masters and particularly eighteenth-century paintings, whose popularity in around 1900 he helped to create. Under his son Georges (1892–1963) the firm expanded to cover the Impressionists. Their stocks in New York (they opened their gallery on Fifth Avenue in 1902) consisted at one time of some 2,000 paintings, including 8 Rembrandts, 79 Fragonards, 20 Renoirs and 250 Picassos. Dealers, however, did not create

[1] Mrs. Linda Whiteley is writing a doctoral thesis at Oxford on Durand-Ruel.

taste; their influence spread only slowly; economic conditions
and changing fashions could destroy their work. After the First
World War, for example, the Barbizon school, which had
steadily increased in value, collapsed (with a few exceptions);
and no propaganda could attenuate the effects of the great
depression. The provinces continued to provide a steady market
for traditional painting, particularly in cities like Lyon and
Marseille which had their own favourite local schools. There
can be no doubt, however, that dealers did create reputations:
a good example is that of Villon, whose paintings sold very
cheaply until 1942 when Louis Carré became his propagandist,
organised twenty-seven exhibitions for him all over the world
in the space of sixteen years, and his price increased more than
a thousandfold. But one should not glamorise these dealers too
much into prophets of future taste. Paul Rosenberg said modestly in 1948: 'I made a fortune by mistake, because all my life I
had to keep pictures I could not sell, by Picasso, Braque and
Juan Gris', which all of a sudden became priceless.' Le Barc de
Boutteville, who was one of the main dealers of the Nabis, cared
little about what he sold, and often expressed amazement at the
strange pictures that passed through his hands. Tostain, who
advertised in the *Figaro* in 1858 that he always had 4,000 paintings in stock, to suit all tastes, at 20 francs for four, framed,
English spoken, was perhaps not unrepresentative. Ambroise
Vollard at his death was said to have over 700 Rouaults, and
hundreds of Impressionists, but he also owned the complete
works of painters like Iturino who have never been heard of
since; and he was heartily disliked by many of the young
painters, who complained that he used his exhibitions of their
works to attract clients interested in established names; he had
a filthy shop, and himself wore threadbare clothes and broken
shoes. Berthe Weil, who sold many of the Fauves, began as a
second-hand dealer, and though she eventually had three gal-
leries, she never made much money out of her flair. Other
dealers who supported the Fauves were Soulié, a former clown,
and Druet, who originally ran a bistro patronised by painters,
and then took up photography.[1] Nevertheless, the dealers often

[1] A. Vollard, *Souvenirs d'un marchand de tableaux* (1948); Gustave Cogniot, *Les
Indépendants 1884–1920* (3rd edition, n.d.), 29–30; D. H. Kahnweiler, *Confessions
esthétiques* (1963); Rheims, op. cit. 105; Crespelle, op. cit. 336.

did have both faith in their protégés and a feeling for art, which has influenced the history of painting.

The influence of art critics on taste is more difficult to assess. Monet wrote in 1883 that 'nothing can be achieved nowadays without the press'; he cared nothing for what it said, but 'it is from the commercial point of view that one must look at it . . . for even intelligent connoisseurs are sensitive to the least noise made by the newspapers'. But an art critic had already written in 1859 that 'criticism has little power today and it is seldom that anyone listens'.[1] The press was certainly important in the process of selection of fashionable painters, particularly as the number of painters increased, but it is possible that those it condemned benefited as much from their publicity as their favourites. It tended to discuss painters more than painting, and it is not clear that it aroused interest in the arts among those who cared nothing for them. The critics to whom it opened its columns met with hostility from an early stage, and not only among complete philistines. A professor of the Paris faculty of letters published a satirical commentary on their style in 1861, suggesting that those who felt lost at exhibitions could acquire the vocabulary and mannerisms of connoisseurs in a couple of hours.[2] The profession of art critic was a comparatively recent one, begun in the eighteenth century and developing fully only with the growth of the Salon and the press in the nineteenth. There were about a hundred art critics under Napoleon III and nearly 350 in 1961; in 1899 they formed themselves into a trade union. Most of them were part-time writers, journalists, academics, novelists, failed painters, and leisured civil servants. Because of that, they could be expected to reflect what was said at the Salons; but by developing their own jargon, fancy phrases and platitudes, which their pretentious readers aped with more or less success, they attempted to make the appreciation of art more complex; they may have explained things to some people, but they also turned others away with insults about their bad taste. The most fashionable critics, writing for the newspapers with large circulations, seldom formed taste, but rather

[1] M. H. Dumesnil, *Le Salon de 1859* (1859), quoted Joseph C. Sloane, *French Painting between the Past and the Present. Artists, Critics and Traditions from 1848 to 1870* (Princeton, 1951), 33 n.

[2] Nicolas Martin, *Le Parfait Connaisseur, ou l'art de devenir un critique d'art en deux heures, imité de l'allemand* (1861).

embroidered around the orthodoxies familiar to their readers, confirming prejudices that already existed, but backing them up with moral considerations and seeking to show how the style they approved was the inevitable one. The critics who wrote for small journals often played a different role. They sought to vindicate the claims of new painters and new styles to public attention, and sometimes set themselves up as interpreters or even guides of new work. The paper battles of the critics consolidated factions and friendships and exacerbated disputes. It is above all to the critics that the division of painters into schools, with opprobrious titles, is due. In the process, aesthetic theories were developed which sometimes stimulated the artists to whom they were attributed, but just as frequently left them indifferent or protesting that their aims were being over-simplified, over-clarified. The categorisations the critics popularised gave their world a framework which did not accurately contain the variety within it, but which was nevertheless influential as a myth that neither painters nor public could escape. The critics who are now most esteemed are those who were, in their day, considered the most biased and the least learned. Certainly, Baudelaire's knowledge of art history was superficial; Zola was only twenty-six years old, and his experience was limited to advertising for Hachette the publisher, when he launched his unmeasured praise of Manet; Apollinaire, as Braque said, could not even recognise a Leonardo when he saw one; he knew nothing of painting, but he loved originality, change, fantasy and the painters with whom he associated; his advocacy of a succession of new artistic schools was the product of a temperament. The enthusiasms of Baudelaire and Zola did not last; they were each seeking more than what the painters offered; and they ended by condemning the modern art which they had helped create. What critics of this kind did was to bring new theories and words from other disciplines, like philosophy, or mysticism or science, to add the same kind of weight to new painting styles that morals gave to the academic painters. In course of time—it often took as much as thirty years—the critics of the provinces absorbed their doctrines. Thus it was only around the 1880s that realism was accepted and indeed espoused by provincial critics, whose articles then reproduced almost word for word what Thoré had written a generation before in Paris. They resisted innovation, at least till it had become familiar and had moderated its eccentricities. They liked to understand what the painters were trying to do, and it is a measure of the failure of the Parisian critics that their provincial colleagues took so long to get their message. The difficulty new painters had in being accepted came in some measure from the fact that these critics insisted on painters speaking the language of ordinary men: the Impressionists were rejected by provincial critics because, as *Le Dauphiné* put it in 1886, they had something wrong with their eyes: they could not see 'the sights commonly visible to humans, to you and to me'.[1]

Critics thus on the one hand formulated the resistance of the public to the painters' claim to an independent and original view of the world. On the other hand some of them helped the public to build a bridge between their ordinary perceptions and those of painters, and to extend the range of their sensibilities. Baudelaire held up as the ideal the art lover who was 'partial, passionate and political, amusing and poetic', who can analyse and translate the shock of pleasure he experiences in front of a picture, and whose imagination is capable of penetrating beneath the surface, to perceive hidden analogies between the different arts. He urged the painter to interpret the age he lived in to itself, to be the philosopher of modernity. He made temperament—or individuality—the crucial quality that a painter needed.[2] This was to make art the preserve of the happy few. Zola, who repeated Baudelaire's injunction when he said 'a work of art is a corner of nature viewed through a temperament', added however that the public's reactions were as important as the picture. He wanted the artist to 'conquer the crowd' by the force of his genius, though without making any concessions.[3] These two critics set up a debate on the status of art which was never resolved.

One constant and decisive factor in the world of art was the artists' determination to win independence and recognition of themselves as a superior creative profession. All these economic

[1] *Le Dauphiné* (12 Aug. 1886) quoted in R. Moulin, *Lex Expositions* (1967), 216. Cf. L. Venturi, *History of Art Criticism* (New York, new edition 1964).
[2] Charles Baudelaire, *The Painter of Modern Life and other Essays* (1964, English translation).
[3] E. Zola, *Salons* (ed. F. W. J. Hemmings) (1959).

and social pressures upon them had to battle with the way they wanted to see themselves, with their ambition for a kind of life which involved much more than selling their pictures. Their whole history, indeed, had been dominated by a remarkably steady determination in the same direction; though each successive victory also brought with it unexpected difficulties, which tied them up in new knots. In the middle ages, they set themselves up as a guild, and this protected them against their principal employer in those days, the Church, but this also had the effect of cutting them off from another corporation, the University. The fine arts and letters as a result remained separate for many centuries, and artists were weakened by their isolation. The guild in course of time became oppressive and the king set up an Academy of Fine Arts as a rival to it, in which his court painters could work free of its restrictions; but though this body gave an élite of artists the benefits and prestige of royal protection, it soon got embogged in rules it formulated in the hope of strengthening and safeguarding that prestige. In the eighteenth century a division was established between the fine arts and the applied arts; this appeared to the court painters as a great triumph; but the long-term result was to isolate painters still further, this time from industry and science. Many people who might have become good artisans were condemned to remaining bad and embittered painters. To make itself more respectable, the Academy laid down rules about what art should be, which inevitably caused almost every generation to rebel against it. Internal feuds were built into the art world's institutions. When the Academy was revived after its temporary abolition at the Revolution, it had lost much of its power, but it retained and strengthened its hold on art education. The academicians were professors at the School of Fine Arts, and artists continued to be divided into pupils, *agréés* and academicians, preserving the old apprentice, journeyman and master division. But this was a system which could no longer work in modern conditions. There were now too many students and the chances of becoming an academician became increasingly remote. In the seventeenth century one could hope to be elected to the Academy while still in one's twenties. In the nineteenth century the average age of new members was 53. The competition for the prix de Rome, the top annual scholarship which set a painter on the path of success, dominated the training of young painters; the near-inevitability of failing weighed them down into a feeling of helplessness, which they concealed behind the bohemian *joie de vivre* they cultivated—a façade of assumed frivolity that covered up insecurity and brutality. The relationship of master and student collapsed when the former could no longer guarantee jobs to his disciples; and the Renaissance and Baroque practice of working together as collaborators had died under the assaults of individualism. Courbet's studio, where there was no teaching, marked the crisis of the system, as also did the other independent studios—which the Impressionists were to attend. Many students not unnaturally responded to the crisis by opting out of a rat race they could not win, and that was the basis of independent art.

However, the belief that the revolutions in artistic style of this period were essentially rebellions against the Academy is mistaken. The idea that there was academic art on the one hand and progressive or modern art on the other—represented by that famous succession of groups whose -isms summarise the art history of this century—is a misleading simplification. It is true that the Academy saw itself as the guardian of doctrines evolved in the seventeenth and eighteenth centuries. These were that the subject-matter of art had to be selected with great discrimination, that only 'noble' themes should be painted, that these were to be found above all in classical or Christian history, that the human figure expressed ideal beauty best, and that it should be presented in ideal form, in traditionally admired poses, that harmonious composition and accurate drawing should prove the painter's skill. The Academy tried to make painting appeal to the intellect: a work of art should translate 'a profound thought or an ingenious idea'. Poussin had said that those who painted 'mean subjects take refuge in them because of the meanness of their talents'. A painter had to be a moralist, to point out what was worthy of admiration. That is why academic art was identified with 'grand' pictures, depicting 'battles, heroic actions and divine things'.[1] That, too, is why such pains were taken to fill paintings with accurate historical and mythological detail. Erudition raised the painter to a much higher level than a decorator. Meissonier declared that if he were not a painter, he

[1] Sloane, op. cit. 16 n.

would wish to be a historian. Copying old paintings was an essential part of the artist's training, which maintained reverence for the skills and the methods of the old masters. These doctrines, whatever might be thought of them aesthetically, were defensible if art was seen as a servant of the state, and if the state's duty was seen as the preservation of order and morals. The state was by far the most important patron of the arts, and it commissioned 'grand' art, which was both impressive and edifying. Historical painting was much encouraged by King Louis-Philippe for the decoration of the palace of Versailles, and in the 1830s such paintings formed the bulk of state commissions. In the 1840s about 85 per cent of the state's purchases were of religious paintings and in the 1850s about 45 per cent.[1] In all, between 1851 and 1860, the state bought about 2,000 pictures. These were by no means all different pictures, for favourites were ordered in many copies: at least thirty-two churches, for example, were sent copies of Prud'hon's *Christ en Croix* and thirty-two others of his *Assomption de la Vierge*. Only about one-sixth (319 in all) of the state's purchases were originals; but the difference between an original and a copy was not all that great. The painters who were commissioned to do an original painting were told what to paint—for example the thirty local saints, commissioned to satisfy the requests of *curés*, and the portraits of the Holy Family, commissioned from nineteen different artists. One of the Second Republic's most grandiose ideas had been to establish a Museum of Copies in Paris, which would reproduce the best paintings of the whole world, and in 1851 four painters were dispatched to copy the works in the National Gallery in London.[2] Under the Third Republic, the decoration of town halls and public buildings, raised up in great numbers, continued the demand for moralising works, with a new 'social' element added to them.

The Academy, however, did not monopolise the patronage of the state, and it is not true that the 'modern' painters were totally rejected and, as it were, thrown into opposition. Between 'academic' and 'modern' art, there was a middle ground of 'official' art which attempted a reconciliation between them.

---

[1] Pierre Angrand, *Monsieur Ingres et son époque* (1967), 165.
[2] Id., 'L'État mécène, période autoritaire du second empire 1851–60', *Gazette des Beaux-Arts* (1968), vol. 71, 303–48.

Delacroix, who was long rejected by the Academy and not elected to it until he was an old man, nevertheless received important commissions from the state. The Barbizon painters, though they broke the academic rules, included the king's son, the duc d'Orléans, and the prime minister, Casimir Périer, among their first patrons. The Second Empire favoured watered-down versions of their style, and then watered-down realism, which was what a large number of middle-of-the-road painters were producing. The extreme innovators had difficulties, but they soon attracted moderate imitators, who made them respectable by marrying moderation with their eccentricity. Delaroche made romanticism acceptable, and later the highly esteemed Bastien-Lepage adopted the lighter palette and looser style of the Impressionists—these men seemed, in their day, to be the protagonists of modernity. As Henry Houssaye said in 1882: 'Impressionism earns every form of sarcasm when it takes the names Manet, Monet, Renoir, Caillebotte, Degas, [but] every honour when it is called Bastien-Lepage, Duez, Gervex, Danton, Gœneutte, Butin, Mangeant, Jean Béraud or Dagnan-Bouveret.' The real innovators in any case were not permanently ostracised. Manet was eventually given a medal under the Third Republic, and Millet's work was bought by the state in the 1870s. It was the same in politics: the electorate was frightened by the extreme Reds, except in certain traditionally extreme circles, and it was the moderate radical-socialists who were admitted to apply their ideals of social justice in suitably diluted form; it was fifty years after their death that the utopians became heroes. In art, the division between apparently opposing sides was really almost as false as it was in politics. On a personal level, many academic and Impressionist painters were friends; the Impressionists had a great admiration for some 'official' painters, like Puvis de Chavannes; and on the other hand they did not get on too well with others who were more 'modern': Manet was hated by Courbet. The invention of labels to characterise and categorise painters confused the issues enormously. The more artistic rebellions of the century are examined, the more their debt to and their links with the art of their predecessors is seen to be crucially important. Thus it used to be thought that Manet, who spent many years as a pupil of Couture, hated all that Couture stood for, and that the rise of Impressionism could be epitomised in the clash of their contrasting doctrines. But now that Couture's painting and teaching have been more carefully examined, it has been discovered that, in his day, Couture was seen as the antithesis of academic ideals: he urged his pupils to ignore the intellectualist attitude of the Academy and to concentrate on pictorial technique, on purity of colour, on spontaneity and self-expression. 'Produce with a fresh mind and a hearty spirit whatever you feel like doing', he used to say. He had a little group of loyal admirers around him, but he was 'so violently attacked', as he himself said, that he gave up teaching. The battle the Impressionists fought was not a new one: Couture's happens to be less famous. Couture was a product of the Academy, but one who had narrowly missed success: he had been runner-up in the prix de Rome competition. How different would he have been if he had won? Couture, in denouncing 'serious painting', was himself repeating the iconoclasm of Delacroix, who ended up in the Academy.

The Academy should not be seen as the enemy of good painting because of these quarrels. Its rules were not as absolute as they were in theory, and it in fact encouraged tendencies with which its theory conflicted. Thus landscape painting was, according to its teaching, an inferior form of art; but in 1817 it was made part of the academic syllabus for students; it was the academician Valenciennes who wrote the first textbook on landscape painting, which was recommended by Pissarro to his son some fifty years later; and most academicians of the nineteenth century painted landscapes. Gleyre, in whose studio several Impressionists studied, emphasised landscape painting, and Couture took his pupils on field trips to paint from nature. The rigid hierarchy of subject-matter had been greatly attenuated in the face of the romantic sensibility in both artists and public. Again, the Academy laid enormous theoretical stress on perfect finish as an ideal, on line as opposed to colour, and indeed it did not allow its pupils to paint at all until they had mastered drawing. It criticised the romantics for producing mere sketches, which it condemned as being morally as well as artistically inferior, as a dishonest way of reducing the amount of labour put into pictures, and of increasing output. Nevertheless it did establish a special competition for compositional sketches, which had a great influence on the development of painting. The cult of copying old masters was modernised by doing more sketches of them, thus combining veneration for the past with the cultivation of originality. The sketch, which the romantics had valued for its expressiveness and spontaneity, was gradually seen as a valid work of art, and not simply as a preparation. When applied to landscape painting, it led to the shift of interest from the objects painted to the study of light and the representation and juxtaposition of colour. It was from this basis that the Impressionists developed the idea of the outdoor sketch, produced in a few hours, as a self-sufficient work of art. What used to be condemned as amateurism was now raised to a new status; and this opened up great possibilities for genuinely amateur painters too. It was not a pure coincidence that amateur painting now suddenly became a popular hobby and that long, academic training no longer seemed essential—as the flood of Teach Yourself Painting books testified. In 1872 there were already twenty art schools for girls in Paris.[1]

What emerged from these conflicts was the triumph of self-expression as the artist's main preoccupation and this was at the root of the new styles from the romantics onwards. This culmination of the artists' struggle for independence marked a very important transformation in the criteria of taste. The Academy had in theory set out clear ideas about what good painting was, and the artist's function, if its doctrine was rigorously interpreted, was simply to approximate to that ideal. But the Academy also believed in originality. Its interpretation of originality was, however, aristocratic; it considered that only some people were original and the vast majority were definitely not so; to be original was to be a member of a superior élite. Now a democratic view of originality challenged this. As early as 1819 Alexandre Lenoir in a paper on this subject declared, 'Originality belongs to every human being and to every genre. It is independent of talent.' During the Second Empire Viollet

---

[1] Horace Lecoq de Boisbaubran, *Coup d'œil sur l'enseignement des Beaux-Arts* (1872) 69 ff.; J. de La Rochenoir, *La Couleur et le dessin appris seul* (1857); R. de Lasalle, *L'Aquarelle en six leçons* (1856); Mme Veuve Cavé, *L'Aquarelle sans maître* (1856); J. P. Thénot, *Le Pastel appris sans maître* (1856); Victori, *Tout le monde artiste. Procédé pour faire de jolies peintures sans avoir la moindre notion de dessin* (1898); Camille Bellanger, *Le Peintre; Traité usuel de peinture à l'usage de tous le monde* (1898); Madame Bourdox-Sody, *Nouveau Procédé de l'art de peindre, sans maître et sans notions du dessin* (1882).

le Duc added that originality was 'the most important of qualities'.[1] The sketch, the artist's impression, constituted the expression of this originality. Once again, however, this victory for the
artist had a high price: his relationship with the community
was altered. On the one hand this new doctrine meant that
everybody could be an artist: to be an artist no longer meant to
cut oneself off. But now everybody was entitled to his opinion,
and the shift of emphasis from communication with the public
to self-exploration meant that the artist became a more isolated
and lonely figure than he had ever been. The proliferation of
sects and groups was partly a compensation for this, but the
labels artists adopted have never been enough to explain them
or to summarise their individual ambitions. 'Good taste', as a
result, became more elusive than ever; it no longer followed
from membership of the ruling class or polite society.

Already in 1848 French art, as illustrated in the Paris Salon
of that year, which was open to all artists without restriction,
was declared to be 'distinguished by such a variety of styles that
no one looking at it would believe in the existence of a French
school.' There were already different avenues to success and
different markets for the specialisations into which artists divided
themselves. The controversies which raged about the merits of
particular individuals and particular styles show that there was
never any unanimity of judgement. Though grand historical
and religious art was held in the highest esteem, in the sense that
success in it led to official honours, the majority of private buyers
wanted pictures of scenes from daily life, and it was these that
fetched the highest prices. For long, the painters who were most
successful financially were those who managed to combine the
lofty idealism of the former with the anecdotal relevance of the
latter. The Impressionists were derided for eliminating the intellectual content from art; they were condemned as 'materialists'
by Catholics, as 'democratic' by the royalists, as 'mad' by the
Figaro, the organ of well-to-do men of the world.[2] But their
crime was more one of exaggeration than of innovation, more
in the way they made their statements than in what they said.
If one takes Bouguereau (1825–1905) as the representative of

[1] Albert Boime, *The Academy and French Painting in the Nineteenth Century* (1971),
important.
[2] Jacques Lethève, *Impressionistes et symbolistes devant la presse* (1959), 23, 73, 76.

the successful academic painter, one sees that, though he was an artist as sincere as any 'modern', he was more modest, willing to adapt his work to satisfy convention, without any sacrifice of his integrity. Bouguereau's passion was the study of nature; he would spend hours admiring and meditating about a passing cloud or a wild flower. He believed in the importance of the artist's personality as an equal source of inspiration, in so far as composition was concerned. One was born an artist, according to him, because an artist was 'a special kind of creature with a special sensitivity, that of seeing form and colour, spontaneously and together, in perfect harmony'. The skills of the painter had to be learnt by practice and hard work, and he himself did almost nothing but work. His enormous fees led people to accuse him of painting only to make money, but he denied this, and indeed he lived very modestly and avoided fashionable society, having only a few painters as friends. Far from instilling any doctrines into his pupils, he urged them to follow their natural bent, to find their originality by individual research and by the development of their special gifts. He thought that there was no point in trying to produce painters on the model of those of the Renaissance, with encyclopedic knowledge. He was himself uninterested by philosophy, or politics, or literature; he cared nothing for theories about painting and disliked analysing it too much. He knew a lot about mythology, but though his paintings were often of mythological or classical subjects, they were not primarily or essentially about their ostensible subjects, the gods and goddesses. He painted, above all, beautiful women with beautiful skins, and it was only afterwards that he found titles for them, labelling them Venus, or Magdalen, or 'La Rêverie'. The long conversations he had with his wife about these titles are said to have been full of humour. He aimed at simplicity in his allegories, addressing himself to 'all intelligences and imaginations'. His painting came to be considered too perfect, but his sketches show he had more to him than technical mastery. He has been in eclipse for nearly a century but a recent exhibition of his work in New York indicates that he is on the way back into fashion.[1]

It will be a long time and will need a great deal of research before Bouguereau's contemporaries—whose work is nowadays

[1] Marius Vachon, *W. Bouguereau* (1900).

dismissed contemptuously as *art pompier*—are properly under-stood. The richness of their legacy was shown in a striking way when the paintings which were in the Luxembourg Museum (the Museum of Living Artists) in 1874 were, in 1974, brought out of their cellars and exhibited once again. It is no longer possible to maintain that it was only the 'modern', as opposed to the academic painters, who expressed 'modernity'. Gérome (1823–1903), who came to be seen as the incarnation of reaction in art, was nevertheless a representative figure, even if, or rather precisely because, his eroticism was clothed in erudite epigrams. Meissonier's precision was a source of endless interest to his contemporaries. Adolphe Leleux (1812–91) and Gustave Brion (1824–77) recorded the folkloric aspects of provincial life in a way that went beyond the suburban horizons of most Parisian painters, while Jules Breton (1827–1906), regarded as the lead-ing landscape painter of his day, sought to defend dignity and grandeur in rural existence. François Bonhommé (1809–81) was one of the increasingly numerous painters of industry and machines. Charles Chaplin (1825–91) produced pictures that people liked to put in their bedrooms and boudoirs. J. J. Henner (1829–1905) and Jules Lefebvre (1836–1911) specialised in female nudes, with great success. Fromentin (1820–76) was famous for his subtle colours: his rose-greys and delicate mauves were copied by many admirers. Gleyre's (1806–74) remarkable studies of light should not be overlooked because they were out-done by his pupils Renoir, Monet and Whistler. Ernest Hébert (1817–1908) was condemned by Baudelaire for trying to please his public, but he deserves to be remembered, perhaps, because he was so successful in doing this. Bastien-Lepage created a new synthesis of styles which was for a time regarded as the vanguard of modernity; and it is not irrelevant, if one wants a comprehen-sive notion of what modernity was, to remember that he was also a great expert on music-hall songs.[1]

What painters represented, in social or political terms, cannot be easily stated. It is tempting to identify art which was revolu-tionary in its technique or new in the treatment of its subject-matter with revolutionary ideas in general, but the connection is not always there. J. F. Millet (1814–75), for example, is

[1] Cf. Francis Jourdain, 'L'Art officiel de Jules Grévy à Albert Lebrun', *Le Point* (Apr. 1949), with numerous reproductions.

celebrated as the painter of the peasantry, whom he depicted without sentimentality. He was therefore regarded by some as a demagogic socialist, by others as teaching that 'art should confine itself to copying servilely ignoble models'. Who would want to hang a picture of a dirty, sweating, gloomy labourer on his wall? But Millet ultimately emerged from the traditional near-starvation of the unrecognised painter to become a very successful painter, and that was because, despite the boldness of his art, he stood only partly on the side of modernity. He painted real life, but he commented on his work with learned citations from old authors; his paintings could variously be given biblical or contemporary titles. His peasants could appeal to romantics like George Sand, for they contained idealisation as well as sadness. He said that he painted peasants because they were the section of society he knew best. He was indeed the son of a peasant, but he had formed a liaison with a Breton servant-girl, who bore him four children, and he preferred to break with his parents rather than reveal either her or their existence. The peasants in his pictures were thus partly nostalgic symbols of the way of life he had abandoned, as well as being partly illustrations of biblical and classical pastoral life, which greatly interested him. He did not in fact either like or even get to know the peasants among whom he lived in Barbizon: he considered them narrow-minded, insensitive to the charms of nature. Millet mocked the idea of labour being a source of happiness, and that was one reason why he worried the critics; but he said he did not paint the joyful side of life, because he had never seen it. The only happiness he knew was rest, calm, silence—the opposite of work. He was deeply conscious of the pain that life involved. He painted peasants beaten down by hard labour because the sight of pain was what moved him most. His view of the world was sad, he admitted, but he drew no conclusions from this. He was no philosopher, he said; he had no desire to suppress unhappiness nor to find a formula to make men stoical or indifferent towards it. As an artist, he believed his function was to express what he saw, to give things their true character. The subtlety of all this could not be readily appreciated by his critics, by his admirers or his detractors. He made his reputation eventually, though it was foreigners—Belgians—who recognised his power first.[1]

[1] Étienne Moreau-Nélaton, *Millet raconté par lui-même* (1921); R. L. Herbert,

The link between politics and painting can perhaps be established more firmly in the case of Gustave Courbet (1819–77), but Courbet was not only a socialist: he was also a narcissist, doing self-portraits over and over again. What irritated his critics was that he did not make it altogether clear what message he was conveying. He declared that art should have a social purpose, but also that it could not be taught, for it was strictly individual, and the result of individual inspiration.[1] There were equally painters who identified themselves with new radical ideas, with a religious outlook or with the technical changes of their times, but also others who rejected all such relationships. Impressionism was not the application to art of the optical discoveries of Chevreuil, but when the painters of this school learnt of these, some of them found a justification in them. Pissarro and Seurat declared that art, which sought harmony, should use science to find it.[2] Renoir on the other hand, who was very attached to his status as an artisan, deplored rationalism as 'incompatible with any conception of art', and attacked the 'mania for false perfection that is tending to make the unadorned cleanness of the engineer the ideal'. He had no use for politics either. To exhibit side by side with 'the Jew Pissarro' and Gauguin was to be 'revolutionary' and 'at my age, I do not want to be revolutionary: the public does not like what smells of politics'.[3] Puvis de Chavannes, whose father had been a mine engineer, likewise had a horror of machines: he had nightmares after a visit to the Exhibition of 1889 and exclaimed: 'What will become of us artists in the face of this invasion of engineers and mechanics?'[4] For him painting was about painting: 'I am an

'Millet Revisited', *Burlington Magazine* (Apr. 1962), 294–305; L. Le Poittevin, *J. F. Millet, portraitiste* (1971).

[1] For the links of art, politics and society, see the ingenious and stimulating work of Timothy J. Clark, *The Absolute Bourgeois: Artists and Politics in France 1848–51* (1973) and *Image of the People: Gustave Courbet and the 1848 Revolution* (1973).

[2] J. Rewald, *The History of Impressionism* (New York, new edition 1961) and *The History of Post-Impressionism* (New York, 2nd edition 1962); L. Venturi, *Les Archives de l'Impressionisme* (1939); Pierre Francastel, *Art et technique au 19ᵉ et 20ᵉ siècles* (1956).

[3] Sven Lörgren, *The Genesis of Modernism. Seurat, Gauguin, van Gogh and French Symbolism in the 1880s* (Stockholm, 1959), 81; cf. also Jean Renoir, *Renoir my father* (1962).

[4] Maurice Vachon, *Puvis de Chavannes* (1895), 62; cf. Jon Whiteley, *Puvis de Chavannes* (forthcoming).

ignoramus,' he said. 'I know nothing about philosophy, history or science. I busy myself only with my own profession.'[1]

Art was so inventive in these years neither because of politics nor because of science—though both of these affected it—but because artists were able to paint with more independence than ever before and because their right to individuality was turned into the basic principle of their work. This meant that art became, more than anything, the means by which they expressed their feelings and their attitudes. Courbet proclaimed their independence in his typically flamboyant way, saying 'I too am a government'. Van Gogh used his painting as a means of spiritual salvation and emotional release: he called it 'the lightning-conductor of my illness'; it was the logical extension of his restless and tortured years as a missionary.[2] That meant also that art became a more searching investigation into the nature of reality. With the Impressionists, this involved the study of appearance and the fleeting moment. For the Symbolists, it was more ambitious: Moreau thought he had a 'synoptic message' and would reveal 'the truth underlying all myth and all religion in his paintings'. Cézanne, for his part, said he could not paint a landscape until he had studied its geological structure. Gauguin turned away from civilisation in order to rejuvenate it, through a new vision. Distortion became a vitally important element in painting, because it enabled the artist to express his own interpretation: inaccuracy could reveal, as Van Gogh said, truth that was more real than literal truth. Cubism was thus 'an art of realism', which enabled more information to be included than traditional methods allowed, though it also required more effort from the spectator to reconstruct the subject-matter; it was a more intellectual approach, showing the world not as it appeared to be, but as the painter knew it to be. It was significant that it was a socialist member of parliament, J. L. Breton, who in 1912 denounced the Cubists as 'obviously anti-artistic and anti-national' and demanded that they should not be allowed to exhibit in the Salon d'Automne.[3] But Cubism was

[1] P. Jullian and A. Bowness, *French Symbolist Painters* (catalogue of the exhibition at the Hayward Gallery, 1972), 17.

[2] Meyer Schapiro, *Vincent van Gogh* (1951), 96; cf. Jean Leymarie, *Van Gogh* (1951).

[3] John Golding, *Cubism. A history and an analysis 1907–1914* (2nd edition, 1969) is the best guide; cf. Christopher Gray, *Cubist Aesthetic Theories* (Baltimore, 1953) for philosophical links.

also a stage in the process by which the object ceased to be of interest: abstract art allowed the painter to construct his own world. Delaunay made colour, on its own, his preoccupation. The Paris exhibition 'Art d'Aujourd'hui' in 1925 declared in its manifesto: 'the purpose of this new technique [is] to relieve art of the weight of reality, which is essentially anti-lyrical. Mankind needs an escape from reality.'[1] Matisse said that the colours he chose for his paintings had no explanation in any scientific theory: they were designed to express his emotions, not the object on which they were based. His goal was to reorganise and simplify his perceptions so as to produce harmony, equilibrium, tranquillity, which was what he was trying to find in life, and he hoped that the tired businessman would obtain calm and relaxation—without intellectual effort—from looking at his pictures.[2]

Artists were not necessarily the best persons to explain what they were doing, but the critics who grouped them into schools performed an equally suspect task.[3] A potted history of each -ism would give a false account of the development of art. A whole string of biographies—and there would need to be a very large number of them—would not be adequate either, but it would, perhaps, stress that the art of this period found, as Rodin said, beauty in everything.[4]

Music

'Music is, without a possibility of contradiction, the most popular of all the arts.' So wrote one of the ministry of education's experts in 1889. Musicians, said the newspaper Le Monde in 1964, are the poor relations of the arts.[5] Both statements were true. Together they show how wrong it is to judge French taste by its reputation, how false an indication of popular values is given by state support for officially favoured manifestations of

[1] M. Semphor, Abstract Painting (1964), 92.

[2] Henri Matisse, Écrits et propos sur l'art (1972), 50. Cf. C. E. Gauss, The Aesthetic Theories of French Artists, 1855 to the present (Baltimore, 1949); Marcel Brion, L'Œil, l'esprit et la main du peintre (1966).

[3] Cf. Rudolf Arnheim, Art and Visual Perception (1954).

[4] Auguste Rodin, L'Art. Entretiens réunis par Paul Gsell (1924), 217. Cf. Alan Bowness, Rodin: sculptures and drawings (Hayward Gallery exhibition, 1970).

[5] A. Cornet, L'Enseignement du chant (1889); Le Monde (7–11 Aug. 1962).

them, and how necessary it is to distinguish, in studying attitudes and loyalties, between different groups in society.

The taste for music was not inculcated at school. When primary schools were reorganised in 1833, even singing was not made a compulsory part of the syllabus, and there were indeed, at that time, no song books specifically for children. It is true women teachers (but not men) were required in 1836 to study singing, but between 1851 and 1866 this was defined as religious chanting. The law of 1850 placed singing in schools at the very end of the optional subjects, together with gymnastics. Only in the 1880s was an effort to stimulate it made, but the results seem to have been negligible and, despite a further reform in 1922, there could be no disputing the statement made in 1941 that 'musical education has failed to find a place in the school'. However, in the eastern part of France, under German influence, the situation was different: in the 1820s it was said that there was a piano in every school in Alsace and the schoolteachers, who were frequently organists, were often skilful musicians. The city of Paris also showed great, and exceptional, interest in the teaching of music. In 1819 it appointed L. G. Bocquillon (1781–1842) director of singing in its schools. He (having adopted the more German-sounding pseudonym of Wilhem) used the mutual system of teaching (by which older pupils taught younger ones) to make up for the lack of teachers; but despite the efforts of his successors Gounod (1818–93), Jules Pasdeloup (1819–87) and François Bazin (1816–78) Paris had during the Second Empire only fifty music teachers for all its schools, who gave three hours to each school, and they were paid roughly half of what drawing masters got. France was way behind Germany in producing songs for children, and indeed the first successful song book for schools was an adaptation by two Alsatians of German ones with moralising lyrics, 'Let us chase away sorrow', 'Life is good', 'Be happy'.[1]

The proselytes in the cause of music had much more success outside the schools, particularly in the formation of choral societies. During the July Monarchy Wilhem brought together his best pupils into a choir of 1,200 voices, called the Orphéon;

[1] M. Delcasso and M. Gross, *Recueil de morceaux de chant à une, deux et trois voix à l'usage des écoles normales et des écoles primaires* (first published 1856, reprinted 11 times by 1870).

within a few decades similar societies had blossomed all over France. Paris took the lead with its Athéniens de Montmartre and its Carlovingiens (who became the Montagnards in 1848 and the Tyroliens in 1852). By 1868 there were 3,243 choral societies in France, with 147,000 members. In 1859 Eugène Delaporte, organist of Sens Cathedral and one of the leaders of this movement, took 3,000 singers to the Crystal Palace for an international competition. The government gave its backing, since the idea was to 'moralise the worker' and bring about a 'fusion of youth', but this support only resulted in a split of the movement into three. In Paris, the choirs were composed mainly of workers and clerks; but in the provinces the bourgeoisie, civil servants and clergymen also took part. The singers were praised as model citizens who were quick to lose their provincial accents and to wear smarter clothes; the railways gave them reduced fares and they travelled widely to take part in competitions. There were also politically inspired, left-wing societies. In the 1840s the choral societies used to parade through the streets of Toulouse singing, but the police later forbade this; so they took to giving concerts, which high society patronised. Individual groups, like the forty Chanteurs Montagnards des Hautes-Pyrénées, or the Chanteurs Béarnais, toured the whole of Europe giving concerts in the 1840s. A large number of composers arose to produce songs and music for them. Villages increasingly participated in competitions held in towns, but a new fragmentation soon appeared. Military music became a rival of the *orphéons*, and in many places it grew so popular that it replaced the choirs.[1] Francisque Sarcey claimed that these societies existed more to encourage drinking than singing, and people commented that few of the members could read music; much effort was put into inventing easier ways of teaching it. It seems that the choirs reached the peak of their popularity towards the end of the Second Empire. Never before has there been so much singing in France, it was said; 'France has become at least as musical as Germany; melomania has invaded us on

[1] Ch. Poirson, *Guide manuel de l'orphéoniste* (1868); P. Marcel, *L'Art du chant en France* (1900); 'De la musique dans les campagnes', *Journal d'Amiens* (20-1 July, 29-30 Aug. 1864); Édouard Garnier, 'La Musique de chambre', in *La Phare de la Loire* (8 Dec. 1868, Nantes); F. G. Hainl, *De la musique à Lyon depuis 1713 jusqu'à 1852* (Lyon, 1852); Oscar Comettant, *Les Musiciens, les philosophes et les gaietés de la musique en chiffres* (1870).

all sides.'[1] The obstacle to further development seems to have
been that they sang songs which never won popularity; perhaps
they were dominated by bad composers; at their competitions,
they had to sing the songs of the unknown Kucken and
Schwahal. There was a gap therefore between their activities
and the vulgar ditties and patriotic and revolutionary hymns
that the workers and peasants liked. When the Vichy regime
regrouped these choirs into its Jeunesses Musicales de France
in 1941, it collected only 130,000 members.[2]

The experience of the choral societies is important because it
shows the transition from music as a constituent part of a religious or social ritual to music as a recreation and as an end in
itself. In the eighteenth century music was used largely as a
background for conversation, for theatrical performances, for
religious or military ceremonies. The romantics gave it a totally
different significance when they claimed that its function was to
plumb the secrets of the universe and the deepest emotions of
man: composers emphasised the expression of their own feelings
and music was now expected to produce private ecstasies,
reveries, essentially personal and egocentric sensations. At the
same time the number of musical instruments multiplied and
public performances became increasingly grandiose spectacles.
In the seventeenth century, the orchestra in the Opéra had
about twenty members; by 1860 it had increased to eighty-four
and Meyerbeer caused a sensation by using a hundred players
for his *Africaine*. In the Second Empire it was still common for
fashionable people to arrive at the Opéra during the second act,
to watch the pretty ballet girls, to meet and be seen by their
friends, rather than to listen to the music, at most to be amazed
by the richness and splendour of the costumes and the settings
—which was what Meyerbeer was particularly good at. But the
interest in Italian music, stimulated by Rossini, created a circle
of passionate devotees who gave the Théâtre italien a totally
different atmosphere. The Concerts of the Conservatoire
(started in 1828) were attended by an even more refined
audience, who were more silent than churchgoers and who
indeed seemed to look on the concert hall as a sort of temple.

[1] J. M. Bailbé, *Le Roman et la musique en France sous la monarchie de juillet* (1969),
105.
[2] Bernard Gavoty, *Les Français sont-ils musiciens?* (1950), 165, 168.

In due course, therefore, there developed a breach between serious and popular music; and music lovers adopted the characteristics of initiates. At first this was not apparent. Pasdeloup started his popular Sunday concerts in Napoleon III's reign with the aim of introducing the workers to the symphonies of Haydn, Mozart, Beethoven and Mendelssohn, who were barely known; but when Lamoureux founded his orchestra (1881) he requested his audience to avoid giving marks of approval or disapproval until the performance was over. Concerts, and particularly opera, used to be noisy affairs, as theatres were too. The presence of the claque, who applauded or hissed at the order of the leader, could make them almost like public meetings. The claque was difficult to eradicate, because it was not the theatres which hired it; on the contrary it was the *chef de claque* who paid the theatre, which of course needed the money. He sometimes described himself as an 'entre-preneur of theatrical success'. He visited impresarios, composers, authors, actors and singers and promised them applause in return for a fee; he then bought blocks of seats, which helped ensure a full house. He could become so powerful that even major artists were forced to give him regular protection money. Auguste, *chef de claque* at the Opéra, made so much out of his profession that he retired with an income of 20,000 francs a year. When Queen Victoria went to the Opéra during her visit to Paris in 1855, the whole of the pit was occupied by the claque, and they all wore full evening dress to ensure that their applause was appreciated. Usually the claque at the Opéra-Comique consisted of fifty people on ordinary days, but as many as 300 on first nights.[1]

The changes that occurred in the financial bases of music-making produced an increasing specialisation of audiences and of performers. In the eighteenth century, the main patrons of musicians were the court and the very rich. Now these ceased to keep private musicians. The opera, the theatres and the churches, which at first provided the general public with the bulk of their musical fare, were in the course of the eighteenth century supplemented by professional concerts—like the Concerts Spirituels of Paris which already specialised in German music and at which the world's greatest instrumentalists appeared,

---

[1] Auguste Laget, *Le Chant et les chanteurs* (Paris and Toulouse, 1874), 332.

or the Concerts des Amateurs, held in a Masonic lodge, which went in for 'progressive' music. The difficulty of finding an audience in this period is illustrated by Mozart's getting only 176 subscribers for his series of subscription concerts in Vienna in 1784. But by the Second Empire Parisians had a very large choice. In 1866, for example, they could take their pick from the Opéra's performances of *Don Juan*, *La Trouvère*, *Robert le Diable*, *Giselle*, Halévy's *La Juive*, Weckerlin's *Paix*, *Chante et Grandeur* and the first performance of *Le Roi d'Yvetot* by Massa Petipa and Labarre. The Opéra-Comique put on five new operas, including Gounod's *La Colombe* and Victor Massé's *Fior d'Aliza*, based on the novel by Lamartine. The Théâtre italien had Verdi and Donizetti as well as six new operas by other Italian composers. The Théâtre lyrique had eight new operas including a new version of *Don Juan*. Offenbach offered six new operas at the Bouffes Parisiennes (one of them by himself); and the Fantaisies Parisiennes had about a dozen operas by young composers. There were in addition about ten 'non-lyrical' theatres which put on operettas. The Conservatoire gave eleven concerts, of its usual repertory, though it added three works to it this year. Pasdeloup gave twenty-four popular concerts of Haydn, Meyerbeer, Weber and Liszt. The Philharmonic Society of Paris, started in 1865, played modern music, while the Société des concerts de chant classique, in its seventh year, performedthe choral works of dead composers only. Weckerlin's Société Ste Cécile, in its second year, gave six concerts of music by himself and others. Deledicque, first violinist of the Théâtre italien, also ran a Société des Symphonistes, in its sixth year; Lalo and Saint Saens played for the Société de musique de chambre; the Société de quattuors, in its sixteenth year, devoted itself exclusively to the last works of Beethoven. Various composers and virtuosi gave personal concerts in addition; while the musical schools held numerous competitions. The provinces of course usually had to make do with local talent, but at least ten new French operas were performed in the provinces this year.[1] It will be noticed that opera still dominated the musical scene at this time, as it had done a century before, and that the concert societies were largely new; music was still a social event, combined with other forms of entertainment and attracting

[1] *Almanach de la musique* (1867).

an audience of very mixed tastes and origins. A lot of money could be made from the spectacular shows and opera singers in particular received very large fees. Naudin, the greatest tenor of his day, was paid 110,000 francs in 1865 to sing in Meyerbeer's *Africaine*, which was about six times as much as the country's leading tenor got thirty years before. The new director of the Opéra, appointed in 1866, received a salary of 100,000 francs, which made him one of the highest paid men in the country. The status of singers was accordingly transformed. France's most famous tenor in the eighteenth century, Garat (†1823), had been cut off by his family for becoming a singer: now singers were lionised, and even took to writing their memoirs. The discovery of the American market increased the rewards still further: the company of the Théâtre italien toured the U.S.A. in 1891 and came home with a million dollars' profit.[1]

By the twentieth century all this had changed. The symphony concert replaced the opera as the major attraction. The distribution of the musical events in Paris was as follows:

	1924–5 season	1938–9 season
Symphony concerts	451	321
Piano recitals	296	121
Chamber music	142	125
Miscellaneous	921	452

In 1913 there had been in all only about 700 concerts of all kinds in Paris; in the 1920s this figure more than doubled to as much as 1,880; but in the 1930s it fell sharply, and was only 1,009 in 1938–9. What happened was that an increasing number of groups were formed to play different kinds of music, beginning with the Société Nationale de Musique (1871) to perform the works of new French composers, the Concerts Calonne (1873) to spread the taste for the symphony, and especially Berlioz, who was then more famous abroad than in France, and the Concerts Lamoureux (1882) to advance the cult of Wagner. In the prosperity of the 1920s small sects could flourish; in the depression they collapsed; in 1945–6 about 85 per cent of

[1] Victor Maurel, *Dix ans de carrière 1887–1897* (1897), 151–2, 246; A. Laget, op. cit. 45–7.

recitals given in Paris lost money. There was increasing difficulty in finding audiences for new works. In Angers, with a
population of 80,000 just before the Second World War, there
were only about 400 regular patrons of the local concerts, but
the attendance doubled for Bach, Beethoven and Wagner and
quadrupled for the *Damnation of Faust*. In Lyon, with a population of 600,000 at the same time, older traditions survived, for
there was an Opéra, which performed five times a week, but
its audience (there were 1,500 seats) was directly proportionate
to the classicism of its repertoire; and the Lyon Philharmonic
Association gave ten subscription concerts a year, to, on average,
an audience of 800. The result of music being an increasingly
specialist activity, with a small circle of increasingly erudite
listeners, was that composers lost their social function as general
organisers of entertainment, and became isolated figures, without regular contact with either performers or audience; and
their music showed less concern with popularity. Debussy began
by saying that 'music must humbly seek to give pleasure' but
later despaired of art being appreciated by the masses; his work
became more abstract and he declared 'One can no more order
the crowds to love beauty than one can ask them to walk on
their hands'.[1]

In 1780 Paris was a major international centre of musical
publishing: it had forty-four firms specialising in this. That was
the time when European and especially German firms were
beginning to develop, and these soon outstripped their French
rivals. There are now only some twenty-three publishers of
classical music, and seven or eight of them produce three-
quarters of the total output. The demand for sheet music barely
justifies even this number, for editions are often limited to a few
hundred copies and they may take fifty years or more to sell out.
Georges Auric's Three Impromptus for piano, published in 1946
in 500 copies, had sold only 330 by 1962; and this was typical.[2]
How long the bourgeois cult of the piano as a necessary symbol
of respectability lasted and how many pianos were produced to
enable idle daughters to acquire the accomplishments of a lady,
would be worth calculating, for it would help to establish the

[1] Bernard Gavoty, *Les Français sont-ils musiciens?* (1950), 50, 136.
[2] Alicia de Schwarzer, 'Certains aspects de la sociologie de la musique en France
1960–70' (unpublished mémoire, École Pratique des Hautes Études, 1972).

size of the musical constituency. Pleyel started making pianos under the Restoration and by 1890 had produced 100,000;[1] he was one of many. Today, 8·2 per cent of the French population own pianos (but one-quarter of the managerial class have them). The guitar (12·9 per cent) and wind instruments (12·7 per cent) are more popular.[2] But the French have almost completely ceased to make musical instruments. In 1969 only about 13,000 new pianos were bought (compared to about 220,000 in the U.S.A.).[3]

Music has clearly been transformed by the radio. Already in 1939 there were about 1,500 shops selling radios, compared to about 160 selling pianos.[4] In the 1940s the radio stations interpreted popular taste, or popular needs, by broadcasting (hours per annum):

1,622	hours of	light music
1,555	,,	songs (variety and folkloric)
1,369	,,	symphonic music
942	,,	chamber music
916	,,	dance and jazz music
463	,,	opera
229	,,	operetta
61	,,	religious music

Opera has fallen low after the supremacy it enjoyed a century ago. The present-day opera-goers constitute only 2·6 per cent of the population, compared with 6·9 per cent who go to symphony concerts, 5·8 per cent who go to the ballet, 4·4 per cent who go to operettas and 6·5 per cent who go to jazz or pop concerts; though it is true that opera-goers tend to be fanatics, and attend twice as often as other music lovers. The effect of broadcasting on musical taste has still not been worked out.[5] But broadcasting and gramophone music have undoubtedly increased the amount of music, and the breadth of choice, available. This is all the more true because the old music teacher,

[1] Oscar Comettant, *Histoire de cent mille pianos et d'une salle de concert* (1890); L. E. Gratia, *Les Instruments de musique du 20ᵉ siècle* (1931).

[2] *Pratiques culturelles des Français* (1974).

[3] Elizabeth Lion, 'L'Offre et la demande de musique. Essai d'analyse économique' (unpublished mémoire, École Pratique des Hautes Études 1970), 94–6.

[4] *Annuaire O.G.M. (ex-Musique-Adresses) du commerce et de l'industrie de musique, radio, phono* (1939).

[5] Cf. Paul Beaud and Alfred Willener, *Musique et vie quotidienne* (1973), 12.

who was once a not unimportant part of bourgeois households, has become a much rarer figure. In 1921 there were 14,105 teachers of music and singing in France; in 1936 there were 10,305; in 1946 6,941. There were in addition about 12,000 musicians, 6,000 singers and 700 composers between the wars. Their numbers have fallen too, but the most dramatic loss has been that of the singers, who were down to under 3,000 in 1962.[1] The effect of new technology has been a great centralisation (and, accordingly, 56 per cent of musicians live in Paris). The same famous artists reach an enormous audience, and the obscure provincial teacher cannot compete with them. Music, more than ever, has become an individual experience and the meaning given to it probably varies more than ever before.[2]

It is impossible to write a satisfactory history of musical taste in France, first of all because so many of its composers have fallen into complete oblivion, and only a few names, surviving from this period, have been heard by the present generation.[3] The paradox that needs to be explained is why German and Italian music was so popular, why (as Romain Rolland said, with much exaggeration) all great French composers were foreigners, but why at the same time a distinctly French kind of music—distinguished by a characteristic lightness—continued to be produced and to remain immediately recognisable. French painting soon became international: French music did not.

This chapter has suggested that ideas of beauty were moving in two opposing directions simultaneously: the increasing individualism of artists was paralleled by strong pressures, on the side of their public, in favour of conformist taste. These pressures can be understood more clearly if one looks at the newspapers, which acted as the intermediaries between the two.

[1] Schwarzer, op. cit. 30–6.

[2] R. Francès, *La Perception de la musique* (1958); A. Silbermann, *La Musique, le radio et l'auditeur* (1955); id., *Introduction à une sociologie de la musique* (1955).

[3] André Coenroy, *La Musique et le peuple en France* (1941), for an inquiry into the most popular songs of that period, p. 76. Henry Raynor, *A Social History of Music* (1972) unfortunately stops in the early nineteenth century.

4. Newspapers and Corruption

THE press, more than anything else, created reputations. Reputation, said Balzac, is a crowned prostitute; it has to be bought. There is a great deal to learn about the frustrations of France by looking at who was keen to buy reputation and who was willing to be bought. The press brought information to the masses, but a lot of bargaining took place between the journalists and the people as to the kind of information they were willing to pay for. This was an age of education, but the people seemed to demand relaxation and entertainment instead: what one witnesses in the history of the press is the clash of Parisian culture and primitive taste. The press, finally, was an astonishing world in itself, attracting strange, deluded and disillusioned men; and their adventures are worth investigation even if their impact on the masses was not as great as they believed it to be.

The character of the press was shaped by three forces—the journalists, the newspaper owners, and the readers, whose interests and aspirations were far from coinciding. One cannot talk simply of the former exercising an influence on, or leading, the latter, nor can one accept the view that the press expressed the opinions and attitudes of its readers, mirroring 'public opinion'. Each of the pressures in the newspaper world was itself infinitely complex and varied.

Journalists

No clear image of the French journalist is possible, because he had too many faces. To begin with, the journalist, born (in a professional sense) in the eighteenth century, had an ambiguous and dubious origin. In his most primitive form, he was a news-seller, who wandered around Paris, picking up and repeating whatever gossip he could find: the Tuileries and Luxembourg gardens were his favourite haunt; in different parts of these, scientists, economists, literary men met to hear and discuss the latest events. Montesquieu was contemptuous of these *nouvellistes*: 'they are useless to the state,' he wrote, 'but they believe themselves to be important because they discuss magnificent projects and deal with great interests. The basis of their conversation is a frivolous and ridiculous curiosity; there are no offices too secret for them not to be able to penetrate into; they refuse to be ignorant of anything . . . all that they lack is good sense.'[1] But one of these news-sellers was revealed in 1774 to have been a former royal counsellor and intendant's subdelegate, who found it worth while to remain in the business for twenty years, employing fifty copyists and pedlars, and having 280 subscribers to the manuscript service he provided: among his clients were the archbishop of Paris and several dukes. However, the printed newspaper had serious obstacles to its rise. The king employed no less than 121 censors in 1763, and he gave a monopoly to the *Gazette de France* and the *Journal des savants*: all those wishing to compete with these had to buy their permission and a licence; and even foreign papers entering the country had to pay them a fee. Manuscript newspapers were theoretically altogether forbidden, under pain of flogging. But such was the demand for news, and such were the profits to be made, that this new challenge to serious literature grew rapidly. The great minds of the eighteenth century were divided in their attitude towards this development: on the one hand their principles favoured free speech and the freedom to publish, but on the other hand they had a profound contempt for the low quality of those who sought to profit from this freedom. Voltaire said journalism was discredited by the 'multitude of papers which mutually competing and greedy booksellers have published and which obscure writers fill with incorrect extracts, stupidities and lies . . . to the extent that there has developed a public trade in praise and criticism'. Diderot remarked, 'People discovered that it was easier to write a review of a good book than to write a decent line of prose of one's own, and many sterile minds have therefore applied themselves to this.' Newspapers, he said, were invented 'for the solace of those who are either too busy or too lazy to read whole books. They are a means of satisfying

---

[1] Montesquieu, *Lettres persanes* (1719), Letter 130; F. Funck-Brentano, *Les Nouvellistes* (1905).

curiosity and giving learning at a small cost.' Rousseau thought
journalism a labourer's task, and a periodical 'an ephemeral
work, without merit and without utility, which cultivated men
avoid and despise and which serves only to give women and
fools vanity without instruction: its fate is to shine in the
morning at the toilette and to die in the evening in a cupboard'.
But already in 1749 the marquis d'Argenson was attributing
'the great ferment among the people' to their reading newspapers. This was too prophetic an explanation, for most
newspapers sold only 300 to 500 copies an issue under the
ancien régime, and the *Gazette de France* itself never had more than
12,260 subscribers. These small sales were enough, however,
to make journalism a profitable business. The editor of *Le
Patriote français*, with only 5,000 subscribers (1790), earned
6,000 livres a year and the publisher made 24,000.[1] Newspapers
were expensive, a luxury product. In the 1830s a subscription
to most papers cost about a tenth of a worker's wages.

Journalists became much more ambitious and much more
dangerous as a result of the French Revolution. The complete
freedom temporarily won by the press meant that 500 new
papers were published between 1789 and 1792. Not only were
many of the most distinguished leaders of the Revolution, from
Mirabeau to Marat, active in journalism, but almost every
group started a paper, and seemed to acquire influence from it.
The press became a political tool as never before. The Revolution established the tradition by which, in 1830 and in 1848,
journalists played leading roles in overthrowing governments.
The freedom of the press became a major political issue. But
precisely because the number of newspapers multiplied greatly
in the course of the nineteenth century, the quality and functions of journalists became much more varied; their position
became much more ambiguous; the contrast between what
they actually achieved and the pretensions they put forward
was accentuated.

Émile de Girardin (1806–81), perhaps the most influential
figure in the history of the modern French press, illustrates
well the heights journalists aspired to. He was the illegitimate
son of a distinguished noble general by the beautiful Madame

    [1] C. Bellanger *et al.*, *Histoire générale de la presse française*, vol. 1 (*des origines à
1814*) (1969), 159, 439.

Dupuy (whom Greuze painted, as *The Girl with the Dove*, in the Wallace Collection), but both father and mother found his existence inconvenient, gave him a fake birth certificate in the name of Émile Delamothe, sent him away to be brought up by strangers, and neglected to have him educated. When he grew up his father saw him once a month, gave him lunch in his gardener's cottage, refusing to let him into his house. Girardin grew up obsessed, as he said, by 'the triple longing for a name, the affection of a father and the love of a mother'. At the age of twenty-one he published his autobiography, a plea for the rights of bastards, affirming his determination to 'draw upon him the eyes of the masses and so revenge himself for having been abandoned . . . to win an honourable situation which I shall owe to no one but myself, a situation in the world which will be so brilliant that I shall hear people say: Though without family and without fortune, he surmounted the obstacles which condemned him to obscurity: he succeeded in overcoming his misfortune, and having no name, he made himself a reputation'. His parents would then come running to him, and he would not repulse them. The way to become famous, he said, was not to help people, but to flatter the passions of the masses. Merit was useless unless backed up by money and he had to become rich too.[1] He achieved these aims with extraordinary rapidity. At eighteen, another beautiful lady, Madame de Sesonnes (painted by Ingres), taking a liking to him, got him a job in the civil service; a few years later he was appointed assistant inspector of Fine Arts, but this was unpaid; so he abandoned the safe paths of bureaucracy to make himself a living in journalism and literature. He founded a newspaper called *The Thief*, which, without hypocrisy, made clear that it provided summaries of other newspapers. He raised 500 francs, just enough to print the first issue, but instead of paying the printer, he used the whole sum to advertise the paper and this brought in several thousand francs in subscriptions: very soon his paper was giving him an income of 50,000 francs net. At twenty-three, he established *La Mode* (1829), as a paper for the fashionable world, which he had illustrated by Gavarni, and for which he obtained contributions from a host of writers who were soon to reach the front rank of literature—Balzac among

[1] E. de Girardin, *Émile* (1828).

them. Two years later, his *Journal of Useful Knowledge* (1831) obtained 132,000 subscribers within a year, yielding an income of 200,000 francs. It issued an *Almanach de France* in 1,300,000 copies, with the motto 'Health, Prosperity and Knowledge'. This was Girardin's programme. He presented himself as a pioneer of mass education, through mass journalism, and he sought to educate the people in every aspect of life. His *Musée des familles*, *La Musée rustique* and a host of other periodicals made him one of the most important publishers of his day. In 1834 he was elected to parliament (falsely declaring himself older than he was so as to qualify: he had endless trouble with his birth certificates). He crowned his achievement in 1836 by founding *La Presse*, a daily newspaper costing 40 francs a year, instead of the 80 francs which was normal at the time; he proposed to make advertisements pay the difference. This inaugurated a revolution in newspaper production, beginning the steady fall in the price asked of the reader, and increasing dependence on advertising. Like most revolutions, other people had the same idea at the same time, and a rival paper, *Le Siècle*, was founded on the same basis simultaneously, and it was in fact somewhat more successful. But Girardin was as remarkable a journalist as he was an entrepreneur; he wrote his paper as well as managing it; and unlike the masters of *Le Siècle*, he saw in *La Presse* a stepping-stone to higher things.

He was a member of parliament for much of his life, under successive regimes. He had no particular preference as between them, making his programme simply Liberty. He consistently fought on behalf of anybody who suffered at the hands of governments, pressing for the release of political prisoners, demanding amnesties. 'What is the State?', he asked. 'Everything. What should it be? Nothing.' He had vague ideas about abolishing centralised government, partly echoing the ideas of Proudhon; but he never joined any party. Independence was his watchword; 'an idea every day' was what he offered in his paper. He had a universally recognised genius for journalistic strategy, in the sense that he was a brilliant polemicist, a master of controversy, whose articles, always written in short sentences, bursting with striking formulae, kept him continuously in the public eye. But all this made him incapable of obtaining political power, which was the unfulfilled ambition of his life.

He regularly supported compromise policies and compromise politicians: he was a 'progressive conservative' under Louis-Philippe, which pleased neither conservatives nor progressives. He played a decisive role in persuading Louis-Philippe to abdicate, but got him to proclaim a regency, which never materialised. He supported the Provisional Government of 1848, but soon fell foul of it, and was arrested by General Cavaignac. He took up the cause of Louis Napoleon, the first major paper to do so; but he was cruelly disappointed when the latter failed to give him the ministerial portfolio he longed for. He then became the most active supporter of Émile Ollivier's liberal Empire, but again failed to have a post offered to him. He never concealed that active participation in government was what he wanted. He had quickly lost his illusions about the power of the press; its scribblings, he said, were condemned to immediate oblivion; 'the so-called tyrants of opinion were really only busy-body flies', living on the surface of events. The time for discussions was over, what he wanted was action, and that was the function of government, not journalism. The great men of the day, he declared, were 'Garibaldi and Kossuth, not Proudhon or Girardin'. But because he held himself aloof from all parties, because he appeared a speculator as well as a journalist, because he was haughty and cold, he never got beyond the fringes of politics. Émile Ollivier said he 'had neither the wide knowledge of Proudhon, nor his skill as a writer, nor his integrity, but he equalled him in his passion and his hard work and he appeared more practical because he was more pedestrian'. His unashamed advocacy of material well-being, industrialism and *Universal Prosperity* (the title of another of his periodicals) made him a crank in a political world which placed more emphasis on grand rhetoric and principle. His newspaper empire expanded considerably during the Third Republic and he died worth well over eight million francs, but in old age he lamented to Villemessant, the editor of the *Figaro*, 'I have everything and yet I have nothing'. His was perhaps an ambition that could not be satisfied.[1]

[1] Maurice Reclus, *Émile de Girardin* (1934); E. de Girardin, *L'Abolition de l'autorité par la simplification du gouvernement* (1851), *L'Abolition de la misère par l'élévation des salaires* (1850), *L'Impôt* (1852), *La Liberté* (1857), *Le Désarmement européen* (1859), *Pensées et maximes* (1867), *L'homme et la femme* (1872), etc.

This combination of business and politics that characterised the press can be seen in another important journalist of the Second Empire, Adolphe Guéroult (1810–72). The son of a textile manufacturer, whose old-established family business collapsed in 1814, Guéroult was converted to Saint-Simonianism while a law student. He abandoned himself, as he wrote to a friend, 'without reservation to the influence' of the leader of the sect, Enfantin, but 'there was always a part of me, the best part perhaps, which remained outside the affection I bore him and . . . which always resisted him'. Guéroult had a muddled political life and a muddled private life. He fell in love with a leader of the women's rights movement, Pauline Roland, who refused to marry him, but decided to have an illegitimate child by him; then just before the child was born she left him for another man, by whom she had four other children, before leaving him to marry someone else. Guéroult in time got over this and married another girl whom he met at a Saint-Simonian club. But he had some difficulty in deciding what to do with his life. On the one hand, he had his political convictions; on the other his love of music 'which is art *par excellence*, the most popular, the most powerful, the most inspired of all arts', which led him to specialise for a time as a music critic; but there was also his desire for a career and a conventional family life. He was much abused when he took a job on the conservative *Journal des Débats* and then accepted appointment by Guizot's reactionary government as French consul in Mexico, and then (because he could not stand the food there) in Moldavia. He did not resign at the revolution of 1848, saying he had a family to support, and it was only when he was sacked the following year that he returned to journalism. He now made a name for himself with articles attacking the Catholic Church, and in favour of industrial expansion and material prosperity; he denounced, like Girardin, the fear of the useful and the comfortable. The capitalist Millaud offered him the editorship of *La Presse* (1858), though requiring an undated letter of resignation before he started, just in case things went wrong. This was a pro-government paper, but Guéroult accepted its political line, though he added anticlerical and pro-Italian touches of his own. In 1859 the emperor's radical cousin, Prince Jérôme Napoléon, started up a new paper for Guéroult with the help of a printer, a banker and probably with secret funds from Piedmont. In *L'Opinion nationale* Guéroult was able to give free rein to his advocacy of nationalism (the unification of Italy and Germany), anticlericalism, and the reorganisation of Europe into a federation. In 1863 he was elected to parliament for Paris, showing the leading role that newspapers were playing at that time in political life. But Guéroult's publication of a series of articles by Champfleury on the seedy side of fashionable life 'La Mascarade de la vie parisienne' was considered indecent; his chief assistant and two other journalists employed by him were dishonest; the paper failed to win a mass circulation despite the considerable skill with which it was written; it appealed, apparently, as a police inspector reported, to 'second-class railway travellers' (at a time when there were three classes). Guéroult's friendship with Prince Napoléon made him suspect to the republican opposition he was supposed also to be friends with; and in 1867 he (and the editors of four other papers) was accused publicly of being in the pay of the Italian and Prussian governments. The investigation into the charge was never completed, but his name was sullied; he lost his parliamentary seat in 1869, returning to a paper whose circulation had been halved by his preoccupation with politics and by internal feuds. After the revolution of 1870 he rallied to the republic, saying he was willing to serve all governments, because something of value could be drawn from each, whatever its politics. Guéroult was a very active partisan of the rights of the press, a sober, courteous, persevering man. He looked the 'very archetype of the bourgeois, a mixture of blooming health, malice and complacency'. He bequeathed his paper to his son as a family business; another son became an inspector of finances and *trésorier payeur général*; a third was an engineer.[1] The biography of Guéroult illustrated how journalism acquired a dubious reputation, despite the talent that went into it, and how its influence was therefore equivocal, despite its occasional political and commercial triumphs.

One can see the same in the career of the colourful, amazing, but equally ambivalent Henri Rochefort (1831–1913), who

[1] Bernard Coste, 'Adolphe Guéroult et l'Opinion nationale' (doctoral thesis, unpublished, in the library of the Paris Faculty of Law, 1968).

made his fortune by whipping up journalistic polemic to unprecedented heights of violence, audacity and wit. He was the son of the marquis de Rochefort-Luçay, a ruined aristocrat who had become a successful vaudevillist; he was one of the very rare people who abandoned, instead of adopting, a title. His mother 'generally saw everything as gloomy': he was himself sad, nervous and rebellious at school; his family condemned him as stupid; he seems always to have been a lonely man, who said 'adults have not always liked me, though children have'. He had a constant feud with his father and allowed him to die in poverty; and his own elder son committed suicide. A fellow journalist wrote of him: 'Every time I saw Rochefort . . . I always found him frantic to escape from a formidable bore, suggesting both a permanent anxiety of mind and very violent stomach pains. He sought pleasure in every form, tracked down all the emotional thrills. He gambled at roulette, at the races, at cards, in the stock-market; suppers, girls, theatre and journalism. The dominant feature of his character was vanity and what vanity . . .'[1] Rochefort denied this, saying he neither smoked, drank nor gambled; but he certainly seems to have had difficulties with women, for all his three marriages ended in divorce or separation and he had three illegitimate children. There can be no doubt that he was one of the sharpest wits of his generation; his journalism was an unending show of brilliant and dangerous fireworks, that found many lesser imitators. But it was rather by accident that he found his way into the newspaper world. He began as a clerk in the patent department of the Paris Hôtel de Ville, and then in the department of architecture, where his colleague was Drumont, father of another journalistic incendiary. His job left him with plenty of leisure to cultivate his interest in art, or more precisely in art dealing and restoration, which he learnt about from another ruined aristocrat, who kept himself by restoring old paintings for those who were still rich. This was a time when people like Dr. Lacaze, another of Rochefort's friends, who left his collection to the Louvre, could buy up a Frans Hals for 300 francs, because the dealers were so ignorant: Rochefort mocked them in a series of articles for *Le Charivari*, reprinted as a book

[1] Quoted in R. L. Williams, *Henri Rochefort, Prince of the Gutter Press* (New York, 1966), 130.

entitled *The Mysteries of the Sale Rooms*, saying they attributed a head of Christ inscribed with the words Salvator Mundi to 'the painter of the Bolognese school, Salvator Mundi'. But it was the time also when these antiquarian art lovers painted extra objects on to the paintings they discovered, saying they needed improvement. Rochefort earned his first 100 francs from writing by producing a novel for Mirecourt, who churned them out like a factory. He tried his hand also at vaudeville, following in his father's footsteps, and altogether produced eighteen light comedies. He started journalism as a theatre critic; when he lost his civil service job, he joined *Le Nain jaune* at 100 francs a week, moved to the *Figaro*, where he was so successful that in 1868 its editor raised the money to set up a separate paper for him, *La Lanterne*, to do the things the *Figaro* dared not do itself. The editor, Villemessant, liked Rochefort because, as he said, he was the only journalist in his employ who was not trying to write so as to get elected to the French Academy: 'Tease and make them laugh' was his advice and Rochefort had followed it. He fought lots of duels, including one with the cousin of the emperor, Prince Achille Murat, and that gave him his fame. *La Lanterne* which he now brought out, writing it almost entirely himself, sold 100,000 copies of its first issue, which alone gave the investors behind it their money back. Its first sentence was 'France has 36 million subjects, not counting the subjects of discontent', and that was typical of the bitter jokes Rochefort produced inexhaustibly. His readers were entranced not only by his outrageous humour and his pitiless satire, but also by the boldness of his attacks, and none could tell what retribution each issue would bring from the government and from the people he insulted. He was a kind of stunt man who was funny as well as frightening. He helped to stir up the largest demonstration against the Second Empire in 1870; he was exiled to New Caledonia for his part in the Commune; he escaped dramatically; he got elected to parliament in 1885 where he was a violent anti-Semite and Boulangist, until he was exiled again. But he had created a style of satirical and rebellious journalism so successful that, even without him, his paper earned enough to send to him in London 242,000 francs a year. The journalists who tried to ape him, lacking his humour and reproducing only his violence, made the French press one of the most vituperative in the world. That politics so often confused opposition with insult, and mistook words for deeds, owed much to the tradition he helped establish.[1]

One could certainly make a lot of money out of journalism. In the middle of the nineteenth century, when a good worker or successful artisan could earn 1,000 francs a year, a poor weaver half of that, a sub-prefect three times as much and the rector of an Academy around 7,000 francs, there were famous journalists whose earnings were among the highest in France. Zola as a young man had earned 6,000 francs a year but by 1867 was getting about 10,000. Théophile Gauthier is said to have earned 20,000 francs over twenty years from his books and his plays, but 100,000 in fifteen years from his journalism. La Gueronnière, editor of the government-backed La France, got 20,000 a year, and that also is what Prévost-Paradol, once a professor on a pittance, earned by supplementing his French journalism with articles for the London Times. When Edmond About ran the Dix-neuvième Siècle his salary shot up to 30,000, five times what he had started with on the Opinion nationale. Villemessant, the phoney aristocrat who made the Figaro the record of the frivolities of the idle rich, said that he had been accused of raising the price of the journalist and that he was proud of it: he poached his authors from other papers, doubling their salaries. But it was in the new popular press that the largest sums were to be obtained: the master of sensation journalism, Léo Lespès, made as much as 40,000 francs. Even Jules Vallès, though he never got over his rage with society, reached 24,000 francs.[2] A newspaper could not only finance a popular politician, but keep him in some style, as Gambetta discovered. Gambetta was a very poor man when he entered political life, but La République française, with a sale of only 18,000 in 1873, made enough profits to keep him, and even to buy itself a house in the rue de la Chaussée d'Antin, where Gambetta was given a free flat. In 1876 Gambetta was such a power in politics, it was decided to launch a popular daily under his aegis. A Swiss businessman, Dubochet, president of the Eastern Railway Company and of the Gas Company, offered to put up the money

---

[1] Henri Rochefort, Les Aventures de ma vie (5 vols., 1896); Williams, op. cit.

[2] Pierre Denoyer and Jean Morienval, 'La Condition sociale du journaliste française', Études de presse (15 Jan. 1952), 10–20, and Bellanger, op. cit. 2. 343.

needed, though he was completely uninterested by politics and only wanted a good investment. Gambetta refused his offer; instead, he got an Alsatian industrialist of republican sympathies, Scheurer-Kestner, to write 129 letters to suitable capitalists, from whom 300,000 francs were raised. Gambetta was given shares in the new company worth 300,000 francs too, though he contributed only his name. It does not appear that he even contributed his pen, or his managerial skill, for he limited himself to having the ideas for the major articles and it was his Achates Spuller who wrote them. By the time he was prime minister, therefore, journalism had given him financial independence. Of course, it was a fragile one, depending on his political popularity. After his death, the paper had financial difficulties and a new set of businessmen came to its rescue, under Joseph Reinach's leadership; in 1893 a third set took it over, to back another rising star, Jules Méline, in his anti-free-trade campaign. Journalism could be highly profitable for some people.

But these were the top names, and they were exceptions. The majority of journalists earned only a tiny fraction of these salaries. Brazier (1783–1838), who later kept himself by writing over 200 vaudevilles, started as a collector of 'the little misfortunes of Paris', and he was paid three francs for each misfortune published. Victor Considérant's Fourierist paper, *La Démocratie pacifique* (1843–51) paid its staff daily according to its receipts—usually between three and five francs—little more than a carpenter could earn—and when it was out of funds, they contented themselves drinking sugared water spiced with rum. When Jules Vallès was at the beginning of his career and wrote for the *Journal de la cordonnerie*, he was paid with a gift of a pair of shoes. In 1893 Aristide Briand started on *La Lanterne* at 250 francs a month; after five years he reached 1,000 francs a month. The rewards of the majority of journalists were very modest indeed, and between the wars, when inflation struck, they were even worse. Between 1914 and 1925, while the cost of living rose fourfold, the wages of journalists rose on average between two and two and a half times. A reporter in 1925 earned more or less the same wage as a primary school master; a *secrétaire de redaction* started at the same level as a junior secondary teacher; an editor might not earn very much more, though a successful one could earn several times as much. There was nothing unusual in the French situation: the wages of the reporters and the printers on English provincial papers were also roughly the same.[1] Paris reporters might earn twice as much as provincial ones, but they had a higher cost of living to bear. Their poverty was unchanged in 1950, when reporters were still on the same level as *instituteurs*; they bitterly complained that they earned less than sewer workers, but then there was intense competition for very few jobs. Even in 1970, there were still only 12,000 journalists in France (at a time when there were 65,000 doctors). Theirs moreover was the only profession—apart from banking—for which no prior professional qualifications were required.

Balzac had the most profound contempt for journalists and left scathing portraits of them in his *Illusions perdues*. Theirs was an occupation, he said, from which it was no more possible to emerge pure than it was when one went to a brothel. During the Second Empire, there was general agreement that they enjoyed, as a class, little prestige. They were condemned as bohemians, who were redeemed only by their wit. They were placed on the same level as actors 'whom people both despise and envy'. They were, to some degree, even performing bears, in that, to attract publicity, they made a habit of fighting duels; a room for fencing practice was often provided next to that in which they wrote their copy; and one of the leading experts on duels, who tried to continue them into the twentieth century, was Paul de Cassagnac, the Bonapartist editor. Everyone knew that the violence of their polemic was a mask, that the insults they hurled at each other through their papers were a game, simply serving as an entertainment for the bourgeois. There were very few journalists, as there were bankers, notaries and priests, who had made themselves notorious as criminals, and yet, as one provincial journalist wrote, 'There are few professions which are the object of more widespread discredit.'[2] The reporter, said Larousse's Encyclopedia in 1875, was an 'inferior writer', whose legs were more important than his style, and who 'is in general rather poorly

---

[1] Bureau International du Travail, *Les Conditions de travail et de vie des journalistes* (Geneva, 1928), 147–9.

[2] Anatole Willox, *Le Journalisme en province* (new ed. 1887), 130.

thought of by serious people who regret seeing news taking on exaggerated importance, expelling the serious article from newspapers. He is generally held in little esteem by those who read him with the greatest assiduity.' But Larousse conceded that he was nevertheless a useful person, however despicable 'the intimate dramas and the loves of fashionable *cocottes*' about which he collected information, because, if the press was to survive, these stories were needed to win the readership of 'the indifferent part of the public'.[1] Barbey d'Aurevilly, in his study of *Journalists and Polemicists* (1895), said journalism 'diminished the faculties, when it did not kill them, after having depraved them'. It destroyed budding writers by giving them bad habits, frivolity, inconstancy, party passion, false judgement and worst of all it made them fool themselves, so as to be able to fool their readers better. They were dominated by the search for pretty formulae, but though they aimed to be amusing, their vehicle, and the instrument of their success, was always the banal idea. He was not sure whom he hated more, the frustrated rebel, whose opinions were no more than the expression of hurt pride, or the pompous editorialist looking at the world through drawn curtains, or the gossip writers, unable to distinguish what was important, or to make any judgements at all. The spoilt child of journalism was the young man of wit, who made his appearance during the Second Empire, and who at least could make fun of the world, to leaven the doctrinaire sententiousness so many papers still adopted, but he was regarded as being on the fringes of the profession.[2] A professor of medicine, in a work on *The Influence of Journalism on the Health of the Body and of the Mind* (1871), classified journalists as 'jealous, ambitious for popularity, and infatuated with themselves; they excite themselves by writing, taking the risk of overstepping boundaries as the drinker who drinks thoughtlessly and befuddles himself in despite of the stupor that threatens him'. The violence of their language did not mean they were brave, as they imagined themselves to be, but that they lived in a state of 'pathological excitement and hot fever'.

---

[1] *Grande Encyclopédie Larousse* (1875), s.v. Reporter.

[2] J. Barbey d'Aurevilly, *Les Œuvres et les hommes. Journalistes et polémistes, chroniqueurs et pamphletaires* (1895), 20, 204, 231–2, 342. For examples of this light journalism, see Louis Duchemin, *Durand et Cie, scènes de la vie parisienne* (1878).

They were dangerous people, because they spread their nervousness to their readers.[1] They were dangerous people also, as one of them pointed out, because they had it in their power to harm those who got on the wrong side of them, and that is what saved them from being completely ostracised by good society. By fighting against each other and by their fake duels, they had won attention as entertainers, but they had also lost in dignity. There would always be more respect for authors of books than for the mere journalist: 'The job of journalist is suitable only for vagabonds and men without any means of support.' It could be a perfectly honourable occupation, though one in which ambition was out of place. What brought it so low was 'advertising, camaraderie and blackmail', using newspapers to advance the cause of their friends, writing reviews and praising artists and actors corruptly.[2]

By the twentieth century, however, the power of the journalist had become too obvious for these moral doubts to matter too much, just as the *nouveau riche* financier was eventually welcomed into the aristocratic society that had once disdained him. In 1910 it was said that 'whereas twenty years ago a bourgeois would have had scruples about finding himself in the company of a journalist in a *salon* of high society, now the journalist is everywhere respected and it is to him that one almost always turns to obtain a favour, knowing very well that he has his own ways of getting at influential personages'.[3] Too many famous men of letters had dabbled in journalism; too many journalists had become politicians and ministers; too many people in the liberal professions earned supplementary income from part-time journalistic activities: in 1930, indeed, a professor of literature—it is true not a representative one— wrote that it was time that it was realised that newspapers were not the enemy of literature, but one of the forms of literature, the form that the general public loved best, and 'the most vigorous of all literary genres'.[4] It also now appeared as one of

---

[1] I. Druhen, *De l'influence du journalisme sur la santé du corps et de l'esprit* (Besançon, 1871), 20–1.

[2] N. Fourgeaud-Lagrèze, *La Petite Presse en province* (Ribérac, 1869), 12, 19, 38.

[3] Alexandre Guérin, *Comment on devient journaliste* (1910), 19. Cf. René Perlat, *Le Journalisme poitevin* (Poitiers, 1898).

[4] Léon Levrault, professeur au lycée Condorcet, *Le Journalisme* (1930), 7–10. But cf. N. Nikoladzé, *La Presse de la décadence. Observations d'un journaliste étranger* (1875).

the most exciting of occupations, having attractions for young people which were frequently compared to those of sport. The hunt for news, and the race to be first with the news, was an exhilarating adventure. The reporter who was sent off to some distant country sometimes won the prestige of an explorer, record breaker and fighter for just causes. It is true that the first reporter to carry out one of these grand assignments, involving travelling round the world in sixty-three days, came back so worn out, that he immediately accepted a job as a provincial librarian. But the generation that grew up just before the 1914 war, which thirsted for adventure and found it in sport or war, also revelled in the opportunities provided by the popular press; and it was a job that girls could enter also. Geneviève Tabouis, one of the most successful of these girls, loved the power: 'With his pen and his notebook the journalist is the censor and the equal of the greatest people in the world.'[1] Paul Bodin made the hero of his novel about a journalist say he had chosen the profession because 'I discovered in it the privileges of our function: we are witnesses and spectators but we can, whenever we wish, mix with the actors. We choose the moment when their passions can be made public. We join the participants in events; though we are barely noticed, even the greatest of these send us away only with extreme prudence: the journalist is one of the powers of the modern world.'[2] The fact that they might write rotten prose, or even make imbecile mistakes revealing crass ignorance (and one of them published a curious collection of these)[3] no longer mattered much. The new breed of reporter did not always take his job all that seriously: he might start as a sports writer and move on to every speciality in turn, but he would continue to praise the sporting spirit as the key to good journalism.[4] Sometimes he burnt himself out in constant, restless travel, like Albert Londres (1884–1932), one of the most famous of the early 'grands reporters'. The grandson of a pedlar, he claimed that he became a journalist in order to lead the same kind of wandering existence. His ideal was always to live out of a suitcase, to feel that he would be

[1] Christian Brincourt and Michel Leblanc, *Les Reporters* (1970), 347.

[2] Paul Bodin, *De notre envoyé spécial* (c. 1950), quoted in *Études de presse* (15 Oct. 1951), 325.

[3] Marcel Schwob, *Mœurs des diurnales. Traité de journalisme* (1926).

[4] Renée Pierre-Gosset, *Cochon de métier* (1950).

moving soon. 'I am not a weak man', he wrote, 'but an unquiet one.' He liked doing only three or four large articles a year, so he was often broke; he sometimes went without meals; he had no interest in luxurious living. He made his name with an investigation of conditions in the prisons of Cayenne; he got intense pleasure when the articles were printed as a book. Another of his great successes was *The Road to Buenos Aires* about the white slave trade. He wrote in the style of a popular novelist, but at forty-five he decided he would stop writing fast and would compose 'like a writer'. When he was accused of having an insufficiently formed style, he went out and bought a textbook on *The Art of Composition.* He was apparently a manic depressive, greatly dependent on the encouragement of his editor. He was a great believer in Justice, but had no definite political or religious ideas. He was drowned in a shipwreck at the height of his powers.[1]

The variety of characters that were attracted by journalism may be seen from the case of Eugène Lautier (1867–1935) who joined *Le Temps* at the age of eighteen and stayed with it for thirty-five years, becoming its pontiff on internal politics. He was a large fat man, a bachelor with an enormous appetite, whose favourite saying was 'I am never wrong'. His infuriating, genuine self-confidence went with an inexhaustible ambition for honour and power. At *Le Temps* he came to know everybody who mattered in politics, finance and literature; he helped to create the idea that the journalists on his paper were a power in the world; and when a former member of its staff, Tardieu, became prime minister, Lautier hitched himself on as under-secretary for Fine Arts. He was certain that he had the makings of a statesman: but he was only briefly a deputy for the corrupt constituency of Guyana. He knew all about political intrigue, but he offended too many people as a result. Because he had only his journalism to base himself on, he failed as a politician. He is a curious example of the frustrations of a certain kind of journalist.[2]

---

[1] Florise Londres, *Mon père* (1934); Paul Mousset, *Albert Londres: l'aventure du grand reportage* (1972); Albert Londres, *Au bagne* (1923), *Le Chemin de Buenos Aires* (1927), *Pêcheurs de perles* (1931).

[2] Victor Goedorp, *Figures du Tempes* (1943), 9–58. For other attitudes to the press, see Henri Béranger, 'Les Responsabilités de la presse', *Revue bleue* (4–25 Dec. 1897), quoting leading public figures.

Jules Vallès, a journalist who had other talents too, when accused of vanity, replied 'One does not become a man of letters from modesty'. Vanity was no doubt common among journalists, as it was in many of the liberal professions, and the journalist Edmond Texier (1816–87) was also probably right that 'it is sometimes because you have a cruel father who, when you were young, had a coat made for you out of his old breeches, that you are driven to write elegies'.[1] But journalism was to many people a job much like any other, which they not infrequently entered because their fathers had worked in it before them, or because they simply longed to escape from the civil service or teaching. The memoirs of some provincial journalists are, contrary to Vallès's dictum, very much the work of modest men. Arsène Thévenot, editor of *Le Vosgien*, recorded that 'in 1883, as a result of a reverse of fortune, I was obliged to seek my living from my pen'.[2] J. M. Villefranche, editor of the *Journal de l'Ain* (circulation 2,200), who spent fourteen years on the paper, attacking its anticlerical rival (circulation 1,600), said that there were two kinds of journalists, those who were convinced and those who were sceptics, willing to write to order: the latter were far more numerous. Despite the status in local politics that his editorship gave him, he valued his obscure poems and novels more highly than his daily polemic; and in his memoirs, of which he realistically had only 300 copies printed, he said 'One writes for the papers to earn a living or to serve truth, but neither is valued as much as a book, in the eyes of posterity.'[3] Likewise, Edmund Claris, though he went quite far in Parisian journalism, had no illusions. The son of the editor of the obscure *Dépêche de Paris*, he entered journalism as an adolescent, with a series of articles on the week's suicides for an ephemeral illustrated periodical, *L'Œuvre sociale*; he worked part-time as a research assistant to historians, while also

---

[1] Firmin Maillard, *La Cité des intellectuels: scènes cruelles et plaisantes de la vie littéraire des gens de lettres au 19ᵉ siècle* (3rd edition 1905).

[2] Arsène Thévenot, *Souvenirs d'un journaliste 1883–9* (Arcis-sur-Aube, 1901).

[3] J. M. Villefranche, *Photographies contemporaines. Souvenirs et menus propos d'un vieux journaliste* (Bourg, 1890), 271:

> On écrit journaux pour vivre
> Ou pour servir la vérité
> Mais aucun d'eux ne vaut un livre
> Auprès de la posterité.

selling 'news in brief' items to *Le Matin*. He then at last got a job with a regular salary on *La Petite République*, where he defended the rights of Algerians, trade unionists and madmen, and helped to start a shop, 'The Hundred Thousand Overcoats', whose profits were designed to save the paper from bankruptcy. He had friends in the art world of the Latin Quarter, so he became an art critic, and at the same time he published a serial novel and edited the speeches of Jaurès. He had to turn his hand to whatever task presented itself. Though a socialist, in 1909 he became the editor of *Le Radical*, but after obtaining a contract which stipulated that he should not be obliged to follow the radical party line slavishly: the owner of the paper was not too much of a radical either, for he employed a priest as tutor to his children. But after a quarrel, Claris moved on to *Le Journal*, where, because he was not paid much, he was allowed to have lunch daily for only five francs at Maxim's Restaurant, which tended to be empty at lunch time, and which his employer partly owned. From his socialist days, Claris had many friends who were now becoming ministers, like Viviani and Briand, and these gave him an entrée into the government offices; when Millerand became prime minister, Claris, who had long known him, became his assistant *chef de cabinet*. But all the while he kept on several other jobs, because pay was low: he worked for a news agency Agence-Radio, for *La France d'Outre Mer*, and for various provincial papers. He knew Clemenceau and Mandel, too, from his youth, so he was never short of news; but he never got more than a modest living from journalism; despite his experience and his contacts, he had to take work wherever he could find it.[1]

Journalists were ultimately wage earners with no security, at the mercy of arbitrary proprietors; many did not even have regular wages, but got paid by the line, and sometimes a small retainer. Some associated themselves with barristers, to whom they brought cases for a commission. They had to pick up what earnings they could, and they competed in a profession in which, it was said, there were six times as many people as were needed.[2] At the extremities of the journalistic world were a host of amateur part-timers, whom the professionals looked on

[1] Edmond Claris, *Souvenirs de soixante ans de journalisme 1895–1955* (1958).

[2] Paul Pottier, *Professions et métiers: Les Journalistes* (n.d., about 1907).

as interlopers, but the professionals were too individualistic to be able to organise themselves effectually.[1] They began forming unions in the 1870s, but Catholics, republicans, specialists each formed separate associations.[2] The National Union of Journalists was founded only in 1918 and by 1939 still had only 2,750 members. It spent about ten years negotiating for a collective contract for journalists, but in vain. However, in 1935 it succeeded in getting a law passed[3] which gave the journalist a professional status, entitled him to an official press card, annual holidays, compensation for dismissal, even when the journalist left his job for reasons of conscience following 'a notable change in the character or orientation of his paper or periodical, if this change creates for the employee a situation which endangers his honour, his reputation or, in a general way, his moral interests'. This was an important first step in the process which was to lead journalists, after the 1939–45 war, to strike against their employers and even in some cases to take over the running of the papers they worked on. But the exceptional power that the journalists of *Le Monde* and *Le Figaro* have won remains an exception, and the capitalist newspaper owners remain supreme. Even though they were temporarily dislodged by the Resistance in 1944, they have returned virtually omnipotent.[4]

Advertising

The power of capital behind the press was one of the great obstacles that stood in the way of journalism becoming an independent and influential profession. In 1836 Émile de Girardin, the pioneer of a cheap press for the masses based on advertising, killed, in a duel, Armand Carrel, who represented the identification of journalism with politics, and whose newspaper indeed had played a decisive part in overthrowing King Louis-Philippe in 1830. This duel has, rather fancifully, been taken as symbolising the victory of the new press—a commercial, profit-making industry—over the old doctrinaire press, devoted

[1] Robert de Jouvenel, *Le Journalisme en vingt leçons* (1920); Georges Bourdon, *Le Journalisme d'aujourd'hui* (1931); Joseph Folliet, *Tu seras journaliste* (1961).
[2] Syndicat des journalistes français, *80 ans, 1886–1966* (1966), for a brief history.
[3] Law of 29 March 1935. See F. Terron, 'L'Évolution du droit de la presse de 1881 à 1940', in Bellenger *et al.*, *Histoire générale de la presse française*, vol. 3 (1972), 42–4. [4] Jean Schwoebel, *La Presse, le pouvoir et l'argent* (1968).

mainly to party polemic, and justifying itself not on financial grounds but as an essential part of democratic government. No such victory was ever won, both because purely political newspapers have survived—even if they have usually been on the verge of financial collapse—and also because the commercial press was not in any case properly established. Girardin hoped to get most of the income for his paper from advertising but he did not entirely succeed. Advertising developed very slowly in this period and never attained anything like the proportions it reached in the U.S.A., Germany or even England. Even in 1970, after a decade during which expenditure on advertising had risen by between 8 and 15 per cent per annum, the annual amount spent in France was still only 80 francs per inhabitant, compared to 150 francs in the United Kingdom, 220 francs in Germany and 419 francs in the U.S.A.[1] This has had a profound effect on the character of the French press, and indeed on French life.

It has been seen how in politics, bureaucracy and industry, favouritism and personal recommendation remained of great importance.[2] Though careers were gradually opened to talent, no one believed that success in open examinations was enough to enable a man to get on in the world; and most politicians realised they had to be of personal service to individual electors to secure their votes, however attractive their programme was. The same kind of attitude prevented the rise of advertising. In 1848 Girardin assured his readers that there was nothing to be ashamed of if one advertised in a newspaper: in England at any rate 'people no longer blush' when they place advertisements.[3] But the tradition of mutual exchange of services was not eradicated. In the first French newspaper, Renaudot's *Gazette* (founded in 1631), advertisers did not pay anything, but simply gave the publisher a few copies of the object they advertised. Publisher and advertiser were considered to be in league, and with time advertising did indeed develop into something of a conspiracy, because so much trouble was taken to conceal its true character from the consumer. During the French Revolution, some newspapers offered their readers space not simply to advertise goods, but to publish their

---

[1] Bernard Voyenne, *L'Information en France* (1972), 59.
[2] See my *Ambition and Love* (1979), ch. 7.   [3] *La Presse*, 3 Oct. 1848.

opinions on any subject they pleased. In the course of the nine-teenth century, this system was standardised so that news-papers came to offer four different kinds of advertising space. First was what was known as the 'English advertisement', which was an advertisement which did not pretend to be any-thing else. These were generally grouped on the fourth or back page and were the cheapest of all. But they were not very popular, precisely because they were cheap. Girardin tried to develop the 'small ad.', arguing that he would prefer to have a vast number of these than a few displayed ones; but in 1845, when the London *Times* was publishing about 1,500 advertise-ments a day, the most successful French papers were still unable to find more than forty or fifty each. More expensive than the open advertisement on the fourth page was the *réclame* on the third page, which usually cost two-thirds more, or a *faits divers* news item on the second page, which cost another 30 per cent, and most expensive of all was an article on the front page. These were known as 'editorial publicity', as opposed to 'advertisements': their purpose was to convey information about a product but without letting the reader know that he was reading an advertisement, until the last line. Sometimes, especially in articles or *chroniques*, the advertisement was totally camouflaged: a recommendation of a particular share would appear to result from an independent and objective assessment of the stock-market, and a review of a book would apparently have only the values of literature in mind. Villemessant, editor of the *Figaro* during the Second Empire, declared himself to be satisfied with an issue of his paper only when every single line in it had been paid for in this way.

One reason why the advertisement invaded the whole paper was the way advertising agencies developed. Newspapers were generally established with inadequate capital; because they needed income at once, they often started by farming their back page out to an agency. The pattern was set very early on by the *Société générale des annonces* founded in 1845 by Charles Duveyrier (1803–66), an enterprising Saint-Simonian, who had been in turn a missionary of his sect to England and Belgium, and a journalist—until he was sentenced to a year's imprison-ment for outraging morals in an article on women; but a revolution had then made him Inspector-General of Prisons, and between times he was also a playwright and a businessman. He offered the three leading Paris papers 300,000 francs per annum each, plus half of his profits, in return for control of their advertising; and he offered the public an advertisement in all three papers, which together had 60,000 subscribers, at only 6 francs a line. Over 200 shopkeepers all over Paris were appointed sub-agents to collect advertisements. Havas, who had taken over Duveyrier's firm, became overwhelmingly powerful by amalgamating with two other leading agencies. Havas also owned (as will be seen) a news information service. His expanded agency now offered provincial newspapers a free news service by telegraph, in return for the right to insert advertisements free of change. Since this enabled provincial papers to do without their own Paris correspondents, the scheme was attractive and successful. But the growth of this formidable advertising monopoly (or near-monopoly) left the newspapers with a fixed income from advertisements (and in the case of those who exchanged advertisements for news, no income at all). Having lost control of their back pages, they therefore attempted to raise more revenue by selling space in the rest of the paper, and they did this by in effect becoming advertising agencies themselves, offering to write advertisements and pass them off as news. But another middleman now arose in the form of rival agencies which offered to put clients in contact with newspapers willing to sell themselves in this way. These agencies differed from British or American ones in that they did not charge their clients the cost of the advertisements they advised, and add 10 per cent for their services. Competition between them was not based on the quality of the advice or service they offered, but solely on price. They obtained discounts from the newspapers for whom they secured advertisements; the advice they gave was usually determined by the amount of money they could make from the deal themselves. Since throughout this period the newspapers refused to allow audited circulation figures, it was impossible to have objective criteria on which to base advertising policy; and, of course, this made it possible for a whole host of papers to appear, whose aim was simply prostitutional, to sell space and articles at the highest possible price. Advertising agencies tended to have a group of assorted papers, a few well-known ones and other obscurer ones, with whom they had arrangements, and they usually tried to sell their clients package deals—an advertisement in seven different papers, for example, for what they claimed cost little more than a single advertisement in one high-circulation daily. This uncertainty as to what press advertisements really cost resulted in a general belief that they were expensive, more expensive than in other countries, and this was often adduced as the reason for the failure of this activity to grow in the same way as it did abroad. In fact in 1911 it was calculated that a square centimetre of advertising space, per 100,000 copies, cost 91 centimes in the U.S.A., 68 centimes in England and only 54 centimes in France. It is true that the French price was impossible to state accurately, both because circulation figures were unreliable and because rates varied, as much as fivefold, depending on where the advertisement was placed. Large advertisements were proportionately much cheaper in France than small ones; enormous discounts encouraged clients to take half or whole pages, and the newspapers got little profit. It was true that advertising in provincial newspapers was expensive if done from Paris, for the Paris agencies often charged two or three times the rates payable in the provinces itself. In this industry, as in the retail food trade, the middlemen inflated costs in a quite disproportionate way. They asked a different price from every client, and the clients not surprisingly sought alternative avenues.[1]

Only certain sorts of people advertised in the press. In 1938 advertising space was distributed as follows:

Pharmaceutical products	29·87 per cent
Department stores	17·46
Food	8·85
Furniture	7·28
Household goods (produits d'entretien)	5·43
Cars	5·18
Alcoholic drinks	4·35
Soaps and cosmetics	4·20
Clothes	3·30
Miscellaneous	14·08[2]

[1] Émile Mermet, avocat, *La Publicité en France. Guide manuel* (4th edition, 1880), by one of the first advertising consultants; Henri Vathelet, *La Publicité dans le journalisme* (doctoral thesis, Paris, 1911), 67–89.

[2] Claude Bellenger, 'La Publicité dans la presse en 1938 et en 1951', *Études*

The most striking omission is industry and finance. The great failure of the press was its inability to obtain public advertising from the wealthiest firms and indeed from most sections of business in general. There were several reasons for this. Really large firms with expansionist ambitions preferred to buy up newspapers, or to obtain secret support from newspapers. Usually they did not see newspapers as a means of increasing demand in the general public, but rather as a way of stimulating public contracts and influencing politics. For purely trade purposes, they tended to advertise in trade journals, which accordingly flourished in very large numbers and which were often no more than collections of advertisements. There were a few manufacturers who believed in general advertising, of whom perhaps the most famous was Menier the chocolate a manufacturer, who had discovered—when he temporarily stopped advertising—that it really did pay; but Menier was also something of an eccentric and not the usual kind of business-man. Advertising by foreign manufacturers—like the Belgian Esders clothes chain, or Scott's Emulsion—did not compensate for the general wariness towards the papers. Even the department stores, who used press advertising so much, seem to have done so with some reluctance and from fear of blackmail. When one of them once stopped advertising, the newspapers replied by announcing that the store was stricken by the plague, imported with its Oriental carpets: it was forced to resume. Firms usually preferred to pay the newspapers to keep quiet about them rather than to parade their wares. Thus the suicide of the head of one firm was passed over in complete silence, and marked only by the fact that advertising by the firm suddenly filled the papers. The Société des Bains de Mer de Monaco was said to have spent large sums getting the papers to praise the merits of the south coast and to avoid mentioning the disasters caused by gambling in its casinos. But generally, apart from certain trades, businessmen looked on advertising as an extra expense, which would reduce profits and raise prices.

Press advertising was discredited because it was indeed used

de presse (Spring 1953), 37–40. In 1951 pharmaceutics were temporarily down to 8 per cent because of legislation limiting their advertising, clothes were up to 14·50, food to 16·88, cosmetics and soaps to 6·22.

most noticeably by dubious businesses and by obvious charlatans. Among the regular advertisers were usurers, into whose
hands no sensible man would entrust himself, small contractors, seeking domestic outworkers at exploitative wages, estate
agents, particularly those selling small shops, cafés and hotels
—where the advertisement was usually a way of extorting a
high advance fee from the seller, much larger than the actual
cost of the advertisement. Attentive readers could see that
advertisements were not infrequently a form of blackmail: press
campaigns in support of noble causes, for the extirpation of
various vices, turned out to be simply methods of forcing people
to advertise, as when *Les Nouvelles* waged an attack on a casino
on the outskirts of Paris, and then suddenly stopped, sporting
instead advertisements for the casino. The result was that in
1938 only 41 per cent of advertising expenditure went to the
press, compared to about 50 per cent in Britain and 80 per cent
in the U.S.A.

Perhaps it was because newspapers were a favourite place for
advertisements by charlatans offering every kind of medical
cure and elixir that the pharmaceutical industry was forced to
compete with them and advertise in the papers too. Pharmacists were originally forbidden to advertise, by the rules of the
College of Pharmacy founded in 1801; members of the society of
Pharmacists of the Seine, founded in 1819, likewise had to give an
undertaking not to advertise—though some broke this rule. But
a Pharmacists' Congress in 1867 voted to allow advertising and
from that time on the pharmacists were leaders among the
newspaper advertisers.[1] This decision marked the triumph of
the pharmaceutical industry, manufacturing patent drugs, or
'secret remedies' as some people still called them, over the
individual local pharmacist, who made up prescriptions to the
doctor's order. In the period 1900–14 these firms were said to
be spending about thirteen or fourteen million francs annually
on press advertisements, which appeared to be an enormous
amount.[2] When radio stations started to take advertisements,
one-half of these were pharmaceutical.[3] It did not enhance the

[1] Eugène Guitard, *Deux siècles de presse au service de la pharmacie* (1913).

[2] 'La publicité pharmaceutique', special issue of *Le Courrier graphique* (May
1938), no. 15.

[3] René Mante, *La Publicité pharmaceutique au point de vue de la déontologie et de
l'hygiène publique* (Paris medical thesis, 1939).

prestige of the media that they were willing to accept advertisements which were, strictly speaking, illegal, for the law forbade 'secret remedies'.

Another source of revenue for the press was the theatre,
though in a more roundabout way, which again reflected little
credit on either party, and in the end brought in comparatively
little actual cash. The announcement of the titles and times of
plays was inserted in most papers free of charge, or rather in
return for some free tickets, but the *chronique des théâtres* was
paid for by the theatres though it purported to be an independent gossip column. The great literary figures whom the major
newspapers employed as theatre critics had a free hand to write
what they pleased, and the papers paid them large sums for
their articles; but many minor journalists were in the pay of the
theatres, and used by them to announce that every play was a
great success, so as to attract more custom. There was no safer
way to ensure that one got one's own play put on if one was a
playwright, than if one was also a theatre critic at the same
time, with a regular column in a paper. So, for example, Henri
Rochefort discovered, when, in his early twenties he had a
play accepted: he was incensed to discover that it was put on
only to placate *La Presse théâtral*, the journal for which he worked.
The same principles applied also in book reviews. Publishers
were among the first people to use newspapers for advertising.
Originally they simply gave two free copies of the book they
wanted advertised: one went to the editor and the other to the
reviewer, who wrote his article free. In time, stronger induce-
ments became necessary. In 1845 a Paris artisan with literary
pretensions and Maratist sympathies, Constant Hilbey, published a revealing account of his attempts to have his work
recognised by the press. He sent a play he had written to the
newspapers but it was ignored. He went to the offices of *La
Presse* to protest, but he was assured that 'one must either pay,
or else be a friend of one of the staff' to be noticed. So he paid
to have a verse inserted in the paper, as a sample, and he nego-
tiated to have a review printed; but difficulties arose about the
price: they were willing to give him only one and a half columns
for a hundred francs, but he demanded a longer article. The
editor, Granier de Cassagnac (a well-known author of historical
works, and a Bonapartist member of the legislature throughout

the Second Empire), heard about the dispute, agreed to write the review himself, and refused any money, though he asked instead for 'a present'—and he later sent a clerk to suggest a silver teapot costing 200 francs. However, he put off writing it and in the end sent word that Hilbey should write it himself. When Hilbey asked what he should say, Cassagnac replied, 'Please yourself: say, for example, that the first edition is sold out.' In the end Cassagnac wrote the article and Hilbey, who had refused to pay anything until he had seen it, was pleased and gave him silver cutlery for four, with which Cassagnac declared himself very satisfied. While all this negotiation was in progress, Hilbey had inserted a note, for 6 francs, in *La Presse*, to prepare the readers: 'People may say that this century is not interested in poetry, but a new printing of the poems of the young tailor M. Constant Hilbey has just appeared . . .' When the review was published, a journalist from another paper, *La Patrie*, wrote to Hilbey offering to publish extracts of his work in an anthology he was bringing out, and indeed to manage all his publicity. Hilbey agreed to pay him forty francs to write an article about him in *La Patrie*. This process of buying reviews kept Hilbey busy for some time, until, for a bribe of 800 francs, he got a promise from the director of the Odéon Theatre to give his play twenty-five performances; but the director, having taken the money, dropped the play after only a few showings, demanding a further fifty francs for each night. Hilbey tried to insert a (paid) article denouncing this, but no paper would take it, fearing a libel suit. Hilbey's lawyer, the famous republican Emmanuel Arago, advised him against making a fuss, because no author could afford to offend the press.[1]

As the number of books published continued to increase, and as critics formed higher views of their status, their attention had to be won less by money and more by connections. George Sand wrote to the journalist Guéroult saying she was publishing a book and needed his assistance: would he come to lunch?[2] Marcel Proust got a favourable review written by a friend

[1] Constantin Hilbey, ouvrier, *Vénalité des journaux. Révélations accompagnées de preuves* (1845).

[2] B. Coste, 'Adolphe Guéroult' (law thesis, unpublished, in the library of the Faculté de Droit, Paris, 1968), 21.

reprinted in several papers, by putting pressure on his connections in the literary world. No money seems to have changed hands in these cases, but the Catholic writer Fonsegrive claimed in 1903 that when, for example, the *Figaro* published a review of a novel by its critic Albert Wolf, this would cost the author or publisher at least 2,000 francs, half of which went to the newspaper and half to Wolf. Fonsegrive published a book on *How to read a Newspaper*, to enable the reader to distinguish between advertisement and independent comment, but he concluded that it was precisely the papers which claimed to be most impartial, to be purely literary or simply to give news, who should be the most suspect. 'One is never sure, except when an article appears over the signature of a few names, and they are very few indeed, that one is not reading an advertisement, a piece of advocacy for which the paper has been paid and often for which both the author and the paper have been paid. An article which appears completely objective, even if it deals with nothing but chemistry or geography, serves to prepare, in the following issue or even in another column of the paper, the launching of some industrial company or some exotic mining enterprise.'[1] The gossip columns of the newspapers, which were supposed to meet the demand of readers anxious for more entertainment and less dull politics, were also frequently a new way of making money. When a paper reported the famous or not so famous people seen at the theatre, this enabled it to get paid by the decorators and costumiers it mentioned; the mention of the tradesmen involved, particularly when accompanied by a flattering epithet, was a sure sign of money changing hands. Thus it came out in court that Arthur Meyer, the *Figaro's* colourful editor, had paid his florist's bill of 4,000 francs by mentioning her in his reports of society parties. Gossip about actors was often paid for, or at least recompensed with free tickets. The reporting of sports was another case of commercial forces making it worth while, as much as a concession to readers' interests.

This petty corruption is difficult if not impossible to prove, and no accurate assessment of its extent can be made. But more substantial evidence does exist about corruption on a larger scale. A very considerable proportion of the advertising obtained

[1] G. Fonsegrive, *Comment lire les journaux* (1903), 22.

by the press appeared in the form of apparently independent stock-market commentary. There was so much of this that it had a major influence on the solvency of the press, and indeed a number of secret institutions grew up to organise the distribution of this financial advertising. Very early on, the papers farmed out their financial page, as they had farmed out their back, small-ads. page. Banks and financial institutions wishing to raise money from the public were thus able to insert articles in praise of themselves, in return for a subsidy to the paper. The man who had first got this going on an organised scale was Jules Mirès, who bought the *Journal des chemins de fer* in 1848 for the express purpose of getting banks and companies to pay him to boost the shares they were trying to sell. In the course of the Second Empire, he obtained control of five more similar papers; backed by the Péreires, his ambition was to create a Saint-Simonian *omnium*, which would be master of all financial advertising in the country. This was a time when the value of shares on the stock-market increased threefold, and until the crash of 1882, the press took full advantage of the competition for the investments of the small saver. Girardin and a few other press magnates formed a National Bank which acted, in effect, as a financial advertising agency. Soubeyran, the Bonapartist Governor of the Crédit Foncier, was particularly effective in manipulating the financial columns of many newspapers, with a view to raising the value of stocks he dealt in; when he launched his Discount Bank in 1878, he allocated almost 10,000 shares to journalists so as to win their complaisance; by 1880 he was said to have obtained control of the financial pages of no less than sixty-four papers.[1] In the 1880s specialised advertising agencies grew up to exploit this lucrative game, and to share with the newspapers the profits which were to be made by hoodwinking gullible provincials. Batiau (publicity agent for the Crédit Lyonnais and the Crédit Foncier), Gustave Laffont (publicity agent for Rothschild), Alphonse Lenoir (connected with the Havas agency) were unknown to most readers, but they played a highly important role in the newspaper world. Lenoir, for example, was not simply a financial agent: as a police report had it, 'When individual ministers or even a whole cabinet needed the help of newspapers in some

[1] M. B. Palmer, *Some Aspects of the French Press* (Oxford D.Phil. thesis, 1973), 45.

matter or other, for some parliamentary vote for which public opinion had to be prepared, it was Lenoir who undertook to visit the newspapers and to distribute special subsidies to them. When the papers waged campaigns either against important financiers or against famous individuals, like the Reinach family for example, or against members of the government, it was Lenoir who was very often asked to arrange the matter and end the campaign, when the campaign was inconvenient to those who were the object of it.'[1] In 1909 Léon Rénier (1857–1950), one of the directors of the Havas agency, tried to consolidate all the financial advertising in the country into a monopoly and he was, indeed, for a time, the distributor of largess to the major Paris papers—half a million francs a year, or more, to the *Petit Parisien*, the *Petit Journal* and *Le Journal* for example, down to a mere 10,000 francs for the royalist *Action française* and the Bonapartist *Autorité*; and in addition he was master of the financial advertisements of eighty provincial newspapers. It was not inappropriate, considering his influence, that Rénier was made a Grand Cross of the Legion of Honour in the decorations list of 1929, which promoted only one other person to this exalted rank—Bergson. These financial agents certainly became rich men, since they exacted large commissions from the banks for their services; and it became accepted practice that no bank could even consider raising money without bribing the press. Occasionally, the details of individual bribes would be made public in some scandal. Thus it was revealed that over the years 1875–90, the Crédit Foncier spent sixty million francs a year on press subsidies, twenty-two million paid directly and thirty-eight million through various intermediaries. In 1887–9, during the Boulangist crisis, the money seems to have been paid to ministers, who used it to encourage the press to defend the republic. The Panama Canal Company gave about twelve million francs to the press to boost its shares. The most fully documented instance of bribery is that carried out by the Russian government. To assist it to raise its loans in France—of over five milliard francs during the period 1889 to 1904—it distributed at first between

---

[1] A.N. F(7.) 13969, quoted by P. Albert, in *Histoire générale de la presse française*, ed. C. Bellanger *et al.*, vol. 3 (1972), 265. New light on the inter-war period by J. N. Jeanneney, in *Revue française de science politique* (1975), 717–38.

70,000 and 110,000 francs a year, but when the Russo-Japanese war and the revolution of 1905 made raising money much harder, its subsidy was increased to two million francs. It employed as its Paris agent Raffalovitch, grand officer of the Legion of Honour, corresponding member of the Institute of France, a prolific writer on economics with a high reputation. Raffalovitch's correspondence with the Russian government, preserved in the archives opened up by the Soviets, was published by *L'Humanité* in 1923–4, and showed that a large number of highly respectable journalists accepted and solicited bribes, as a condition for writing articles in favour of Russia. They included Leroy-Beaulieu, a distinguished economist, who demanded and got 4,000 roubles a year as a subsidy for his journal *L'Économiste français*. Hébrard, owner of *Le Temps*, supposedly a dignified independent, conservative daily, had, as Raffalovitch reported, 'mad pretensions' demanding 10,000 francs, but his circulation figures were too low and he was given much less. The secretary of the journalists' trade union seems likewise to have sold his support, suddenly shifting from pro-German to anti-German articles. The Association of Paris Stockbrokers passed an official motion refusing to handle Russian loans unless the Russian government placed 200,000 francs a month 'at the disposal of the press' for the duration of the Russo-Japanese war. Blackmail was not practised only by journalists.[1] Nor was Russia a lone victim. The Turkish government, for example, had to spend three million francs in 1914 on publicity to raise a loan on the Paris market; over two million of this sum was distributed to the press through Léon Rénier, who kept 490,000 francs out of it as his commission. During the 1914–18 war, the Germans distributed large sums to a number of French newspapers, who were not deterred from accepting even though these bribes now involved treason. *Le Journal*, which had one of the largest sales in Paris, received ten million francs through the German ambassador in the U.S.A., or rather it got five and a half million, because the intermediary, Bolo Pacha, a Marseille businessman, kept the rest as his commission. The editor of *Le Journal* was tried but narrowly acquitted by a majority vote; the owner of the paper—Pierre Lenoir,

[1] A. Raffalovitch, *L'Abominable vénalité de la presse, d'après les documents des archives russes 1897–1917* (1931), vii–xvi, 28, 38–9, 57–8, 64, etc.

playboy son of the leading advertising agent of the previous generation, Alphonse Lenoir—was convicted and executed, as too was Bolo Pacha. The left-wing *Bonnet rouge*, which had a daily sale of around 50,000, had before the war been encouraged in its pacifist line by regular subsidies from Caillaux. In 1916 it accepted money from the union of manufacturers of alcoholic drinks to assist its campaign against the temperance leagues; it got a further 45,000 francs from Cinzano, 60,000 francs from Martini-Rossi and 200,000 francs from other similar firms. Its editor, Almereyda, either committed suicide or died of drug addiction; its manager, Duval, who had received subsidies from the German ambassador in Switzerland, was executed for treason. It is by no means clear that the Germans got much in exchange for their bribes; one could claim that the newspapers simply used them as a milch-cow; but secret subsidies came to be regarded by all except a very few papers as a normal source of revenue. Between the two world wars several newly created countries were added to the list of the major powers which continued as benefactors of the French press.

The French government, far from disapproving of this bribery, took an active part in it, in the hope of deriving short-term political advantages itself. There had always been pro-government papers which owed their existence to ministerial benevolence: secret funds were always available to help a few newspapers; prefects had the power to give their favourite the monopoly of official advertisements; and individual ministers had often had their own papers to support them. Grévy had *La Paix*, Freycinet *Le Télégraphe*, Jules Ferry *L'Estafette*; Waldeck-Rousseau, who was rich, spent, just in the years 1882–4, no less than 135,000 francs on *La Réforme de Paris* and *L'Opinion*. Governments always wanted the news presented in a way that suited them and the press kept up the illusion that it was doing them a favour by publishing it. Ministerial press offices began to appear in a rudimentary form in the 1920s, but the idea of favouritism in the distribution of news remained, so that in the 1930s it was a regular practice for the main ministries to give the journalists they dealt with monthly 'envelopes'. The journalists became unofficial civil servants— but they also got 'envelopes' from banks and businesses. Jean Luchaire, editor of *Notre temps* (founded in 1927), said in 1946 at his trial for collaboration with the Germans: 'Before the war political newspapers and journals could not exist without subsidies. They had the choice of getting them from abroad, or from capitalist firms. The source that was least bad was the state.' He gave details of the sums he had received from a whole succession of French foreign ministers, which he combined with a regular income from the Germans, who, in addition, bought 4,000 copies of each issue. Blum in 1936 created a special department to consolidate and control the allocation of state advertising: this naturally went mainly to sympathetic papers, but not entirely. Some newspapers were set up simply to collect subsidies from anyone willing to pay, and the way to attract attention was to wage violent campaigns against likely benefactors. It is surprising what totally insignificant papers, with tiny circulations, were able to pick up by this method. It was the same method that non-political papers, as for example *Gil Blas* (founded 1879), used against prostitutes, gambling houses and men of fashion: Maupassant, who worked on this journal, which was at once scurrilous and served by famous literary figures, left a fictionalised account of it in his novel *Bel-Ami*.[1]

A more vigorous advertising industry might perhaps have saved the French press from this corruption, even if it created other problems, but there was a rival to the press which needs to be mentioned briefly, because it took a lot of advertising income which might otherwise have gone to the press. This was the poster, in which the French claimed to lead the world. Certainly advertising agencies tended to recommend posters in preference to press announcements, because they were much cheaper and lasted longer. Newspapers themselves, after all, were often posted up on walls before they became cheap enough for almost everyone to buy. In 1950 there were about 200 firms specialising in poster advertising, and controlling about two million square metres of hoardings on which to place them. Posters had the added attraction that they were often artistic. Perhaps the press should have shown itself more appreciative of the power of the artist.[2]

[1] Pierre Albert, in C. Bellanger *et al.*, *Histoire générale de la presse française*, vol. 3 (1972), 249–50, 259–75, 380, 432, 435 n., 439–40, 487–9, 493, 496–509, 529.
[2] Pigier, *Cours pratique de publicité* (2nd edition, 1928), 33; B. de Plas and H. Verdier, *La Publicité* (1951), 11.

The Press Magnates

The press magnates were not all that different from the journalists. At first, they included successful journalists who turned out also to have great skill at financial manipulation, and Girardin is the best example of one who was both a journalist and a newspaper tycoon. With time, it is true, they were increasingly financiers or industrialists who dabbled in journalism. The first example of this latter kind was Moïse (alias Polydore) Millaud. He was a man of great originality, in the sense that he was responsible for the major change which took place in the character of the press during the Second Empire: the foundation of a newspaper which was sold not to subscribers but on a daily basis and at a lower price—5 centimes, equivalent to an English halfpenny—than any paper in the world had yet reached. Millaud was a member of a group of Bordeaux Jews who were behind a whole series of radical changes carried out under the Second Empire. The Péreire brothers were the most famous of these, because their democratisation of banking, and their leadership in railway building, were combined with Saint-Simonian sympathies. Jules Mirès was another member of the group; though usually remembered as a speculator, because his schemes collapsed in the end, he had, as has been shown, a most important place in the history of advertising. Millaud, about whom personally little is known, was associated with Mirès in his advertising adventures, from which they had made eight million francs between them. Millaud then went on to establish *Le Petit Journal* (1863), a totally new kind of daily newspaper. It was specifically designed for the masses and not for those interested in politics. It would be non-political also because in this way it would not have to deposit any caution money (which could be as much as 50,000 francs), nor pay stamp duty (6 centimes a copy): it would be distributed not by post but by the paper's own criers, and Millaud employed 1,200 of these. It distinguished itself from other papers by starting out with no intention of influencing its readers, or of leading opinion: its editor, Henri Escoffier, was given the mission of 'expressing what everyone is thinking', and assured that he must be 'bold enough to appear stupid'. 'Do not try to impress, or to achieve *tours de force*,' Millaud told his reporters. 'You should spend your time in buses, in trains, in theatres, in the street. Find out what the average man is thinking. Then let yourself be guided by this. At the same time keep up with all the latest discoveries, all the latest inventions. Publicise all the knowledge that gets buried away in the serious "heavies" . . . Your job is to report what most men are thinking and to speak of everything as if you know far more about it than anybody else.' He invented 'Timothy Trimm' to give expression, in a personal way, to these banal opinions—daily articles, written at first by Leo Lespès, who said 'I teach things I know nothing about' and who became one of the highest-paid journalists in Paris. Millaud signed on Ponson du Terrail, and other famous novelists, to produce a daily serial, providing 'the excitement that the masses love'. He made sensationalism the criterion of what the paper included. He advertised his paper's stories with brilliant use of suspense, printing mysterious posters, for example, saying simply 'Monsieur Lecocq, who is this Monsieur Lecocq?'. Eventually a poster revealed: 'Monsieur Lecocq, the great, the brilliant, the famous, the learned Cop, Monsieur Lecocq, Monsieur Lecocq by Émile Gaboriau, the popular author. It is *Le Petit Journal* that will recount the exploits of Monsieur Lecocq.' This 'mouthpiece of all who work, save and progress, the supporter of all who seek to become capitalists but also the defender of existing property-owners', as it called itself, attained an unprecedented circulation of 582,000 in 1880, four times that of its nearest rival and more than a quarter of all the Paris dailies put together. Millaud, however, did not reap the rewards of his ingenuity. He died in 1871, leaving his firm heavily in debt to the printer Marinoni, who had invented the machines which provided the technical basis of this newspaper revolution. The heavy investment needed was not covered by the profits. *Le Petit Journal* was bought up, bankrupt, by a trio of newspaper magnates—Marinoni, Girardin and Jenty, owner of *La France*—who planned to expand into a giant press consortium, with provincial offshoots.[1] Concentration of newspaper ownership was, however, very slow to come to France. Agreements between the major dailies were attempted from 1916 onwards, but they were repeatedly

[1] Michael B. Palmer, 'Some Aspects of the French Press 1860-90' (Oxford D.Phil. thesis, 1973), 78–128, shortly to be published.

broken. Monopolies were achieved only in the news agency (Havas) and distribution (Hachette) sides of the business.

No single paper was ever able to obtain a dominant position. One of the characteristics of journalism was that papers existed in rival pairs almost from necessity, like political parties for whom an enemy was as important as a programme. At the turn of the century there were still fifty dailies in Paris alone, though five-sixths of their total circulation was provided by five major papers. *Le Petit Journal*, abandoning its political neutrality and becoming fiercely polemical under Ernest Judet, found its rival in *Le Petit Parisien*. This latter paper has been the subject of a doctoral thesis which has made public a wealth of detail about the profitability and management of newspapers, which is quite unique in French press history. The reason this has come about is that the paper, the property of the Dupuy family, was closed down in 1944, accused of collaboration; it was bought up by Émile Amaury, a former advertising tycoon, who owns *Le Parisien libéré*. Normally, newspaper archives are either lost with every change of ownership or concealed from historians by the descendants of their proprietors, for fear of scandalous revelations. In this case, however, Amaury had nothing to lose by allowing his daughter—but no one else—to use the archives he bought, to obtain her doctorate. She has shown that between 1880 and 1914 *Le Petit Parisien* distributed sixty-eight million francs to its shareholders, and a declining but not negligible amount thereafter, as the difficulties of the Paris press increased.[1] From 1909 Charles Dupuy owned 53 per cent of the shares, but he had already obtained a stake in the paper in the early 1880s. Charles Dupuy, in contrast to Millaud, had very little originality about him; he repeated and developed the methods of *Le Petit Journal* and he was very handsomely rewarded for his perseverance, but personally he was a singularly unmemorable character. He was prime minister of France but has been totally forgotten. He was one of those hard-working, self-made businessmen who helped the Third Republic to appear to be a meritocracy, but who, by founding a vigorous dynasty of plutocrats,

[1] 41 m. francs 1929–27, 49 m. 1928–32, no profits distributed 1936–44. Dividends accounted for 80·5 per cent of profits, the rest being reinvested. Profits represented 30 per cent on turnover 1890–1900, and 23–30 per cent in 1914.

gave the lie to its pretence that it was democratic. Dupuy was descended from a line of humble serge weavers; his father was a well-to-do village shopkeeper; he himself married the daughter of an artisan. He began life as a solicitor's clerk, rose to be a tipstaff (*huissier*), made so many contacts that his firm became one of the most successful in Paris, with 25,000 cases a year; finally in 1882 he abandoned law and became a 'business consultant'. So when *Le Petit Parisien*, founded in 1876 by a radical politician, and soon on the verge of bankruptcy, came to him for advice he was able first to arrange a banker's loan, and then to offer it accommodation in a building which his mortgage work placed at his disposal. In this way he became its principal shareholder, though he only gradually obtained a majority holding. The profits came in quickly however; he bought a château; he got himself elected as a senator. With Lourdes in his constituency, he had to play a careful role between defending the rights of pilgrims and supporting the republicans' anticlericalism. In his paper, he similarly succeeded in offending as few people as possible: that was essential to achieve a mass circulation. *Le Petit Parisien* had a sale of 1,453,000 in 1914 and in 1916 had the largest sale hitherto reached in any country: 2,183,000. It played down the Panama scandal, was prudently reserved about the Dreyfus Affair, approved the republic's foreign policy, and was always a reliable supporter of the establishment. It saw itself as unifying the country. 'To read one's newspaper', it declared in an editorial on 13 October 1893, 'is to live the universal life, the life of the whole capital, of all the town, of all France, the life of all nations . . . The worker, with the earnings of a few minutes [for the paper cost only a *sou*] buys his paper, and he sees all, and he knows all: his mind surveys the whole universe. It is thus that in a great country like France, the same thought, at one and the same time, animates the whole population . . . It is the newspaper which establishes this sublime communion of souls across distances . . . It is *par excellence* the instrument of discussion from which enlightenment emerges . . . It teaches men to reflect and to judge.' In fact, though its success was founded on an impressive distribution network—which rose from 330 sales depots in 1881 to 23,000 in 1939, and which gave wholesalers a discount of 30 per cent, and sellers 20 per cent, buying back unsold copies—it failed to penetrate into either the extreme east or west of France, or into the south. In 1921 40 per cent of its sales were bought within fifty kilometres of Paris. It was unable to meet the challenge of the rising provincial dailies and in vain tried to set up a regional offshoot in the west: its *Ouest-Journal* (1931) lost seven million francs and had to close down in 1936. As a result, in the inter-war period, its circulation fell from one and a half million to half a million. On Charles Dupuy's death, the control of the paper passed to his son Jacques-Paul Dupuy, who succeeded him also as a senator for the Hautes-Pyrénées, while sharing ownership with his other children, Pierre Dupuy, deputy for the Gironde, and Marie, who married François Arago, vice-president of the Chamber of Deputies. This family illustrates well the interconnections of politics, money and the press. But its income was derived from newspaper selling in the strictest sense. Advertising revenue accounted for only between 7 and 10 per cent of profits before 1914, and never more than 25 per cent (1928). *Le Petit Parisien* was a family business which steered clear of involvements with other financial interests; it manufactured its own paper; it did not farm out its advertising columns; it made minimal use of Hachette's distribution service. What distinguished it was its exceptionally sound commercial sense. In 1925, it was the first paper to establish a radio station: it was always alive to the opportunities around it. Perhaps the one important mistake it made was to take its cult of independence too far, rejecting co-operation with the other Paris dailies, so that they all, by their rivalry, destroyed themselves.[1]

A rather different approach to newspaper ownership can be illustrated from the case of *Le Matin*. This was founded in 1884 by an American, Sam Chamberlain, backed by two English financiers; but it was rapidly sold to Alfred Edwards, the son of a rich Levantine, who pretended to be English, though he had a French passport. Edwards was quite genuinely a journalist, who had tried to make *Le Matin* essentially a *news*paper. He had

[1] Francine Amaury, *Histoire du plus grand quotidien de la troisième république: Le Petit Parisien 1876–1944* (1972), 271–2, 366, 511, 1326, a very rich source of information; Micheline Dupuy, *Un Homme, un journal: Jean Dupuy 1844–1919* (1959), a more personal, much briefer biography.

leaders written in turn by politicians from different parties. But he used the paper above all as an instrument of blackmail, making much more money from this activity than from the proceeds of sales. He collected 200,000 francs from the Panama Canal Company, but then he got tired of the game and sold to a banker and advertising agent, Henry Poidatz, and another profiteer of Panama, Maurice Bunau-Varilla (1897). Bunau-Varilla, who ran *Le Matin* for forty-five years, was one of the most remarkable personalities of the French press. He was an Auvergnat, originally called Varillat, but he had changed his name to make it sound more exotic and vaguely South American. He was an actor taken in by the role he assumed. Having made a fortune by dubious means, he longed to be considered the disinterested defender of noble causes, the benefactor of his country—to purge the magistracy of corruption, to speed up the slow bureaucracy, to clear the streets of orange peel, to purify milk, to eliminate pornography from the theatre—and he could never see the hypocrisy that underlay the press campaigns he was constantly waging. He was an acute businessman: he increased the circulation of *Le Matin* more than tenfold, raising it to 1,610,000 copies in 1916 and keeping it at around a million for several years; but he wanted the credit for himself. 'What the state cannot do, *Le Matin* can,' he said. His conceit verged on megalomania. He treated his journalists like servants, paying them very well, but demanding obsequious obedience to his every command: he made them write under pseudonyms to prevent their having any false notions about their importance. 'At *Le Matin*', he told them, 'there are no journalists, only employees.' One of these employees, F. I. Mouthon, has left a vivid description of their relationship. Mouthon joined the paper as a greenhorn graduate of the Catholic faculty of Lyon, an enthusiastic Christian socialist, happy to accept a low starting wage because he saw journalism as a cause. Bunau-Varilla summoned him to his office one day and said gravely 'The King of Belgium has committed suicide. (Pause) He has committed moral suicide. He has abandoned his wife and children to live in infamous concubinage. He has given himself up to trafficking in rubber, ivory and white slaves. This royal scandal can no longer be allowed to weigh on the conscience of Europe and it is the duty of *Le Matin*, the defender of all noble causes, to bring about its end.' Varilla, who had large shareholdings in the Belgian Congo, asked Mouthon to go and collect anything he could discover that might embarrass the king. They published 'The Memoirs of Leopold II which might be authentic'. Bunau-Varilla waged another of his 'moral' campaigns against absinthe: he called a public meeting of 5,000 scientists and sociologists to discuss this scourge but suddenly his campaign ceased. The reason was that the National Federation of Paris Wine Merchants replied by plastering the walls of the city with a counter-attack, and their own shops with posters saying 'Here *Le Matin* is no longer taken'. In four months *Le Matin* lost 95,000 readers. Bunau-Varilla relented and gave the wine sellers 25,000 francs in 'damages'. That interest group was too powerful for him, but it was very reluctantly that he acknowledged that anyone could stand in his way. Once one of his reporters extracted some correspondence from a house in which a crime had occurred and *Le Matin* published it. He and the reporter were prosecuted for theft of the correspondence. Bunau-Varilla asked the minister of justice to sack the officials responsible for the prosecution. The minister, Chaumié, refused. *Le Matin* waged a campaign against him. Chaumié sued it. It replied by sending reporters to collect all possible scandal against him, to discover whether a piano teacher in his constituency owed his Legion of Honour to the fact that he was a friend of Mme Chaumié; every case of favouritism, every female friend of Chaumié's was investigated; every juryman was visited. *Le Matin* published its discoveries in the name of morality, in the interests of eliminating corruption and favouritism. 'My paper', said Bunau-Varilla, 'is, one may say, without limits. What it wants, it accomplishes; and it never wants anything but good things, useful to the greatest number.' All the while, Bunau-Varilla was involved, together with his associate Poidatz, in several of the most shady speculations of his day. He represents the flamboyant, mad-dictator type of press magnate.[1]

Between the wars it was far less easy to make money out of newspapers, at least in Paris; and newspapers now tended to attract millionaires whose aim was not so much to increase their

[1] F. I. Mouthon, *De bluff au chantage. Les Grandes Campagnes du Matin. Comment on fait l'opinion en France* (n.d.).

wealth as to win power and influence. François Coty (1874–1934), born François Spoturno, had made an enormous fortune out of his perfumes, thanks largely to America's appreciation of them, but he formed the view that his destiny was to go much farther. In 1922 he bought *Le Figaro* and spent eighty-five millions on it over the next eleven years; he raised its circulation from 20,000 to 50,000, though by making it the organ of his personal opinions, he lost its traditional audience and sales sunk in 1932 to 10,000. At the same time, he subsidised half a dozen extremist papers, including the *Action française* (to which he gave over five million francs), Cassagnac's Bonapartist *Autorité* and *Le Flambeau*, the organ of the Croix de Feu. In 1926 he founded a new daily of his own, *L'Ami du peuple*. He fixed its price at about half that charged by other papers, so all the press turned against him; Havas refused to sell him news and Hachette to distribute his paper. Coty sued them and won ten million francs in damages. By 1930, *L'Ami du peuple* was printing one million copies, even though it was full of long articles of polemic, had few pictures and no serial novel. Coty was appealing to the small man, holding himself up as the enemy of the state, the capitalists and every possible bogy man. But he could not go on subsidising losses for ever, particularly after his divorce in 1929 forced him to settle 425 million francs on his former wife; his press empire had virtually collapsed by the time of his death in 1934. Coty's megalomania had increased with the years; because he was a Corsican, he claimed to be descended from the Bonapartes. He had bought himself a seat in the Senate, but his election having been declared invalid, he had borne the Republic a bitter grudge ever after; and the communists in particular were his *bête noire*. Never before, perhaps, had so many millions been spent on printing newspapers to satisfy the neuroses of a single individual.[1]

The inexorable grip of the capitalists on the press, even the left-wing press, was revealed in the disillusioning career of Henri Dumay. He was the man who organised two major left-wing publications, *Le Progrès civique* (1919), a serious weekly which he ran in co-operation with left-wing leaders like Ferdinand Buisson, the historian Alphonse Aulard and Pierre

[1] Alfred Kupferman, 'François Coty' (unpublished Paris thesis, 1965).

Renaudel, and *Le Quotidien* (1922), which had the distinction of being largely owned by its readers. But Henri Dumay was an advertising agent by profession. He had been in charge of publicity for Barnum's Circus in the U.S.A. and Buffalo Bill's tour of Europe; he had joined Dupuy's *Petit Parisien* and launched *Nos loisirs* for his group; but he then quarrelled with his employer, was sacked, extracted an enormous golden hand-shake and went into parliament instead (1919). *Le Progrès civique*, which he founded, was so successful (50,000 copies) that he decided to found his own daily, and he invited his readers to subscribe shares of 100 francs to raise the money for 'an honest paper for honest people'. Twenty-five thousand readers sent in between 200 and 500 francs each. *Le Quotidien*, thanks to the enthusiasm of its readers, was able to overcome the obstacles placed in its way by the consortium of the five main dailies and by Hachette's distribution network and by 1925 it had 385,000 readers. It became the main organ of the Cartel, in whose electoral victory of 1924 it was considered to have played an important part. The leading politicians of the left wrote for it and it became a political power to be reckoned with. But in 1927 it emerged that Dumay had tricked his readers: the shares held by him and his friends, worth 1,600,000 francs, had ten votes each, while those of ordinary shareholders, who had subscribed 9,900,000 francs, had only one each. Behind the democratic, co-operative façade, Dumay was master of the paper, and he had used it to extract (unknown to his readers, but in the typical traditions of advertising in this period) subsidies from the railways, the Gas Company and the Bank of France, to mitigate his attacks; he had farmed out his financial columns to an adventuress, Marthe Hanau, and kept a large commission for himself on the deal. When his financial empire collapsed, it all came out. Dumay had in addition secretly sold half his shares to a right-wing politician, the cognac distiller Hennessy; as his paper's circulation declined, he appealed for help to the very people he was attacking.[1] *Le Quotidien* ended up an organ of the right. *L'Œuvre* (1915), its principal radical rival, with a circulation of between 125,000 and 274,000, was also owned by Hennessy. The left wing indeed

---

[1] René de Livois, *Histoire de la presse française* (Lausanne, 1965), 2.463; and Albert in Bellanger, op. cit. 570–1.

had a great deal of difficulty in supporting a daily, and the socialists most of all. Their *Populaire* (1920) collapsed in 1924, was revived in 1927 but regularly made a loss, and the proportion of unsold copies sometimes reached 30 per cent. In the provinces, too, many obscure local journals were preferred to it by the faithful, for it was much more a doctrinal than a news paper. But that a political party could run a paper efficiently was shown by the Communists, who made a commercial success of *L'Humanité* (1904), raising its circulation to 300,000 in 1936 and even adding an evening paper, *Le Soir*, in 1937. A whole host of periodicals for women, children, peasants, etc. made the communist press a counterpart to that of the Catholics—all with the minimum of advertising.[1]

The most successful press magnate was probably the only one who liked journalism for its own sake, as a profession and a skill. Jean Prouvost (1885–   ) was a textile manufacturer. His grandfather had founded a wool-combing factory which became the largest in France. Prouvost expanded his inheritance by marrying a rich cousin, modernised his equipment with the proceeds of war compensation, modelling himself on American and British examples, and opening up subsidiaries in New York and Czechoslovakia. But though he successfully transformed his business into one of international importance he had since boyhood longed to be a journalist, and in the U.S.A. he admired above all the press magnates. The key to his success in journalism was that he had no axe to grind, and no professional training to fix him in any tradition: he always took the viewpoint of the reader, stressing the market above all. His main idea was that 'a newspaper must do all it can to obtain the largest possible circulation. Once it has this, no one can do anything against it, because it has the power. Advertisers will be obliged in the end, despite boycotts, to bring it their advertisements, whatever price it asks. Then, its investment will be paid off and profits could be considerable.' This straightforward commercial approach, with no illusions about educational missions or political apostolates, was rare at this level. No one would believe that he had no ulterior purpose, and they wondered what game he was playing when he refused

[1] Claude Estier, *La Gauche hebdomadaire 1914–62* (1962); 'Les Problèmes financiers de *l'Humanité* 1920–39', *Revue d'histoire moderne et contemporaine* (Oct. 1973).

subsidies from foreign embassies and decorations from the government. His purpose was to sell a new product, for which he was sure there was a demand: 'people are no longer content to know, they want to see'. *Paris Soir* came out in 1931 with no less than nine photographs on its front page alone. The stress on pictures was combined with exceptional coverage of sport, a final edition with two extra pages of horseracing results, easily inserted and numerous small advertisements and a daily horoscope. But it combined its gift for sensational reporting with serious articles by famous people; its staff included not only Pierre Lazareff, who had entered journalism at fourteen and who was a master of the popular style, and not only the crime reporter Georges Simenon, but also graduates of the École Normale, like the historian Georges Perreux. It saw the commercial advantages to be derived from independence, when the rest of the press was largely corrupt. By 1939 it had a sale of 1,800,000, which was more than the two leading Paris morning dailies put together; and its success was multiplied by the magazine *Match* (1938), modelled on the American *Life*, which had a sale of 1,400,000 within a year, and *Marie-Claire* (1937), for women, which sold a million. It had all the capital it needed thanks to the backing not only of Prouvost's own fortune, but also the Beghin sugar and paper firm. Jean Prouvost became minister of information in 1940.[1]

It is inevitable that the press magnates of Paris should be most famous, but to concentrate on them is to form a distorted picture of the French press in general. For the provincial press was extremely active; in terms of readership, provincial dailies already had in 1939 as many readers as the Paris dailies; but the variety of provincial papers was so great that, apart from a few local monographs, historians have been unable to get far beyond compiling long catalogues, and doing that has proved difficult enough. In 1884 there were in the provinces 258 dailies, 363 papers which appeared two, three or four times a week and 601 weekly journals. In 1914 there were still 240 dailies; in 1938 there were 175 dailies and 1,160 weekly or semi-weeklies.[2]

[1] Raymond Barrillon, *Le Cas Paris-Soir* (1959); Pierre Lazareff, *Dernière édition* (n.d., memoirs published in New York during the 1939–45 war).
[2] The readership of the provincial daily press was in 1868 25 per cent of the

Local papers were originally essentially advertising sheets; they could be profitable even with small circulations, and so they expanded to accommodate the ambitions of local printers, politicians and men of letters. They thrived on local gossip, on the reporting of local events and the announcement of property sales—all of which were extremely popular; and they enabled men with a relatively small amount of capital to acquire local importance. Almost every member of parliament, actual or prospective, thought he needed a local paper in order to succeed, and some papers were little more than electoral posters. Thus the department of Pas-de-Calais, with a population of one million, had 692 local papers between 1865 and 1944. Two-thirds of these lasted less than two years, but there were times when it had seventy papers existing simultaneously. Every interest liked to have one, so that there was even a *British Continental Mercury* for the British colony and a *Narodowiec* for the Poles.[1] Local pride kept some periodicals going, in small towns, with circulations of well under a thousand, sometimes even only 300. But some local papers blossomed to become successful and influential on a regional scale. The Catholic *Ouest-Éclair* (Rennes) and the radical *Dépêche de Toulouse* are perhaps the best known, but in 1939 there were nineteen regional daily papers with circulations of over 100,000 copies each.[2] These papers became the focus of local political life and controversy, and the slanging matches between rival ones in the same town were an endless source of entertainment and anxiety. But one must distinguish between the small town paper, which had to be very careful not to offend anyone and to record every celebration, and the political rag, which was designed to be just that, an incitement to frenzy, the local advertising weekly, which was essentially a money-spinner, and finally the regional dailies, which won their popularity by

total readership of French dailies, 35 per cent in 1914, 50 per cent in 1939, 62 per cent in 1969—Pierre Albert, *Documents pour l'histoire de la presse de province dans la seconde moitié du 19ᵉ siècle* (roneoed, n.d., about 1973), 3.

[1] G. Bellard, *Pas-de-Calais: Bibliographie de la presse française politique et d'information générale 1865–1944* (1968). This is volume 62 of a series, published by the Bibliothèque Nationale, each volume covering one department.

[2] The other major ones were *La Petite Gironde* (Bordeaux), *L'Écho du Nord* (Lille), *Le Progrès de Lyon*, *Le Réveil du Nord* (Lille), *Le Petit Dauphinois* (Grenoble), all selling over 200,000 copies a day. For a list, see Albert in Bellanger, op. cit. 604–5. Henri Lerner is writing a thesis on the *Dépêche de Toulouse*.

doing what the Paris mass circulation dailies did, providing sensational news, but adding the local news too—a combination that proved irresistible.[1]

However, the variety of French newspapers concealed a common source of information, particularly for foreign news. The Havas News Agency made it possible for these newspapers to survive. As Balzac said, 'Every paper places its own colour, white, green, red or blue, on the news that is sent to it by Monsieur Havas, Jack of all trades to the press. [From the point of view of foreign news] there is only one newspaper, written by him, and all newspapers draw from its source.' In 1832 Havas, a former newspaper owner and son of a government book censor, founded an agency which summarised the news taken from foreign papers. By 1852 Havas had 200 subscribers among provincial newspapers. In the course of the Second Empire he made agreements with similar agencies in other countries (notably Reuter in England and Wolff in Germany), and later with Associated Press, for a mutual exchange of news, which made it possible for them to share the world between them, with Havas covering South America, the Balkans and the French Empire. Havas was not the only news agency in France, and Reuter's rivals, Dalziel, established an agency in Paris in 1891 which, in alliance with some right-wing papers, for a time posed a serious threat. Havas had well-established connections with all the French ministries, which provided it with news in return for giving publicity to information the government wanted to make known. At the turn of the century, Havas was able to provide a provincial newspaper with 1,760 lines of text daily for an annual subscription of around 10,000 francs. Foreign news was something French newspapers were for long weak on; they depended on occasional articles, and selected

[1] Raymond Manevy, *L'Évolution des formules de présentation de la presse quotidienne* (1956). The classic on the local press is Jacques Kayser, *La Presse de province sous la troisième république* (1958). On the non-political press, see N. Fourgeaud-Lagrèze, *La Petite Presse en province* (Ribérac, 1869). For a general survey, André Demaison, *Lex Voix de la France. La Presse de province au 20ᵉ siècle* (1932). For examples, see Paul Mansire, 'La Presse en Seine-Inférieure sous la troisième république 1871 à 1939', in *Études de presse* (1955), no. 12, vol. 7, which describes the *Dépêche de Rouen*, for which Alain wrote. It had a circulation of only 25,000, as compared with the 75,000 of the *Journal de Rouen*. Also André Parrain, *La Presse dans le Puy-de-Dôme de 1870 à 1914* (Clermont-Ferrand, 1972).

their news arbitrarily. Some newspapers made a speciality of it, and the obscure *Messager du Midi* of Montpellier, for example, was very well informed about Italian affairs in the 1859 war. *Le Temps* had some notable foreign correspondents, like Clemenceau, Louis Blanc and André Tardieu. *Le Matin*, under Edwards, gave a new stimulus to interest in foreign news. Havas was able to benefit from this and his became a highly profitable business. The family was bought out in 1879 for seven million francs, by a group of forty subscribers, mainly bankers. The agency's prosperity increased steadily until the 1914 war, but after that, because of increasing costs, it was kept going largely by its advertising side, and eventually it could no longer pay its way: Radio Luxembourg, which it owned, was still too insignificant to make good the loss. In 1938 the French foreign office gave it a subsidy; in 1940 its news service was nationalised as the Office Français d'Information, and so it continued to turn out its 40,000 words a day. After the war, it was succeeded by the Agence France-Presse, founded as a rival during the Resistance; in 1957 the problem of monopoly was at last resolved by placing this agency under the management of a board representing the country's newspaper editors.[1]

But there was a slightly different ending to the story of the other great monopoly behind the French press, the Messageries Hachette, the French equivalent of England's W. H. Smith. Hachette had obtained the exclusive right to open kiosks to sell books and newspapers on railway stations in 1852–5 and it kept the concession, except for a partial interruption in 1896–1905, until the Second World War. The business took some time to get established, and the kiosks were at first staffed by the wives or widows of railway employees, but as from 1865 newspapers became more important than books, in terms of turnover. The number of stalls reached 442 in 1874 and around 1,100 at the turn of the century, when newspaper sales accounted for about four-fifths of their business. There were a few newspapers which avoided using Hachette's services, but it required enormous resources to do so, and Hachette was in a position to place serious obstacles in the way of new papers which threatened the equilibrium it supported. The war of 1939–45

[1] Pierre Frédérix, *Un Siècle de chasse aux nouvelles. De l'Agence d'Information Havas à l'Agence France-Presse 1935–1957* (1959).

put an end to its stranglehold: in 1947 a new distribution system was set up, in which a co-operative of all newspapers had a 51 per cent shareholding, and Hachette 49 per cent. But Hachette has compensated by not only expanding its book-publishing activities, but also by buying control of several major newspapers and journals, from *France-Soir* to *Mickey* and *Elle*. It remains a major force in the newspaper world.[1]

Newspaper Readers

The final force in the making of the press was the reader, first because newspapers often claimed to be speaking on behalf of public opinion, and to be reflecting their readers' wishes, and secondly because the frantic competition to increase sales meant that the reader's demands had to be discovered and met. However, what readers thought is, and was, very difficult to ascertain. Only very general ideas are possible, for example, as to who these readers were: no paper seemed to have any accurate analysis of its readership. Not all sections of the community were newspaper readers. In 1858, the Paris dailies sold only about 235,000 copies; newspapers, at that date, were clearly still an interest of a small minority. By 1870 the rapid expansion of popular dailies raised the sales figure to one million, and by 1880 to two million. In 1910 the figure was up to five million and in 1939 to six million. To this one should add the provincial press. In 1868, the provincial political papers had 343,700 subscribers—though many of these papers appeared only twice or three times a week; they reached one million by about 1885, four million by 1914 and six million by 1939. So in 1939 there was a total sale of twelve million copies. Since the war, this total figure has remained roughly constant, the only change being that the provincial press has made headway against the Paris press and captured two-thirds instead of half the sales. This means that the French read far less newspapers than many other countries, indeed only half the number of papers the British read. In 1956, UNESCO's statistics placed France twenty-third in world rank for the number of copies sold per head of population.

---

[1] Jean Mistler, *La Libraire Hachette de 1826 à nos jours* (1964).

Comparative Newspaper Sales 1956

	Number of dailies	Total print copies (millions)	Copies per 1,000 inhabitants
Great Britain	114	29·1	570
U.S.A.	1,765	55	339
France	137	10·6	246
West Germany	598	12·5	254
Italy	107	5	107

In 1955, 75 per cent of the population of France (or at least of a representative sample) said they read a paper every day, and only 12 per cent said they never read one. But 24 per cent of people over sixty-five never read a daily paper, nor did 17 per cent of peasants, nor 15 per cent of people in small towns with under 5,000 inhabitants. In one province, only 51 per cent of agricultural labourers read a paper daily, as compared with 90 per cent of members of the liberal professions. Twice as many women as men did not read papers. It is clear therefore that newspapers have been a predominantly urban and masculine interest. This comes out strikingly in the way people answered the question of how far they felt deprived by the disappearance of newspapers as a result of a strike for a month in 1947. Fifty-seven per cent replied that they felt no deprivation, but their answers differed markedly according to the size of the towns in which they lived. Only 32 per cent of Parisians felt no deprivation: the figures rose steadily as the size of town fell, reaching 78 per cent in villages of under 2,000 inhabitants.[1] It is probable that the majority of the peasantry did not read papers regularly till after the First World War.[2] A more detailed and carefully phrased questionnaire revealed in 1965 that only 53 per cent of those questioned had read all the last six issues of the paper they regularly took. This finding needs to be balanced against the fact that newspapers were passed around: 23 per cent said they gave their newspaper to someone else, outside the family.[3] On the other

[1] No deprivation: Paris 32%; but 44% in cities over 100,000; 46% in towns of 40,000–100,000; 52% in towns of 20,000–40,000; 64% in towns of 2,000–20,000 and 78% in villages of under 2,000.

[2] *Sondages. Revue française de l'opinion publique* (1955), n. 3, 'La Presse, le public et l'opinion', 31–3.

[3] Groupement des grands régionaux, *Enquête par sondage sur l'audience de dix grands quotidiens régionaux* (1965), 29.

hand, newspapers were clearly not read with uniform attention: on average people spent thirty-eight minutes a day on their papers in 1947, about an hour in 1949 and 1954, about fifty minutes in 1965. Nor did all subjects attract the attention of readers. The earliest sociological investigation of readers' interests, made by the *Petit Parisien* in 1938, showed that its readers looked at the illustrations first (68 per cent); 65 per cent said they were most interested by the *faits divers* (human interest stories) and pictures, 55 per cent by general news, 37 per cent by the serial novel, 27 per cent by the *contes*, and only a tiny fraction by politics. In the north and in Normandy, the serial novel came unashamedly at the top of the list.[1]

It is not clear, indeed, just how important a part newspapers played in disseminating news: the generalisation that they made democracy possible by educating the country politically, and spreading the message of the politicians, needs qualification. Some people no doubt did absorb what they read about Paris politics, but when in 1954 the sample of newspaper readers were asked how they heard of the fall of Mendès France from power, only 20 per cent said they got it from the newspapers: 28 per cent said from conversation and 49 per cent from the radio. The role of gossip and the café may well have been larger before the age of the radio. It is certainly significant that when this sample was asked what they thought was wrong with the press, the criticism which was voiced most frequently was that newspapers had too many pages. The inquiry of 1965 is most instructive about how different sections of the population responded to the varied content of newspapers. This was a survey carried out in the provinces, to determine the character of the readers of regional newspapers, but by that time of course there were more of these than Parisian papers. It showed the following order of priorities in what interested readers most:

Local news	86%
News of France and the world	62
Comic strips	39
Radio programme timetables	34
Small advertisements	33
Local sport	31
Women's page	30

[1] Francine Amaury, *Le Petit Parisien 1876–1944* (1972), 1.290.

National sport	29%
Serial novel	23
Social, economic and financial	19
Agricultural news	18
Horse-racing	15
Travel	14
Camping	7

There was a surprising uniformity in these answers as between the different regions—except that, among the readers of the *Dernières Nouvelles d'Alsace*, 67 per cent were most interested by the small ads. and only 7 per cent in horse-racing. But men and women differed very much in their attitude to sport— 50 per cent of men were interested but only 10 per cent of women. The serial was read by twice as many women as men, while horse-racing interested 21 per cent of men but only 10 per cent of women. Rural readers were less interested in national and international news (51 to 56 per cent) than were the upper classes and liberal professions (79 per cent). Peasants were less interested in sports than other classes; clerks and workers were very keen on horse-racing.

It was not easy for the press to satisfy the wishes of its readers, even if it could discover them accurately, because it had to reconcile those wishes with several other pressures—the desire of newspaper owners to further their own political ambitions, the need to win advertisers, the expense of buying news. Since one of the well-established rules of press management was that readers tended to remain loyal to their papers from habit, the scope for innovation was limited; new methods tended to be tried out by new papers, and they were not always universally copied even if they were successful. To satisfy the desire for illustrations, *Excelsior* (1910) was created, full of photographs (backed by the arms-dealer Basil Zaharoff), but it was not a great success; photographs were not exactly what the masses wanted and it was only later discovered that drawings were preferred—comic-strip cartoons. This suggested that the old *images d'Épinal* which had provided just this, and which used to be sold by pedlars, still had a faithful following: the old style had become outdated, it illustrated mainly old and traditional stories, so it came to be read mainly by children, but when revived as comic strips in newspapers, it was instantly popular, and it contributed considerably to the success of *Paris-Soir*. In 1974 the comic strip was even admitted into the sober pages of *Le Monde*, a paper which has no photographs at all. Behind the reader of popular newspapers, who tended to be regarded as the newly educated offspring of the Third Republic's schools, there clearly lurked the old superstitious peasant, who could always spare a copper for an almanac with frightening stories and prophecies of future catastrophes. But it was not a discovery of his ghoulish tastes that led the newspapers to devote so much space to crime stories, but rather a perpetuation of the tradition of obsession with the marvellous and the unusual, which the old almanacs had long catered for. The popular newspapers which began to develop their *faits divers* rubrics from the 1860s, took over from where the *canards* left off. The *canard* was a flysheet, much used in the first half of the century, to distribute sensational news; it told stories about visions of the Virgin, fantastic animals, national disasters, the ravages caused by passion, gambling and debauchery, the perils of travelling, the return of prodigal sons and missing persons, and every kind of crime. They were very much in the medieval tradition, appealing to the love of the marvellous. A typical title would be: *Horrible details of the misfortunes occasioned by rabid animals*. Journalists out of work used to invent these stories, for the *canard* was a way of printing money. One story, for example, about a woman shipwrecked in the Pacific, captured by a monster with whom she lived until rescued, published in 1849, was the subject of no less than fifty-two different editions. Larousse said the *canard* was designed to discover just how far the reader's credulity would stretch; but what was important about these stories was that they were interesting, rather than that they were true.[1] It became immediately clear that newspaper readers, beyond the small circles who were personally involved in politics and administration, were keener to have this kind of entertainment from the press, rather than an education in democracy. *Le Petit Journal* was able to boost its circulation by over 200,000 in a few weeks by giving predominant attention to the *affaire Tropmann*, involving sensational multiple murders. The selection of the news that was printed was, however, far from being an automatic process, in which

[1] J. P. Séguin, *Nouvelles à sensation. Canards du 19ᵉ siècle* (1959), 157.

journalists simply applied a formula.[1] There was roughly one suicide in France (in 1970) every hour, but it was the journalist who selected the very small number which were in fact reported. The attitude of local and national papers differed: the larger the circulation of a paper, the less did it matter where things happened, provided they were odd enough; and that is one reason why international news was for long so sketchy and arbitrary. But the local paper felt it had to concentrate on giving the news about people whom readers knew, even if there was very little new to report. Thus the *Sud-Ouest* of La Rochelle thought it proper to print this item: 'In the rue Grade, Monsieur X's car collided with Madame Y's dog. The dog was unhurt. The car sustained no damage.' The increasing popularity of the regional newspaper suggests that this kind of local news was highly valued. Simone de Beauvoir recalled how when she and Sartre were teachers in a provincial *lycée* 'we had few friends, almost no social life. It was partly to palliate this lack that we developed an ardent taste for the human-interest stories in the newspapers.' It was in the same way that she frequently bought *Detective* (founded 1928, circulation 250,000), a fiction magazine which had the added advantage that, in its early days at any rate, it made a practice of attacking the police and the establishment.[2] Newspapers, like novels, did not provide simply an aid to escapism, for they were also an aid to a different kind of participation in life. Politics was a means by which some people found a role for themselves in the world around them, but it did not appeal to every temperament: the newspaper provided, through its *faits divers*, both alternative subjects of conversation, of a less abstract or distant nature, and also opportunities for readers to exercise their imaginations and give vent to their emotions in less systematic ways than politics required.[3] They also helped to reconcile the contradictions which people's hypocrisy created. They worked on the assumption that people liked reading about vice, but that they were also ashamed of doing so: and the popular newspaper provided a combined package, which contained both vice and

---

[1] On the process by which news is selected, see Edward J. Epstein, *News from Nowhere* (New York, 1973).

[2] Simone de Beauvoir, *La Force de l'âge* (1960), 131.

[3] Georges Auclair, Le 'Mana' quotidien. Structures et fonctions des faits divers (1970), 33.

moralising united. Thus *Le Journal*, at the turn of the century, always adopted a puritan and austere tone: it was fond of lamenting that the world was going to the dogs; it complained, for example, that girls were no longer what they used to be, but had become 'flirtatious, brazen and easy-going to the point of impertinence, saying things which would make a monkey blush' (24 April 1895), but it simultaneously published short stories which were full of pornography, sexual perversion, adultery and violence.[1] *Le Journal* had literary pretensions and gave much space to literature, aiming to attract the middle classes, but though it never printed any manifestos saying so, it obviously believed that its readers both aspired to culture and were bored by it, that their cultural, intellectual life was only one side of them and that eroticism and sadism were in no way extinguished by this. That is why it also gave them plenty of xenophobia, nationalism, anti-Semitism and scandals. It seems that the press, as it gradually shed its concentration on politics, was accurately responding to a demand from its readers which obsession with politics had temporarily masked. These newspapers tried to be accurate reflections of the conflicting aspirations and anxieties of their readers.

In 1902, the distribution of space in newspapers as between different subjects was as follows.

	Paris newspapers	Provincial newspapers
Home news	13·05	19·55
Literature	9·95	14·35
Crime	8·80	8·75
Internal politics	7·15	5·75
Foreign news	8·35	4·35
Theatre and other 'spectacles'	6·45	2·55
Arts	4·50	2·95
Useful literature	3·90	4·0
Sports	3·20	2·80
Moral and charitable works	2·65	4·65
Science	1·85	2·0
Foreign politics	1·8	1·2
Travel	0·8	0·55
Advertisements (appearing as such)	23·9	27·95
,, (disguised)	3·6	1·1

[1] Patrick Dumont, *La Petite Bourgeoisie vue à travers les contes quotidiens du Journal 1894–5* (1973), 21.

These statistics[1] are averages, but as such they show that if the interests of readers at the turn of the century bore any relation to those which readers admitted to fifty years later, newspapers still gave readers what they did not want. The amount of space devoted to crime was in 1902: 670 lines daily in *Le Petit Parisien*, 500 in the *Figaro*, 310 in *Le Petit Journal*, 160 in *Le Matin* and 40 in *Le Temps*; 330 in *L'Écho du Nord* of Lille but only 75 in *La Dépêche de Toulouse*. By contrast, in 1937, *Paris-Soir* had established its fame by giving no less than 1,250 lines to crime; *Le Petit Parisien* had gone up to 1,110, *Le Petit Journal* to 775; most papers indeed had almost exactly doubled their ration. But papers were now 8,000 lines long as opposed to 3,200, so the proportion devoted to crime did not actually increase. It is wrong to talk of an increasing demoralisation of the public by the press. One should not contrast the popular press with the political press of the July Monarchy. The popular press was an industrialised version of the old almanacs and *canards*: if it did innovate, it was probably in the direction of forcing a lot of facts, of a new kind, down its readers' throats.

What did change somewhat was the freedom the press enjoyed. During the Second Empire, and indeed till 1881, political commentary had been strictly controlled, with a severity which was only slightly less than that of the *ancien régime*. But instead of employing censors to read papers before they were published, the Second Empire distributed punishment for wrongdoing after the event: the threat of this, combined with a system of official warnings and culminating in the closing down of the paper altogether, was fairly successful in restraining the press.[2] The prefects, who were the principal instruments of this repression, carried their censorship well beyond politics, in that criticism of any kind could be seen as a threat to the established order. Thus the prefect of the Côtes-du-Nord, for example, ruled that 'polemic about artificial fertilisers causes indecision among buyers' and he warned newspapers against exciting discontent in any form. As a journalist said on the publication of Renan's *Life of Jesus*: 'One can

[1] H. de Noussanne, *Ce que vaut la presse quotidienne française* (1902).
[2] For the history of press legislation, see Irene Collins, *Government and Newspaper Press in France 1814–81* (Oxford, 1959).

no longer attack anybody except Christ.' This was one reason why non-political journalism developed so rapidly in this period: whereas political papers had to give the government a large sum as caution money for their good behaviour, non-political papers were freer—and much comment on public life was therefore rephrased in allegorical or satirical language. The censors were always on the look-out for political references, as Victorien Sardou discovered in 1863 when in one of his plays he was unwise enough to insert a tirade against blonde women. Four censors summoned him to say that could not be allowed: did he not know that the empress was blonde. And, added another of them, so too was Madame Walewska (the emperor's cousin).[1]

The abolition of censorship in 1881 gave the press a free rein, almost untrammelled even by libel laws. The freedom was not total, for what really allowed anyone to say almost what he pleased was the feebleness of sanctions. Thus after 1881 there were still several kinds of offence journalists could commit. The law of libel, as far as private citizens were concerned, was far-reaching. The courts ruled that a report of a rumour that a certain mayor had wrongly allowed some people in his village to pay less taxes than they should have done was a libel (1884); they held it was libellous to accuse someone of sorcery (1909), or even to assert that a doctor held philosophical and religious opinions contrary to the beliefs of the majority of the inhabitants of his locality (1905). The law assumed that there was an intention to libel, unless the defendant proved the contrary. There were even more stringent rules about attacking members of the civil service or government—an offence known as *outrage*. It was an outrage to accuse these depositaries of authority of whistling (1903), of making obscene gestures, or to call the government a collection of bandits and the judges a group of thieves (1910). It was still seditious to shout 'Vive le roi' (1909), and anarchist propaganda was nominally forbidden by the law of 1894. It was possible for a newspaper to be prosecuted for spreading false news or corrupting morals, though the courts varied in their attitudes: in 1908 an advertisement of a brothel, under the guise of a massage parlour, was held to be innocent, but in 1928 it was not. However, all these

[1] Roger Bellet, *Presse et journalisme sous le Second Empire* (1967), 16.

threats held over the press were mitigated by three factors. First, the reluctance of juries to convict meant that prosecutions were infrequent, though libel litigation was far more active than is realised. Secondly, there was the right of reply, which was pre- ferred as a means of settling disputes. The law required news- papers to give persons it had mentioned the right of reply; and this reply must be published in the same place and in the same characters as the article which provoked it; though if the reply was longer than the original article, the writer of the reply had to pay for the extra space at advertisement rates. Civil servants had the 'right of rectification', and this right allowed them twice as much space as the libellous passage. However, thirdly, the theory of provocation modified this right. It was held that a person who stood for election to public office provoked criticism and so had less right to protection against libel: the divulging of defamatory facts about him, designed to enlighten the voters, was therefore legitimate. The question of whether this principle of provocation applied to literature was long controversial. Some held that the mere fact of publishing something invited people to criticise it and so literary or artistic criticism should not be liable to the right of reply. When in 1897 Jules Lemaitre wrote a totally damning review of a play by Dubout, a banker of Boulogne-sur-Mer, which had been put on at the Comédie-Française, the appeal court forced the *Revue des Deux Mondes* to publish Dubout's reply, arguing that whatever the principle of provocation, Lemaitre had written in 'a moment of malice' and that the play had in fact been enthusiastically applauded by the audience. Again, in 1923, when Dunoyer said in the *Revue universelle* that Nordmann's book on Einstein was a 'scandal' and its success 'incomprehensible', the court ordered the review to publish a reply, judging that Dunoyer had, in jealousy, gone beyond just criticism. All this meant that the papers could get away with a great deal, and if their victims pro- tested, that only served to add vivacity to the polemic.[1]

The extent of this liberty can be seen in the way the press dealt with crime. In France, as elsewhere, the reporter rose up as a rival to the policeman, searching for criminals, or missing

[1] Marcel Hoursiangou, *Le Journaliste en France. Conditions économiques et juridiques de son activité* (Bordeaux law thesis, 1936), 113–214.

persons, at least when there was a sensational aspect to the story; but in France the press was probably freer in its hostility to the police, and that added to its popularity. In the case of the *curé* of Châtenay, for example, who disappeared in 1905, the papers attacked the police violently for failing to find him; they cried murder, offered large rewards for information, and stimulated a shower of anonymous letters in which neighbours accused each other of the crime. In the end the poor *curé* was discovered in Brussels, where he had gone, as he hoped, to live in peace with his mistress. The fact that a case was *sub judice* seldom worried the press, which published full details of sensational trials and of relevant documents, even when the law forbade it. The *Figaro* in 1899, for example, illegally published full reports of the Dreyfus trial in the court of cassation: it was fined 500 francs, and it then continued to publish them. The press regularly revealed every intimate fact about accused persons, so that people wrongly accused nevertheless seldom escaped unscathed. It reported verdicts with approval or disapproval, passing its own sentence on the judge and on the accused. Judges and barristers quickly saw that it was necessary to keep on good terms with journalists, who distributed praise or blame to them, or were totally silent about them, in proportion to the amount of co-operation they received: journalists said they had no need to seek out information, they got it without asking; leaks were common; court officials allowed the press to look at their files; they were all on terms of *tutoiement*. A law of 1849 forbade the press to publish details of charges before the public trial; another forbade it to publish facts about private life (11 May 1868, article 11); but in vain. The press waged a war against the secret inquisitorial procedure of French law, in the name of the liberty of the press and of the individual, but without much success, and perhaps in the process it damaged the lives of many individuals whom it tried in its own columns. Its hypocrisy was revealed in the way it treated public executions, whose immorality it attacked, but to which it devoted a great deal of space. In 1909 scenes of appalling savagery occurred at an execution at Béthune, which the press had publicised, to which it sent an army of reporters, and which photographers captured for the cinema. On three successive days *Le Petit Journal* devoted seven columns on its front page and three on its second page to the execution, publishing eight photographs of it. The conclusion of a legal commentator on the relations of the press and the law was that 'the judiciary has been not only defeated in its duel with the press, but it has completely capitulated. The press reported almost exactly what it liked between 1881 and 1940 and prosecutions were rare.'[1]

Smaller Worlds

Books about the press have tended to be above all about the political press, but this gives a very incomplete view of the activities of journalists, the vast majority of whom were not political. In 1881, for example, 1,343 periodicals were published in Paris. Of these only seventy-one were political. A far larger number were financial (209), medical (97), general illustrated papers (88) or fashion magazines (81). These statistics give one a curious hierarchy of the interests of newspaper readers. During the next fifty years financial journals increased slightly in number, and it was only in 1930 that they were outnumbered by political journals (252 against 281).[2] The medical press more than doubled (236), so that it remained very important. Literature had remarkably few journals devoted exclusively to it: in 1881 only 30, in 1900 only 46, in 1930 73. But at the turn of the century an additional category of 'political and literary reviews' suddenly blossomed into importance: at these three dates there were respectively 46, 188, and 161 of these in Paris alone. What gave the impression of intense literary activity was the large number of little ephemeral literary reviews: from 1914 to 1939 no less than 269, which lasted for less than ten issues, are recorded.[3] By the 1930s there were more journals devoted to photography than to the fine arts, and almost four times as many devoted to sports. Though religion had been nominally defeated by the anticlericals, it still found

[1] Georges O. Junosza-Zdrojewski, *Le Crime et la presse* (1943).

[2] On the financial press, see above, page 521; and also J. Gascuel and R. Sedillot, *Comment lire un journal économique et financier* (1957, 2nd edition 1960), and Francine Batailler *et al.*, *Analyses de presse* (1963), part 3, 'Sociologie de lecteurs de la presse économique et financière', 177–232. These deal with the 1950s and 1960s; there is room for an interesting historical study of this subject.

[3] Richard L. Admussen, *Les Petites Revues littéraires 1914–1939. Répertoire descriptif* (St. Louis, Missouri, and Paris, 1970).

readers for its very numerous journals, with their own independent parochial distribution system. A rough list of the Parisian press, arranged by subject, may give an indication of the variety of preoccupations in the capital, which belie any generalisation about France as devoted to literature, or the arts, or free thought, or politics. (The list is illustrative rather than exhaustive; there are many difficulties in classifying newspapers.)

The Press in 1881, 1901 and 1930[1]

	Paris 1881	Paris 1901	Paris 1930	Provincial 1930
Politics	71	178	281	?
Political economy	3	40	85	11
Administration	28	35	65	2
Diplomacy	6	10	12	..
Colonial	..	46	71	6
Military	17	41	75	27
Naval	8	11	32	9
Literature	30	46	73	..
Literary and political reviews	46	188	161	28
Fine Arts	19	45	43	..
Photography	5	28	45	..
Music	14	37	46	2
Theatre	13	37	32	8
Architecture	26	14	31	3
Humour	..	26	34	7
Sports	21	46	219	45
Catholic	61	83	108	40
Protestant	24	22	30	22
Jewish	2	3	8	..
Freemason	..	4	?	..
Financial	209	219	252	15
Professional, industrial and commercial	?	?	243	..
Technology	38	..	..	..
Industry	27	44	67	20
Metallurgy	..	12	29	3
Mines	5	6	12	11
Petrol	..	..	8	..
Electricity and radio	..	..	56	..
Gas and electricity	..	25	..	..
Gas	..	..	7	..
Printing	..	14	20	..
Science	41	89	103	..
Sugar	..	3	4	..

[1] Based on the *Annuaire de la presse française* (1882, 1901 and 1930).

	Paris 1881	Paris 1901	Paris 1930	Provincial 1930
Motor cars and cycles	..	22	?	..
Textiles	..	9	8	6
Transport	..	..	25	..
Public works	..	23	34	2
Commerce	32	56	96	17
Agriculture	34	70	121	148
Insurance	18	25	35	..
Fashion	81	127	166	4
Feminist	?	17	18	..
Illustrated	88	130	109	33
Stenography	..	16	20	..
Medicine	97	219	236	26
Pharmacy	9	9	11	5
Jurisprudence	61	98	122	14
Education	38	50	85	7

The history of medical journalism shows how one section of
the country used the press to develop its sense of community.
It is a subject so extensive that it will require a whole team of
researchers to reveal its full variety and the richness of the
talents that expressed themselves through it. Doctors in
France were—as indeed they still are in most developing countries—intellectual leaders, whose contribution to man's view
of himself has never been adequately assessed; they were often
men with leisure, whose hobbies were more literary and artistic
than those of businessmen or landowners. The first French
newspaper was started by a doctor in 1631; the first French
medical journal followed soon after, in 1679, founded by
Nicolas de Blégny, a surgeon, who was also a seller of drugs,
author of books on venereal diseases, manager of a clinic and
of a bathing establishment, publisher of the Paris directory
which later became the *Bottin*, and, inevitably, an enemy of
the Paris faculty of medicine: he got his doctorate from the
faculty at Caen and collaborated with a graduate of Montpellier to produce the *Journal des nouvelles découvertes en médecine*.
By 1848 another eighty-one medical journals had been started
in Paris alone, to which one should add twelve more on popular
medicine, seventeen on magnetism, fourteen on specialised
branches of medicine, and thirty-two provincial journals. Between 1848 and 1867 another fifty-seven medical journals had

been founded.[1] In 1950 it was calculated that there were about 300 medical journals, excluding trade union organs and publications for private circulation.[2] Many journals originally began as a means of propagating the views of a particular doctor, famous or eccentric: thus the controversial Dr. Broussais (1772–1838) had his *Annales de la médecine physiologique*, which lasted from 1822 to 1884, and which, to begin with, published one of his faculty lectures each week. Daily medical newspapers were even founded, mainly by students. *La Lancette française*, founded in 1828 and renamed *La Gazette des hôpitaux* in 1850, appeared three times a week. The *Moniteur des hôpitaux* (1852–6) published the lectures of Claude Bernard, and to cater for Spanish students in Paris, there was even a *Gaceta medica clinica de los hospitales de Paris* (1850–4). Dr. Amédée Latour founded *L'Union médical* in 1845 as the first periodical designed to defend the pecuniary and professional interests of doctors. Some medical men had journalistic gifts and they were able to use them; Dr. Charles Bouchard, founder of *La Gazette hebdomadaire de médecine et de chirurgie* (1859), had a career which was as much journalistic as medical. Writing was often a consolation for obscure country doctors who had not won the fame they had dreamt of: as one wrote: 'Medical journals, when they are not the organ of a *camarilla*, fulfil a role which allows us to participate, even the least important among us, in the great movement of contemporary thought and scientific creation. They offer a *chair*, to which all may accede and from which they can make themselves heard. . . . They are thus a *compensatory chair* for those who will never enter any post, for those whom seem condemned to silence, even though their minds and hearts boil with activity.'[3] There was always room for doctors to produce humorous magazines, or journals devoted to gastronomy, and there was even a periodical devoted exclusively to advising doctors on investment in the stock-market—and it was said that its recommendations always produced a noticeable movement in share price.

[1] Dr. Achille Chéreau, *Essai sur les origines du journalisme médical français suivi de sa bibliographie* (1867).

[2] Marcel Lhopiteau, 'Contribution à l'histoire des journaux médicaux' (Paris medical thesis, 1950, unpublished, in the library of the Faculty of Medicine, Paris).

[3] *Bulletin mensuel de l'Association professionelle des journalistes médicaux français* (March 1932), 3.

As medicine became more specialised, an increasing number of journals appeared devoted to new sciences, like the *Archives d'opthalmologie* (1883), the *Revue neurologique* (1893), or *La Médecine infantile* (1894). These were very substantial publications, each issue being longer than an average book. The *Annales des maladies vénériennes* (1906) was 400 pages long in its first issue, but 950 pages by the 1930s. The development of the social services added a further crop, as too did colonial and military medicine, and even the history of medicine had four journals devoted to it.[1] This meant that an increasing number of doctors became involved in part-time editorial duties, and publication was a normal part of the professional lives of even more. The *Journal de pharmacie et de chimie* (1809), which was already producing over 1,100 pages a year, and 1,500 by 1910, had been founded quite humbly by a group of six people to help pharmacists 'perfect themselves in their art', which was necessary if 'they wanted to be distinguished by public esteem', but as the different branches of these sciences became more specialised, it needed twenty-one people to run it.[2] Many of these were professors, but an independent profession of medical journalists also arose, who formed their own association. In 1933 it had 114 members, but they were more powerful than this figure might suggest. At least, the pharmaceutical industry realised that they could have a considerable influence on the habits and expenditure of their contemporaries; and it accordingly gave regular subsidies to the medical journalists' pension fund, which was maintained very largely by these gifts, rather than by the subscriptions of the journalists themselves. The mineral-water firms of Vichy and Évian were also important benefactors. This made sure that the medical press was not unfriendly to them, or to new pharmaceutical products placed on the market.[3] It is clear that in medical journalism, as in all other forms of journalism, periodicals were sometimes started with the express intention of blackmailing manufacturers into adver-

[1] 'La Presse et l'édition médicale', special issue of *Le Courrier graphique* (Dec. 1938), especially 65–71.

[2] Émile Bourquelot, *Le Centenaire du Journal de pharmacie et de chimie 1809–1909* (1910), 24.

[3] *Bulletin mensuel de l'association professionelle des journalistes médicaux français* (there are copies of this rare publication, for 1932–5, in the library of the Faculty of Medicine, Paris).

tising in them. It became essential to collect an editorial board of distinguished practitioners to ensure that pharmaceutical firms and clinics dared not refuse to advertise in a new journal. Masson, which published about sixty medical journals, derived its strength partly from the advertising arrangements it was able to make. But there was no monopoly in this field. There was a great deal of local journalism by doctors, which survived on a strictly provincial readership. Thus Montpellier—admittedly the most important medical faculty after Paris but still only a small town—had forty different medical journals in the period 1791–1958. The proceedings of the faculty were the basis of these, but individual professors published separate journals to publicise their lectures and their theories. In 1840 a *Gazette médicale de Montpellier* was founded, which lasted fifteen years, to attack the professors of the faculty, edited by a doctor who could not get a job in it. The *Gazette hebdomadaire des sciences médicales de Montpellier* (1879–92) was run by a group of local professors to defend the Montpellier brand of medicine against 'the threat of asphyxia caused by the foundation of new rival faculties'. The *Languedoc médical*, started in 1912, became the basis of a family business, passed from father to son, and complemented by *Le Journal des sages-femmes de la Provence* (1924–32). In the 1930s, Montpellier was still producing two medical journals and in 1952 a third was added.[1] This proliferation of literature naturally encouraged the establishment of still more journals to summarise it, so that doctors could keep up with new discoveries. From the 1870s, some periodicals made a point of trying to review foreign discoveries too, but with varying success. It is noteworthy that the major indexes to world-wide research in medicine are published in the U.S.A. and in Germany: there is no French one; and certain discoveries, like penicillin, took some time to be publicised in France.[2] The most successful journals for the popularisation of medical knowledge, perhaps because they were usually started by doctors who were more interested in commerce than in medicine, often repeated, year after year, the same old remedies. The *Journal de la santé* (1893), which

[1] Louis Dulieu, 'Le Journalisme médical montpellérien' in *Montpellier médical* (July–Aug. 1958), 3rd series, vol. 54, no. 1, 28–38.

[2] Lhopiteau, op. cit. 78.

claimed a weekly circulation of 35,000 copies, gave subscribers the right to fifty-two free consultations a year, but it was crammed mainly with advertising and indeed charged the highest advertising rates of any periodical. In 1929, by contrast, the *Droit de guérir* was started to 'defend the interests of the sick' against doctors; it managed to sell almost as many copies.[1]

Women's magazines form another important category about which very little is known. It is too early to say what role they played in shaping the interests and the outlook of women, but there can be no doubt that by the end of the nineteenth century, and even more in the course of the period 1930–60, they provided women with reading matter which consolidated their status as a separate caste. Already in 1774 the *Journal des dames* was complaining about the hard lot of the unmarried mother; and in 1832 the *Journal des femmes* was founded as a paper run and written exclusively by women, but feminism was the cause of a tiny minority and the successful women's papers were those which concerned themselves with women's more immediate preoccupations.[2] *La Mode illustrée*, founded in 1860, lasted till 1937 and contributed substantially to the profits of the printer Firmin Didot who owned it. He had the good fortune to find an editor of outstanding ability in Emmeline Raymond, the daughter of a Belgian officer in the service of Austria and of a French mother who had established a school in Romania. Such was Madame Raymond's success that when she retired in 1902, after forty-two years as editor, her successor adopted her name, to guarantee that continuity would be ensured. Madame Raymond was a writer of considerable talent who had firm opinions which she could state forcibly in clear and straightforward language. Her achievement was to make her journal a link between Paris and the middle and petty bourgeoisie of the provinces, in a way that made her readers imagine that she was their personal friend and adviser, as her voluminous correspondence testified. On her retirement, the journal invited readers to say why they read the paper and

---

[1] The *Annuaire de la presse française* gives curious details about the medical press and the advertisements it carries. Cf., e.g., *L'Actualité thérapeutique* (1890), distributed free, *La Semaine médicale* (1881), *Maman* (1929), etc.

[2] Evelyne Sullerot, *Histoire de la presse féminine en France des origines à 1848* (1966). Continuations of this work are still awaited.

their letters revealed that there were many women who had bought it regularly for thirty or forty years, keeping it in bound volumes on their shelves, treating it as a guide to the practical and even moral problems of life. The journal, as they saw it, preached that it was 'woman's mission to occupy herself with the material and moral well-being of others', to create a home that was always harmonious, gentle and pretty, to achieve this by strict economy, making as many as possible of the things needed in the home herself. From the start *La Mode illustrée* insisted that wealth and elegance were totally different, and that one did not have to be rich to be worthy of respect; it rejected fashions which were too 'operatic', and instead told readers how to remake their old dresses to bring them up to date. It offered them patterns to make their clothes from, detailed instructions on how to produce the thousand knick-nacks that the bourgeois household contained, but it was an 'enemy of all exaggerations'. One reader wrote appreciatively of its understanding that 'we want to dress not luxuriously but with good taste and simply, that is to say in conformity with the rank we occupy'. Another said its moral advice 'frightened and infuriated me', because Madame Raymond seemed 'to know me so well, and I recognised all my faults'. A third approved its ambition to make women see that 'excellence lies in *not* being dazzling or brilliant', and congratulated it on 'trying to make us humble and hard-working women'. But it was not a paper that talked down to its readers. Madame Raymond's numerous books contained a great deal of solid information, common sense and shrewd knowledge of the world. Advertising, of course, assumed an increasing role in the paper, but this also enabled it to double in size (to sixteen pages a week) and include articles on women's careers, child rearing and literature, as well as cooking and gardening, and at the turn of the century it sold 100,000 copies a week.[1]

The connection between the fashion magazines and the fashion industry has still to be investigated; the financial bases of the increasing number of titles remains obscure.[2]

[1] *La Mode illustrée* (see in particular the prospectus of 1860 and the special issue of 1902); *Le Livre d'or de La Mode illustrée* (1904); Mme Emmeline Raymond, *Autobiographie d'une inconnue* (1888).

[2] Henriette Vanier, *La Mode et ses métiers. Frivolité et luttes de classes 1830–70* (1960) is mainly about the clothing industry and its workers. Cf. *Les Dessous*

There were a few publishing firms which seemed to specialise in the market from an early date, like that owned by François Tedesco, who published *La Femme chez elle, Journal des ouvrages des dames, Mademoiselle, Ma poupée, Mon aiguille*; or that of the Catholic senator Huon de Penanster, who bought *Le Petit Écho de la mode* in 1879, when it was selling 5,000 copies, raised its circulation to over 100,000 by 1893, and up to a million by 1923, so founding the prosperity of his family, which still owned this paper in the 1960s. However, the expansion of the mass-circulation women's magazine (in which Cino del Duca's publishing group is now supreme) came only in the 1950s, though the basis for it had been laid between the wars by a few outstandingly successful magazines. Most of them were, significantly, Catholic. *Marie-Claire* (1937) was edited by Marcelle Auclair, who had been educated in a South American convent; *Confidences*, which reached half a million copies within a year of its launching, was based on letters from readers, as though it was supplementing or replacing the confessional.[1]

Children's magazines were also numerous, starting as early as the 1830s. They were given a great impetus by the publishers Hachette and Hetzel under Napoleon III, with Jules Verne as an outstanding contributor; they were modernised first under the influence of *L'Épatant* (1908) and then with *Le Journal de Mickey* (1937) which popularised the comic. These magazines were, however, read very largely by the middle classes, and they reflected the values and morals of the middle classes. In 1958, 38 per cent of children's papers were still published by political, religious or educational institutions. As a result, their commercial efficiency was not great; *La Semaine de Suzette* regularly had around half its print left unsold, and even *Mickey* had 18 per cent unsold. This meant, also, that the ownership of the children's press was less concentrated than, for example, in England. In 1970 the weekly sale of children's papers in France was only two million, whereas in England, with roughly an equal population, it was nine and a half million.[2] It seems

élégants (founded 1901) as an example of a fashion magazine devoted entirely to corsets and underwear, and full of advertisements.

[1] Evelyne Sullerot, *La Presse féminine* (1963) is mainly an account of the 1950s.

[2] Dominique Prieur and Alain Chahin, 'La Presse enfantine en Grande Bretagne et en France. Étude économique' (unpublished D.E.S. mémoire, in the Faculty of Law Library, Paris, 1970).

likely that French children read the adult press more than papers written specially for them.[1] Children were being gradually turned into a distinct class, but though they were provided with a separate opium to keep their minds off the realities of the adult world, it is probable that it had little effect upon them.

The use of the press as a new advertising instrument by industry can be seen most clearly from the astounding growth of newspapers devoted exclusively to sport. The first such paper was *Le Sport*, founded in 1854, but this was subtitled 'journal des gens du monde': it was a paper for the idle rich, concentrating on horse-racing. However, it found a surprisingly wide audience and it had added swimming, boxing, wrestling, billiards, tennis, cock-fighting and travel to its coverage by the time it collapsed in 1893. By then new developments had changed the situation. In 1869 the cycle manufacturer Fabre founded *Le Vélocipède*, partly to refute the attacks of doctors who were saying that cycling was unhealthy because it tired the legs while leaving the rest of the body 'in dangerous immobility', and partly to reply to *Le Cocher français* which denounced cycling as mad. In 1876 the president of the Nautical Club of France founded *La Revue des sports* and several more journals quickly followed, sustained by plentiful specialised advertising: *La Bicyclette* (founded 1892 and soon selling 20,000 copies a week) had as many as seventeen of its forty-two pages filled with advertisements—all but two of them about cycles. *Les Sports athlétiques* (1890), started by the founder of the Olympics, Pierre de Coubertin, was sustained by railway advertisements. The profits to be made were such that in 1891 a daily devoted exclusively to sports, *Le Vélo*, was launched and within a few years it had a sale of 80,000, considerably more than many respected political dailies. This paper was backed by the car and cycle manufacturer Darracq. In 1900 Adolphe Clément, a rival cycle manufacturer, in association with a number of leaders of the motor-car industry—the comte de Dion, Édouard Michelin, the baron de Zuylen de Nyevelt (president of the Automobile Club de France) and the comte de Chasseloup-Laubat—started another daily, *L'Auto-Vélo*.

[1] Béatrice de Buffevent, *Qu'attendent de leurs journaux les 11–14 ans?* (1963); Elisabeth Gérin, *Tout sur la presse enfantine* (Bonne Presse, 1958).

There was bitter competition between these two dailies: the latter was forced to change its name to *L'Auto* following a court case brought against it by *Le Vélo*. But *L'Auto* had a remarkable man as its editor in Henri Desgrange (1865–1940), who had started life as a notary's clerk, became a fanatical cyclist and world champion, got appointed publicity manager to the Clément Cycle Company, and opened a new velodrome in the Parc de Prince. *Le Vélo* refused to report the races held there. *L'Auto* appointed 542 correspondents in France and abroad and sent in addition special reporters to every big meeting. *Le Vélo* was slower with the news, but it replied to the challenge by giving reductions of between one-third and one-half on its advertising rates to firms which undertook not to advertise in any other sporting journal. *L'Auto* was unable to rise much above 20,000 until in 1903 Desgranges had the brilliant idea of organising the Tour de France cycling race, with a prize of 20,000 francs. His paper's circulation at once more than doubled and its fortune was made: in July 1914 it sold 320,000 copies a day, in July 1923 495,000, in July 1933 730,000 (the July figures, during the Tour de France, were at least 50 per cent higher than the average sale). *Le Vélo* long refused to mention this race.

Newspapers gradually realised how they too could benefit from having a sports page: in 1914 political dailies usually gave a quarter of a page to sport, and conceded a whole page only around 1930. Their weakness was that they paid attention mainly to the great races, ignoring the amateurs, and this is what allowed the specialist papers to survive. *Paris-Soir* was the first general daily to exploit sport with real commercial acumen: in 1939 it employed no less than eighteen sports reporters and it sent as many to cover the Tour de France as *L'Auto* did. It made sport sound more dramatic, emotional, sensational; it regularly gave sport a whole page, and three pages on Monday. As a result *L'Auto*'s circulation had fallen to 200,000 by the beginning of the war: its attempt to stave off disaster by adding general news failed; and at the end of the war it was closed down as part of the general collaborationist purge. *Élans* was founded in 1946 with the express intention of ending the influence of *L'Auto*, which, it claimed, had deliberately, for commercial reasons, given more publicity to certain sports, like cycling and motor-car racing, to the neglect of football. But *Élans* failed, and so too did *Sports* (1946), started with similar intentions by the communist party. *L'Auto* re-emerged as *L'Équipe*, making good its earlier shortcomings by publishing a weekly supplement, *France-Football*, which at once obtained a circulation of 140,000. The *Dépêche du Midi* of Toulouse replied by publishing a weekly devoted to rugby, *Midi olympique*; and the communist party renewed its attack with *Miroir-Sprint* and a host of other *Miroirs* devoted to individual sports, which kept up the attack on *L'Équipe* as the cause of all France's sporting troubles. *L'Équipe* continued to prefer professional sports, but football, which now surpassed cycling in popularity, had become professional too. The rivalry of the sporting press gives a good reflection of the complex motivations behind recreation; divisions were far more intricate than this brief account may suggest: in 1958 there were at least 231 periodicals devoted to sport with a total sale of 1,457,000 per issue. This was so even though the main Paris newspapers devoted 14·7 per cent of their space to sport, as compared with 9·9 per cent to general news, 8·9 to internal politics and 8·8 to foreign politics;[1] and the provincial press was even more lavish, for on Mondays some of them gave as many as five pages to sport. What this signified in terms of the interests and attitudes of their readers will need separate attention. But the press certainly co-operated in developing a sub-culture of entertainment and relaxation.

Religion, too, had a formidable collection of periodicals to support it. Nearly all of them were consistently moralising, in the sense that they made a practice of relating ephemeral events to the teachings of the Church; and yet the question of just how influential they were is not easy to answer. The most famous Catholic papers had very small readerships. *L'Univers*, started in 1833 by Abbé Migne, who was the editor also of a Catholic encyclopedia in 171 volumes, was taken over in 1843 by Louis Veuillot (1813–83), one of the most pungent and talked-about journalists of the century; but its circulation was only 4,700 in 1845 and around 7,000 in the 1870s. This is a good example of a newspaper which was essentially the organ of an individual, who had style, firmly held ideas and a determination to express them. Veuillot was considered to express the views of the

---

[1] Figures for 1947. Édouard Seidler, *Le Sport et la presse* (1964).

backwoods clergy who read him, but he hardly represented the Church's official line. His paper had perhaps received some financial help from the Vatican, but it was really an independent and profitable family business, which Veuillot handed over to his brother Eugène in his old age. Similarly *La Croix* was founded in 1880 by Vincent Bailly, who was the son of Emmanuel Bailly who had helped start *L'Univers* in the 1830s and who had succeeded Migne as its editor. *La Croix* was maintained as a polemical paper by the Assumptionist Order, vigorously attacking the republic until it was expelled from France; it was then kept going by a Catholic industrialist, Paul Feron-Vrau, till 1914, but it subsequently came under the control of two able editors, Abbé Bertoye and Professor Jean Giraud. The political line of the paper was always vigorous, though it changed from support of liberal Catholicism to advocacy of the Action Française. Its circulation varied between 150,000 and 180,000, which it achieved thanks to the support of a unique distribution system (run by parish workers), low costs (by having nuns print it) and very loyal subscribers (it had the lowest rate of unsold copies of any paper). But it was too serious a paper to be able to compete with the mass-circulation dailies, even though it showed considerable business acumen and sensitivity to its readers' demands. In 1960 it came second only to *Le Monde* in the amount of space it gave to foreign and economic news, but second only to *Paris-Jour* for the space occupied by photographs. At that date it sold a larger proportion of its copies in the provinces than any other daily (81 per cent, as opposed to *Le Monde*'s 44 per cent): but it was not a great commercial success. Its advertising income in 1960 was the same as that of the communist *L'Humanité*, about a quarter of that of *Le Monde* and one-twentieth of that of *Le Figaro*.[1] Its more popular Sunday editions sold roughly twice as many copies, and regional editions widened its impact.

What, however, was most impressive about the Catholic press was the way it catered for every taste, every level of intelligence, every type of reader; instead of trying to please everybody with one large daily, it produced numerous specialised journals. For purely religious purposes, the *Petit Messager du Cœur de Marie*

[1] J. and P. Godfrin, *Une Centrale de la presse catholique. La Maison de la Bonne Presse et ses publications* (1965), 161.

(1875) (with a circulation of 39,000 in 1936) kept up the zeal of the followers of the Virgin Mary; *Le Petit Bulletin de la croisade eucharistique* (1916) sold 300,000 copies monthly; and there were a host of other similar ones for different fraternities. The clergy had *L'Ami du clergé* (1878), which sold 6,000 at the turn of the century and 25,000 in the 1930s, and which had the virtue of being particularly cheap, but also *L'Ouvrier de la Moisson* (1927, 3,600 sales), *Les Annales des Prêtres adorateurs* (1888, 8,500 copies), etc. More intellectual Catholics could read the Jesuits' *Études* (1856, whose circulation rose from 3,000 to 13,000), or *La Vie intellectuelle* or *Sept* published by the Dominicans; and Abbé Bethléem's *La Revue des lectures* (20,000 copies, 128 pages monthly) gave advice on what books to read and what to avoid. There were special magazines for different professions, like *Le Postier catholique* (1922, 4,500 copies), others for pharmacists, for teachers, for soldiers, one even for people in hospital, *L'Ami des malades* (1928, 10,000 copies). There were at least thirteen educational journals, but also many others specially written for the young, like *La Semaine de Suzette* for the very young, *Les Veillées des chaumières* for older girls (this one, established in 1877, sold 200,000): every age group was catered for, and every class: *Noël* for the children of the bourgeoisie, *Bernadette* for poorer ones. Advice on entertainments was available in *Nos spectacles*, *Nos chansons*, *Choisir*, etc. *Le Sel* (1932) provided a humorous paper to rival those which might be too dirty for pious readers. All these journals were successful because they catered for definite groups of people, most of whom were organised to buy them. But the Catholic press, like the left-wing press, was suspicious of advertising and did not rely on it. Seventy-five per cent of the advertising revenue of La Bonne Presse, which was by far the largest Catholic publisher of periodicals, came from one daily paper, *Le Pèlerin* (1872), originally founded for pilgrims to La Salette, but quickly transformed into a successful popular family paper.[1] The Catholics converted no one with all this vast output. Their journals were read by the faithful; they were indeed a mark of solidarity. This is clearly seen from the wide regional variations in their sales. They were most successful in the west and least so in the Paris region.

[1] Anon., *Les Revues catholiques françaises à l'exposition internationale de la presse catholique au Vatican en 1936* (1936).

The Catholic Press in 1936[1]

North	10 dailies and 31 weeklies. Sale 668,000 for a population of 5,200,000

North	10 dailies and	31	weeklies. Sale	668,000 for a population of			5,200,000
East	29	,,	49	,,	,,	536,000	,,	3,900,000
South-East	5	,,	37	,,	,,	596,000	,,	8,117,000
South	1	,,	14	,,	,,	124,000	,,	2,160,000
South-west	6	,,	25	,,	,,	304,000	,,	4,240,000
West	7	,,	49	,,	,,	942,000	,,	6,730,000
Centre including Paris	4	,,	30	,,	,,	315,000	,,	19,759,000

It would be quite wrong to imagine that this was in any way a unified Catholic press empire. The French press was characterised by extreme fragmentation and, apart from a few combines, each journal was individual, representing the eccentricities and ambitions of writers, businessmen, politicians and men of leisure of very different kinds. One can see this, for example, in the history of *Le Nouvelliste de Lyon*, which in the early Third Republic was the most successful Catholic regional daily. It was founded in 1879—when there were already several well-established dailies in Lyon—by a group of fifty-one Catholics of the city. Twenty-nine of these were members of the Catholic Association of Employers of Lyon, each of whom subscribed between 500 and 2,500 francs; thirty-seven of them were old boys of the fashionable Jesuit boarding-school of Mongré. There were no professional journalists or politicians among them. The main organiser, Joseph Rambaud (1849–1919), was an industrialist and landowner, who in his spare time taught at the Catholic Faculty at Lyon and was the author of a textbook on economics —which he hoped would replace that of Gide—designed to show economic development as the accomplishment of the divine will. Rambaud, who went to church every day, was a conservative Catholic, a disciple of Bishop Pie and of Le Play but an enemy of the Social Catholics, whose reliance on the state he disapproved of. Within a year, his paper had a circulation of 40,000, at a time when in Paris the respectable *Journal des Débats* sold only 6,500 and the *Figaro* 97,000. In 1886 the paper bought out the printer, so great were its profits. It had started

[1] Based on Paul Verschave, *La Situation de la presse catholique en France en 1936* (1936).

with only 125,000 francs of capital; within ten years the value of its shares had almost trebled; by 1899 it was paying a dividend of 30 francs on each 100-franc share, and it owned buildings and reserves worth over a million francs. The paper took the view that religion was the answer to all problems, but that was not why it was successful. Despite its high principles, it borrowed the methods of the popular press and gave a lot of space to sensational news, 'sad and violent dramas'. Rambaud acknowledged that this was wrong, but explained that charity must 'bend to the needs and weaknesses of those it wished to serve'; he personally would prefer to print serious articles, but to do so in a popular paper would be egoism, which was the opposite of charity and love. He drew the line only at rape, adultery and seduction, which were never mentioned.[1]

This was a paper in which the shareholders allowed one man to make money for them unhindered, while also defending a cause they held dear, but when control was shared by a number of people, Catholic papers were just as liable to be torn by internal rows and rivalries as those of any other persuasion. The *Ouest-Éclair*, for example, was started by two radical priests in Rennes at the turn of the century, with the help of four local dignitaries, barristers and merchants, each of whom invested a sizeable part of his savings in the enterprise. They soon had trouble with the bishop, who disapproved of their democratic tendencies, and with their professional editor, who was an unpractical bohemian, with no head for business. The paper established itself not because of its religious character but on the contrary because the priests who started it discovered that its rivals failed to give enough news about prices at local fairs and practical, local information of that kind. This was the gap they filled. Endless personal and doctrinal bickering, however, left the paper unstable, until the politician Louis Loucheur and the Havas news agency gave it the capital it needed for expansion.[2] The *abbé*-journalists who entered this fray had no illusions about the press. They realised that newspapers were essentially businesses. As one of them wrote, with resignation or complacency,

[1] Louis de Vancelles, '*Le Nouvelliste de Lyon*' *et la défense religieuse 1879–1889* (Lyon, 1971), 85, 212.
[2] Paul Delourme, *Trente-cinq années de politique religieuse ou l'histoire de l'Ouest-Éclair* (1936).

'Everything in the newspaper world is venal, even silence; everything in it is bought, everything has to be paid for.' It was impossible to resist the offers of printers and paper merchants, and of advertisers who made sure that even when a murder was reported, the article ended with the assurance that it would not have happened if the victim had used the soap made by X, or the umbrella of Y and Co. The press, said one *abbé*, was accused of engaging in blackmail, and he could not deny it; it was forced to do so; but the public was a willing accomplice of the game.[1] In religious life, as in so many other aspects of life, the press was one way by which people obtained a sense of belonging to a group, easier to identify with than the nation as a whole; but the question of who was fooling whom was left unanswered.

All these newspapers and periodicals were dependent on the printing industry, whose efficiency, or at least whose cheap rates, made it possible for almost anyone who was determined to get himself before the public eye to do so. This is an industry, however, about which virtually nothing is known. The emphasis in the study of typographical history has been almost exclusively antiquarian: much more is known about the eighteenth and earlier centuries than about the modern period. There are some books about individual firms but they are mainly commemorative; a fair amount has been written about the new kinds of printing machines, but little about the men who exploited them. Printing workers were among the most sophisticated members of the proletariat; their employers, who were often former workers, were, one suspects, additionally endowed with shrewd business sense. Printing had been a regulated corporation under the *ancien régime*, and until 1870 there were only a limited number of printers who were allowed to practise. The *brevets*, or government licences, were family property, or could be sold, like notary's *études*, so dynasties of printers were common; but their prosperity depended on how many new *brevets* the government issued. The July Monarchy was generous with them, but there was then still plenty of work to go round. But when the Third Republic ended all restrictions, many workers set up on their own and competition forced down prices. There remained

[1] Abbé P. Fesch, *Les Souvenirs d'un abbé journaliste* (1898), 218–34. Cf. Georges Hourdin, *La Presse catholique* (1957).

an important distinction between the small printer and the large firms equipped with expensive machines.[1] The former were often antiquaries interested in local history, typography and bibliography, like Adolphe Grange, deputy librarian of Dijon, who in 1861 bought a local printing works, on which he printed the *Journal de la Côte d'Or*, until, persecuted because he gave it a republican slant, he sold out to become one of the authors of Larousse's *Grand Dictionnaire du dix-neuvième siècle*.[2] The firm of Caillard of Narbonne, established in 1790, was handed down from father to son until 1920, when the last descendant gave up printing and devoted himself exclusively to bookselling.[3] There were many printers who were one-man businesses, or employed only a couple of workers; some were part-time, printing when there was work. The small town of Valence (population about 20,000) had eight printers at the turn of the century; and that sort of number meant that the town could publish, in the course of the previous fifty years, eight Catholic journals, seven Protestant ones, twenty-five political ones, fifteen financial, commercial and advertising papers, ten artistic and literary journals, ten humorous ones, one educational one and eleven miscellaneous reviews.[4] Bordeaux in 1852 (population 180,000) had eighteen printers, forty-two lithographers, twenty-eight booksellers. Here there were opportunities for the growth of larger firms, as the history of the Gounouilhou family showed. They were Protestants, artisan armourers and watchmakers, but a member of the family was apprenticed to a printer, married his daughter and in 1851 bought the firm of Faye-LaCourt, which went back to the seventeenth century, and had valuable contracts as printers to the archbishop, the courts, the faculties and various learned societies. Gounouilhou continued to print for the archbishop but he also printed a Bonapartist journal established in Bordeaux by a Paris speculator, Delamarre. This paper, however, lost money, so Gounouilhou bought it from its owner for a song. He replaced

---

[1] Georges Dangon, 'Sociologie du maître imprimeur', *Le Courrier graphique* (Dec. 1936), 3–12, (Jan. 1937), 3–10.

[2] Clément Janin, *Les Imprimeurs et les libraires dans la Côte d'Or* (Dijon, 1883), 90–4.

[3] H. Malet, *Les Imprimeurs de Narbonne 1491–1966* (Narbonne, 1966); cf. Émile Pasquier, *Imprimeurs et libraires de l'Anjou* (Angers, 1932).

[4] Léon Emblard, 'Les Imprimeurs et les journaux à Valence', *Bulletin de la Société départementale d'archéologie et de statistique de la Drôme* (Valence, 1902), vol. 36, 49–56.

its editor (who went off to become a restaurant manager instead)[1] by his brother-in-law André Lavertujon. The paper, *La Gironde*, became, under his direction, the organ of the republican party. It was very much a family business: Lavertujon wrote it, Gounouilhou printed it, Gounouilhou's wife managed the finances and other relatives did other jobs. Their politics lost them the privilege of printing official advertisements, which the firm had long enjoyed, but the profitability of the newspaper cancelled that out: in five years its circulation rose from 300 to 14,000. With the proclamation of the republic, Lavertujon was summoned to Paris to be editor of its *Journal officiel* and he later became an ambassador; his assistant was appointed to a prefecture; another of its journalists became Resident-General in Tunis. *La Gironde*, and its evening edition, *La Petite Gironde*, became the establishment papers of Bordeaux. By 1900 the Gounouilhou firm was employing 337 people, and was an important publisher, with its *Gironde maritime et commerciale*, *Gironde littéraire et scientifique*, *Gironde illustré*, *Gironde du dimanche*, *Écho du Palais*, and not least *Véloce-Sports* (1885). The firm was taken over by Jules Chapon, a journalist on *La Gironde* who married the boss's daughter, and by their son after him.[2] Printers had an important influence on the press. They were often the decisive factor in determining whether a particular town had its own newspaper, though many, and often elusive, forces must be investigated to explain the erratic birth and irregular life of newspapers.[3] The economic basis of the French newspaper industry is still very obscure.

Any historical study of the press must inevitably be unsatisfactory because there is no way of measuring the influence it has had. In the past, it has simply been taken for granted that the press was an important force in politics; and historians still quote newspapers as expressions of public opinion, no doubt

---

[1] This was Jules d'Auriol, who ran Les Dîners de Paris, a large restaurant founded by the press magnate Émile de Girardin. D'Auriol then married the widow of the founder of the Bouillons Duval restaurant chain and died a millionaire.

[2] G. Bouchon, *Histoire d'une imprimerie bordelaise. Les Imprimeries G. Gounouilhou* (Bordeaux, 1901).

[3] Georges Auclair, 'Conditions d'existence d'une presse quotidienne départementale: le cas de La Rochelle', *Revue française de sociologie* (Oct.–Dec. 1962), 415–31.

because they can find no alternative source for discovering this. The French have not, to this day, investigated the question of the influence of the press in any systematic way. One is therefore forced to turn to American studies, of which there have been a very large number. Their general conclusion has been that the press has had the effect much more of reinforcing existing opinions than of changing them, that minor changes in attitude have occasionally followed from reading the press, but that conversions are rare. People expose themselves to the press selectively, choosing papers which are in accord with their existing views; they avoid exposure to information they do not like and if they come into contact with this, they tend either to distort it, so as to make it fit in with their existing views, or they remember only acceptable parts of it. The press can be effective in matters in which its audience has no previous opinions, but the information it conveys often acts as a vaccination, which renders the audience immune to any further opinions. It is true that some people are more persuadable than others, and in particular people under conflicting pressures, with unstable convictions, are open to persuasion; but such people often prefer escapist literature to reasoned argument. It seems to have been clearly established that personal conversation or contact is most effective as an instrument of persuasion, that the radio is less so, and that the printed medium is least so. The crucial role of 'opinion leaders' and of small groups in creating opinion is stressed, and these tend, on the whole, to work towards reinforcement of traditional views rather than towards change.[1]

The few investigations of detailed incidents in which the press was involved seem to confirm this. In the presidential election of 1848, 190 newspapers supported Cavaignac and only 103 were in favour of Louis Napoleon, but Napoleon nevertheless obtained nearly four times more votes. The influence of the press on this occasion seems to have been virtually negligible; that of clubs, by contrast, was probably considerably greater.[2] In the second half of the nineteenth century, the radicals waged a very vigorous campaign against the Church, using, as one of their main instruments, press propaganda; but investigations of voting behaviour in individual villages show that their invasion by

[1] Joseph T. Klapper, *The Effects of Mass Communication* (Glencoe, Illinois, 1960).
[2] A. J. Tudesq, *L'Élection présidentielle de L. N. Bonaparte* (1965), 145–98.

anticlerical newspapers had virtually no effect.[1] It is quite true that a press campaign directed against Blum's minister of the interior, Roger Salengro, led to his committing suicide in 1936, but that represents a different kind of power—there can be no doubt that the press was able to attack individuals, and sometimes with tragic results, but it does not follow that anyone but its victim was worried by this. The press was very active in propagating anti-Semitism, but it is by no means clear that it did more than give expression in writing to what people were saying in any case; if anything, it may well have been counter-productive, in that it made the prejudice it supported appear all the more unjust, so encouraging the left wing to rally to the defence of a minority which it had hitherto generally disliked.

The most important role of the press was probably to shape the news, and so to modify the way issues were discussed. The press, almost inevitably, presented the news in a sensational, partisan, simplified manner. This was quite separate a matter from the bribery and corruption of which the press was guilty, when it deliberately concealed the truth. Once the press had developed the way it did, with the ultimate emphasis always being on securing the highest possible circulation, journalists were almost automatically the victims of a technical pressure, of the rules of a game which required them, impossibly, to reconcile conflicting demands of professionalism, truth and popularity. Newspapers became obsessed with being first with the news, and their rivalry concentrated their attention, therefore, on the ephemeral and the personal. The press was particularly important in revealing scandals, in creating political crises, and the Dreyfus Affair is the most famous illustration of its power. This was much more a crisis induced and sustained by the press than the result of popular concern. There is no doubt, too, that, as a result of the rise of the newspaper industry, the country knew far more about itself than it had ever done before, but the fragmentary, episodic nature of the information passed on through the press was such that, if the press did make any permanent impact, it may well have been more to confuse than to enlighten. The newspapers were frequently, indeed usually, critics of government, in a constant relationship of envy and hate towards it, but they were also major supporters of the

[1] G. Cholvy, *La Géographie religieuse de l'Hérault* (1968).

centralising mission and inculcation of uniform behaviour that all governments sought. The progress of this uniformity suggests they contributed to the victory, or at any rate were on the winning side; but the rise of the regional newspapers showed that the local interests and traditional superstitions of the masses were not eliminated. The press was nominally on the side of education, or at least saw itself as one of the instruments of the spread of science and knowledge, but, under pressure from its readers, it also did a great deal to give a new status to sport, relaxation and entertainment. It is partly due to the press, and not simply to politicians—though they were often the same thing—that French politics was seen as the struggle of irreconcilable animosities; the press flattered prejudice and feared to disturb its readers in their habits; it therefore helped to give those animosities a greater reality, preventing people from seeing them in their true light. It was thus ultimately a highly conservative force; it did not encourage its readers to tear themselves away from the past.

There was a good reason for this. The press was not free; it had not, in this period, won its independence, even if the laws hollowly proclaimed the freedom of the press. It failed to find a formula which would allow journalists to write without irresistible pressures weighing upon them, or newspapers to be published profitably without accepting financial servitude. Even today, this formula has not been found. The French press is in a continual state of economic crisis. About half its total revenue is obtained from state subsidies, given indirectly in the form of preferential prices for materials, postal charges, rail freight, etc. This has not altered the traditions of the press, which continues to attack and criticise the government that succours it. The French press is, in some ways, the equivalent of the British institution of Her Majesty's Opposition. But though a few newspapers have secured editorial independence, the press as a whole is very much in the hands of large capitalist combines, whose concentration has increased steadily since 1914–18 and much more since 1945. The blatant corruption of pre-war days has been ended, but less obvious pressures survive, and no doubt inevitably.[1] The very considerable talent, and sometimes even genius, that was expended in the service of this profession almost

[1] M. Mottin, *Histoire politique de la presse 1944–9* (1949).

always ended in frustration; but on the other hand the exceptionally large amount of imagination and wit that went into it added spice and excitement to many lives. Despite its corruption, the press did a great deal to reveal corruption, injustice and stupidity in government and society; because there were so many newspapers in rivalry, it remained immensely active as a defender of the rights of the individual, and of liberal values which it did not always practise itself. Thanks to it, the smoke-screens manufactured by verbose politicians were sometimes dissipated, even if they were more often taken seriously. It was a major factor in liberating literary style from archaic rules, though in seeking to reflect the popular style, it often lost sight of elegance.[1] It did a great deal to undermine the faith that the illiterate originally had in the printed word. It showed up, in short, the resistance of taste, or at least popular taste, against intellect.[2] The press probably did a considerable amount to create fashions, which came and went; and it is in this sense that it created reputations, even if these lasted only for short periods. It was perhaps most powerful in times of national or social crisis, but conversely, it was disgust with its brain-washing propaganda campaigns during the First World War that turned so many people against it. If it is true that opinion is created mainly by small groups mutually sustaining themselves, and by personal influences, then the press should be seen as the mouth-piece of certain cliques, reinforcing rather than creating loyalties. But it is impossible, in the present state of knowledge, to be too precise about the elusive problem of how ideas were transmitted and how tastes changed.

[1] On journalistic style, see Criticus, *Le Style au microscope* (*grands journalistes*) (1953); Charles Bruneau, *La Langue du journal* (1958).
[2] On problems of class and readership see C. A. Tuffal, 'Étude de la presse quotidienne parisienne. Le rapport entre informateurs et informés' (unpublished Toulouse political science doctoral thesis, 1966).

5. Science and Comfort

AT the end of the eighteenth century, there was probably a greater concentration of famous scientists in Paris than in any other city in the world. In 1900 the idea of French scientific supremacy had clearly become an illusion, even if many people still clung to it, and in 1960 only 6 per cent of the French population thought that France could still hope for leadership in this domain.[1] The paradox is that when France did have more scientists than anyone else, the country was taken over by lawyers and soldiers, and men of letters portrayed France to foreigners as being devoted above all to the arts; but when French scientific achievements were clearly lagging well behind those of America and Russia, the technocrats were able to capture power and the whole direction of the economy was altered towards the attainment of essentially materialistic goals. It will be seen that there is of course no paradox, and that the triumph of the technocrats should not cause surprise. It is important to study the role of science in French life precisely because the scientists were for long relatively silent, while literary writers, who did not share their ideals, created dark smoke-screens around the whole subject. Under the cover of this, a division of France between artistic and materialistic ideals was concealed, though it was a subtle, overlapping and unacknowledged division. However, the reason why American ideals, of prosperity before all else, could become the creed of the post-1945 era was that they had silently penetrated into sections of most classes. A trained élite was already available to lead the new order that emerged from the collapse of France.

In the eighteenth century, the study of science was a common hobby among educated men of leisure. It was carried on in much the same way as collecting paintings was, as an alternative or a complement to this. A list has been compiled of nearly 500 people known to have had *cabinets d'histoire naturelle*—aristocrats,

[1] Jean Meynaud, *Les Savants dans la vie internationale. Éléments pour un auto-portrait* (Lausanne, 1962), 14.

priests, actors, collectors of taxes, doctors, factory inspectors, and the duc d'Orléans's chief cook. Lamarck said that the purpose of these was very often to 'provide a show and perhaps to give an idea of the wealth or luxury of the owner'; and they were certainly fashionable among people who knew little mathematics or mechanics, but who satisfied their taste for collecting by accumulating hoards of minerals, plants and animals, and classifying them into species.[1] The division between science and the arts had not occurred. The most popular books of the age were not only Voltaire and Rousseau but also Buffon's *Natural History* (in forty-four volumes, 1749–1804) and Abbé Pluché's *Spectacles of Nature* (1732, in eight volumes).[2] Most scientists, including those who made discoveries of international importance, had other jobs, like Lavoisier (1743–94), who laid the foundations of modern chemistry but who was also a senior tax-collecting official and was guillotined as such in the Terror. Scientists were closely associated therefore with public affairs. Napoleon made Laplace (1749–1827), the leading mathematician of the age, minister of the interior; on his expedition to Egypt, he took with him a large group of brilliant scientists, whose researches remain as the most impressive monument of the war. This was almost to be expected, because scientific discovery was seen as an integral part of progress and of military power. The great Encyclopedia of the eighteenth century was produced jointly by the philosopher, playwright and art critic Diderot and the mathematician d'Alembert, author of an important *Treatise on Dynamics* (1743). The prestige of French science was such therefore that Frederick II, the king of Prussia, modelled his Berlin Academy on the French Academy of Sciences and successively invited three Frenchmen—Maupertuis, d'Alembert and Condorcet—to direct it. Science was so fashionable in Paris high society that a *grande dame*, the marquise de Chatelet, undertook the translation of Newton's *Principia*. There were few branches of science to which France did not make major and fundamental contributions in the century 1750–1850.

[1] René Taton, Charles Bedel *et al.*, *Enseignement et diffusion des sciences en France au 18e siècle* (1964), 669.
[2] D. Mornet, 'Les Enseignements des bibliothèques privées 1750–1780', *Revue d'histoire littéraire de la France* (1910), 449–96.

Scientists produced such a profound transformation in men's view of themselves that they had every right to expect a dominant role in society. Their discoveries led to more radical changes than the theories of philosophers because the implications could be demonstrated in such dramatic and convincing ways. Politicians might preach an end to resignation—the dominant attitude that Christianity had fostered—but scientists could show that it was possible to change one's environment, to alter what seemed to be rigid decrees of nature, to travel at unprecedented speeds. Politicians might blame the nation's misfortunes on human error and argue that man could put an end to his miseries, but it was scientists who proved that disease was not a punishment from heaven, but the work of germs, and they showed that they could destroy them. Optimism took on a new strength when the mass of people were, in consequence, able to live twice and three times as long as they had previously done. The claim that God had created the world at a particular time was challenged in such a way that the very basis of religious authority seemed to be undermined; scepticism on the one hand, determinism on the other, were given a wide popularity. The idea that men existed in order to fulfil some divine purpose, that they were different in kind from animals, or indeed from ordinary matter, was so weakened that both government and morals had to turn in new directions. The physical well-being of the masses assumed a much higher priority than it had ever done. Science set up a new pattern of attitudes, in which the possibility of change was an essential element.

However, though in the early nineteenth century the Saint-Simonians suggested that scientists should take over government, this did not come about. The explanation is to be found, first of all, in the very conditions that scientific progress created, which paradoxically limited the ability of scientists to seize the full implications of their work, or to convey these to the public. Specialisation reached a turning-point around the middle of the nineteenth century, after which not only did laymen become incapable of understanding what the scientists were doing, but the scientists themselves branched off into separate disciplines, with only the gifted few being able to keep up in more than one. It is too simple to say that, as a result, two cultures developed. That was a slower process, particularly in France, where the tradition of science as part of culture survived, where leading scientists continue to be elected to the French Academy—a body that epitomises the union of literature, the arts and all forms of public service in the defence of style and taste—and where a smattering of philosophy and of rhetoric were required accomplishments from all educated people, as piano playing was from well-brought-up girls. But precisely because scientists continued to mix, to a certain extent, with men of letters, they grew increasingly modest about their capacity to philosophise about their work, and they were profoundly influenced by the positivist theories that the men of letters developed for them. The essence of positivism was that people should not draw metaphysical conclusions from their observations and should confine themselves to studying observable facts. French science took on characteristics which were the opposite of those found in other fields of endeavour. It grew frightened of general theories, even of working hypotheses, and scorned the Germans for making so much use of these, even though they were sometimes highly fruitful.[1] The basis of its early success was the advanced state of mathematical teaching in France, and this mathematical bias was long preserved. The result was that French scientists favoured mathematical research more than investigations of industrial applications. They were of course not unique in despising, or being ignorant about, the work of engineers—Rutherford was too—but because the best scientific research was concentrated in Paris and in a few non-university institutions—the faculties of science for long remaining essentially teacher training establishments—a serious gap grew up between scientists and the rest of the world. The scientists were themselves largely to blame for their growing impotence, because they cherished their independence so much. Condorcet had argued that the scientific community deserved a privileged position in the state but had insisted that it should receive no money from it, so as to be completely autonomous. The result was that throughout the nineteenth century scientific research was carried on with very limited financial resources, and in 1933 Jean Perrin was still able to say that the allocation of money for research in the university was 'an irregularity' which the government consented

[1] Maurice Caullery, *La Science française depuis le 17e siècle* (1933, 2nd edition 1948), 198.

not to notice. The government could hardly be blamed, because most of the scientists behaved like artists, absorbing themselves in their researches oblivious of the practical consequences.[1] Whereas in Germany industry quickly took charge of scientific research and forced it to devote time to technological applications, there was less contact in France. It was claimed in 1914 that 'unfortunately there is a very widespread prejudice [among French industrialists] today that it is in every one's interest to retard the progress of science, so as to preserve more easily one's advantages over one's competitors'. This was perhaps an exaggeration, and there were instances of grants from industry to assist scientific research, but they were of small sums. The Conservatoire des Arts et Métiers, moreover, which was founded (1794) to copy its German equivalent, developed in a totally different way and avoided research on subjects of general utility.[2]

It is incorrect, however, to ascribe the relative decline of French science from the heights it reached around 1800 to financial or institutional causes, to suggest, that is, that science became a minor interest of the country, to which little value was attached. The whole question of the 'decline' of French science is, to begin with, confusing. A sociologist has counted the number of papers published on medical science in the nineteenth century, and has shown that France led in 'productivity' up to 1840, when it was overtaken by Britain; in 1850 it was overtaken also by Germany, and in 1890 by the U.S.A. This should not be surprising. In 1800 France was still the most populous nation in the western world, and probably the richest; the latest view of the economists is that though Britain is supposed to have been the pioneer of the Industrial Revolution, statistics prove that French industrial production in the eighteenth century was greater than that of Britain. These dates simply reflect France's changing international situation as its population ceased to grow.[3] The real question is whether France

[1] J. J. Salomon, *Science et Politique* (1970), 60–5.

[2] Henry Le Chatelier, *Les Encouragements à la recherche scientifique*, Mémoires et documents du Musée social (1914), 58–88.

[3] J. Ben-David, 'Scientific Productivity and Academic Organisation in 19th century Medicine', reprinted in B. Barber and W. Hirsch, *The Sociology of Science* (New York, 1962), 305–28; T. J. Markovitch, 'L'Évolution industrielle de la France', *Revue d'histoire économique et sociale* (1975), 266–88; P. K. O'Brien, *Two Paths to the 20th Century* (1977).

came to place less emphasis or value on science. The answer is not clear, because of the war of words between arts and sciences and between religion and science. But if one considers what happened, as opposed to what was said, and if one ceases to give special attention to the opinions of literary men, simply because they were artistically eminent, the decline of science can be seen to have been a withdrawal into discreet obscurity rather than a collapse into insignificance. Science continued to have its admirers and its adepts, but they kept to themselves more. This did not mean that science became less important in society, but only that society was more fragmented, and the results of scientific activity were experienced more than they were written about. A great deal has been made of the influence of the École Normale Supérieure as a nursery of writers and politicians; a certain amount has been said about the crucial positions that graduates of the Polytechnic came to occupy; but very little has been written about the École Centrale and the schools of applied science. Yet France was the world's pioneer in the organisation of technical education.[1] However it did not expand this into a mass system, but kept it within the bounds set by the demands of industry. The results were nevertheless very considerable. The first calculation of the number of scientists and engineers trained at university level was made only in 1950, but the figure then was 137,000, to which should be added 145,000 'technicians'.[2] This army of over a quarter of a million people was, comparatively speaking, small. Even though the proportion of science degrees in all university degrees rose between 1950 and 1959 from 29 to 42 per cent, France in 1959 still had less than half the number of science graduates, per head of population, than the U.S.A. had. But the French scientists were a more cohesive and united group, even with something of the characteristics of a caste. The École Centrale was to the industrialists of France what Oxford and Cambridge were to the ruling class of England, but even more so. In the nineteenth century, about

[1] F. B. Artz, *The Development of Technical Education in France 1500–1850* (Cambridge, Mass., 1966).

[2] 24,000 natural scientists, 95,000 engineers, 18,000 agricultural engineers, of whom 53 per cent worked in industry, 40 per cent in services (mainly teaching and administration) and 7 per cent in agriculture. O.E.C.D., *Resources of Scientific and Technical Personnel in the O.E.C.D. Area* (1963), 147, 69; O.E.C.D., *Shortages and Surpluses of Highly Qualified Scientists and Engineers in Western Europe* (1955), 52.

80 per cent of its students came from bourgeois families, and mainly from those running industry. Between 1831 and 1900, seven Japys, seven Peugeots and seven Dollfusses were educated at the École Centrale. There was much intermarriage between the families of its graduates; it had a very strong old boys' association which virtually dominated recruitment into technical and management posts in industry. But the graduates of the École Centrale on the whole kept out of politics, unlike the Polytechniciens, and contented themselves with supremacy in a limited world.[1] The Polytechniciens, and the graduates of the schools of applied science, of course had their own *esprit de corps*, which, however, was more tied up with control of the state administration.[2] There were rivalries and jealousies between all these sub-groups, but together they did have a recognisable individuality. Because they were so comfortably ensconced in one sector of the economy, they took care not to draw too much attention to their privileges, and they adopted a system of live and let live towards the rest of society. The consequence was that, as an eminent biologist has put it, science won its place in the practice but not in the hearts of society at large.[3] Science and ethics remained separate. But that is not to say that science's place was inferior.

The history of France's scientists and engineers has not yet been written. The attention of historians of science has been concentrated on the period around 1800, because this is considered France's golden age in scientific achievement. But the French were the first to make science a professional career and the results of that deserve study.[4] The achievements of French scientists were far from negligible, even against the competition of larger countries. Jean Perrin, Louis de Broglie and Frédéric Joliot, for example, played a decisive role in the development of nuclear physics. French science continued to be distinguished by important discoveries, even if they were not often applied for purposes of mass production. In 1930 France was still the second

---

[1] Michel Bouille, 'Enseignement technique et idéologies au 19ᵉ siècle' (unpublished thesis, École Pratique des Hautes Études, 1972).

[2] J. C. Thoenig, *L'Ère des technocrates. Le cas des ponts et chaussées* (1973).

[3] Jacques Monod, *Chance and Necessity. An Essay in the Natural Philosophy of Modern Biology* (1972), 158.

[4] M. Crosland, 'The Development of a Professional Career in Science in France', *Minerva* (Spring 1975), 38–57.

largest exporter of patents in the world after the United States; though by 1938 it had dropped into fourth place, after the U.S., Britain and Germany.[1] The activity of French engineers abroad made highly important contributions to the economic development of many of the smaller European countries. At present, it is possible only to illustrate the problem of the relationship between science and society by taking the cases of a few notable individuals, on whom there is something approaching adequate information.

The way scientists could be extremely bold in their own specialities, but nevertheless very modest in drawing any general conclusions from their work, for the guidance of general conduct, can be seen in Claude Bernard (1813–78). He placed physiology on a new footing by chasing vitalism out of it—the old notion that a mysterious vital force ruled the body, making it radically different from the inorganic world. Bernard showed how the body produced the energy it used, how digestion worked, how the blood supply to different parts was regulated; he destroyed the view that the body was simply a bundle of organs, each with separate and appropriate functions, and instead argued that it was one chemical and physical mechanism, whose activities were interrelated and subordinate to its over-all physiological needs. Life was thus defined mechanistically as the maintenance of the equilibrium of the body. Bernard's *Introduction to the study of experimental medicine* (1865) defined the principles that should guide the research worker, emphasising experiment, methodical doubt and the avoidance of unjustified system building. Bernard thus made the physiology of man as precise and exact a science as physics or chemistry. But he firmly refused to draw general conclusions about the world from his particular discoveries. He insisted that man had three faculties—believing, reasoning and experimenting—and that these produced three distinct disciplines—religion, philosophy and science. His fundamental idea was that the limits of each of these must be strictly observed, and that progress could be measured in terms of their more exact delimitation. The rule of reason would make man a monster. All men—even scientists

[1] Harry W. Paul, 'The Issue of Decline in 19th Century French Science', *French Historical Studies* (Spring 1972), 416–50, is a valuable critique of Robert Gilpin, *France in the Age of the Scientific State* (Princeton, 1968), 35.

—needed metaphysics and religion, and their problem was simply how to reconcile their ideas. Science itself was in any case only a provisional belief, and it did not exclude the search for first or final causes, though it never reached them. Ignorance was the lot of man; progress in science was not linked to the progress of humanity; the determinism he saw in phenomena did not affect the liberty man's thought and actions enjoyed. Claude Bernard, the son of a wine-growing peasant, educated by his village priest and by the Jesuits, died in the faith of his boyhood, asserting his belief in the immortality of the soul. Science did not solve his personal problems: 'Science absorbs and consumes me', he said. 'I ask no more if it helps me to forget.' His wife and daughters protested against his refusing to be an ordinary medical practitioner and contributed to the anti-vivisection societies which harassed him; and it was a Russian, Madame Raffalovitch, who sustained his confidence. Despite the modesty of his conclusions, he was held up as the champion of a new attitude to knowledge and his *Introduction* became a textbook in the schools. In their enthusiasm, his positivist popularisers omitted to point out how much he disagreed with them.[1]

Pasteur (1822–95) is another example of scientific genius united with the most conservative political and social ideas. Pasteur's views—outside his laboratory—may indeed be taken as typically representative of the average man of his time. He was a scholarship boy, the son of a tanner who had been a sergeant-major under Napoleon I, and Pasteur inherited an admiration for the emperor. The educational system, said Pasteur, should be based on the principle of the cult of great men. He had a profound faith in hard work as the means of rising in the world, and when he had a cerebral haemorrhage at the age of forty-six, from too much of it, he read Samuel Smiles's *Self-Help* during his convalescence. *Laboremus* was his motto. Another of his favourite books was Joseph Droz's *The Art of Being Happy*, in which he found confirmation for his view that life consisted of 'will-power, work and success', success

[1] C. Bernard, *La Science expérimentale* (1878); C. Bernard, *Philosophie*. Manuscrit inédit présenté par Jacques Chevalier (1937); Joseph Schiller, *Claude Bernard et les problèmes scientifiques de son temps* (1967); Reino Virtanen, *Claude Bernard and his place in the history of ideas* (Lincoln, Nebraska U.P., 1960).

being a 'brilliant and happy career'. He married the daughter of the Rector of the Academy where he was a professor; he replied to her protests against his dedication with the assurance that he was leading her to eternal fame. But there was no greed or selfishness in him. When Napoleon III asked him why he did not try to profit personally from his discoveries and their important industrial applications, he replied that he thought this would take up too much time and would impair his spirit of invention; besides 'in France scientists would consider that they would be demeaning themselves by trying to make money'. He had no philosophical ideas, and he said that 'my philosophy is one of the heart, not of the mind'. He had read very little philosophy, and thought scientists should avoid being influenced by it, since it might make them *hommes de système*; but, he added, 'I admire them all, our great philosophers'. He made a clear distinction between himself as a scientist, basing himself on observation, experiment and reason in his search for truth, and himself as 'a man of feeling, of tradition, faith or doubt, a man of sentiment, a man who cries for his dead children, who cannot, alas, prove that he will see them again, but who believes and hopes this, who does not want to die as a vibrio dies, who tells himself that the strength in him will transform itself. The two domains are distinct and woe to him who wants to make them infringe on each other in the present very imperfect state of human knowledge.' In his work, therefore, he found 'the sole distraction from such great sorrows'. He saw no affinity between the revolution he was carrying out in science and the political agitations of his time. He was strictly authoritarian in his dealings with students, and passionately patriotic. The influence he exercised was therefore totally at variance with his ambitions. He became France's most famous scientist, because the practical results of his research were so dramatic. He showed that diseases formerly attributed to some inner failing were due to infection by microbes—a new word and a new idea, which placed life at the mercy of new, almost invisible beings. He developed 'pasteurisation' as a defence against them, and vaccines also. His work on fermentation had a profound effect on the methods of making beer, wine and vinegar; but it also destroyed the notion of spontaneous generation. However, he did not like the broader generalisations that were developed from this. He was an example of a scientist who undermined, without seeking to, the religious and philosophical principles of his society, who showed how research could increase the well-being of his fellow men more efficaciously than political agitation. He held science up as the instrument of 'wealth and prosperity', but showed also that its discoveries could not solve emotional or moral problems. He gave prestige to materialist solutions despite himself.[1]

Marcellin Berthelot (1827–1907), the pioneer of chemical synthesis, gave detailed expression to the hopes science raised in this direction. In his fantasy on *The Year 2000* (written in 1897) he prophesied that chemistry would by then make agriculture and mining unnecessary; food would be eaten in the form of small synthetic pills; industry would be powered by inexhaustible energy from the sun and from the heat of the earth, reached by wells five kilometres deep; air transport would replace all other forms. Man would become gentler and more moral because he would cease to feed himself by carnage and the destruction of living creatures. The world would become an immense and beautiful garden. Everything would be all set to 'realise the dreams of socialism'. But he admitted two difficulties. There would be less work to do, but idleness was bad. This was surmountable: since labour was the source of all virtue, people would work harder than ever all the same, because they would get the full rewards of their efforts. Nevertheless, the condition for this transformation was still 'the discovery of a spiritual chemistry, which will change man's moral nature'. He had no method for finding this.[2] Science thus held out the prospect of all the conditions of bliss, though never bliss itself. Berthelot, having written thirty volumes and about 1,500 articles, which showed above all that organic matter was subject to the same chemical laws as inorganic, went into politics as a radical, as though with the pretension, as his enemies put it, of annexing science to his party's electoral programme. The results were disquieting. As minister of education, he defended censorship of the theatre and maintained the ban on a play based on Zola's *Germinal*. As minister of foreign affairs his ineptitude was held up as disproving the claim that scientists had a contribution to

[1] *Discours de réception de M. Louis Pasteur* (1882); R. Vallery-Radot, *La Vie de Pasteur* (1900).

[2] M. Berthelot, *Science et morale* (1897), 508–15.

make to the maintenance of peace. Outside his own subject, Berthelot was a conservative. He was for long a staunch enemy of the atomic theory and prevented it being fully admitted into the school syllabus until the 1890s, in the same way as Claude Bernard and many others remained sceptical about Pasteur's theory of microbes. The disputes among scientists—the long and violent battles in the Academy of Medicine on the subject of contagious diseases were the most celebrated—encouraged a section of the lay public to resist the new doctrines. And even the scientists themselves did not seem to find full satisfaction in what they preached. Berthelot confessed he was often sad: 'I do not know . . . how to deal with life as it is and to produce harmony from all its parts.' His research involved a constant struggle against doubts; and only intense intellectual work gave him 'moral peace'. Privately, he admitted that the belief in progress was perhaps an illusion and his unhappy conclusion was that 'We must drain the cup to its dregs, because, outside that, there is only worry and absence of dignity'.[1]

As scientists gradually transformed more and more aspects of daily life, they increasingly came to be seen as benefactors of mankind and as national heroes. A new kind of hagiography developed, which praised them for their genius and disinterested devotion to their work, in the same way as medieval saints had been extolled for their piety and asceticism. Marie Curie (1867–1934), the discoverer of radium and popular above all because that promised a cure for cancer, was hailed as 'a lay saint of science'. A large number of biographies have been written of her, most of them simple and edifying ones for children, which built up a whole legend around her name. She was presented as a pure, altruistic woman of supreme intellectual gifts, working for the benefit of her fellows, 'giving all and taking nothing . . . gentle, stubborn, timid and curious', refusing wealth, enduring honours with indifference, uncorrupted by fame. All this was not far from the truth, but no nuance or reservation was allowed to modify the picture of perfection. She was raised to heroic status not only because her research contributed to the transformation of the very notion of 'matter' and the inauguration

[1] A. Boutaric, *Marcellin Berthelot* (1927), 197–8; R. Virtanen, *Marcellin Berthelot. A Study of a scientist's public role* (University of Nebraska Studies, New Series, no. 31, Lincoln, 1965).

of new methods in medicine, but partly also because she was a woman. One should not conclude that scientists were more open-minded in their attitude to women and willing to admit them to a share in their work. Marie Curie was helped by the fact that she was of Polish origin and foreign girls could do things in France which French girls, watched over by parents with pretensions, could not: a sizeable proportion of the first female university students were for that reason foreign. Many more women exercised power in the worlds of commerce and industry than in the scientific community. But Marie Curie was the first woman to reach the very peaks of achievement in the field of discovery, and she owes her popular fame in good measure to that. In scientific circles, she was treated less generously. Her life was dogged by the sordid rivalry and competitiveness which was an inescapable part of the academic, as of other worlds. She herself took great pains to ensure that she should personally get all the credit that was due to her; she carefully distinguished between what she and her husband had each achieved. Her relationship with her fellow scientist Rutherford, for example, was friendly, but behind her back Rutherford complained of her 'constitutional unwillingness to do anything that might directly or indirectly assist any worker in radioactivity outside her own laboratory . . . it is a great pity that some people are so darn sensitive about criticism and the Madame apparently has the idea that anyone associated with her laboratory is a sort of holy person'. He had doubts about just how great a scientist she was, and there is still disagreement as to whether she deserved to be the only person to be awarded the Nobel Prize twice. Harvard University at any rate refused to give her an honorary degree, its physicists protesting that 'since her husband died in 1906, Madame Curie has done nothing of great importance'. But after his death, she revealed very considerable gifts as an administrator of research, a status to which so many scientists were raised by success. She had the good fortune to be discovered by an American journalist who arranged for her to tour the U.S.A. and who organised a campaign to raise money and buy equipment and materials for her. She showed herself to be an unusually determined and successful fund-raiser, only occasionally giving way to complaints that she was being exhibited 'like a wild animal', or resorting to putting her arm in a sling to save her from constant handshaking. The institute founded in her honour—like that founded in Pasteur's—was, significantly, financed by international rather than French benefactions. By American standards both were of course mean and tiny establishments, but they were very important in that they enabled a few more scientists to devote themselves purely and simply to research. Marie Curie's own life, indeed, was totally absorbed by research. She had no interest in politics, or even in feminism. Her private life, though affectionate, was efficiently organised so as not to interfere with her work. She shows how many scientists created closed worlds around them in which they moved untroubled by external events. She came of a family of doctors and teachers. She married a scientist who was the son and grandson of doctors. Her daughter became a scientist and married a scientist. It was not surprising that some people became suspicious of such charmed magician's circles, and that when Marie Curie, in her widowhood, had an affair with another famous scientist, Langevin, the newspapers, which saw scientists as dangerous people, should ruthlessly and mercilessly make her private life public, so as to discredit them as morally outrageous also. Langevin fought a duel with the editor of the anti-Semitic magazine which published his private correspondence with her ('The Sorbonne Scandals'). This editor, significantly, had been Langevin's fellow student at the École Normale and then a teacher of philosophy until sacked for political extremism. The scientists frequently had the same origins as their enemies, but they sometimes cut themselves off in later life, and they were then treated like a medieval heretical sect.[1]

Marie Curie's distinguished family shows, however, how complex the reality was behind the appearance. Her husband Pierre Curie (1859–1906) was indeed the son of a Protestant who had close associations with the radicals of 1848, and all his political sympathies were on the left, but he believed that men were 'powerless to change the social order and would probably do more harm than good if they tried to interfere with "inevitable evolution"'. To concentrate on science was safer; every

[1] Robert Reid, *Marie Curie* (1974); Eve Curie, *Madame Curie* (1939); P. Bignard, *Paul Langevin* (1969); Maria Sklodowska-Curie, *Centenary Lectures* (Vienna, 1968), 13–23, 125–35; Marie and Irène Curie, *Correspondance 1905–1934* (1974).

discovery at least would remain acquired knowledge. In his youth he wore only blue shirts, so as to look like a workman, but he was too gentle and modest to seek to influence political events. Their son-in-law Frédéric Joliot (1900–58), later known as Joliot-Curie, was, similarly, the son of a Communard, but one who had done well enough in business to be able to devote himself to shooting and fishing, a passion which, he argued, was not cruel or incompatible with his hatred of violence, because it was a survival of man's natural method of searching for food. Joliot-Curie's mother (a Protestant, daughter of Napoleon III's sauce-cook) was also very republican. He was active in left-wing political demonstrations from his earliest youth; in the 1930s he was a leading member of the Committee of Anti-Fascist Intellectuals and in 1942, when Langevin's son-in-law, Jacques Solomon, a brilliant young scientist, was shot by the Nazis, he joined the communist party. He complained that he was, as a result, ostracised as a class traitor: 'I was born into a middle-class family; I received a good education; I have been successful; I am comfortably off; in their eyes [those of the middle class] I have no excuse. . . . They could have forgiven me any error, any crime, but not that of being a communist.' But the belief that he was totally opposed to the society he lived in simply showed how the divisions in that society were misconceived and confused. Joliot-Curie said, 'I am a communist because I am a patriot.' His radicalism or communism was not the expression of a carefully thought-out plan of subversion. He frequently insisted that he was not an intellectual, being too fond of working with his own hands for that. If he could choose his life freely, he would like to be a professional fisherman. He said he was surprised to find himself classified as an intellectual and it had been an effort to learn to be one. He always found it difficult to write, partly because he could not concentrate and partly because 'expressing my ideas to other people risks committing other people. It is a great responsibility [whereas] preparing fishing nets makes immediate sense to me, it concerns only me. . . .' His politics were essentially instinctive, and also the product of mistrust of political thinkers: 'There is one word I never like to hear used in my presence', he said, 'and that is philosophy.' His breach with the blasé writers and cynical profiteers of the capitalist system reflected a time-lag that had developed between scientific research and the world of letters. Scientists were achieving such rapid and stimulating advances in knowledge that, as far as their work was concerned, they could not help being optimistic, and they carried forward something of the youthful naïvety of the eighteenth century, with which moralists, endlessly rotating around the same insoluble problems, had become disabused. The temperaments of science and arts specialists failed to coincide, paradoxically, because the arts men were trying to become more scientific while the scientists, for all their methodological rigour, increasingly saw themselves as poetic creators. Henri Poincaré the mathematician had had, it is true, a profound contempt for the 'metaphysical' studies of his brother Raymond, who became president of the republic, saying that 'science should alone rule our actions'. This was the simple form that the quarrel assumed on a banal level. But Joliot-Curie insisted that the qualities needed for fundamental research in science were 'close to those which favour artistic creation: a sure grasp of basic techniques and solid craftsmanship (Van Gogh was not an inspired dauber—he had learned his craft meticulously) at the service of a creative imagination and intuition'. As director of the Centre National de la Recherche Scientifique, he abolished the distinction between pure and applied science but he was very concerned that the researcher's independence and personality should not be stifled by the pressures of a society that had moved from the artisan to the industrial stage: 'one cannot do original work in chains', he wrote. The value of science, for him, was that it enabled man to understand himself better, in the sense that it showed him that he was a creature still in extreme youth; it banished superstition and the fear of invisible forces; it gave its researchers a sense of collective effort, and ultimately therefore he was hopeful that science would do more good than harm. This was a confident declaration of faith by the man whose discovery of nuclear chain reactions was, as he realised, potentially as dangerous (and beneficial) as Marie Curie's discovery of radium. His stormy career showed that the gaps in understanding between scientists and the rest of the community continued to increase. The scientists were partly responsible for that gap, because most of them ceased to be able to communicate with laymen. Laymen got too involved in quarrels about the philosophical and religious consequences of scientific discoveries to understand what scientists were like in temperament and imagination. Indeed so little has been written about the scientists of this period, that it is too early even to attempt a description of them.[1] When Léon Blum appointed Marie Curie's daughter, Irène Joliot-Curie, as the first under-secretary for scientific research, the identification of science with left-wing ideals seemed complete, but it is by no means certain that the majority of scientists were socialists. It is very probable that they were to be found in all parties, and there was certainly a significant number of Catholic ones. The divisions of politics, religion and science did not coincide.[2]

The chief characteristic of the scientist, wrote the biologist Charles Richet in 1923, is that he does not try to apply his work in practice. He is above all disinterested, seeking truth for its own sake, and treating science as a religion. He lectures as little as possible, because he much prefers research. All this 'places him apart in our venal society'. Whereas British and American scientists were 'men of the world' who knew how to play their part in public affairs, the French were different. The scientists of Paris nearly all lived isolated in the Latin Quarter, but did not form a united community. There were watertight partitions separating their family from their laboratory lives and 'we rarely know whether a colleague is married'. What emotional energies they spared from their labours they devoted to mutual criticism and to jealousy, becoming enemies of all those who disagreed with their theories. The advice that Richet gave his pupils was: 'Never think about the possible practical consequences of your discoveries'. The result was that other people had to do this thinking for them.[3]

The simplification of the issues involved in scientific discovery was largely left to people on the fringes of the scientific world or

---

[1] Pierre Bignard, *Frédéric Joliot-Curie. The Man and his Theories* (1961, English translation 1965), 70, 81-2, 141, 157. Cf. Liam Hudson, *Contrary Imaginations* (1966), a psychological study of the difference between arts and science specialists based on interviews with English schoolboys.

[2] Dr. Louis Fleury, *Science et religion* (1868); François Russo S.J., *Pensée scientifique et foi chrétienne* (1953).

[3] Charles Richet, *The Natural History of a Savant* (1923, translated into English 1927 by Sir Oliver Lodge).

even wholly outside it. These were of three kinds. First there were professional popularisers; secondly the philosophers; and thirdly the moralists. Each deserves separate examination.

Few of the great scientific names of this period wrote for the general public. Professional popularisers did this work for them; a vast number of popular scientific periodicals was published, increasing rapidly during the Second Empire. Historians of science have not got round to reading them and assessing the accuracy or bias of the picture they painted; but these popularisers were interesting men. Some were simply journalists who specialised in science because there was a demand for articles on the subject. Such a man, for example, was S. H. Berthoud (b. 1804), famous for his scientific column in *Le Pays* and, later, in *La Patrie*. He was also a novelist, a playwright, a historian, an organiser of adult education, and a collector of children's toys, of which he founded a museum. He was one of those highly prolific writers now totally forgotten, whose works ranged from treatises on the problems of marriage to histories of *Man over the last five thousand years* (1865) and whose *Village Botany* (1862) and *Scientific Fantasies* (1861–2) combined wonder at modern miracles with dour Protestant moralising. Another populariser was Victor Meunier (1817–1903), a Fourierist, who wrote the scientific articles for the republican papers of the Second Empire. He predicted in 1865 that 'before long the popularity of the sciences will not yield to that of letters', books about science would be read like novels and people would attend lectures on it in the same way as they went to the theatre.[1] This was an admission that science had still not reached that position, even in the eyes of those who were most enthusiastic about it. But journalists like Meunier helped to make it more exciting by the battles they waged in the press in favour of or against the theories scientists put forward: the scientific journalists of different persuasions attacked each other with great verve, so that the political diatribe between newspapers was matched by constant polemic about the latest discoveries in geology or zoology.[2] Meunier claimed that each subject was a fief of some specialist, who established dogmas and stopped his opponents from obtaining

[1] V. Meunier, *La Science et les savants en 1865* (1865), premier trimestre, 212.
[2] For disputes about evolution, for example, see R. E. Stebbins, 'French Reactions to Darwin' (Minnesota Ph.D. thesis, unpublished, 1965).

jobs; he revealed a lot about the sordid politics of science.[1] The most widely read populariser of the Second Empire was, however, probably the Abbé Moigno (1804–84), a Jesuit, whose weeklies, *Cosmos* and *Les Mondes*, provided very solid summaries of the latest experiments and theories. Moigno knew twelve languages and had travelled all over Europe to report on scientific advances. He was a serious mathematician in his youth; he then devoted himself to reconciling science and religion. He argued that the threat of irreligion was still capable of being snuffed out, for whereas the national subscription to raise a memorial to Voltaire had collected only 30,000 francs, that to celebrate Pius IX's jubilee had produced ten times as much. His work on the *Splendours of faith, showing the perfect accord of revelation and science* (in five volumes, 1883) collected the testimony of many leading scientists to support this view.[2]

Under the Third Republic, the most widely read populariser may perhaps have been Camille Flammarion (1842–1925), whose *Popular Astronomy* (1879) was for long a best-seller. He was entirely self-taught. Had his father, a well-to-do peasant, not been ruined by an unsuccessful business venture, he would have stayed on at school and become a priest. Instead he came to Paris and got a job in the Paris Observatory (while his father started a new life in Nadar's photographic studio). He was horrified to find that his scientific colleagues were pious, unimaginative civil servants, who felt no sense of wonder at the mysteries of the universe; for them astronomy 'was simply a table of logarithms'; they did their mathematical calculations, but all of them were dissatisfied with their jobs and looking for better ones. Flammarion at once rebelled against this specialised view of science, which, he said, was purely mechanical and ignored life. At the age of nineteen, he published his *Plurality of Inhabited Worlds* (1862) which sold 41,000 copies and was in addition translated into Arabic, Chinese, Czech, Danish, English, German, Italian, Polish, Portuguese, Spanish, Swedish and Turkish. Flammarion's fame abroad was probably even greater and he received many foreign decorations. The impact his book

---

[1] V. Meunier, *Essais scientifiques* (1857), esp. vol. 1, 'L'Apostolat scientifique'.

[2] Abbé Moigno, *Les Splendeurs de la foi* (1883), 1. 35, 3. 1446–59; *Cosmos: Revue encyclopédique hebdomadaire des progrès des sciences* (1852–63); cf. *La Science populaire* (1883–4) edited by a royalist.

created may be judged from the remark made by Napoleon III, that the thing that had struck him most in it was the engraving showing the comparative sizes of the earth and the sun: 'Is this possible?' he asked. 'How insignificant we are! It is better not to think about it; it makes us invisible; it is enough to destroy us.' The empress refused to believe it. At the end of his long life, Flammarion noted that despite his efforts 'the general ignorance about astronomy is really stupefying' and he gave examples of the absurd questions famous people had asked him. Meunier's prophecy that science would be the most popular subject was not fulfilled. Flammarion said that it had been overtaken by pornography. He declared himself surprised by 'the general indifference of the inhabitants of the earth' to its mysteries, and to the question of what life meant; men, busy with their little jobs or pleasures, were no different from snails. For him, understanding everything was a passion, reading an obsession (he accumulated a library of 10,000 volumes); 'thinking and loving' were the essential parts of life. The astronomer Le Verrier (who discovered Neptune) sacked Flammarion, telling him he was a poet not a scientist, and Flammarion admitted that for him astronomy was 'the poetry of life'. He was dominated throughout by 'the conviction that there is no death', or rather he was determined to prove this. He lost his Christian faith but he became a leading advocate of spiritism: he greatly admired Allan Kardec (author of *The Book of Spirits*) and was invited to succeed him as president of the Société Spirite. He combined these interests with the presidency of the Paris branch of the republican Ligue de l'Enseignement. He wrote seven books criticising Catholicism but also positivism. He was firmly 'anti-materialist' and published a 'Declaration of the Rights of the Soul'. He was an unorthodox, enthusiastic, generous optimist who illustrates well the confused views that amateurs who interested themselves in science formed. Most professional scientists were suspicious of him: the popularised version of their work that he produced in his many publications was far from being an accurate reflection of what they believed. But Flammarion was representative because there were so many different strands in him. He fell in love with Victor Hugo's niece when he was fifteen; he courted her for ten years and finally persuaded her to leave her husband. They lived together for many years and were married only much later, after the husband's death, spending their honeymoon in a balloon. When she reached the age of sixty—she was ten years older than him—he fell in love with a young girl, one of the many admiring women who attended his lectures, and established a *ménage à trois* with all parties consenting. But he said not a word about this in his memoirs, which are an important source for scientific speculation outside the laboratories.[1]

These memoirs show how people did not simply transfer from religion to science. They emphasise that credulity was not the monopoly of those who rejected scientific method. This credulity needs to be remembered: one can illustrate it with the story of the forgery scandal in which Flammarion was marginally involved and which tore the Academy of Sciences in 1867–9. The inventor of modern geometry, Michel Chasles, professor at the Polytechnic and the Sorbonne, Copley medallist of the Royal Society of London, presented a paper to the Academy arguing that Pascal had discovered the law of gravity before Newton. He produced letters from Pascal to Boyle proving this. Many Academicians were convinced. The astronomer Le Verrier denounced the letters as forgeries. The chemists examined them and declared them to be at any rate very old. Chasles supported their authenticity by yet more letters. It turned out that he had accumulated a collection of 27,320 autographs, by some 660 famous people, from Thales, Pythagoras, Cleopatra and Julius Caesar downwards, including 2,000 by Galileo. The world of science was shaken by the totally new light this placed on the history of discovery, showing in particular that France had played a much larger part than hitherto realised. Chasles resisted all the arguments attacking their authenticity for two years, until the forger was finally unmasked.[2] Great scientists made fools of themselves often enough for their opponents to be able to refuse to believe them even when they were right.

Philosophical reflection on science attempted to give it a much more precise significance than these popularisers achieved.

[1] Hilaire Cuny, *Camille Flammarion et l'astronomie populaire* (1964); C. Flammarion, *Mémoires biographiques et philosophiques d'un astronome* (1911).

[2] Henri Bordier and Émile Mabille, *Une Fabrique de faux autographes ou récit de l'affaire Vrain Lucas* (1870).

There were three thinkers in particular who took the lead in this effort of interpretation, Comte, Taine and Renan. Auguste Comte (1798–1857) came to be regarded, by people of almost all parties, and with the virtually official agreement of the university, as possibly the most important thinker of the nineteenth century. It was said of him, during the Second Empire, that he 'inaugurated a new mental regime for humanity'; and in 1925 it was still argued that Comte 'really founded a new conception of human life'.[1] A leading anthology on political thought in the nineteenth century, published in 1924, gave him more space than anyone else.[2] Men like Gambetta and Ferry acknowledged themselves to be his disciples. Through him, therefore, the influence of science may appear to extend over the whole thinking of society and the Third Republic may almost seem to be, as some people claimed, the offspring of science. But this is a superficial impression. Comte was indeed a scientist, a pupil and later examiner in mathematics at the Polytechnic, a popular lecturer on astronomy; and he did have quite exceptionally wide knowledge of the different sciences of his day. No man was better qualified to interpret them. Comte, however, declared that no existing science, not even mathematics, was capable of producing a synthesis to guide mankind, either on the intellectual plane or, still less, on the plane of daily conduct. He undertook his researches indeed precisely because he found his own scientific knowledge so emotionally unsatisfying. The importance of Comte was that he extracted from science a methodology for tackling human problems. He argued that all knowledge passed through three chronological phases, the theological or fictional phase, the metaphysical or abstract phase and the scientific or positive phase. Men, in other words, have employed three different ways of thinking: first interpreting what they saw in terms of divine intervention, seeking the primary causes and ultimate purpose of things and finding them in supernatural forces; and secondly, replacing theology by philosophy, they explained behaviour in abstract terms. The third, positive attitude, which was just beginning to penetrate the natural sciences, involved the renunciation of the possibility

---

[1] E. Littré, *Auguste Comte et la philosophie positive* (1864, 2nd edition), 32; D. Mornet, *Histoire générale de la littérature française* (1925), 204.

[2] Bayet and André, *Écrivains politiques du 19ᵉ siècle* (1924).

of discovering the origin or purpose of the universe and confined itself to the study of observable phenomena only, and to the establishment of regular relationships between them. Societies were theological in their infantile or primitive state, metaphysical in their youth (which was what France was) and finally positive in their prime.

Positivism meant a concern with the real as opposed to the chimerical. It meant a search for the useful—for knowledge was worthwhile only if it led to the improvement of individual or collective life, and not simply to the satisfaction of sterile curiosity. It involved also a search for both certitude and precision (though accepting that knowledge was always relative), the establishment of harmony between individuals, their fellows and their environment, and above all a determination to organise rather than to criticise. What Comte reproached the liberalism that had emerged from the Revolution for was intellectual anarchy, which he found intolerable. The natural sciences could not cure this themselves, but the creation of a new science, which he first called social physics and then sociology, could do so, by applying the methods of science to politics. Comte's major book began with a long review of scientific knowledge. He argued that a scientific background was an essential training for politicians, but government was an independent science, in the study of which they then needed to specialise. Comte arranged the different sciences in hierarchic order with sociology as the supreme science. His method was the distillation of all human knowledge, which it arranged in an order that revealed both the unity and the connections between the parts; it allowed those who applied the method to see the significance of every problem, because it taught them to identify what kind of problem it was. He believed that politics could be made into a science with fixed laws, based on the observation of human behaviour in the past and capable of predicting the future, in general terms. Historical study should be its basis, but history seen in terms of civilisations. Though he understood the growth of specialisation, he argued for an interdisciplinary social science saying that it should not blindly copy the natural sciences: its fragmentation into isolated subjects would render it sterile.[1] Comte's immense erudition, his grasp

[1] A. Comte, *Cours de philosophie positive* (1830–42, 1894 edition), 4. 282.

of a vast range of problems, his ability to sustain his argument through a mass of detail, throwing off innumerable insights as he went along, could not fail to make a profound impression on his readers. His clearly was a quite exceptionally powerful intellect, and those who could keep up with him shared, to some extent, in the ecstatic feeling that he was indeed opening up a new way of understanding.

Comte was a typical intellectual, critical of the society around him, proposing radical reforms for it, but finding it difficult to agree with other intellectuals, feeling that his genius was unappreciated by them or by the establishment he was attacking, proposing a higher status for the intellectual élite but full of contempt for that which existed around him. He was a man who both loved his work and found it unsatisfying. He was able to illuminate the problems he tackled with great clarity but he was obsessed by illusions where his own person was concerned. He could, at times, be infinitely gentle in his relationships but he generally had great difficulty in living harmoniously with others. He never succeeded in getting a proper job, and his part-time employment at the Polytechnic was terminated; he was forced to live off the charity of a few admirers, notably some English benefactors whom J. S. Mill rallied round him. When he descended into the political arena, he did grave damage to his reputation.

Comte's second major work, *The System of Positive Politics* (four volumes, 1851–4), claimed to apply the principle of positivism to the organisation of society; but his bitter experience of life modified the conclusions he drew. Intelligence, he now decided, was not enough. He remained enough of an intellectual to insist that traditional revolutions, which overturned political institutions, did not achieve much in practice and that what was needed was a revolution of the mind, in people's ideas. The great need was to make people see that egoism was an unsatisfactory basis for conduct, and that it should be replaced by the idea of service to others, by living for others. However, one could not convert the masses to altruism by argument: it had to be a question of emotion, not of intelligence. Comte, rather to the amazement of his intellectual disciples, concluded that what was needed was a new religion, which he called the religion of humanity to indicate that it aimed at binding the world together in mutual love. He insisted that ritual and feasts were things man could not do without and proposed elaborate institutions to provide them. Family life must be strengthened, to lay the basis for a new emotional security. The aim of politics should not therefore be equality, but the acceptance of the facts of life, and the adaptation of institutions to them. Inequality of wealth and of intelligence should be recognised as inescapable. Government should be by those most fitted for the task, not because Comte favoured the dictatorship of intellectuals, but because he believed there should be a specialisation of functions. The masses knew what they wanted, and no one had the right to speak for them. But the formulation of plans for bringing about their wishes should be left to 'publicists' and the execution of these plans to a government. 'Sociocracy' was therefore not democracy, but, rather, the end of democracy. Science could not tolerate the chaos of individualism; liberty, equality and fraternity could not be accepted as a satisfactory motto and Comte proposed instead Order and Progress.[1]

The result of Comte's arguments was that science ended up by proposing something very similar to the Catholicism it sought to dethrone. One might wonder why Comte did not simply become converted to Catholicism, for whose organisation he had great admiration. The answer seems to have been largely personal, in the sense that Comte had a personal antipathy for Christ, whom he hated as an impostor or adventurer, 'a mixture of hypocrisy and charisma'. He regarded Christianity as muddled, incomplete, mystical, even if it was the precursor of the true religion, which was the scientific religion of humanity. He looked forward to preaching the doctrine of positivism himself from the pulpit of Notre-Dame. He thus made positivism anti-religious, but also aroused hostility because he wanted a church of his own. He placed a great emphasis on the role of women in the development of altruism, arguing that they understood affection far better than men, but he took this to the point of insisting that they should therefore remain at home, to devote all their energies to being mothers. Comte was so certain of the importance of family love because he had never enjoyed it: he broke with his own father (a tax-office clerk) in early life and refused to see him again; he decided his marriage was the

[1] A. Comte, *Système de politique positive* (1854), vol. 4, appendix p. 5.

greatest misfortune of his life and he finally left his wife, declaring that she was 'despotic and incapable of being disciplined, having a false notion of the necessary condition of her sex in the human economy'; only in later life did he finally fall in love, with a divorcée who died eighteen months later: it was she who, he said, taught him the value of 'the influence of feminine sentiment on masculine activity'.

Comte considered himself superior to Bacon and Leibniz, but not to Descartes. His self-confidence, and his personal eccentricities, have produced strong reactions against his claims. There could be no denying that he was, like all original thinkers, greatly indebted to others who had come before him, and notably Condorcet and Montesquieu. Renan, who had his own debts to Comte, denounced him nevertheless for saying 'in bad French what all scientific minds in the past two hundred years had seen as clearly as he'. A historian has described him as combining 'many of the worst and weakest aspects, often in exacerbated form, of the eighteenth century *esprit de système*, Kantian phenomenalism, the Hegelian coherence theory of truth, scientism and garbled scientific method, pseudo-romantic evangelical sentimentality and totalitarian notions of social engineering'.[1] It is certainly true that positivism, as he formulated it, was capable of creating difficulties not very different from those he wished to remedy. He became an advocate of 'cerebral hygiene', which meant that he stopped reading almost entirely, distracting himself only with opera and some poetry. His science therefore remained the science of the 1820s. His ideas on science have, apparently, been influential on the development of biology; but he reduced psychology to phrenology, and he downgraded geometry in his hierarchy because he was at war with the geometricians of the Polytechnic.[2]

Comte's followers fell into two distinct schools. The orthodox positivists, who accepted the whole of his work, founded churches and practised his religion. They were led at first by Laffitte, a man with remarkable gifts for lucid exposition who did much to make the master's doctrines more intelligible. Not surprisingly these men, who accepted Comte's politics, moved to the right of the Republic and a third of their ruling committee were

[1] W. M. Simon, *European Positivism in the Nineteenth Century* (Ithaca, 1963), 46.
[2] See *Bulletin de la société française de philosophie* (1958), special issue on Comte, 15.

members of Action Française in the early twentieth century.
Since the Second World War the Church of Humanity in Paris
has been maintained by donations from Brazil, where positivism
has found its main refuge. The more important section of
Comte's heirs, however, were those who rejected his politics.
Émile Littré (1801–81), the author of the famous dictionary,
was their leader, again a man with a clear style, who popularised
an expurgated condensation of Comte's writings. Littré became
a highly influential figure in the Third Republic. He was a
senator and editor of an important journal, *La Philosophie positive*
(1867–83), which greatly broadened the appeal of positivism,
precisely because it did not make it into an organised movement
or sect. He saw positivism as simultaneously revolutionary, conservative and socialist—just the kind of broad and vague ideal
to appeal to radical republicans sobered by the acquisition of
power. He kept it firmly parliamentarian and disowned Comte's
later opinions as an aberration. But his election to the French
Academy in 1871 led to the resignation of Bishop Dupanloup,
who saw in it a triumph of anticlericalism. The significance of
science was confused by political animosities.[1]

Just how limited faith in science was, and just how complex
and muddled its votaries were, may be illustrated from the life
of Ernest Renan (1823–92), the author of the *Life of Jesus* and
the *Future of Science*; he was the champion of the 'progressive
ideas' of the second half of the nineteenth century, and in him
were reflected also a large number of common opinions. His
ideas were called 'the most contagious of his time.' 'There is no
example in literary history', it has been said, 'of a man—not
even Voltaire—who so occupied the attention of not only the
educated but of the whole public.' But Renan was well aware
that he was a confused man. 'I am a romantic protesting against
romanticism, a utopian preaching down-to-earth politics, an
idealist vainly giving himself much trouble to appear bourgeois,
a tissue of contradictions.'[2] Renan, for all his intellectual inde-

[1] H. Gouhier, *La Jeunesse d'Auguste Comte* (3 vols., 1933), excellent; E. Littré,
Auguste Comte et la philosophie positive (2nd edition, 1864), for Littré's interpretation;
T. Chiappini, *Les Idées politiques d'Auguste Comte* (Paris thesis, 1913); Stanislas
Aquarone, *The Life and Works of Émile Littré* (Leyden, 1958); E. Littré, *Conservation,
révolution, positivisme* (1852); D. G. Charlton, *Positivist Thought in France during the
Second Empire* (Oxford, 1959); Pierre Arnaud, *La Pensée d'A. Comte* (1969).
[2] E. Renan, *Souvenirs d'enfance et de jeunesse*, ed. Jean Pommier (1959), 51.

pendence, never lost the characteristics imprinted on him by his background. He had been destined for the priesthood but did not take orders, partly because the study of exegesis made him doubt the reliability of the Bible but partly also because he was too cold towards the Church, too sceptical, more interested in truth than in prayer. The worldly religion he was taught in his Paris seminary had nothing in common with that of Brittany, where Catholicism was mixed up with mythology and superstition—interests which continued with him all his life. He was a Breton and he attributed to this his lack of interest in the practical side of life, his taste for dreaming about ideal worlds, which he regarded as the inevitable lot of an isolated population. The classical education he received gave him a lifelong obsession with antiquity and an admiration for Greek values which conflicted with his Christianity; but it also left him time to read the romantic poets of his own day and to cultivate enthusiasm: he voted for Lamartine in 1848. He did not feel he belonged to any one class: he despised the bourgeoisie ('the rule of businessmen, industrialists, workers—the most selfish of classes—Jews, Englishmen of the old school, Germans of the new school') but he also sought to reassure it; he considered himself a son of the people and thought that was why he could understand Christ, who shared this popular origin with him; in practice, however, he lived a thoroughly bourgeois life. Because he had been so chaste in his youth, he found merit in libertinage at an age when other men took to frowning upon it. The way he lived and what he preached conflicted; he was incapable of sincerity in conversation; he lived uneasily with his opinions. He sought a compromise between science and Christianity, scepticism and faith, liberalism and tradition, optimism and pessimism.

His hesitations and confusions may be illustrated from three of his most important books. His *Future of Science* was regarded as a manifesto of confidence in science as man's necessary instrument in the search for truth and happiness. He wrote this book in 1848 and published it only in 1890. It shows how ideas about science could remain static for half a century, how his notion of it was an eighteenth-century one, and how equivocal he was about it. 'The triumph of science', he said, 'is in reality the triumph of idealism.' In 1848 he wrote 'Science alone can give man vital truths, without which life would be insupportable and society impossible.' In his preface of 1890 he was much more cautious: 'No one knows, in the social order, where the good is to be found . . . Science preserves man from error rather than telling him the truth; but it is something to be certain that one is not a dupe.'[1] His philosophy of history was that man had passed through the ages of faith and criticism and was now moving on to that of synthesis: he did not seek to jettison the past; he respected superstition and feeling. He could never get away from traditional vocabulary: he believed in God, the soul and immortality, though he used these words in the most diverse and often pagan senses.[2] He was not keen on the realist novel, saying that since reality was unpleasant enough, there was no point in representing it in fiction. His favourite novelist remained George Sand.

Renan's *Life of Jesus* (1863) won the reputation of being the first major attack on Christ's divinity, based upon the fruits of modern biblical scholarship. It made an impact which, it was said by a contemporary newspaper, could be compared only to Luther. It argued that the Scriptures should be studied critically, like all the ancient writings, that they were full of inaccuracies, and in effect history mixed with fiction; miracles could no longer be accepted. Christ was only a man, though the greatness of his work could justify his being called metaphorically a god. Renan claimed in his preface that his book was the result of great labours; in fact he wrote it rapidly in a Lebanese hut, with only five or six books at hand, inspired by a sudden vision and by the atmosphere of Nazareth. His long dissertation on the historical value of the Scriptures he thought up and wrote afterwards, and it was not the result of personal research but of reading other books. He was much influenced by certain German Protestant theologians and by the views of the Protestant circle into which his marriage with Cornélie, the sister of the painter Ary Scheffer, introduced him: these looked on Christ not as a god but as a superior man in whom religious feeling reached its highest form and whose essentially moral preaching was quite different from the dogmatism and ritualism of the Catholic Church. Ary Scheffer's painting *The Temptation of Christ* to a certain extent served him as a model. His book was more a work of art than

[1] E. Renan, *L'Avenir de la science* in *Œuvres complètes*, vol. 2 (1949), 726–7, 758.
[2] Jean Pommier, *La Pensée religieuse de Renan* (1925) has a good analysis.

of science. His notes show him to have been moved by impressions rather than by logical arguments; he wrote brief notes summarising his feelings, which he later combined when he had a 'general sensation'. His Jesus was really an idealised self-portrait—not a Galilean but a nineteenth-century Frenchman. One can recognise Renan himself in his view of Christ as a man who 'had risen from the ranks of the people, of a family of artisans', among a population given to 'ethereal dreams and a sort of poetic mysticism' (reminiscent of Brittany). Jesus, said Renan, was (like himself) a great master of irony and eloquence who appeared to submit to the established powers outwardly, though really derisive of them: he replied to questions with 'the fine raillery of a man of the world combined with divine goodness'. He was a 'delicious moralist' and a 'revolutionary in the highest degree', who proclaimed 'the rights of man and of the freedom of conscience'.[1]

However, even on this question of the rights of man, Renan did not hold consistent views. In his *Intellectual Reform of France* (1871) he attacked democracy as the cause of his country's defeat, and urged the re-establishment of monarchy and the rule of an élite, as the solution for its decadence. Renan had the misfortune of being repeatedly let down by the ideals he cherished. After Christianity came the Germans, whom he had worshipped as the representatives of modernity and science. That is partly why by the end of his life Renan became the embodiment of scepticism, though he was not simply that. 'Renanism' meant a mixture of seriousness and mockery, unctuousness and blasphemy. He was held to be responsible for the dilettantism of the last years of the century—a dilettantism which his pupil Anatole France carried to the point of nihilism. The evocative and dramatic power of his style helped greatly to popularise his teaching. He became a hero to every party— which is perhaps a decisive mark of his importance. Combes unveiled his statue in 1903 in an emotional speech; Clemenceau in 1917 said, 'I do not show deference to many but I do to him, for he made us what we are'. His anticlericalism however was

[1] Prosper Alfaric, *Les Manuscrits de la* Vie de Jésus *d'Ernest Renan* (Publications de la Faculté des lettres de l'université de Strasbourg, fascicule 90, 1939), introduction; P. M. J. Lagrange, *La Vie de Jésus d'après Renan* (1923). See also the preface to the 13th edition of the *Vie de Jésus*.

only one side of him. Barrès and Maurras looked on his *Reform*
as a key work in the movement for national regeneration. Sorel
praised him for having seen that the salvation of the world
would come from the proletariat. Bourget praised him for his
monarchism, forgetting what he said also on the other side. His
forty volumes, 24,000 pages long, are a monument that points
in every direction, revealing that if this was the age of science,
it was equally the age of uncertainty.[1]

The man who most successfully showed how science could be
a guide in everyday conduct, in morals and in art, was Hippolyte Taine (1828–93). Taine was probably the most talented
writer among the so-called positivists: he wrote about the most
difficult and dry subjects with an astonishing vivacity: he had
a gift for making abstract ideas clear and even dramatic; he
illustrated his arguments with vivid and varied examples. He
was interested in contemporary literature and art (in a way in
which Renan was not) and so he won a strong following among
a wide circle of young writers. Anatole France recalled how
around 1870 'the thought of his powerful mind inspired in us
an ardent enthusiasm, a sort of religion, for what I would call
the dynamic cult of life'.[2] Taine gained his ascendancy because
he was first of all a brilliant demolisher of the doctrines of the
past, in a way that liberated and excited the men who read him.
His book on *The French philosophers of the nineteenth century* (1857)
can be compared in importance with Renan's *Life of Jesus*, as
the popularisation of an intellectual attitude. In it Taine ridiculed the reigning philosophers of his day with a measured wit
and vigour that were profoundly effective. Taine was the enemy
of the classical view of man—the universal type with a clearly
defined character which was to be found in whatever time or
place he lived. This, he argued, made impossible the accurate
study of man, based on observation. Taine equally castigated
the romantic way of life ('The taste for general terms, the loss
of precision in style, the forgetting of analysis . . . the passion
to see without proof . . . the theatre and novels accepted as
manuals of science . . . every poet explaining man and the world

---

[1] H. W. Wardman, *Ernest Renan* (1964); Henriette Psichari, *Renan d'après lui-
même* (1937).

[2] Victor Giraud, *Essai sur Taine: son œuvre et son influence* (Fribourg, 1901), 138,
quoting from *Le Temps* of 7 Mar. 1893.

and in addition, claiming to be the saviour of humanity', a constant buzzing of metaphysical dreams and God transformed into an interior decorator, employed to make life more agreeable). Above all Taine vilipended the eclecticism of Cousin, whom he described as 'the most admirable tragedian of the century', an orator not a philosopher, whose work was admirably elegant but totally devoid of genuine thought or inquiry. Cousin, said Taine, was interested in maintaining order rather than in finding the truth; he took the need to preserve existing morality as the basis of his arguments, and deduced that God existed because morality needed him; art was justifiable only if it expressed moral beauty. The success of Cousin, he argued, was due to the country's exhaustion with the critical spirit of the eighteenth century, its determination to restore some sort of agreement, its having greater interest in morals than in science, but also its continuing to cherish a taste for abstract words and empty phraseology.

Taine had good reason to be so bitter in his invective. His career had been almost ruined by his rebellion as a student against eclecticism. His prospects had been brilliant. Born the son of a solicitor, the grandson of a sub-prefect, he had been called by his teacher, the philosopher Vacherot, 'the most hardworking and distinguished student I have known at the École Normale Supérieure. [He had] prodigious learning for his age; an ardour and avidity for knowledge the like of which I have never seen.'[1] But he did not succeed at the school because he would not accept the orthodox doctrines; he was sent to a junior post in Nevers, though he eventually made the grade by writing a thesis on the inoffensive subject of La Fontaine. It was only some ten years later that he obtained a job as examiner for Saint-Cyr—involving three months' travel and the rest of the year free; in 1866 he succeeded Viollet-le-Duc as lecturer in the history of art at the École des Beaux-Arts, where he remained for twenty years. Taine all his life felt himself torn between the vocation of artist and philosopher. A semi-autobiographical novel he wrote shows how he worked hard as a boy because of an overwhelming sense of isolation. He read Stendhal's *Le Rouge et le noir* over thirty times, and identified himself with the

[1] Sholom J. Kahn, *Science and Aesthetic Judgement. A Study in Taine's Critical Method* (1953), 13.

explanation of Julien Sorel: 'He could not please: he was too different.' In science, he found, as he said, 'an alibi. In the east, they have opium and dreams. We have science. It is a slow and intelligent suicide.'[1] 'Science is an anchor which holds man.'[2] He did not seek happiness: 'We shall reach truth, not calm . . . The more I enter real life, the more it displeases me.'[3]

Taine argued that 'all states of the human soul are products having their causes and their laws, and that the whole future of history consists in the search for these causes and these laws. The assimilation of historical and psychological researches to physiological and chemical researches, that is my object and my principal idea.' Man must be studied as an individual and in nations, in the same way as plants and animals were; the methods of science must be applied to all human activity. Taine summarised these methods in two striking formulae. First, all things could be explained in terms of their *race*, their *milieu* and their *moment*; that is to say, a plant owed its peculiar characteristics to its being a certain species, to the environment in which it grew and to the time in which it existed; and human activity could be analysed in the same way. Secondly, the accumulation of these details should be crowned by the discovery of the *qualité maîtresse*, the principal quality of the object studied, in which all its characteristics were summarised and from which all the facts about it followed. The impact Taine made was due to the simplicity of this method and to the consistency with which he illustrated its application to different forms of human behaviour. He applied it to history in his *Origins of Contemporary France* (1875–93). He showed how societies should be looked at in the same way as trees, the product of a long history and therefore not capable of radical or rapid change. The culprit of French history was, to him, classicism resurrected in the revolutionary spirit and in Jacobinism: its inflexible logic, he said, 'installed in narrow minds which cannot hold two ideas at the same time, . . . became a cold or furious monomania, determined on the destruction of the past which it curses and the establishment of a millennium it seeks; all this in the name of an imaginary contract, at once anarchic and despotic, which

---

[1] H. Taine, *Étienne Mayran* (1910), 35.
[2] Id., *Vie et correspondance* (1901–7), 1. 83.
[3] Id., *Histoire de la littérature anglaise* (1863).

lets loose insurrection and justifies dictatorship; all this to end up with a contradictory social order resembling now a fanatics' Bacchanalia and now a Spartan convent'.[1] As a result Taine became an admirer of English politics, an advocate of conservatism, decentralisation, and a two-tier voting system to limit the influence of the ignorant. His historical conclusions, reached by supposedly scientific methods, were immediately attacked by the Sorbonne professor, Aulard, who pointed out innumerable errors of fact, the neglect of everything that did not fit in with his theories, and above all a tendency to make vast generalisations based on preconceived ideas: Taine, Aulard claimed, was just another romantic, in the school of Michelet, loving the picturesque and abnormal and capable of appalling bias. The only difference was that unlike Michelet, Taine, under the influence of the horrors of the Commune, called the masses of the Revolution 'an epileptic and scrofulous rabble', 'a grimacing, bloody and lewd monkey'.[2] Positivism was thus once again reactionary.

Taine applied his method to literature in his *History of English Literature* (1864–9), the introduction to which was a concise summary of his doctrine. He argued that literature provided the best material for writing 'moral history' and for discovering the 'psychological laws on which events depend'. His ultimate aim was to discover, through literature, 'the psychology of the nation'. His conclusions were therefore inevitably the opposite of Renan's, in that the importance of individual genius and initiative was minimised, and great general laws stressed instead. Taine is a precursor of the sociology of literature, even though he was never quite able to achieve what he set out to do. He is important also in the history of art criticism, his views on which were given in his *Philosophie de l'art* (1865–9). He saw one ideal as supreme in each period—the beautiful young athlete in Greece, the Christian knight or pious monk in the middle ages, the perfect courtier in the seventeenth century, Faust or Werther in the romantic age. Artists gave expression to this ideal, which was responsible for producing harmony between the different arts in any one period. The moral climate of an age caused art

[1] H. Taine, *Les Origines de la France contemporaine* (24th edition, 1902), 2. 76.

[2] A. Aulard, *Taine, historien de la révolution française* (1907); L. Halphen, *L'Histoire en France depuis cent ans* (1914), 100–3.

that was in keeping with it to succeed and the rest to die, in the same way as climate and geography caused plants to survive. The value of a work of art depended on the faithfulness with which it gave expression to this climate; for example, if it represented the essence of romanticism it was more important than if it reflected only a superficial and temporary fashion; it was most successful if its various parts harmonised to produce a coherent effect. This theory was based partly on Taine's idea of the *qualité maîtresse*, but also on a study of what works in the past were great. It was a historical approach, seeking to be impartial, in that it refused to judge; but it was much more ambitious in simplification, seeking to explain everything in a formula.

Taine did much to make positivism, understood in a wide sense, attractive and prestigious. He gave his disciples the illusion that their judgements were scientific; he taught them how to proceed further, beyond his own researches. His most famous comment, 'that vice and virtue are products like vitriol and sugar', gave him the reputation of being a complete materialist. Though he was a materialist, an atheist and a pessimist, he also respected the individual in a way his philosophy did not allow and he believed in the values of humanism and Christianity. He influenced men of all parties; and it was largely through him that the ideas of positivism entered literature. When Barrès and Bourget in their novels wished to describe the positivism they were rebelling against, it was Taine they used to incarnate it, even though they both owed a great deal to him. However, while his teaching gave faith to some, it also inhibited a lot of human emotions. 'Taine taught us', wrote the philosopher Boutroux, 'that science is not made to satisfy our desires, nor to oppose them, but to find and show the truth.'[1] This, as Taine realised, was not enough to console his generation.

Just as there was a considerable difference between the truth as scientists saw it and the simplifications that the popularisers

---

[1] 'Quelques opinions sur l'œuvre de H. Taine', Enquête, *La Revue blanche* (15 Aug. 1897), 263–95; André Cresson, *Hippolyte Taine. Sa vie, son œuvre, avec un esquisse de sa philosophie* (1951), a useful summary; André Chevrillon, *Taine, la formation de sa pensée* (1932); R. Gibaudan, *Les Idées sociales de Taine* (1928); Maxime Leroy, *Taine* (1933); Alvin A. Eustis, *Hippolyte Taine and the Classical Genius* (California U.P., 1951); P. G. Castex, *La Critique d'art en France au XIXᵉ siècle: Taine et Fromentin* (Cours de la Sorbonne, 1964).

spread among the public, so there was also a discrepancy between the intentions of the popularisers and the message that the public absorbed. This can be seen particularly in the novels of Jules Verne (1828–1905) which became not only standard reading for virtually all French children who read books, but also an international best-seller: in 1953 UNESCO placed him fourth as the world's most translated author, after Stalin, Lenin and Simenon. Verne's books were deliberately written to take advantage of the interest in the wonders of science and they had a strong didactic element, aiming to convey information as well as to appeal to the century's sense of adventure. Verne transformed the fairy-tale into science fiction and in the place of the traditional excursions into mythology, animal fantasy and folklore substituted stories which could give their readers the feeling that they had it in their power to transform the world. It is, however, only in a simple reading that Verne appears to be the optimistic herald of a new age. Unlike his successor in the genre, H. G. Wells, Jules Verne was a conservative, who hated the Communards, the Dreyfusards and the suffragettes. He was not by training a scientist, but a lawyer and stockbroker, who escaped into playwriting before becoming a novelist; he wrote surrounded by encyclopedias, for he had hardly travelled at all and his only participation in the world around him was a period of service as municipal councillor of Amiens, where he lived a quiet bourgeois life. Jules Verne did believe that knowledge of science was important and that science would bring more comfort to daily life, but his optimism was romantic, and therefore of a kind that could go sour, as it did. He was a utopian of the 1848 vintage, so that he was ultimately more concerned with moral than with material progress. He came to the conclusion indeed that every invention contained within it a germ of evil, that technology could not solve man's spiritual contradictions, and that despite the undoubted power that machines gave him over objects, they left him as helpless as before in the face of the uncontrollable forces around him. The omnipotence of 'accident' was thus one major theme of his works, and there was much ambivalence in his attitude to the virtues and ideals of his society. His heroes were usually either orphans or bastards, men without family or name, escaping from the normal world, in search of mysterious places or unknown islands, fighting against

monstrous forces, seeking to unravel impenetrable enigmas.
Beneath his bourgeois exterior, Verne thought of himself as an
orphan and an outcast, and his life was dominated by rebellion
against his father, whose solicitor's practice he had refused to
continue. 'I am not what you would call a civilised man,' he
wrote. 'I have broken with the whole of society.' His books
reflect his aggressive attitude to men in general, and even more
towards women, who very rarely appear at all in them. His
marriage broke down; a nephew shot him and made him lame;
he was, increasingly, a recluse.[1] It is curious, and typical of the
unpredictable influence of authors—which is so often like a shot
that misfires in the wrong direction—that the product of Verne's
tormented imagination should have been taken as symbolic of
confidence and hope and recommended to children. But then
that is only further evidence that one should not too readily
assume that literature reflects its age, or that its message is
understood.

It was Émile Zola (1840–1902) who did most to publicise the
introduction of scientific methods into novel-writing. In *Le
Roman expérimentale* (1880) he called the novel naturalist rather
than realist to give it the suggestion of a natural science. He
claimed he was applying the theories of Claude Bernard's
Médecine expérimentale to literature. Zola developed the view that
all things were interesting: 'the first man he comes across will
do as a hero: examine him and you are sure to find a straightforward plot'. He took over Flaubert's principle of scientific
detachment: 'A novelist . . . has no right to give his opinion
about the things of the world . . . The author is not a moralist
but an anatomist who confines himself to stating what he finds
inside the human corpse . . . He believes that his own emotion
would interfere with that of his characters.' Zola was particularly interested by the effect of heredity and environment on
human conduct. He was influenced in this by Lucas's *Traité
philosophique et physiologique de l'hérédité* (1847–50) and by the
theories of Taine. He believed that man's life was determined

[1] Jean Chesneau, *Une Lecture politique de Jules Verne* (1971); Simone Vierne,
Jules Verne et le roman initiatique (1973); Marcel Moré, *Le Très Curieux Jules Verne*
(1960) and *Nouvelles Explorations de Jules Verne* (1963). Cf. Robert Fath, *L'Influence
de la science sur la littérature française dans la seconde moitié du 19ᵉ siècle* (Lausanne, 1901)
and J. J. Bridenne, *La Littérature française d'imagination scientifique* (1950).

by his physical constitution, which he received mainly from his parents, according to the laws of heredity. Physical defects were carried on from generation to generation, often accentuated, so that people almost inevitably became alcoholics, cretins and prostitutes. He accordingly wrote a series of twenty connected books, *Les Rougon-Macquart* (1871–93), tracing the history of a single family through many situations, designed to illustrate these theories. Each book portrayed a different social class or a different aspect of life, so that the whole presented a comprehensive portrait of French society in what appeared to be a factual way. Far from deifying his heroes, he stressed their animality. He did not go in for careful psychological analysis but painted with large brush-strokes, showing the supremacy of insuperable natural forces. He excelled in describing crowds, because he sought powerful effects and he found the greatest violence and passions in masses. The terrible effects of drink, poverty, hard toil and the struggle for wealth and power were shown to be inexorable, with tremendous force. He sought to be impartial, on the whole, revealing vice everywhere, among workers and the rich classes, so that, despite his liberal sympathies, some of his books, especially *L'Assommoir*, were criticised by the socialists for giving an unduly black picture of the workers. Others criticised him for his inaccuracy. He made considerable efforts to collect material on which to base his supposedly factual studies but, given that he wrote on average a book a year, his knowledge was inevitably superficial. His study of mining life in *Germinal* was based only on a week spent at Anzin, and on about three books on miners' diseases and conditions. Research was not the inspiration of his writings: he did it only after he had worked out a story.

Zola did not have the temperament of a scientist. He was the son of a Venetian immigrant, an orphan at six; he failed his *baccalauréat*. He had a romantic passion to be recognised as a leader: 'all that matters is to stir the crowd'. But he always led an isolated life, and in journalism and novel-writing he obtained the illusion of contact with men. He longed for popularity. He adopted causes that drew attention to himself: he felt he existed with a real identity, above all, when he was the object of attacks. He led a blameless life but filled his books with sexual excess. He was a hypochondriac, superstitious and melancholic. There is much that is artificial in his books, and his opinions often seem to be shallow or poses. He wrote in praise of Fourierism (*Le Travail*), of science (*Dr. Pascal*), of Dreyfus; he attacked the Church (*Lourdes* and *Rome*) and was placed on the Index. After the birth of his illegitimate children late in life, by a girl twenty-eight years younger than himself, he lost most of his misanthropy (*Fécondité*). His life represents an attempt to cast off illusions—because dreaming had led him nowhere—and an acceptance of things as they were, a willingness to leave them as they were and to confine himself to describing them. But there was some conflict between this attitude, which goes with his 'scientific' impartiality, and the faith he also had in progress. He cannot be taken as a reliable source about his times. Ultimately he was popular for the same reasons as the romantics were popular: the power of his imagination, which endowed reality with 'a sort of brutal poetry and symbolic grandeur'.[1]

Science thus failed to make as much impact on men's minds as it did on their practical lives. The scientists were unable to find in it an adequate guide to conduct. They did not, in this period, dare to claim superiority in fields outside their own, and indeed retreated into a specialisation which limited their influence. They thus strengthened the cellular nature of this society. The writers who tried to interpret science made great claims on its behalf, and put its message into some striking formulae, but they were all ambivalent in their attitude to it, for their enthusiasm usually concealed anxieties for which science had no effective remedies. The hopes placed in science were far from being fulfilled, and not even in the material sense. This latter aspect, the physical changes wrought by science, needs to be examined now.

Comfort

The consequences of scientific and technical advances on the daily lives of Frenchmen is not a subject that has received much attention. The history of science is generally written from the

[1] F. W. J. Hemmings, *Zola* (Oxford, 1953); I. M. Frandon, *La Pensée politique de Zola* (1959); R. Ternois, *Zola et son temps* (1961); H. Mitterand, *Zola journaliste* (1962); Guy Robert, *E. Zola* (1952) and *La Terre d'E. Zola* (1952); E. M. Grant, *Zola's Germinal* (1970); D. Baguley, *Fécondité d'E. Zola* (Toronto, 1973).

point of view of the scientist, or as part of the development of knowledge. The consumer, however, has yet to find a historian. Science viewed from the receiving end had a different appearance: what was important in the realm of theory took decades, or even centuries, to make an impact, and it has been seen how difficult people found it to reorganise their mental habits to take account of new theories. The immediate result of technical improvements, however, was greater productivity, more goods on the market and eventually more money to buy them with. A new kind of consumer was therefore created, with far more choice than he had ever had. How he exercised that choice can throw light on the question of how much importance he placed on different aspects of his life. Did the consumer society have its origins in this period?[1]

The masses could get a sight of the latest advances in technology and the practical results of science in the international exhibitions, which were events of great importance in several different ways. The exhibitions were voluntarily attended by more people than went to any other attraction or entertainment that was organised in this period. That of 1862 was visited by 6,200,000, that of 1867 by 9,000,000, that of 1878 by 16,000,000, that of 1889 by 39,000,000 and that of 1900 by 50,000,000. The exhibitions brought the industrial portion of the nation out of its traditional secretiveness and enabled it both to boast of its achievements and to receive public acknowledgement of the value that people placed on them, despite all the attacks on profiteering and chimney smoke. They drowned, even if only while they lasted, the pessimistic complaints of the poets and moralists in exclamations of awe and self-congratulation; and the delight in technical progress that they stimulated should not be overlooked simply because there were few great writers who echoed it.

Industrial exhibitions had first started in 1798, which was an important date, because for the first time industrialists received honours hitherto reserved for the fine arts; in 1801 when a second one was held, the artists refused an invitation to exhibit together with industrialists; in later years they agreed provided they had a special section. In 1798 only 110 manufacturers

[1] For the complicated question of rising living standards, see J. Fourastié, *Machinisme et bien-être* (1962).

showed their wares; at the seventh exhibition in 1827 there were
1,600; by 1878 there were 52,000 exhibitors, of whom half were
French. Those who were admitted to exhibit, moreover, represented only a fraction of those who were anxious to (one-fifth in
1867). A great attraction was not only the orders that businesses
could expect, but also the honour of medals and decorations,
which constitute a kind of nobility peculiar to the nineteenth
century; it is only recently that labels listing prizes won at international exhibitions have been replaced by advertising slogans
as proof of a product's merit. Admission as an exhibitor gave
one a very good chance of getting a medal: in 1844 there were
3,960 exhibitors and 3,253 prizes. The large manufacturers
dominated the selection process and got most of the honours.[1]
Successful manufacturers were increasingly recognised as the
equals of any other profession. In 1819 the king awarded the
Legion of Honour to twenty-three of them and made two of
them barons. In 1849 fifty-one exhibitors were given the Legion
of Honour.[2] Contempt for the 'mechanical arts' no doubt continued in some quarters, but manufacturers began to enjoy an
increasing sense of pride, rationalising their activities with the
defence that 'work is the greatest moraliser in the world'. Technology had its own morality also.

One of the uses of the exhibitions was that they made it possible to take stock of the relationship between inventiveness and
public demand, and to discover, if not what the public would
buy, at least what aroused its curiosity most. In the 1839 exhibition, French heavy industry occupied a very minor part, and it
was Belgium which impressed most in this field: France distinguished itself in perfumery, jewellery, craftwork, music—
'noisy music is the veritable mania of the century' wrote an
official observer. The problems for which visitors came seeking
solutions were things like inefficient heating ('smoke is one of
the curses of our homes') and better lighting (Thillorier, inventor
of the 'hydrostatic lamp', sold hundreds of thousands of them).[3]
In 1849 a gold medal went to the inventor of a calculating
machine, which no one bought, and to Sax, the inventor of the

[1] A. Chirac, *Lettres d'un Marseillais sur l'exposition universelle de 1867 à Paris* (1868).
[2] Achille de Colmont, *Histoire des expositions des produits de l'industrie française* (1855), 56, 317.
[3] J. B. A. M. Jobard, *Industrie française. Rapport sur l'exposition française de 1839* (1841), 1. 3, 2. 95.

Saxophone, which no one played. In 1855, there were 128 exhibitors of agricultural machines, but the report on them declared they were thirty years behind England and there was comparatively little interest in these. 'France', it said, 'is, by taste, military, artistic, literary'; it was forcing itself to become industrial and commercial; but it had still not got round to applying science to agriculture.[1] More excitement was roused by central-heating systems and by metal beds, now considered to have 'reached perfection'. Above all, it was the enormous reduction in prices of articles of daily use, which were once luxuries, and which now came within the reach of the masses, that seemed important. Industrialisation meant, more than anything else, cheaper goods. Textiles led the way in this. Shawls, for example (which were to the nineteenth century what pullovers became for the twentieth) used to cost as much as 450 francs for the best 'cashmere' quality—a labourer's annual wage. By the middle of the century Reims had taken up the manufacture of Scottish tartan shawls which were sold for only 8–12 francs and 'Kabyl' ones for 14–25 francs. Sizes had to be diminished and the number of colours used reduced from six to three, but these cheap parodies of luxury now became the pride of every working woman. French manufacturers exploited these opportunities with varying speed, because it took some time for traditional tastes to be abandoned and new standards to be accepted. Thus in 1867 the peasants were said to be resisting the wool–cotton mixtures of poor quality which manufacturers thought ought to be the material for the clothes of the masses. Peasants wanted clothes that lasted. It was the better-off fashion-conscious buyers who took the lead in preferring clothes of poor quality, which they could change frequently. The workers followed them, demanding clothes that appeared to be fashionable. So because the demand for 'cheap' clothes was so great, prices remained relatively high, despite the fall in the cost of raw materials. One could buy pure wool cloth for only 1 fr. 40 a metre in Périgueux but there was very little of it; in Sedan there were some wool mixtures at 3 francs a metre; but 9 francs was still considered a low price. English goods were both cheaper and of better quality.

Mass production thus roused ambivalent feelings from its earliest stages; and it did not at once become possible to enjoy

[1] Colmont, op. cit. 368.

its benefits. The mass production of shoes, for example, still involved only shoes with the uppers screwed or nailed on; American machine-sewn shoes were a novelty, inspected with great curiosity, though vulcanisation brought the price of rubber boots down by 40 per cent in the 1860s. Wooden clogs were then in the process of disappearing in the towns, but they were being replaced by galoshes with wooden soles, because these were still one-third of the price even of mass-produced leather shoes. Cheap products for household and kitchen use had been a major theme of the 1855 exhibition, and that of 1867 laid particular stress on 'objects for the improvement of the physical and moral condition of the masses', but only one-third of the space allocated to this was taken up. Some cheap crockery and cutlery was shown but the iron furniture exhibited met with almost universal disapproval from the workers who saw it: they insisted that furniture must be varnished and ornamented. One trouble was that the large gap between wholesale and retail prices prevented these goods from being really cheap, and the gap increased as the object was cheaper. The most successful article of cheap mass production in this period was perhaps the sewing machine, which was down to 300 francs. By contrast a mechanical drill, which could have appealed to the male population as that did to women, cost twice as much as a piano. The section of the exhibition in which workers could show things they had made themselves significantly contained almost nothing but *objets d'art*, for use by the rich. Despite the curiosity aroused by the typewriters, phonographs and rubber tyres, and despite the emphasis on machines in the propaganda about the exhibition, these occupied only 4,600 square metres of space, compared to 2,500 given to textiles, 3,000 to furniture and domestic goods, 3,100 to art and 769 to 'objects for the improvement of the masses'.[1]

The exhibition of 1900 was the most magnificent that had ever been staged, but it brought to a head the tensions that had revealed themselves in earlier ones. This was symbolised by the difficulty the organisers had in deciding what its theme should

[1] *Exposition universelle de 1867 à Paris. Rapports du jury international publiés sous la direction de M. Michel Chevalier* (1868), esp. volumes 1 and 18; C. A. Oppermann, *Visites d'un ingénieur à l'exposition universelle de 1867* (1867), 16–18, 141, 189, 446; Jules Mesnard, *Les Merveilles de l'Exposition de 1867* (1868), 1. 39.

be. In 1889, the Eiffel tower, the electrically illuminated foun-
tains, the huge Gallery of Machines had paid unreserved hom-
age to modernisation, and the protest signed by many writers
and artists, like Dumas, Maupassant, Bouguereau and Meissonier, against the 'ridiculous tower dominating Paris like a
gigantic black factory chimney . . . a dishonour to the city' did
not prevent Eiffel, who had the rights to the profits from it for
twenty years, from becoming a very rich man, for the crowds
were enthralled. In 1900, however, the theme chosen was retrospective and whimsical: at the front gate a statue of 'La Parisienne' in a tight skirt and hat of the latest style symbolised Paris
as a centre of fashion, and the major exhibition was one of Old
Paris. France's particular contribution was nationalist rather
than scientific, with expensive reconstructions of an Algerian
and an Indo-Chinese village, to show off colonial might. It was
the Germans who made the most profound impression from the
technological point of view, with their huge dynamos and whole
factories producing synthetic chemicals. The French had organised the exhibits in order of the importance they had, in the
French view, for the development of mankind: they placed
education first (but its pavilion in fact attracted very few
visitors) and art second (but only a few large paintings held the
attention of the crowds). All this was too serious: the exhibition
was treated as an entertainment by most. There was now too
much to see and many people declared themselves overwhelmed.
A frequent tendency was for people to go and look only at the
exhibits of objects in their own specialities. France felt itself
humiliated by the industrial superiority of other nations—some
talked of 1900 as an 'industrial Sedan' and reacted by losing all
enthusiasm for exhibitions of this kind. The next one, held in
1937, was dedicated to 'Arts and Technology' and the emphasis
was as much on the former as the latter. The French pavilion
contained virtually no heavy industry. There was, however, a
section on folklore, which expressed a revived interest in the
artisan idea, and in traditional feasts, given greater meaning
by the new concern about leisure.[1] All this should not be

[1] Richard D. Mandell, *Paris 1900. The Great World's Fair* (Toronto, 1967);
Georges Gerault, *Les Expositions universelles envisagées au point de vue de leurs résultats
économiques* (1902); G. de Wailly, *A Travers l'exposition de 1900* (1899–1900). The
industrial exhibitions deserve further study and the sources available are large.
Régine de Plinval-Salgues, 'Bibliographie analytique des expositions industrielles

interpreted as showing the 'bankruptcy of science'—a slogan popularised by the literary critic Brunetière in the 1890s. What it shows is the parting of the ways between science and literature. The hold of science—and of the attitudes that it fostered—on the imagination of the majority was not diminished. The intellectuals took fright because they could not control the monster they had helped to create, but the monster was more attractive than they realised.

Science was attractive because it offered the masses comfort, mobility, and health. These were precisely the demands the utopian philosophers had made in the eighteenth century. The scientists brought their demands to fulfilment, but the intellectuals were appalled by the unforeseen consequences that came with them. Material improvements had been intended as a basis for spiritual and artistic growth; but the majority took the means to be the end. That was the source of the antagonism of the 'two cultures'. Moreover, science seemed to bring more obvious benefits than democracy or education. Education, worst of all, became for most people an instrument for improving the level of their earnings rather than a cultural experience. The benefits of democracy were forgotten once they had become an accepted and therefore unnoticed part of everyday life: freedom from arbitrary arrest, for example, increasingly appeared no longer as the triumph of a political creed, but as natural as breathing the air. Science's offerings, which seemed to be the antithesis of Christian abnegation, austerity and resignation, presented the ordinary man with an opportunity to rearrange his attitude to life and to reassess his hierarchy of values. He had to decide whether he preferred ambition or tranquillity, immediate or deferred rewards. The road to wisdom and perfection remained very difficult, despite the enormous efforts of priests, teachers and politicians to point the way, but the ordinary man now had the option of forgetting or postponing these superior goals and

et commerciales en France depuis l'origine jusqu'à 1867' (unpublished mémoire, Institut National des Techniques de Documentation, 1960) lists 1,020 items. See also Colette Famy, 'Bibliographie analytique de l'exposition universelle tenue à Paris en 1878' (unpublished, I.N.T.D., 1962) and Colette Signat, 'Bibliographie analytique des documents publiés à l'occasion de l'Exposition Universelle de 1900 à Paris' (unpublished, I.N.T.D., 1959), which contains a useful guide to the 48 volumes of the *Rapport du jury international* (1902–6).

of contenting himself with more attainable material ends. The unresolved problem is whether science supplied him with the objects and facilities he wanted, or whether, by inventing them, it created needs he had never felt and expectations that became compulsive. This is a problem that will never be resolved, because there is very little evidence about what ordinary people wanted until the public opinion poll arrived (which in France, was in the 1940s), and even then the question asked often forced a certain kind of answer.

By the 1940s, the preoccupation with comfort was certainly overwhelming, though what is even more interesting is that it was still not universal. An inquiry held in 1955 revealed, for example, that one-third of the working class had no desire for what was to become the symbol of affluence, the washing machine, and a further one-fifth philosophically accepted that they would never own one; only one-third hoped to obtain one, and only 13 per cent actually had one. It was not just the workers who felt this way: about 30 per cent of both clerks and managers also had no desire for a washing machine. A fifth of the workers (and a tenth of other classes) had no desire for a bathroom or running hot water; there was even 1 per cent which saw no need for running cold water. The country was thus still divided into four groups, those who enjoyed modern comforts, in varying degrees, those who desired them, those who were indifferent, or who even disliked them, and finally those who were so resigned to never having them that they had no opinion on the matter. Despite the primitive and crowded conditions in which, as will be seen, many lived, only 54 per cent declared that they considered their homes insufficiently comfortable, only 43 per cent complained of not having enough rooms and only one-third thought the buildings they lived in were too old. The ideal of a more leisured life had still not overcome the preoccupation with earning money for basic necessities: only about 5 per cent thought a working week of 35 hours or less was desirable; about half favoured 40 hours, but a third accepted 45 hours or more; 3 per cent were willing to work 50 hours or more.[1] The 'materialism' of this society therefore needs to be qualified, both by the fact that not everyone was obsessed by the same dream, and also by the fact that the options were

[1] *Sondages* (1956), no. 2, 13–32.

irrelevant to many, who were too busy simply surviving to have any choice.

A more detailed inquiry, carried out in Toulouse in 1936–8, showed that the decisive factor in determining how people spent their wages was not simply the size of their pay-packet, nor simply the class or occupation they belonged to. Among workers and clerks earning roughly the same amount, the former spent more on food, while the latter were frequently undernourished and contented themselves with cheaper and preserved foods. However, workers who had recently come out of agriculture put up with worse housing and economised in their eating habits more than those who were long-established townsmen. What mattered, therefore, was how long a worker had been in his class. Once he had accepted the limitation of his prospects, he became keener to spend his money on immediate enjoyment, like food and amusements. It was the worker who reached his maximum earnings quickly who set the pace in consumer expenditure. Already in the 1890s, it was the younger miners at Carmaux who saw fashionable clothes as a necessity. Workers in Toulouse, at any rate in the 1930s, did not use their money to imitate the bourgeoisie: they still wore galoshes in winter and espadrilles in summer, and when they got more money, they simply bought more of these rather than leather shoes. They preferred to use any increase in wages to move to more expensive housing, 'less from a desire for comfort than from a sense of conformity'. The richest workers doubled their expenditure on amusements, but the richest clerks trebled their expenditure on cultural pursuits. There was thus a definite division among Frenchmen between those who had distant ideals, for which they were willing to save (and it was often the poorest workers who, proportionately, saved most in Toulouse) and those who lived in the present. It was not a division of class but of hope.[1]

There were clearly things people wanted that science could not provide, or failed to, and this led to a modification in demand. One can see this in the history of people's attitude to housing, the most basic of needs after food. In 1954, exactly 50 per cent of a sample of people questioned said that what they felt the lack of most was clothes, while 30 per cent said improved

[1] Henry Delpech, *Recherches sur le niveau de vie et les habitudes de consommation, Toulouse 1936–8* (1938), 70–2, 261, 303.

housing was their main need, and 17 per cent more food.[1] This
stress on clothes may perhaps be dated from around 1890, which
is when building ceased to be the country's main activity after
agriculture, and when it was overtaken by textiles.[2] It was
in the eighteenth and nineteenth centuries that the French
equipped themselves with their houses, which meant that when
modern comforts became available in the second half of the
latter century, it was an adaptation, rather than complete
renewal, of housing that was the inevitable choice, because too
much had already been invested in old houses. In 1946, the
average age of houses in Normandy was 137 years, in the Paris
region and the north-east of France about 120 years, in Brittany
and the centre between 95 and 104 years. The rapid increase
in population had made much building necessary between 1750
and 1850. When that pressure ceased, new building became a
largely urban phenomenon. The peasants had a clear order of
priorities: when they had money to spare, they put it first into
buying land, next into improving their farm buildings and only
last into constructing new houses for themselves.[3] The result was
that the modernisation of rural housing was a slow process; and
only certain changes were seen as urgent. The first was separation of the humans from the animals. In 1885–94, when a large-
scale survey of living conditions was carried out, there were still
peasants, in the Aveyron for example, who lived side by side
with their animals, separated only by a partition, in rudimentary hovels with a single window. The way to escape was to
build an additional storey: 'the peasant rises in the social
hierarchy when he puts the twenty or thirty steps of a staircase
between his bed and the many inconveniences of the ground
floor, open to the dust, the mud, the foul smells, the coming and
going of passers-by and of animals.' Many peasants, as in the
Orne and Quercy, built two-storey houses from vanity, but
could not adapt themselves to the change and continued to live
downstairs. In 1856 60 per cent of French houses were bunga-
lows; by 1911 only 48 per cent were; only 1·2 per cent had four or

[1] M. de Clinchamps, *Enquête sur les tendances de la consommation des salariés urbains.
Vous gagnez 20% de plus. Qu'en faites vous?* (1955), 31.

[2] M. Lévy-Leboyer, 'Croissance économique en France au 19e siècle', *Annales*
(July–Aug. 1968), 806.

[3] J. P. Bardet, P. Chaunu *et al.*, *Le Bâtiment: enquête d'histoire économique 14–19e
siècles* (1971), 1–120.

more storeys.[1] The next stage was to make houses more solid. In 1856 about one-fifth of them were thatched. These were mainly in the north—84 per cent of houses in the Manche were thatched, and 62 per cent in Calvados. But by then tiles were already cheaper; thatch began to disappear and by 1941 it was found on only 4 per cent of houses (15 per cent in Normandy). Uniformity of appearance had been impossible until the mid-nineteenth century, because of the cost of transporting building materials (the price of a cubic metre of stone was increased by 80 per cent when carried a mere 21 kilometres). Now the very substantial regional variations in style were progressively modified into a more national uniformity. Imitation of a new kind set in: one village virtually rebuilt itself in brick, following the erection of a brick railway station in it. Traditional methods of basic construction, apart from minor improvements, continued. Science made little difference, except in the cities.

Improved sanitation was not regarded as an urgency, for in 1954 only 27 per cent of homes had indoor w.c.s, and only 10 per cent had baths or central heating.[2] Government investigators complained about the extremely elementary provisions for sanitation in the 1880s but reported that 'what is filth to the townsman is manure to the countryman . . . which delights his eye too much for him to worry about its smell'. But at that period townsmen did not have standards that were very different: 'Even in the finest palaces, we could denounce staircases and corridors, serving the major public administrations, where the most distressing revelations are perpetually inflicted on those whose business takes them there.'[3] Hygiene was imposed by government regulations, rather than voluntarily adopted; and these regulations were one of the major sources of the increased uniformity in the layout of houses. That is not to say, however, that cleanliness was a modern innovation. Housewives in many parts of the country were famous for the meticulous care they

[1] J. P. Bardet, op. cit. 60; *Statistique des familles et des habitations en 1911* (1918).

[2] CORDES (Commissariat général du plan, Comité d'organisation des recherches appliquées sur le développement économique et social), *Recherche comparative internationale sur les critères de choix entre les modes marchands et non marchands de satisfaction des besoins* (Puteaux, Feb. 1973), 2.25.

[3] Ministère de l'instruction publique, *Enquête sur les conditions de l'habitation en France. Les maisons-type*, vol. 1 (1894), introduction by A. de Foville. In 1906 two-thirds of French houses still had no w.c.s (indoor or outdoor).

lavished on their homes, but what they cleaned and polished changed with time.[1] The crucial factor was the theory of germs, which created new taboos about what could be touched and what was dangerous. This theory was no doubt assisted by increasing individualism which also made people keep their distance more. But just how slow these ideas were to gain hold may be seen from the crowding people were willing to tolerate. The government's criterion (in 1911) was that every person ought to have one room: less than that was 'insufficient' and two people to a room was 'overcrowded'. At that date, a third or a half of the population (depending on which statistics one believes) lacked adequate accommodation by this criterion; in the towns, and particularly the growing industrial towns, the proportion was even higher. In Paris, 2 per cent of families even had six or more people living in one room. Privacy for the individual was a national goal, but it was not attained till the 1960s, when, after the enormous building programme of the post-war years, there were at last as many rooms as people. In the previous century, it is true, the country's stock of houses did rise a little more than its population:

Number of houses in France

1847	7 million
1870	$8\frac{1}{4}$,,
1890	9 ,,
1914	$9\frac{1}{2}$,,
1920	$9\frac{1}{4}$,,
1939	$9\frac{3}{4}$,,

But that meant that the accommodation available in the towns, where most of the new population went, became increasingly inadequate.

It is not at all clear how far the development of housing in this century satisfied the wishes of the majority. It is true peasants had more and more space as their numbers fell, but that did not necessarily imply greater comfort. In 1937 only one-third of rural communes had running water, and even fewer had drains.[2] Opinion was still divided as to whether drains

---

[1] Dr. R. Martial, in *L'Hygiène sociale* (25 Jan. 1933), shows that cleanliness did not increase in constant progression.

[2] *Enquête sur l'habitation rurale en France* (1939), 33.

were worth having, and it was only in some parts of the country that they were adopted. The townsmen, for their part, had drains forced upon them. The policy inaugurated by the Second Empire was that the slums the city workers lived in should be demolished and that they should be replaced by blocks of flats, or terraces of small houses in the suburbs. The workers made it plain that they did not like this 'improvement'. 'They attach the highest price' (they said in 1867) 'to the continuous spectacle presented by the boulevards, the public gardens and the main streets of a large town; they find in this a source of enjoyment that costs nothing'; and they preferred to live in an attic in the centre of town, rather than be segregated into estates.[1] It was argued by some that the ideal, at this period, was the detached house. Occasionally this was made available to workers at prices they could afford. Thus the firm of Japy built three-bedroomed detached houses which they sold to their employees for 2,000 francs (£80), payable over eleven years. That however was unusually cheap, and included a subsidy and land at provincial prices. The cité Jouffroy-Renault, erected in Clichy, a northern suburb of Paris, by a philanthropic widow in the 1860s, more typically offered two up and two down accommodation for 4,800 francs. The cost of buying these over fifteen years, including mortgage interest at $5\frac{1}{2}$ per cent, was 381 francs a month, which was more than a worker could afford. These therefore became lower-middle-class estates. Most city workers had to be content with rented flats; some even preferred these because it made it easier for them to move; but the 'modern' blocks put up by Napoleon III in Paris were contemptuously derided by them as 'prison blocks'. When the Co-operative Housing Society experimented with buildings held up by steel frame supports, they complained that their walls were too flimsy, and, in any case, what was supposed to be a cheap substitute turned out to be 50 per cent more expensive. So too did Napoleon III's concrete buildings. Experiment in building techniques was thus constantly resisted, because in building modernity did not also mean greater cheapness, though this may have been a vicious circle. Modern conveniences, as the manufacturers themselves admitted, were so simplified and skimped for mass consumption that they gave much trouble; plumbing was often defective and

[1] *Exposition universelle de 1867 à Paris. Rapports* (1868), vol. 13, 892.

there were drains on the market which were not even water-tight.[1] Speculative building often created houses which were less attractive than those they replaced; and because building costs continued to increase, good, cheap housing for the masses never quite materialised. The laws of 1894 and 1908, codified in 1922 and 1928, by which low-interest government loans were given to encourage *habitations à bon marché*, had only a limited effect. Between 1925 and 1939 about 2,400,000 buildings were put up but only a quarter of a million of these were H.B.M.s. These H.B.M.s moreover were put on the market at rents which the workers considered excessive. They were usually of two or three rooms, with a w.c., but a bathroom was still, in the inter-war period, not considered necessary for workers. Rents were controlled as from 1914: landlords stopped carrying out repairs, with the result that the number of homes declared unfit for human habitation rose from 150,000 in 1911 to 2,800,000 in 1939.[2] Mortgages were difficult to obtain (apart from schemes sponsored by companies for their employees) and were usually for less than half the price of the house.[3]

It was only after the Second World War that the provision of housing was accepted as an urgent national priority. The annual rate of building in the 1960s was almost exactly ten times higher than that in the period 1920–39. In 1968, as a result, France had almost twice as many houses as it did in 1939 ($18\frac{1}{4}$ million). In the process, the proportion of people owning their homes has probably fallen. In the 1880s, 61·3 per cent of houses were occupied by their owners (56·3 per cent by the owner alone and 5 per cent by the owner and tenants jointly). In Paris the proportion was only 29·7 per cent; in rural communes it was 66·6 per cent; in Corsica it was 85 per cent, in the Puy-de-Dôme 83 per cent, but in Brittany only 38 per cent.[4] The full figures for more recent times are not quite comparable, but they suggest that, out of the 14 million 'non-agricultural' houses in 1967,

[1] *Exposition internationale des industries et du travail de Turin* (1911), groupe XII, classes 62 à 70: 'La Ville moderne: rapport général' (n.d.), 119–22.

[2] A. Sauvy, *Histoire économique de la France entre les deux guerres*, vol. 3 (1972), chapter on 'Le logement', 99.

[3] Société des Nations, Services d'Études Économiques, *L'Habitation urbaine et rurale* (Geneva, Aug. 1939), 77–99.

[4] A. de Foville, *Enquête* (1894), op. cit. 1. xliii. A. Pinard, *La Consommation, le bien-être et le luxe* (1918), 91, claims that in 1918 79 per cent of homes were owner occupied.

Map 1. Owner Occupiers (1894). Based on A. de Foville, *Enquête sur les conditions de l'habitation en France* (1894), 1. xliv.

42 per cent were owner occupied; if one excludes those with mortgages, the figure would be about 30 per cent.[1] This shows that home ownership was psychologically but not economically very attractive. One of the main reasons why more houses were not built was that rents were very low; a loan to buy a little house in the 1880s would cost at the very least twice as much as the rent.

The acquisition of material possessions often involved borrowing. The amount people borrowed is a partial indication of the extent to which they preferred immediate to deferred pleasures. In the United States in 1935–6, almost one-quarter of the population were involved in purchasing by instalments; about a third of the purchases were of furniture; but cars accounted for 59 per cent of the total debt. There was, however, even in the United States, an enormous amount of regional variation in the use of this method; it was most common in the cities of the north central part of the country.[2] Very little is known about indebtedness in France, but preliminary researches indicate that there were, similarly, enormous variations from region to region;[3] and the complex interplay of psychology and economics in this has still to be unravelled. The poor, of course, had always bought their food on credit, but what was new was the extension of their interest into consumer goods. A thesis on the subject, written in 1904, observed that 'the taste for comfort, the desire to rise or to appear to rise in the social hierarchy' had launched many humble people into debt and a whole new section of business had sprung up to cater for them. Bakers and grocers were expensive because their customers expected credit; co-operators had little success because they refused it (whereas English co-operators in the nineteenth century often gave credit). French retailers of food, drink and pharmaceutical goods used to offer credit even if it was not asked for. It was a way of increasing sales and of investing their money; they put up their prices by about 20 per cent as a result. But their credit system was based on whim and mutual confidence and it

[1] CORDES, op. cit. 2.22.
[2] Blanche Bernstein, *The Pattern of Consumer Debt 1935–6. A Statistical Analysis* (New York, 1940), 19, 35–6.
[3] M. Philippe Vigier is supervising some research on this subject.

involved no written contracts. The development of purchase by instalments, with regular payments, was invented, or rather developed into a national institution, by Georges Dufayel (1855–1916) who claimed to have the largest instalment business in the world. It all started humbly in 1850 when Crespin, a peasant's son, came to Paris and set up as a photographer, offering twenty portraits for 1 franc, the balance—20 francs—being repayable over several months. He grew prosperous, employed door-to-door salesmen to advertise his services and soon expanded into furniture and clothes. For 25 francs a subscriber had the right to buy 100 francs' worth of goods at a selection of shops. But because Crespin charged 40 or even 50 per cent commission to the shops, they put up their prices accordingly and the scheme was discredited. Crespin's widow associated one of their employees, Dufayel, in the business in the early 1870s, and it was from then that it became important. By 1900 Dufayel had 2,400,000 clients and by 1904 nearly 3,500,000. His system was based on the co-operation of concierges, who answered inquiries about the credit-worthiness of clients, and on inspectors (800 in Paris) who each looked after a few streets, from which they collected repayments. There were 400 shops (including the Samaritaine) from which the clients could buy goods with Dufayel's tokens (on which he made 18 per cent commission); but he then opened his own luxurious stores in the rue de Clignancourt and the Boulevard Barbes, which sold every kind of goods except clothes and food, but including cars; and he had branches in all the large towns. Dufayel defended himself by claiming that he was helping the workers to acquire the comforts of life while preventing them from falling into the hands of usurers. Shopkeepers replied by setting up rival credit companies, especially in the north of France (e.g. the Crédit Lillois, 1885). The department stores of Paris replied by a greater use of advertising, which was an alternative method of increasing sales, or, in the case of the Samaritaine, by establishing, in 1913, its own credit company, La Semeuse. Dufayel, who was, almost typically, a great art collector, also founded an insurance company on the instalment principle and a seaside resort at Sainte-Adresse. His shops were shut down in 1940.[1]

[1] Ch. Couture, *Des différents combinaisons de vente à credit dans leurs rapports avec*

The motor car did a great deal to spread the habit of instalment purchase. In the U.S.A. in the 1930s, at least 60 per cent of cars were bought on credit. In France, only 3 per cent were in 1926, but by 1937 35 per cent were. Just as it was General Motors which developed this in the U.S.A. by setting up a finance house, so in France Citroen, Renault and Peugeot in turn started to lend people money to buy their cars (1923–8). Many independent firms joined in to participate in the profitable business of hire-purchase, because already by 1937 70 per cent of new cars sold involved a part-exchange and 50 per cent of cars were already being resold within two years.[1] At that date, it was claimed that 45,000 second-hand cars were sold every month, to the accompaniment of a vast amount of deception and usury.[2] The manufacturers insisted that theirs was not a luxury article, but a useful one, which stimulated business, expanded markets, increased incomes. Only 15 per cent of purchasers said they bought cars simply for pleasure. But there were those who protested that the car had created needs that had never before existed. Since the price of a new car was twice a worker's annual wage, borrowing was necessary. Borrowing was generally something new for the bourgeoisie, which had hitherto liked to pay cash. It was the rich and the poor who used to buy on credit. The spread of their habit was to a considerable extent the work of women—leaders of change in this too: in 1906 it was said that 80 per cent of instalment buying was by women. Peasants, and bachelors, abstained.[3] But in 1954, an inquiry into the spending habits of townspeople found that only 43 per cent of them had bought goods on the instalment system. Only 11 per cent of them owned cars at that date, but of those who did not, only 44 per cent wanted one. Likewise, only one-tenth of those who did not own bicycles said they would like to have one.[4] One should not exaggerate the pressure for ownership of material luxuries, or even of labour-saving devices. Michel Chevalier, in

la petite épargne (Paris law thesis, 1904); cf. G. Dufayel, Indicateur Dufayel (1901–4), his estate agency's publication, in 28 volumes.

[1] A. C. Dedé, Traité pratique de la vente à crédit des automobiles (1937) (by an employee of Peugeot), 59, 63.
[2] Léonce Daries, Autos d'occasion. Piraterie moderne! (Toulouse, 1937).
[3] Jean Boucher, De la vente à tempérament des meubles corporels au point de vue économique (Paris law thesis, 1906), 138.
[4] Clinchamps, op. cit. 44–5, 68. Forty-seven per cent owned bicycles.

1851, had claimed, as all the Saint-Simonians did, that 'the desire for comfort, an ardent desire which has almost become a passion, has penetrated society in all its parts and there is no class which is not profoundly affected by it'.[1] He also said that the ordinary French artisan was already more comfortable than King Agamemnon had been. That perhaps was one reason why the desire for greater comfort was not as universal as he thought. Another was that prices rose constantly, and even if wages rose faster in certain periods, the poor had great difficulty in adjusting to these changes. They ate more and better food, but when the price of this rose, they felt deprived of what had become necessities, and the struggle to live was not eased. In 1912, there were angry demonstrations by housewives in many parts of the country because the price of butter and eggs had temporarily gone up: they behaved almost as they had done in the middle ages, when threatened by famine.[2] The growth of consumers' associations against *la vie chère* showed many people on the defensive, rather than profiting from abundance.[3]

The difficulties of adaptation may be seen also in people's attitude towards medicine. Better health was one of the most important benefits science offered, and it will be seen that, most noticeably of all, it gave longer life.[4] The longer people lived, however, the more they had need of medicine, particularly in old age. Thus the number of hospital patients increased threefold between 1870 and 1936, when a million and a quarter people received treatment.[5] General practitioners, too, received more visits; in the department of the Indre-et-Loire in 1900 doctors on average gave only sixty-two consultations a month and paid 250 domiciliary visits; in 1936 their average consultations were 180 a month, though their domiciliary visits remained virtually unchanged at 264. The increase since then has been

[1] M. Chevalier, *La Science mise à la portée de toutes les intelligences. Le désir de bien-être est légitime; il peut obtenir satisfaction; mais sous quelles conditions?* (1851), 7.

[2] Émile Watelet, *Les Récents Troubles du Nord de la France au point de vue historique et économique* (1912).

[3] A. Lemonnier, *La Ligue des consommateurs* (1910); M. Deslandres, *Pour la reconstitution de la Ligue sociale d'acheteurs* (1931).

[4] See my *Anxiety and Hypocrisy*, ch. 5.

[5] Number of persons treated in hospitals: 1873 410,000; 1883 448,000; 1893 571,000; 1903 642,000; 1912 775,000; 1923 768,000; 1927 913,000; 1930 1,100,000; 1933 1,153,000; 1936 1,235,000. *Annuaire statistique* (1939), 42.

only in the order of 16 per cent.[1] The explanation is partly that the standard of health people expected rose, and they could afford to look after themselves more, but also that new diseases replaced those that medicine cured. Tuberculosis, from which Frenchmen suffered more than any other nation in Europe, apart from Austria and Hungary, began to decline around 1910, and by 1936 its victims had been reduced by about two-sevenths. Death from typhoid was halved between 1890 and 1908. Small-pox, after a final epidemic in 1907, declined and became insignificant after 1927. Between 1906 and 1930, death from whooping-cough was halved and typhoid reduced by two-thirds. But diphtheria was barely diminished, deaths attributed to cancer rose by a third between 1906 and 1927, and those to heart disease rose by one-fifth in the 1920s.[2] Not only was the French death rate, in the inter-war period, higher than that of most European countries, but in certain regions, afflicted by tuberculosis and alcoholism, it was very much higher. Equality in legal rights may have been achieved, but not equality in the face of death: the death rate was 80 per cent higher in the working-class fourteenth *arrondissement* of Paris than in the wealthy eighth *arrondissement*.[3] In 1930, tuberculosis was killing about 100,000 people a year, but the sanatoriums and hospitals set up to deal with this had only 12,628 beds. Venereal disease, it was estimated, was killing about 80,000 people a year, as well as causing 40,000 abortions and 20,000 stillbirths, despite the 532 dispensaries set up since the First World War in virtually every large town. (When the schoolchildren of the department of the Aisne were medically examined only 51 per cent were declared to be in good health, 25 per cent had signs of tuberculosis and 3·75 per cent suffered from hereditary syphilis.) Six per cent of French deaths were from cancer, but in Paris the rate was 13·3 per cent.[4] Cancer moreover struck in a mysterious manner, affecting women more than men, cancer of the uterus and the breast being the most common forms.[5] Epidemics, such

---

[1] Jean Paul Mercat, 'Évolution de la médecine de campagne en Indre-et-Loire de 1900 à nos jours' (unpublished medical thesis, Tours, 1970), 95.

[2] *Annuaire statistique* (1939), 36*. The figures for heart disease in the 1930s are incomplete.   [3] P. Guillaume, *La Population de Bordeaux au 19ᵉ siècle* (1972).

[4] A. Landry, *L'Hygiène publique en France* (1930), 15, 44, 89, 116.

[5] M. D. Grmek, 'Préliminaires d'une étude historique des maladies', *Annales* (Nov.–Dec. 1969), 1473–83, shows the gaps in our knowledge of this subject. A

[continued on p. 286]

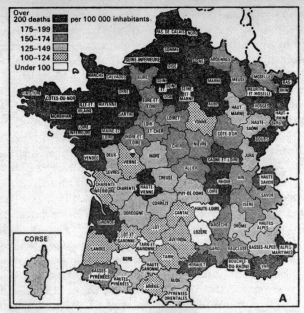

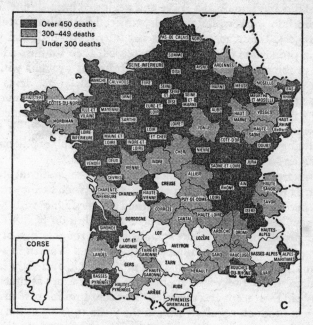

Map 2.

Deaths from Tuberculosis and Cancer
(1913–33).

A. Tuberculosis in 1913.
B. Cancer in 1913.
C. Cancer in 1933.

Based on *Enquête sur l'habitation rurale en France* (1939), 1. 59–69.

as the typhoid which affected several thousand people in Lyon in 1928, could still strike. Viruses replaced microbes as soon as the latter seemed to be in the process of being defeated. Occupational diseases remained a grave and neglected hazard (one-fifth of porcelain workers, for example, suffered from silicosis still in the 1950s). Infant mortality was not fully controlled, and yet, as the proportion of old people increased, their illnesses added new problems. Conquest of the environment brought with it subjection to dangers of a new kind. Industrial accidents increased fourfold between 1900 and 1930, and came to involve over 1 million people a year. In 1930 855 people were killed in railway accidents and 1,506 injured, and railways were just beginning to become safer when motor cars replaced them as a new and much more frequent cause of death.[1]

The transition from a traditional to a scientific attitude towards medicine had only partially taken place at the end of this period. Different groups turned to medicine with very different enthusiasm. Peasants spent much less on health than other people: in 1950 their expenditure was roughly half of the average and in 1960 just under three-quarters. Women in 1960 spent about 50 per cent more than men; people over sixty (and children under two years) spent three or four times as much as people in their teens and twenties.[2] The consumption of pharmaceutical products regularly rose in the years 1950–65 at the rate of nearly 10 per cent per annum. This represented partly increased prosperity, but partly also increased costs and the spread of subsidised medicine. There are no comparable figures to enable one to trace expenditure in the pre-war era, but it is clear that people have recently been more willing to classify themselves as ill. In 1938 insured people were ill for an average of 5·08 days a year and in 1950 for 9·36 days a year.[3] It was only

good comparative study, lacking for France, is Monroe Lerner and O. W. Anderson, *Health Progress in the U.S. 1900–1960* (1963). For regional variations see R. Morot, *Pathologie régionale de la France* (1958), 2. 63, 333, 375; Louis Spillmann and Jacques Parisot, *Guérir est bien, prévenir est mieux. L'effort réalisé en hygiène et en médecine sociales dans le département de Meurthe-et-Moselle* (1925), 179.

[1] *Annuaire statistique* (1939), 199*.

[2] Les Cahiers de l'industrie pharmaceutique, no. 5, *La Consommation pharmaceutique dans les pays du marché commun* (1969), 12, and id., no. 1, *Le Développement de la consommation pharmaceutique* (1967), 15.

[3] Henri Péquignot and J. P. Étienne, *Éléments de politique et d'administration sanitaires* (1954), 25.

in 1902 that smallpox vaccination was at last made compulsory, a victory over mistrust of new-fangled ideas that took three-quarters of a century of agitation to bring about. It was only during the First World War that serious sanitary regulations began to be implemented, and only in 1919 that a law on occupational diseases was passed. It was only in 1922 that a ministry of hygiene was established, but it was part of the ministry of labour until 1930 and in 1939 it still had no technical resources of its own, employing only two doctors and having to rely on the good-will of local authorities. In 1920 one-third of the country's departments did not have the inspectors of hygiene established by a law of 1902; and it was only in 1945 that the compulsory medical inspection of babies and schoolchildren at last made possible an efficient preventive service. The obligatory treatment of venereal disease was introduced only in November 1939. Health thus remained very largely a private matter. In 1951, at a Catholic congress on the subject, a bishop reiterated the traditional view that 'health, though a precious thing, is not the supreme good. Illness, which harms the body, can be profitable to the soul.' A Christian's life did not belong to himself, but to God, and suffering could be beneficial and sanctifying.[1] Even in the 1960s the average Frenchman's view of illness was still not altogether that held by his doctor. Though the microbe had been popularised as the great enemy, it was still more common for people to talk of the causes of disease in a more general and traditional way, as the result of 'poisoning' (*intoxication*), and to blame their environment, city life, stresses of various kinds, noise and unnatural tinned food for their troubles. Death, it is true, was no longer seen as an imminent threat—death was talked of much less—and this was indeed a great change; but exhaustion, which replaced it as the prime complaint, largely transformed health into a battle between the individual and society, rather than something capable of being ensured by science.[2]

Though an important break occurred in the First World War, principally in attitudes to surgery, for this was the first war in which more soldiers were killed by guns than by infection, the really decisive change in the use of medicine occurred in the

---

[1] *Santé et société. Les Découvertes biologiques et la médecine sociale au service de l'homme*, 38e Semaine Sociale de France (1951), 12–17.

[2] Claudine Herzlich, *Santé et maladie. Analyse d'une représentation sociale* (1969).

1960s. Many important new drugs were discovered in the inter-
war period, but they were not much used in the country at large
until much later. Thus in Montluçon hospital the drug used for
blood pressure was, until 1963, still the traditional alkaloid
Rauwolfia Serpentina. It was only in that decade that medica-
tion was drastically revised and put on a more scientific basis.[1]
What characterised the use of drugs before then was a faith in
simple remedies, and their application, almost as cure-alls, to a
large range of troubles. Thus quinine (invented in 1820) was in
turn prescribed for almost all infectious diseases, colds, skin
troubles, anaemia and neuralgia, and a century later the factory
at Nogent-sur-Marne that had been founded to manufacture it
was producing 1½ million kilogrammes a year.[2] Potassium iodide
was the universal panacea for the diseases of middle age—bad
digestion, high blood pressure, heart trouble, obesity. Fashion
changed the emphasis in the use of particular drugs, and introduced new ones, but loyalties died hard. In the late nineteenth
century 'there was practically no dining-table on which iron did
not find its place—in the form of Bland, or Blancard, or Vallet
pills—the girl taking them for her paleness, her mother for her
stomach pains and the father for his breathlessness. . . . Anaemia
was the universal illness' and so iron was prescribed not just for
neurasthenia but also for tuberculosis, renal complaints and
arthritis, though after 1900 it lost popularity. Bicarbonate of
soda was in 1913 still widely and indiscriminately used for all
nutritional and infectious diseases, from diabetes to bronchitis.
Belladonna, which used to be a cure for eye troubles and constipation, among other things, is an example of the drug that has
best survived disillusionment; it continues to be sold as a cure
for colds.[3] The full history of the consumption of pharmaceutical
products has still to be written.[4]

[1] A. M. Batissat-Champomier, 'Évolution de la consommation de quelques
médicaments au centre hospitalier de Montluçon' (unpublished pharmacy thesis,
Clermont-Ferrand, 1969), 31–3.

[2] Anon. [Jacques Makowsky], *Histoire de l'industrie et du commerce en France* (1926),
3. 96.

[3] H. Huchard and Ch. Fiessinger, *La Thérapeutique en vingt médicaments* (1913,
3rd edition); Ernest Léonhart, *La Thérapeutique médicale à Strasbourg de 1800 à 1870.
Évolution des tendances médicales et résultats pratiques* (Strasbourg medical thesis, 1925).

[4] W. Breckon, *The Drug Makers* (1972), 32, gives the following comparative
table of consumption of pharmaceuticals for 1967, in millions of dollars: U.S.A.
3,108, Japan 1,156, France 843, Italy 755, West Germany 716, U.K. 421, Spain
357, Brazil 271, Sweden 112. Cf. also G. E. Trease, *Pharmacy in History* (1964).

Fast travel was another new possibility of this age and a new enticement to expenditure. However, new methods of transport did not destroy the old ones. Throughout this period the number of horses remained virtually constant: about three million farm horses and about one million carriage horses. The number of unmechanised carriages in the 1930s was identical with what it was in 1890.[1] But to these were gradually added first the railways:

Kilometres of Railways

1850	3,083
1860	9,525
1870	17,929
1880	26,198
1890	36,894
1900	43,059
1910	49,628

Then the trams arrived:

Kilometres of Tramways

1870	24
1880	411
1890	1,085
1900	4,231
1910	8,690
1913	10,236

(But only about one-third of these were passenger trams.) Next came the bicycles:

Number of Bicycles

1900	981,000
1914	3,552,000
1920	4,398,000
1930	6,820,000
1938	8,788,000

to which should be added 51,000 motor bicycles in 1920 and over half a million in 1933.

[1] 1891: 1,389,000 carriages; 1913: 1,733,000; 1925: 1,653,000; 1934: 1,352,000. The only change in the animal population was that the number of mules was one-third of what it had been and that of donkeys one-half. Mules fell from 316,000 to 108,000; donkeys from 380,000 to 185,000 (1852–1938).

Finally the motor car:

Number of Motor Cars

	Passenger	Goods
1900	3,000	..
1910	54,000	..
1920	135,000	73,000
1930	1,109,000	411,000
1933	1,397,000	458,000
1939	1,831,000	?
1955	2,472,000	?

In addition, communication by telephone spread at roughly the same pace as the car:

Telephone Subscribers

1890	16,000
1900	70,000
1910	210,000
1913	310,000
1920	439,000
1930	1,113,000
1938	1,590,000

The history of this century could be written around the rise of the railway, which dominated economic life as much as any other single invention. The stimulus it gave to the growth of industry and to the unification of the country, the new relationships it set up between men, and between men and their environment, the transformation it wrought in the landscape and in architecture, make it an influence of crucial importance. Life could almost be said to have come to centre round the railway station more than it did round any other single building, probably more than the church or the town hall. Unfortunately the construction of the railways, the speculation and disputes this aroused, has attracted more attention than the social consequences that followed. In France, only the Northern Railway has been the subject of study thorough enough to reveal the reactions of the public to the new opportunities placed before them. It is not typical, but it shows that under the Second Empire people travelled very largely only when they had to. Some provincials paid a visit to Paris for some special occasion, like the Exhibitions, but on the whole this remained a unique experience. The increase in traffic was due largely to the growth of the suburbs—the commuter to the cities already becoming important—and also to the Sunday trip of the townsman into the suburbs. Already in the early 1870s, 77 per cent of the travellers from the Gare du Nord travelled to suburban destinations. After them, the most numerous category of travellers were businessmen, and international business travel was not insignificant. Gradually, the attraction of Paris as a shopping centre for provincials, to which wives liked to make trips, began to assert itself. In the reverse direction, the introduction of cheap excursion fares 'filled the trains with [Parisian] men and women who had not seen their native province for many years and whose return created a veritable sensation' in their villages. The railways thus strengthened family relations which difficulties of transport had weakened. Railway fares only became really cheap in the period 1883–1913, when they were on average 40 per cent lower than in the previous two decades. The great innovation was the introduction of cheaper return fares for families (1891) and workers' season tickets (1883). The railways, by their policies on fares, created new habits. Commuting from suburbs became possible for all classes, even though commercially the low fares were not justifiable. The railways were already losing money on suburban traffic from as early as 1895, but by doing so they transformed the country's working habits and the location of industry. They set in motion new patterns of leisure by running cheap trains to the seaside. The great increase in traffic between 1883 and 1913 was not in first-class passengers, who remained at virtually the same level, but above all in third-class ones. By the turn of the century, railway travel was not only a banal aspect of life, but it had been so much integrated into working-class habits that only a small proportion of them now travelled at full fare.[1] In 1910 37 per cent of travellers were season ticket holders, which meant over a quarter of a million commuters on the Northern Railway. The result was that when the motor car began to compete with the railway after the First World War, the railways could make no further headway, and since public opinion, government policy and trade union activity made it impossible for them to raise fares

[1] In 1887–91 46·5 per cent of tickets were paid at full fare, in 1909–13 21·8 per cent—the rest benefited from various reductions.

or to keep down the numbers or wages of their staff, they were already heading for insolvency: they had become a social service.[1] The railways had created new needs and had set up patterns of both work and leisure which depended on them. Their staff enjoyed security of employment, and pensions comparable to the civil service. Working on the railways was as attractive as working for the state. This was wholly appropriate, because the country had come to expect services from the railways, in the same way as they took it for granted that the roads would be kept in repair and the schools would provide free learning. Rather oddly, however, no one claimed the 'right to travel' or that the railways should be free also. It would have been a logical conclusion; but that it was not seen as such shows how equality of opportunity applied to very strictly limited fields and freedom in most things was still available only to those who had the money to buy it.

This was even more obvious in the case of the motor car. The history of the motor car provides instructive indications of how Frenchmen viewed and responded to technical modernisation in its most advanced form. The automobile industry refuted the generalisation that the French were too traditional to be capable of rapid economic growth. Between 1890 and 1904 France led the world in the production of motor cars, and until 1930 it made more cars than any other country in Europe. Between 1923 and 1938, when the U.S.A. increased its production of cars by only 20 per cent, France increased its by 180 per cent. But the paradox of this is that the French had not developed a cheap popular car by the Second World War, as every other country had. They clung to artisan methods and luxury standards longer than most. Firms like Dion-Bouton (founded by the marquis de Dion, who built a steam tricycle in 1883), Delaunay-Belleville (founded in 1903, and making 'cars that last'), Rochet-Schneider (1893), Delage (1905), Panhard-Levassor—and there were altogether 155 different manufacturers in France by 1914—have remained famous for their individualist skills. Renault, it is true, got near to mass production. This firm was established in 1899 by Louis Renault, the son of a draper and button manufacturer, after failing to pass the entrance examination into the École

---

[1] François Caron, *Histoire de l'exploitation d'un grand réseau. La Compagnie du chemin de fer du Nord 1846-1937* (1973).

Centrale. He expanded rapidly because he made his cars very largely out of components manufactured by others and because he (or rather his brother Fernand) quickly adopted a very active export policy, with selling outlets all over the world. He specialised at first in taxis and by 1909 two-thirds of the 3,000 taxis in Paris and half of London's 2,400 taxis were Renaults. Instead of reducing prices, he increased sales. He was very much alive to developments in the U.S.A., which he visited in 1911, and he was quick to introduce Taylorisation, but only partially. His prices long remained higher than those of his foreign competitors, and in 1927 it was calculated that whereas it took American firms 70 working days to produce a car, it took the French 300 days. It was only around 1925 that the price of French cars began to drop, long after the dramatic drop started by Ford, whose model T cost almost a third in 1916 of what it had cost in 1909.[1] Renault had the highest ambitions. In 1919 he said that he hoped France would become the 'economic centre of the universe'. But, as one of his collaborators rather unfairly said, his financial skills were those of a peasant. When the great depression struck, he had not overreached himself and he survived the crisis, unlike Citroen, who was the real practitioner of mass production in France, making only one or two models. In 1933–5 the three main car manufacturers in France, Renault, Citroen and Peugeot, were all thinking of launching a cheap popular car, to be sold at about two-thirds or less of the price then current, but partly because of the difficulties created by the depression, and partly because of the resistance of their salesmen, who had got used to dealing with wealthy customers and who argued that the demand was for more powerful cars rather than cheaper ones, the idea was abandoned. The car manufacturers preferred to maximise profits rather than turnover. Renault, despite his genius at seizing commercial opportunities, remained at heart a very conservative employer, anxious to resist the workers' demands and to fight the communists, and his collaboration with the Vichy regime led to the nationalisation of his firm at the Liberation.[2]

[1] The price of a 12 CV in 1913 was 12,000 francs, when the maximum annual salary of an *instituteur* was 2,500 francs and that of a Conseiller d'État 16,000 francs.

[2] Patrick Fridenson, *Histoire des Usines Renault*, vol. 1: *1898–1939* (1972), one of the best histories of a business, with a good guide to the considerable literature on the subject.

There gradually grew up two distinct markets for cars, the new and the second-hand. The very early cars did not last long. Of those built between 1898 and 1908, only 48 per cent were still on the road after seven years and virtually none after fourteen. Of those built between 1908 and 1914, 78 per cent were still working after seven years, and of those built between the wars, 83 per cent survived more than seven years. In 1927 the cutting of the road tax by half for cars of over nine years of age further encouraged people not to throw these away. The result was that in 1930 52 per cent of car sales were of second-hand cars and 68 per cent in 1935. The interesting fact about the people who bought cars was that they were not just the richest. Two-thirds of car owners in 1932 lived in villages or small provincial towns. There were many merchants and doctors among them, but also well-to-do peasants. The car appealed above all to the rural notables, for whom railways had not fully catered, and whom the car freed from their isolation. The middle classes of the cities found the expense of the car less necessary. The idea that every man needed a car, wherever he lived, had certainly not yet established itself; it was in any case an impossible idea, because most people were far too poor even to think about it. An economist calculated the number of families, at various periods, who had an income large enough to run a car, and found that at no time between 1900 and 1952 were there more than about 20 per cent more possible car owners, on this criterion, than actual car owners. Cars were still so expensive that people almost had to choose between having a car and having a child: there is a striking concordance between the map showing areas of low birth-rates and that of car ownership, as there is also with the map showing areas where least new houses were built. Most significantly, perhaps, it was areas with high divorce rates that bought most cars. These relationships were clearly in existence in 1938; it was not until the 1950s that they disappeared, and it was only then that the car established itself as an object whose ownership no longer implied such drastic choices.[1]

The world of the car had by then expanded in two ways.

[1] Janine Morice, *La Demande d'automobiles en France* (1957); Ho-Thoï-Sang, 'Le Marché des voitures de tourisme en France depuis la fin de la guerre' (Toulouse economics thesis, 1958, unpublished).

First there was a growing number of people working in the industry, not only in the factories but also in the garages, which now established themselves in every little town, side by side with and as essential as the pharmacists.[1] Secondly, there was increasing reliance on public road transport, particularly in rural areas. In a rural department like the Puy-de-Dôme, for example, in 1913 cars carried under a tenth of the goods but about a quarter of the passengers on the roads; by 1928 cars carried 25 per cent more goods than horse-drawn carriages but over ten times as many passengers as still used horses. Bus company lines here increased fivefold in the years 1923–9. In the country as a whole, cars and buses were by 1934 transporting as many passengers as the railways, though only one-sixth of the goods that railways carried.[2] The Bordeaux regional bus companies were then carrying 4 million passengers a year. The bus manufacturers encouraged the proliferation of bus services by selling their vehicles on credit, so that there were many bus services run by individuals, with no capital and vague time-tables. Though the speed limit was 50 k.p.h., it was frequently broken, because the bus companies competed against each other in speeding, encouraged by the passengers.[3] It was ironic that the car industry, which began in such a romantic way with characters like Bollée, the bellfounder of Le Mans, who christened his steam car for twelve passengers 'L'Obéissante' (1873),[4] should have developed into the tensest and most inflammable part of the economy, but it was perhaps not inappropriate that the workers in it should have played a leading part in the crucial confrontations of 1936 and 1968.[5] The manufacture of cars would come to symbolise the choice that had been made for the masses by economic forces, by which they sacrificed a third of their day in wholly unenjoyable factory work, in return for greater freedom, during another third of the day, to give themselves up to the enjoyment of leisure. This segregation of work and play had not

[1] See H. M. Astruc, *L'Automobile à la portée de tous (ouvrage de vulgarisation)* (1920, 60th edition 1938).

[2] Maurice Wolkowitch, *L'Économie régionale des transports dans le Centre et le Centre-Ouest de la France* (1960), 188 ff.

[3] André Clavier, *Étude économique des autobus régionaux desservant Bordeaux* (Bordeaux thesis, 1936), 54.

[4] Cf. J. P. Peugeot, *Le Film de l'automobile* (n.d., about 1958).

[5] Pierre Naville et al., *L'État entrepreneur. Le cas de la régie Renault* (1972), on problems of labour relations.

yet come about fully in 1945. But that was perhaps to be the
most important consequence of the growth of industry and of
the technical ingenuity it produced.

The corollary of this was that life became both cheaper and
more expensive—cheaper in the sense that the wages of the
working class rose very considerably, but more expensive also
in the sense that there were far more goods to buy. It is not
possible to draw up a balance-sheet of profit and loss, because
the history of income and expenditure of different classes has not
yet been fully written, and precisely which goods and services
were bought most and by whom is not known. What is clear,
however, is that for the majority of the nation, food still constituted the major item of expenditure (between 50 and 60 per
cent in 1945). Real wages rose for most people, but so too did
the additional demands on them: for transport, furniture, newspapers, entertainment and health. Life involved many more
opportunities, but the advantages created by industrial progress
were distributed in a very unequal way. More food was clearly
what the increased prosperity went into first. The consumption
of wheat and grain per inhabitant rose by about 50 per cent,
1830–70. That of potatoes almost doubled 1840–1940, and in
this period the consumption of sugar increased sevenfold, that
of coffee ninefold, and that of cocoa by more than fifty times.
People next bought more clothes: the consumption of cotton per
inhabitant rose fourfold and that of wool doubled. However, the
prices of different goods fluctuated in a way that pushed expenditure in unexpected directions. The price of cigarettes remained
steady (1891–1915), and so in real terms they became cheaper;
the cost of sending a letter was halved (1849–1907), so was the
price of sugar (1875–1909) and ink (1904–14). Gas cost 50 per
cent less (1880–1907), clinical thermometers fell 60 per cent
(1904–9) and crockery fell by about a third (1907–14); taxi fares
fell 3 per cent (1901–14). On the other hand doctors' fees went
up by 50 per cent (1900–14) and then decupled between the wars.
The price of a man's haircut rose 36 per cent (1900–14), that
of waterproof raincoats by 25 per cent (1899–1914). The price
of eggs rose by a third (1875–1914) and then increased ninefold
between the wars. The conveniences that made up the comfortable life were increasingly expensive: the price of cookers rose

twelvefold (1906–39); when electric irons replaced stove-heated ones (about 1930) they cost three times as much; the price of a mattress was ten times as much in 1939 as in 1914. The money wages of provincial labourers did indeed increase by about eighteen times (1910–39), but those of civil service engineers by only seven times. The real purchasing power of the engineers thus fell between the wars by over a third—and many middle-class people found themselves in the same plight—whereas the workers became considerably richer: the primary-school teacher did best of all, doubling his real income (1914–49). A redistribution of wealth was taking place independently of the policies of governments. The effects of science and technology were thus profoundly revolutionary but in a chaotic way: the kind of life they made possible involved just as much accident and inequality as that which it replaced. It was certainly not the expression of democratic choice, and the scientists had very little idea of the implications of their work.[1]

[1] The difficulty of generalising about prices can be seen from Rémy Alasseur, J. Fourastié, et al., Documents pour l'élaboration d'indices du coût de la vie en France de 1910 à 1965. The following table should therefore be read with reservations.

	Real wages	Industrial prices	Food prices
1840	78·5	57·0	73·1
1850	87·9	51·5	52·2
1860	84·9	65·0	69·8
1870	91·6	55·7	73·1
1880	114·7	46·1	73·1
1890	129·5	40·7	56·6
1900	136·6	43·2	51·1
1910	144·6	45·4	59·9
1920	97·3	266·4	292·5
1930	144·2	268·2	364·4
1938/9	155·9	338·5	449·5
1952	100·0		

Based on J. Singer-Kerel, Le Coût de la vie à Paris de 1840 à 1954 (1961), 104, and tables.

6. Happiness and Humour

IN 1776 the American Declaration of Independence held it to be self-evident that the pursuit of happiness was one of the inalienable rights of man. In 1789 the French Revolution proclaimed, as the American one had done, the importance of liberty and equality, but it did not mention happiness, only fraternity. This is a very significant difference. American history could perhaps be written in terms of that country's search for happiness, from the time when Josiah Quincy, Jr. and Jefferson described this as the main object of society to F. D. Roosevelt's second inaugural address, when he asked, 'Have we reached the goal of our vision? Have we found our happy valley?' Happiness was most visibly made America's ideal in its advertising: one historian counted 257 faces in a single issue of an American weekly magazine, and of these no less than 178 were smiling or laughing, 14 singing and 3 smiling through their tears: the rest were not smiling for a variety of reasons, such as that they were asleep, or 'Arabs or other obvious outsiders'.[1] Laughter has not always met with equal approval elsewhere. Lord Chesterfield wrote that it was a 'low and unbecoming thing', a characteristic of folly and ill manners; it was the way in which the mob express 'their silly joy in silly things', and he denied that he had ever laughed himself a single time since adulthood. That did not stop the English winning fame for their sense of humour, though Taine commented that this was based in melancholy and that 'the man who jests in England is seldom kindly, and never happy'. Happiness and humour require separate attention; but before humour is examined, it is worth seeing why happiness has held such an ambiguous place in French life.

In the eighteenth century, the French were as keen on happiness as the Americans. On the theoretical and literary levels, indeed, they could probably claim to have been the world's experts on it, for they then, suddenly, published about two hundred treatises on the subject. In the process, however, they

[1] Howard Mumford Jones, *The Pursuit of Happiness* (Cambridge, Mass., 1953), 132. Cf. V. J. McGill, *The Idea of Happiness* (New York, 1967).

discovered, or rediscovered, many of the complications that
happiness involves; and their longing for it was therefore
balanced by vigorous arguments about its nature and much
uncertainty about how it could be achieved. Neither Boudier
de Villemert's *Apology for Frivolity* (1750), nor the Jesuit Sarasa's
often reprinted *Art of Tranquillising Oneself* (1664) nor Paradis
de Moncrif's *Essays on the Necessity and the Means of Pleasing People*
(1738), nor any single work can be looked to for a summary of
accepted opinion, because this was in constant evolution. All
that was agreed was that everybody, without exception, wanted
to be happy, but the solutions that were offered to the problems
that this posed were either incomplete, or unsatisfactory even to
those who thought them up, or compromises which involved a
large measure of self-deception. The eighteenth century was not
as straightforwardly optimistic as is often believed, and it bequeathed doubts as well as hopes. Thus the strict Christian view
that happiness should not be sought in this world, and could not
be enjoyed here—except perhaps for the hope of attaining it in
the next world—was vigorously reiterated, as it would continue
to be in the nineteenth century too. The steady flow of young
women into convents showed that renunciation was practised as
well as believed. But there were also Christian authors, like Le
Maître de Claville, from whose best-selling *Treatise on True Merit*
(1734) even Rousseau borrowed, who tried to reconcile the
search for personal salvation with the 'enjoyment of innocent
pleasures' and who held up the attainable ideal of the Christian
gentleman, finding satisfaction in marital bliss and honourable
entertainments. There were thus a large variety of attitudes,
even within the Church itself, towards happiness.

The challenge of the *philosophes* consisted of three propositions
which apparently completely negated the Christian view. They
argued that there was a science of happiness, which could be deduced from an objective study of man and the laws governing both
his emotions and the world around him. Happiness, for them,
was no longer something reserved for an élite, but was attainable
by all, because their science considered the universal man, and
their teachings were not concerned, as the rules of society were,
simply with polite courtiers. Above all, they saw happiness as
no longer to be won by individuals in isolation, seeking their
personal salvation, but as necessarily a social achievement,

depending on the way society was organised, and involving the harmonisation of human relationships. However, when they began to work out the implications of these new rules, as they did in their Encyclopedia and, in greater detail, in Levesque de Pouilly's *Theory of Agreeable Sentiments* (1736), they did not, on many points, contradict Christianity's teaching, though they left out all reference to it. Man, they said, was a machine; if his faculties were used properly, 'agreeable sensations' would result. This meant that mere contemplation was not enough, and the exercise of all sides of the personality was desirable. However, they restricted their praise of pleasure by reviving traditional views about the different value of different pleasures, insisting on moderation and the golden mean in their enjoyment, and above all proclaiming that there was a providential plan which naturally harmonised the diversity of life. So, though morals required man to do nothing which did not make him happy, happiness ended up as not much different from virtue. The ideal of the egocentric saint was replaced by the public-spirited man, seeking the good of his fellow beings, but this did not really substitute a dynamic attitude in the place of Christian resignation. Voltaire illustrated the uncertainties that remained when, in his stories *Zadig* and *Candide*, he showed life as tragic, because the search for happiness was subject to the most absurd effects of chance and of human folly; man was torn 'between the convulsions of anxiety and the lethargy of boredom'. Voltaire ended up with only a moderate optimism, advising sadly that we should 'cultivate our gardens', because boredom was easier to bear; work was the way to avoid thinking, abstention from involvement with the world was the way to reduce suffering. Fontenelle, similarly, argued that man's troubles all came from uncontrolled imaginations; that the way to happiness was therefore to enjoy what one possessed, to know oneself as one really was, to adjust oneself to one's situation, putting aside distracting dreams and phobias, seeking above all repose—cold and boring though that might be. Montesquieu was an advocate of a judicious balancing of human inclinations, to avoid the dangers of exaggerated emotions, for he was particularly conscious of the variety and inconstancy of the individual personality. Helvétius worried about the 'ravages and crimes' of ambition, though he was very much aware of its pleasures. There were many tirades against the ill-effects of money and business, and that was partly why the pastoral life away from the cities, quiet study and gentle friendship, avoiding passion, were so frequently vaunted. The fear of suffering was thus still as strong as, if not stronger than, the hope for better things and the desire to enjoy life to the full.

In the seventeenth century, glory had been held up as something to aim for. Praise for it diminished notably now, many people declaring that it was incompatible with happiness; but there was disagreement about this. Vauvenargues still advocated glory, which involved action, courage, ambition, and Diderot saw applause and praise as man's best stimulant. In the seventeenth century, again, love had seldom been studied in relation to happiness, but it now became 'the great affair of life'. Love was declared to open a new way to self-fulfilment. However, it was now scrutinised in such detail, analysed so coldly, that it emerged full of paradoxes as well as endowed with new attractions. The links of love with vanity, self-love and anxiety were revealed, and much effort was put into freeing it from the myths surrounding it; at the same time, it was idealised in new ways; it was identified with virtue; and a hierarchy of its manifestations was elaborated, so that only its 'pure', 'delicate', and 'true' forms were declared acceptable. Some people nevertheless were bold enough now to sing the praises of its purely sexual side, but the eighteenth century generally was of course not as immoral as its reputation. The materialist physician La Mettrie did indeed argue that the pleasures of the body were the only ones that mattered and that happiness should be sought in them without troubling oneself about problems of good and evil; but though this was how his doctrine was generally understood, and why it was almost universally rejected, he himself made careful distinctions, as far as his own pleasures were concerned, between 'vulgar' and 'estimable' ones. There were advocates of sheer frivolity, even of libertinage, which was indeed part of the education of young men of most classes, but their attitudes were complicated by the restraints of both conscience and propriety, which were seldom wholly absent.

The erotic challenge to Christianity was paralleled by the economic one, but it was not reinforced by it. The commercial middle classes who devoted themselves to the accumulation of wealth seemed to be rejecting not only the idea of the vanity of the things of this world, but also idealism, love and sentiment. However, they were seldom content simply to enjoy their material goods; they wanted esteem also, public recognition of their merit. On the one hand, therefore, they claimed that their economic achievements benefited the whole state, for they were creators of prosperity, and on the other hand they prided themselves on practising most if not all the Christian virtues; they fortified themselves by being models of approved behaviour in their domestic and moral lives, making use of their ill-gotten gains with Christian modesty, seeking to win on all fronts. There was uncertainty, after all, as to whether poverty was a condition of virtue. Rochefort, in his *Critical History of the Opinions of the Philosophers on Happiness* (1778), argued that wealth provided the means which could bring happiness, but that it also destroyed its owner's aptitude to be happy. The philosophers with economic interests justified and praised wealth, as the sign and condition of progress; and the traditional Christian view that, individually, the poor man was the most content, gave way to doubts, as in the works of the abbé Trublet: he thought that there were probably more happy than unhappy people in the world, because there were more poor people, but he wondered whether he would have a different opinion if he knew more poor people, particularly since, when he congratulated them on their gaiety, he was told that they sang at work not because they were happy, but in order to diminish their sorrows and to forget the pain of their labour.

The situation at the end of the eighteenth century therefore was that there was no clear view of how to cope with the conflicts of the heart and the mind, of selfishness and generosity, of natural instincts and the search for virtue, of the desire for repose and the fear of boredom, of the problem of satisfying all these hopes and of finding happiness also. Making money, education, improved hygiene and medicine were put forward as short cuts to general well-being, but the philosophers could not point out obvious cases to prove that their magic cures worked. So meanwhile the aristocracy continued to content themselves with *politeness* as a less exalted way of smoothing human relations and of satisfying the desire to be loved. For them conversation was the prime instrument for the attainment of their goal of making as many friends as possible, or at least not offending too many people. They also believed that society held the key to happiness, but they concentrated on adapting themselves to it, instead of seeking to change it.[1]

In the nineteenth century, adapting oneself was perhaps the most common attitude, partly because it was the easiest course and partly because it incorporated copying the behaviour of one's social superiors, with all the flattering consequences that involved. The counterpart of ambition was imitation. If one confines oneself to what philosophers said about happiness, one is bound to get the impression that this was a complex ideal, never actually achieved, always elusive, even if the formulae for capturing it are simplicity itself. If one turns to other kinds of writers, and particularly novelists and poets, one is faced with the problem of deducing what the average was from the study of exceptional cases; the novelists of this period were personally, on the whole, not particularly happy people: their idealisation of life, or their sombre picture of its difficulties, leave it uncertain whether anybody was happy at all. It is much easier to find records of the pathological, of violence, crime and disaster, than of quiet and contented lives.

Friendship

One can best get an idea of the way changing social conditions bore upon the problem of being happy, for the ordinary man, by looking at the history of friendship. In the chapters on politics, attention has been drawn to the contrast between regions in which family and clan loyalties remained powerful and those where they were replaced by friendship; and it was suggested that it was in these latter regions that advanced republican ideas were most actively propagated. It is often said that in primitive societies all relationships are dominated by family and kin, and the world is divided into the clan on the one hand and strangers on the other, the latter generally being regarded as the enemy. There is very little room in this situation for neutral, intermediary or emotional relationships. France in the nineteenth century had long passed this simple state, but people were still not entirely free to choose their friends where they

[1] Robert Mauzi, *L'Idée du bonheur dans la littérature et la pensée françaises a u 18 siècle* (1960).

pleased, and the idea of friendship, indeed, could only develop slowly against this traditional background. To their obligations to their families, people gradually added obligations to their neighbours and to those with whom they worked: the workshop, the factory, the fraternity, societies, clubs and cafés gradually extended their contacts. The romantic idea was that a man should have free choice in those with whom he associated, and it praised emotional attachments as superior to others which were in various ways imposed; but this was an ideal, to which different classes and different regions were attracted in different degrees. The preference for friends one had chosen oneself over family and social commitments implied that the individual had become self-conscious in a new way, aware more of the peculiarities of his personality than of the status that membership of his family gave him; and it involved experiencing loneliness and the sense of solitude. None of these circumstances came equally to all classes, or at the same time.

This emerged very clearly in a study of the different social relationships of workers, clerks and engineers, residing in Paris, in a middle-sized town and a small town in 1954–5. There were then powerful obstacles still to the formation of friendships. Sexual differences were the most important. Eighty per cent of the sample said that friendship with a person of the opposite sex was possible but only half of them actually had such a friend. Well-to-do professional people were the pioneers in breaking down this barrier—almost twice as many engineers as workers had friends of the opposite sex—while clerks were the most suspicious of such relationships, partly because they saw women as economic rivals.[1] Class was the next barrier. About half of all friends were of the same social class. Workers and clerks kept pretty much apart from each other, for only 15 per cent of workers admitted to having clerks as friends, and only 15 per cent of clerks had workers for friends. Friendships between rich and poor were of course rarer still: only 2 per cent of engineers had workers for friends. This is confirmed by what is known about intermarriage between social classes. About 45 per cent of French people in this period were still marrying within their own social class. This stability varied however with different

[1] 62 per cent of engineers had a female friend, 35 per cent of workers and 26 per cent of clerks.

groups. Thus 64 per cent of peasants married other peasants, 49 per cent of workers married workers, but only 26 per cent of clerks married clerks, and the most ambiguous people were middle management, of whom only 10 per cent married within their own ranks.[1] By now class, or occupation, was not decisive, though it was important: the effect of the Third Republic's work had been to make education even more important: two-thirds of couples were of the same educational level. But though workers and clerks often had the same education and were of roughly the same educational level, they seldom became friends: when they did, it was usually a sign that the worker was treading the path of *embourgeoisement*. This crossing of barriers occurred most frequently in modern industries and in large cities. Miners had far more friends from among their own class than workers in the petroleum industry.[2]

It emerges that friendship did not mean the same thing to the various people who were questioned about it. Workers stressed the reciprocity and the exchange of services as a major element in their view of it; many of them indeed refused to distinguish between *camaraderie* and *amitié*; and manual workers seldom used the word *amitié* at all, preferring to talk about *copains*, mates. Workers liked to form a group of friends, and to have them all

[1] The details are to be found in A. Girard, *Le Choix du conjoint* (1964), and can be summarised as follows:

Profession of wife's father	Profession of the husband						
	Agric. worker	Peasant	Worker	Artisan	Clerk	Middle management	Senior management and liberal professions
Agric. worker	35	27	24	8	6	..	..
Peasant	5	64	14	8	5	1	3
Worker	4	17	49	13	12	2	3
Artisan	1	21	22	34	10	4	8
Clerk	4	16	32	14	26	3	5
Middle management	..	12	21	19	21	10	17
Senior management and liberal professions	1	12	13	18	15	5	36

Elizabeth Glass, *Getting Married: Women and Marriage in Parisian Society in the Later Nineteenth Century* (forthcoming) shows that in 1865, roughly 40 per cent of Parisians in her sample married members of their own social group.

[2] Miners 68 per cent, petroleum workers 39 per cent.

meeting together; they saw friendship as a collective sentiment. In rural areas, *amitié* was used very broadly to mean simply concord or harmony, as in the statement 'There is more *amitié* in this village than the next', meaning more solidarity. Friendship for the workers was thus often closely related to the traditional neighbourly mutual aid, practised most actively in slum quarters. The element of personal choice was limited. The engineers by contrast romanticised friendship much more, making it a kind of substitute for the support of which their escape from community life had deprived them. They saw friendship as more of a personal interchange, in which each friend was valued for unique qualities, so that it was less common for them all to be brought together. This kind of friendship was essentially urban and the product of new classes without traditional organisations. Friendship was still a rare thing. Fifty per cent of all those questioned admitted to having only between two and four friends; 10 per cent said they had no friends at all. The clerks were the loneliest of all, for one-quarter of them said they had no friends. The engineers cultivated friendship most, having twice as many friends as the workers. Three-quarters of the engineers said they often discussed their intimate preoccupations with at least one friend, and only 5 per cent of them never did, but only about half of the workers admitted to these personal discussions and the clerks were even more chary of them: 21 per cent of the clerks indeed never discussed their private affairs with friends. The engineers very seldom broke up their friendships as a result of rows, which the workers did much more often.[1] Almost half of friendships were ended by change of residence and almost a quarter by marriage. The engineers not only formed friendships more, but also broke them more, perhaps because they moved around most. There was obviously a close link between the need for friendship and the sense of isolation; the idealisation of friendship was the work of those who both disliked isolation and feared to show that they suffered from it. The hierarchy of values into which friendship fitted was revealed by what these people said about how it stood in relation to their other commitments. Family still came first, and only a minority would sacrifice it to friendship; work also came high,

[1] Engineers break up because of rows 2 per cent, workers 16 per cent, clerks 10 per cent.

in most cases even higher than family, implying that the need to earn a living, or ambition, were dominant incentives. Political and religious opinions came considerably lower, and 65 per cent said they had friendships with people of diametrically opposed views. This should not be surprising, for though friendship claimed to unite like minds, it seldom did; people have more often sought in friends qualities they admire, rather than those they possess, or some combination of their image of themselves and the ideal they would like to be; and it is only the more confident, those with most self-esteem, who attribute to their friends characteristics they have themselves. Friendship thus did not replace the old ties of neighbourhood and kin in a simple way, for it involved a meeting of ideals rather than of solidly based obligations; it represented a desire for a new security but also for self-transcendence; it was on the fringes of reality and fantasy.[1]

'Sociability' has recently been revealed as one of the key factors in the growth of republicanism.[2] The urban aspect of sociability is certainly emphasised when it is regarded from the political point of view. But, as the chapter on regionalism has suggested, sociability in the south of France had a different significance from what it had elsewhere, and the idea needs to be clarified, for nuances mattered a great deal in something so subtle. The variations of sociability as between classes and professional groups, and the effect of social mobility upon it, need to be borne in mind. There is a need, that is, for much more investigation of the history of sociability. The history of affection between husbands and wives must, moreover, be regarded as closely related to this, for the growth of friendship between husband and wife probably reduced their reliance on support from other members of their families. This is suggested by the way widows were treated. By the Napoleonic Code, widows had very small claims to their late husbands' estates, and it was only in 1891 that a law gave the usufruct of one-half of his property if they had no children and one-quarter if they had. Until then, marriage was often a financial alliance which ended with the death of either partner, and both sides kept as their principal

---

[1] Jean Maisonneuve, *Psycho-sociologie des affinités* (Paris doctoral thesis, 1966).

[2] M. Agulhon, *La République au village* (1970), an essential work for the understanding of modern French society.

heirs their own families. It was the poor, who had least to lose, and whose family ties were least complicated by economic ties, who were the keenest on introducing clauses into marriage contracts providing generously for their surviving partners; it was people with fewest other relationships for whom marriage thus came to mean most in emotional terms. Small shopkeepers very frequently bequeathed their businesses to their spouses, but this was rarer among the rich.[1] The capacity for friendship involved certain preconditions, and it was the same with the capacity for happiness.

It is clear therefore that it would be futile to trace the history of happiness as though this had a constant meaning, but that does not mean that the question of whether people became more or less happy in this period is a frivolous one. The answer must be sought, however, on several levels. Historians have hitherto tended to concentrate on those factors which *should* have made people happier, notably the increase in material possessions and the improvement in physical health. These are very far from negligible; but the conclusions to which they lead are incomplete in themselves, because they do not prove anything about the state of mind of those who have become richer or healthier. Another approach is to consider the manifestations of happiness—joy, revelry and celebration—and work from them to the social relationships with which they were linked. Perhaps the best phenomenon to analyse for this purpose is dancing.

Dancing

Paintings of traditional dancing immediately pose an apparently puzzling problem. Adolphe Leleux (1812–91), a prolific painter of folkloric scenes, has left a most instructive picture of *A Marriage in Brittany* (1863), which was exhibited in the Second Empire's museum of modern art, the Luxembourg. The peasants are shown dancing, but the expressions on their faces give no sign of merriment or joy. There is an explanation of this. There are two opposing sides of happiness, the kind which comes from security, acceptance and conformity, and that which represents liberation from the constraints of daily life. Breton dancing

---

[1] Elizabeth Glass, *Getting Married: Women and Marriage in Parisian Society* (forthcoming), part three.

allows one to see the meaning of this, for though it was not typical of France as a whole, it has the advantage that there was a great deal of it, and it survived long enough for folklorists and ethno-musicologists to record its steps and rituals before it became simply a tourist attraction. Its history to very recent times may be traced, in particular, from a detailed description of Breton dancing compiled on the basis of interviews with old people in 375 villages during the years 1945–60.[1] Many of the informants who were then questioned spoke about the dancing of their youth with exceptional emotion, recalling how people would walk many miles to participate in a dance, arriving all covered in sweat, but at once joining in. 'When I was very young,' said one, 'during the harvesting of the beet, I could barely lift up my overflowing basket; but if I thought about the dance and remembered a tune, I would raise it without effort and I would dance with my load.' An old woman of eighty uttered the proverb: 'Dancing keeps a man standing.' 'Once upon a time,' said a third, 'when one had black thoughts or when one did not feel well, one said, "Let's go and dance the ronde".'

This traditional dancing, which survived up to around 1900 in the Morlaix and Plouaret regions, to around 1914 in northern Finistère and to about 1945 in southern Finistère, was the expression above all of group consciousness, in which bodily movement and gesture, without speech, was the language used to assert the cohesion of the community. Dancing was a collective activity, in which all classes and, most noticeably, all age groups participated. It had little erotic content and most of the old dances could be performed perfectly well by people of the same sex, and many were. It was not done for men to dance frequently with the same women (except for recently engaged couples); and though there were different ways of holding one's partner, the variations were mainly designed to limit contact: if a girl did not like her partner, she would still dance with him, but perhaps hold on to him with a handkerchief rather than by hand, and that is what priests who danced at the weddings of their relatives did. The young never had separate dances in Brittany (though they did in other parts of France). The old

[1] Jean Michel Guilcher, *La Tradition populaire de danse en Basse Bretagne* (Chambéry, 1963, doctoral thesis).

Breton dances were a reflection of the compulsory neighbourliness which was a prime feature of village life. The inhabitants of a village were linked by a common childhood, by much work in common, by frequent use of help from outside the family for the accomplishment of the larger agricultural tasks. Work in the fields, like harvesting, and work at home, like spinning, was often done on a team basis, in which the help of neighbours was sought and subsequently returned. This social aspect made it possible to turn the most back-breaking forms of labour into feasts, so that, for example, the potato harvest was looked forward to by the young, who would find out when each hamlet was planning it, and would come from neighbouring villages to participate in the dancing and games which were the reward of toil. People recalling their youth spoke with great pleasure of these gatherings, the amusements of which had led them to forget the hard labour involved; no task was so exhausting that at least the young did not end the day dancing. Those who sought the help of their neighbours had to provide entertainment afterwards, and much effort was put into ensuring that the pleasure would be greater than the pain.

An example of the way work and feasting were combined was the *renderie*. When a farmer wanted to weave a large amount of cloth, he asked the help of the village girls, to spin enough thread for the weaver; or rather, he asked nine young men, who each had to find nine girls to spin, and a competition was set up between them. The young men attended the competition too; the winning girl won a handkerchief as a prize and her boy friend some tobacco; they then all ate together and danced for half the night. These gatherings were very popular and as many as four or five hundred people might come to join in. They required as much preparation as weddings, which were the other principal form of collective demonstration. Weddings were designed to show off the extent and power of the families involved, but understanding family in the broadest sense, as though it were a Roman clan. Average weddings mustered between two and three hundred guests but attendances of one or two thousand were not rare, and even larger ones are recorded. The religious ceremony would be followed by a dance of honour which, as late as 1935, was still being observed as itself 'a sort of sacred ceremony generally marked by much gravity and dignity'; it was performed in the village square, started off by the bride, alone, until all joined in, including the very old, so that the relatives of the two families were solemnly united. In this region, which was very poor, festivities of this kind stood out all the more by their contrast. No one was completely left out: it was customary to invite the village's poorest inhabitants to weddings, for example, and the couple would dance with them. There were dances even at the *pardons*, the Breton pilgrimages to honour saints, particularly when the clergy did not control them. There were dances after fairs, dances to raise funds for good causes, 'magic dances' and 'marriage dances', the one in Penzé openly having as its function to find marriage partners; but what they all had in common was the staid concentration of the participants. A visitor to Brittany in the 1820s remarked: 'They dance with gravity; the women lower their eyes and the men are serious; no one would guess that they were enjoying themselves.'[1] That was because Breton dances were not designed to give expression to any dramatic idea, or to show off an individual's skill. In a prolonged feast, it is true, the gravity might give way to frenzy, when the dancers were carried away by the atmosphere they had created: most stood between 'the serene joy of the balanced dance and the mad joy of collective excitement'; but all of them were essentially public manifestations of collective security. There was a place in them for all the inhabitants. The dances enabled the community metaphorically to stroke its children, and children to bask in its protection. There was very little change therefore in the steps used. The peasants who participated were not concerned with imitating the aristocracy, and indeed there was only one Parisian dance, out of the thousands the capital invented, which was borrowed by the Bretons, and that only after it had been popular in the towns for over a century. It was only at the very end of the nineteenth century that the rural areas began dancing *la chaîne des dames* or *la chaîne anglaise*, which had then been current in Paris *salons* for about 150 years. It was only when both the authority of tradition and the economic organisation of society began to change that imitation of the towns took a hold. The new kinds of dance allowed the triumph of the individual, or the couple, and they took a hold at the same time as intimate

[1] Boucher de Perthes, *Chants armoricains ou souvenirs de Basse Bretagne* (1831), 187.

friendship, previously described, developed. Dancing competitions were an innovation, beginning only in the late nineteenth century. Till then, dancers simply had to conform; obedience to ritual was the price they paid for security. There were, it is true, some dances, like the *danse du rôti*, which took place during the wedding feast, after a lot of food and drink had been consumed, and which allowed people to show off their strength; but, in general, individual exhibitionism was avoided, particularly in the dance of honour after weddings, where everything was absolutely regulated by strict rules. The idea of pleasing one's partner in a dance, of having personal relations during it, of talking during a dance, was the result of a different conception of happiness.

This can be seen in the way the towns danced, or at least the way Paris danced, for the amusements of the capital are those which are best documented. One needs to distinguish three different kinds of dancing here in the nineteenth century: official, private and public balls. For originally dancing in the towns, like most things, was regulated by the government. Before the Revolution, indeed, the Opéra had a sort of monopoly of public dancing. In 1715 Louis XV authorised public dancing three times a week at the Opéra, dancing, that is, in which anyone could participate by paying an entrance fee. These dances were still very popular under Louis-Philippe and Napoleon III: the Opéra's parterre and orchestra pit were covered with a movable floor after performances for the purpose, and whole families would attend, for these dances were originally a family entertainment. Private family dances, to celebrate marriages, betrothals and feasts, and government balls, with several thousand guests, resembled the dancing of the Breton villagers in the sense that as well as being an amusement, they were also very much concerned with who belonged and who did not; inviting the right people was half the labour, and receiving invitations was a sign of one's acceptance by officialdom or by a particular section of society. The gatherings of small groups multiplied as more small groups were formed by the city's growing population. However, the rituals they enacted were now vigorously challenged by new dances and new forms of organisation.

The traditional *salon* dance was essentially a ballet, with complicated and varied steps, and with the quadrille, for example,

requiring as many as sixteen couples. Long practice and rehear-
sal were needed for them, and dancing lessons were part of a
gentleman's education as much as fencing lessons were. The
dancing masters were however much more than teachers of a
sport, for they taught their pupils also how to walk and salute
properly, how to enter a room, how to give grace and harmony
to every movement of the body. George Sand's dancing master,
the polite and solemn Monsieur Abraham, was still dancing and
still teaching in his eighties, and gave her the same precepts that
he had given Marie Antoinette. The dances which expressed the
fashionable ideals of elegance and decorum were the gavotte—
an elaborate ballet for two, with a set choreography though with
plenty of scope for the exhibition of individual grace and
originality—and the minuet, which had started as a stage ballet
and had then been popularised by the court. These were still
being danced in the 1830s, but by then the standard *salon* dance
had become the *contredanse*, dominant from the First to the
Second Empire. This, renamed the *quadrille*, represented, as
people then thought, a gayer and freer movement, even though
it involved five different figures, each with different steps; but
these were gradually all reduced to a simplified, uniform shuffling backwards and forwards. The great complaint from every
new generation was that *salon* dancing was boring; and in the
nineteenth century there were repeated changes of fashion, in
an attempt to introduce more varied emotions into them. The
waltz represented one of these attempted revolutions. In 1820
it was forbidden at court; in 1857 Flaubert was prosecuted for
describing a waltz without concealing its sexual overtones. The
waltz had in fact been introduced into France in 1787, in the
theatre; a form of it may have existed in seventeenth-century
Provence; but it was welcomed in the nineteenth century as a
sentimental and romantic import from Germany. Originally,
under Napoleon I, it was danced, as old prints show, with
couples holding both hands, or sometimes holding round the
waist, and they moved without turning; only in 1819 did
Weber's *Invitation* give it its modern form. This was shocking,
but innovations of this kind were constantly being introduced,
so that the shock was forgotten under the impact of new audaci-
ties. In 1832 the 'Saint-Simonian galop' modified the quadrille,
by allowing a change of partners. The cotillion, invented in the

1820s, and particularly popular in the early Third Republic, added the clapping of hands and the beating of a drum by the leader of the dance, whom everyone had to copy: it was much used as an ending for balls. The carillon, which had stamping as well as clapping, making a great deal of noise, enjoyed a vogue, until it became a favourite with the children. Another great revolution was that created by the polka, brought to France from Prague in 1844 and instantly copied after its performance on the stage. It made the fortune of its teacher, the Hungarian dancing master Cellarius of the rue Vivienne. 'One needs to have spent the winter of that year in Paris to have a real idea of the dancing revolution that broke like an insurrection in all the *salons*, to understand to what point young and old, mothers and daughters, magistrates and barristers, doctors and students, gave themselves up to the most passionate polkaic *ébats*. Everything was called a polka, from brands of men's and women's clothing to dishes and puddings served in the most sumptuous dinners . . . Boys used to go home from school dancing the polka through the streets, singing the original Bohemian song.'[1]

Fashion took different directions. Sometimes, as in 1830, it meant dancing negligently, shuffling, removing and replacing one's gloves instead of executing a particular step; but this led to dances losing their vitality and becoming unacceptable to the young. So, alternatively, more energetic or rhythmic ways of performing traditional dances were introduced, as for example the Boston, which was a kind of waltz, but less a step than a way of dancing, that could be applied equally to the polka and the quadrille. 'Bostonner' meant to advance or retreat or turn as one pleased, varying one's movements as much as possible, and sliding more than jumping. This became the rage after 1874; and a few years later the old quadrille, rejected as too staid, was replaced by the 'American quadrille', which was more amusing. Innovations were almost invariably foreign, which was the excuse or justification of their break with propriety. In 1892 the Two-Step arrived, in 1894 the Berlin; then the Tango, which was supposed to have been brought by gipsies from China through Spain to Argentina, and at the turn of the century

---

[1] G. Desrats, *Dictionnaire de la danse, historique, théorique, pratique et bibliographique* (1895), 293. Desrats, himself an erudite dancing master, was the son of a famous dancing master, a contemporary of Cellarius.

tango was the word used to describe every exotic dance that
was introduced.

There was a constant conflict, therefore, in Parisian dancing.
The Revolution, which ended the regulation of public balls, had
let loose a dancing mania, as revealed by the 400 and more
dancing places listed in the *Almanach des spectacles* for 1791. The
revolution of 1830 coincided with the invention of the *can-can*,
which was seen as the last straw by civilised society. Voltaire
had said that dancing could be considered an art, because it was
subject to rules. The *can-can*, as one dancing master said, was
'an epileptic dance, a delirium tremens, which is to proper
dancing what slang is to the French language . . . it is subjected
to no musical law, it is the result of the dancer's character as
well as of his suppleness or his agility'. It was declared to be
obscene, and it probably became increasingly so: at least those
who remembered it in its early days complained in their old age
that it had become dirty, and had never been so originally.[1] But
it is from the 1830s that the conflict of taught and untaught
dancing developed; the *bals publics* were abandoned by the
bourgeoisie, and it was there that the livelier new steps were
danced, becoming, in the eyes of the traditionalists, 'orgies and
veritable saturnalia'.

But there was a wide variety of public balls. Though these
represented liberation from one tradition, they were so popular
that they were captured by impresarios who organised them
into a new industry, so that the dancers were now victims of a
more elusive regimentation. *Bals publics* were organised to meet
every taste. Some indeed were specifically designed to revive the
family atmosphere that they once had: the Jardin d'Hiver, near
the Champs Élysées, which flourished during the Second Empire, was such a one; it also organised 'poetic and national
concerts' to popularise the music of the masters, with singers
from the Opéra and the Opéra comique. In the rue des Anglais,
which was only six metres wide, flanked by rotting houses, there
was a shop with the sign 'Dancing for the Family: calm guaranteed, complete propriety required'; and it attracted considerable numbers of Auvergnat families to its accordion music. By

[1] F. de Mesnil, *Histoire de la danse à travers les âges* (1905), v; Charles Narrey,
Ce que l'on dit pendant une contredanse (1863); Pierre Veron, *Paris s'amuse* (1861);
Auguste Vitu, *Les Bals d'hiver* (1851).

contrast the Bal Bullier was an example of a small, dirty, smoke-filled hall, which was stifling but renowned for its 'devilish' atmosphere: it was a family business, the third Bullier inheriting it from the son of the founder in 1882. The Folies-Robert in the Boulevard Rochechouart was founded by Gilles Robert, who had been in turn a ropemaker, a locksmith, a steamboat mechanic, a railway worker and assistant to Monsieur Salvart 'teacher of dancing and of good manners'. He had supplemented his income by teaching dancing in the evenings, until he was picked up by an English major who mistook him for a ballerina and who took dancing lessons from him at a guinea an hour. With the capital accumulated from all these sources, he opened his dance hall in 1856 and made enough of a success of it to have his biography written by a former student agitator.[1] The Salle Rivoli, once known as the Dame Blanche and then l'Astic, was where the boys of the nearby Lycée Charlemagne used to go on Sundays to smoke a cigarette and where famous painters went to seek their models among the exotic girls who came from the Jewish quarter close by. The Grand-Saint-Martin in Belleville, founded in 1800 by Dunoyez (one of whose brothers became a general while another owned most of Paris's taxis), had a different clientele, because it stayed open later than all its rivals.[2] The Élysée Montmartre ball, from the beginning of the nineteenth century, had catered for Parisians who came out of the city on Sundays to amuse themselves under the trees: in 1860 a hall of 1,000 square metres was built by the Serres family, which retained its ownership for several generations—another of the new professional organisers of mass entertainment. La Reine Blanche, a dance hall dating back to around 1850, rebuilt as the Moulin Rouge in 1885, had a reputation as a very gay and amusing place.[3] The Bals Incohérents (1885–98) required compulsory disguise. The Bals du Courrier français, organised by Jules Roques in the same period, after his conviction for publishing pornography, had a different theme each year—pastoral (1890), mystical (1891), transvestite (1892), pagan (1894). The Bal des Quat'z'Arts was the annual carnival of the arts students.

[1] Tony Fanfan [pseud. of Antonio Watripon], *Paris qui danse. Étude, types et mœurs* (1861), 28–35.

[2] Manuscript notes on *bals publics*, with numerous press cuttings, by G. Desrats, in B.N. 8° Z. Le Senne.5544.

[3] André Warnod, *Bals, cafés, cabarets* (1913, 5th edition), 97.

In 1892 it forbade 'formal dress, workers' overalls, bourgeois suits and bathing costumes': the students processed through the streets with four naked models till the early hours, for which they were prosecuted as a result of complaints from the League Against Licence in the Streets. Every year they thought up a new joke.[1]

The war of 1914–18 seems to have had the same effect on dancing as the French Revolution: it greatly increased its popularity, though the Gay Twenties represented relaxation from the austerities of the war rather than enthusiasm of a new kind. In 1921 the Academy of Paris Dancing Teachers issued a statement deploring the 'exotic fantasies executed to the sound of savage music', where each danced according to his whim; they attributed this decay of art to unnamed foreign influences; and they announced that they would refuse to teach the shimmy 'because it resembles too closely St. Vitus's dance and other chronic infirmities'. The headmistress of one of Paris's girls' *lycées* protested that the craze for dancing was producing a 'lowering of the intellectual level' among her pupils: she admitted she knew little about modern dancing but had by accident seen some briefly: she urged the revival of the minuet and gavotte and the dances of ancient Greece. Mgr. Baudrillart, one of the leading Catholic intellectuals, complained that these new dances were 'a direct preparation for the sexual act'. Dr. Bernard, a leading gynaecologist, warned that they brought on dangerous illnesses, like metritis and cystitis in women and impotence in men. Paul Bourget went to visit a dance hall 'for research purposes' and declared that he was horrified by the coarseness and impropriety. The Germans were accused of encouraging the multiplication of dance halls so that they could peddle cocaine in them. The *Revue philosophique* published an article classifying 'the new Argentinian dances' as 'manifestations of satyriasis'. Madame Lefort, a well-known dancing teacher, proclaimed the importance of maintaining the French tradition, of banishing cheek-to-cheek dancing; and if the new steps could not be banned, they could at least be purified: she herself gave lessons in which the shimmy was turned into 'an honest foxtrot and a sort of hygienic and sporting promenade'. The government, however, refused to take action. The Prefect

[1] Georges Pillement, *Paris en fête* (1972), 366 ff.

of the Seine said that personally he found dancing good exercise and he always felt much better the morning after.[1]

But these complaints showed that considerable sections of the bourgeoisie feared and disliked celebrations which broke down too many barriers. Only some people enjoyed themselves in this way. How many is not clear, but in 1962 an opinion poll found that dancing was the favourite pastime of only 13 per cent of young people between sixteen and twenty-four. By then giving dancing parties was a minority, middle-class practice: 68 per cent of these adolescents had never given one; the *lycée* school-boys claimed to go to between eleven and forty a year, while working-class boys very seldom went.[2] The process by which dancing changed its significance and lost its universal appeal still needs to be studied, as too does the system of influences by which modern steps were introduced and copied. One parti-cular problem is how the middle classes ceased to ape the aristocracy and preferred to borrow from foreigners or from the 'demi monde' of which their parents disapproved so strongly. Another is to trace the movement for the revival of traditional dances, complete with dressing up in *ancien régime* clothes, which started as early as the 1880s.

Roles and Etiquette

The attitude of a middle class towards pleasure is always ambivalent, because those who have a social position to safe-guard can seldom afford to ignore the consequences of even their most insignificant actions. In France the ambition to rise in the social scale was not only a very common preoccu-pation but also one within the grasp of most people, so happi-ness, for many, must have meant simply the fulfilment of this ambition. Ambition implied self-control and the renunciation of immediate pleasures; and it usually meant imitating those whose status and manners one admired most. This explains the enormous sales of etiquette books, which are therefore a most instructive source of information: they are the comple-ment of the career books studied in the chapter on Ambition,[3]

---

[1] José Germain, *Danseront-elles? Enquête sur les danses modernes* (n.d., about 1923).

[2] Agnes Villadary, *Fête et vie quotidienne* (1968), 151, quoting J. Duquesne, *Les 16-24 ans, ce qu'ils font, ce qu'ils pensent* (1962).

[3] In my *Ambition and Love*, 87–113.

except that they were written mainly for women, as the career books were written mainly for men. These etiquette books are perhaps a more reliable indication of female fantasies than novels, in that they deal with all those details of daily life which have no dramatic interest but which absorbed the attention of women; they summarise the advice of the women's magazines and enunciate the philosophy which lay behind the endless articles about crocheting and embroidery; they were meant for the women about whom novelists did not write. What is particularly impressive about them is that they—or at least the most successful ones—seldom held out any false hopes. They did not promise happiness to those who carried out their precepts, but only an approximation of it; they urged that women should obtain satisfaction, or contentment, from the observance of rules as a kind of substitute for the bliss that existed only in fairy-tales.

The etiquette books were also much more than that, for they dealt with the general problem of how to conduct one's life, what goals and principles to give it, and not just with how to hold a fork. For about three centuries before this period, the same standard work, *La Civilité puérile et honnête*, based on Erasmus, and endlessly reprinted in various guises, had been given to children, both as a guide to good manners and as a reading text, and the generation of the second Empire had been brought up on it.[1] In 1865 Madame Emmeline Raymond, editor of *La Mode illustrée*, attempted to rewrite it, to bring it up to date at last and to make it a guide for the adult and not just the child.[2] Her book makes clear that old-fashioned politeness was already collapsing and that the rules of good behaviour were far from static. She, however, urged her readers to resist the movement towards informality. She sought to rehabilitate decorum by showing that every one of its rules had a moral basis. She complained that in France, supposedly the land of chivalry, men rushed to the food at parties, and ate it all up, mercilessly, leaving the ladies hungry; and equally women, who

[1] Catalogued in the 'anonymous' index of the Bibliothèque Nationale under Civilité; cf. Mathurin Cordier's and J. B. de La Salle's versions of it and *Le Crapouillot*, no. 19 (1952), issue on Les Bonnes manières; Michelle Calais, 'Répertoire bibliographique des manuels de savoir-vivre en France' (I.N.T.D. mémoire, unpublished, 1970).

[2] Madame Emmeline Raymond, *La Civilité non puérile mais honnête* (1865, 3rd edition 1867).

were supposed to be coquettish, were not infrequently arrogant, over-confident, adopting a military bearing and talking in peremptory tones, quite contrary to traditional ideals. The great culprit, she said was the cult of personality, which was the germ of all defects. 'The personality, a mixture of vanity and egoism, incites us to try and substitute on all occasions our own tastes and our own habits for those of other people.' It produced the desire to dominate and to get one's own way, and gave caprice an almost sacred character. This was an astute appreciation of the growing clash of individualism and established usage. The new generation was happy to go on teaching the old rules to their children, but they no longer wished to obey them themselves. The contrast of children's education and adults' behaviour was being accentuated, with portentous results. Madame Raymond said it was not surprising that 'many young people think politeness is an old bore, from which it is absolutely necessary to free oneself, so as to prove that one has a great brain, incapable of subordinating itself to these futile rules'. She urged women to make themselves the guardians of the chivalric tradition, for as soon as their vanity asserted itself, as soon as they aspired to become reformers, their power would diminish: they would be asserting their will to dominate, their own superiority and so their contempt for others. Women should never contradict. That did not mean they should have no opinions of their own, but that they should make it their overriding aim to please others, to soften the asperities of life, to forget about themselves and to devote themselves to others. They should not cultivate timidity, for that was only fear of being ridiculed, which betrayed excessive concern with oneself. They should obtain their happiness from helping others, and from constantly working to improve themselves morally. Many of the laws of *savoir-vivre* that she enumerated were, as she said, designed to repress women's passions, tastes and opinions. That was a good thing. Happiness for her was repression and self-chastisement.

The Baronne Staffe (*née* Soyer) was perhaps the most suc-cesful of all writers of books on good manners in this period. Her *Usages du monde* (1887) reached its 131st edition within ten years and was still being reprinted between the wars.[1] She, too,

---

[1] Baronne Staffe, *Usages du monde. Règles de savoir-vivre dans la société moderne* (1887).

insisted that 'the more a woman is a woman, the more men like her'. A woman who attempted to go outside her sphere would be in danger of losing her grace and her happiness; she should aim to live in the shade rather than in the bright lights, in the home rather than in the big world; with her children rather than among men. In the opinion of the Baronne Staffe, what women wanted above all was to be loved. She assured them that to achieve this they needed neither exceptional beauty, nor great intelligence, nor even extraordinary virtue: they could acquire the qualities needed, and the first step was to submit. Dependence on their menfolk was a sign of grace. By always being tactful, affectionate, kind, gentle and gay even when they did not feel it, they would create happiness around them. All sensible women knew that 'complete happiness does not exist'; they should not have impossible dreams, or at least they should repress these if they did. A little coquetry was allowed and even necessary in a woman, for it showed a legitimate desire to please others, but 'do not seek dangerous consolations, even in your thoughts. Resign yourself. Lose yourself completely in your children.' But Baronne Staffe was not entirely a conservative. She had no use for 'silly prudery', nor for girls with angelic airs, constantly fainting. She urged her readers to keep their weight down, to avoid being dominated by fashion, to beware of going to seed at forty. Her ideal was, as she said, *la vie douce*. The ideal woman smiled, but seldom laughed, first because laughing made her ugly, and secondly because life was too tough for there to be anything to laugh about. There can be no doubt that this philosophy had many adherents.[1]

Madame Louise d'Alq (1840–1901), another women's magazine editor, sold 100,000 copies of her guide to the art of living because, as she wrote, she did not give her own opinions but simply described what happened in the world; and her description certainly suggested that the Baronne Staffe's ideas were widely held. Madame d'Alq however also revealed the obstacles these ideas encountered. The readers of her magazines, she reported, were wholly absorbed, as adolescent girls, in pleasing men. At eighteen, they wanted to be either actresses, so that they could wear beautiful clothes and be admired in them, or

[1] See also Baronne Staffe, *Mes secrets* (1896) and *Indications pratiques pour réussir dans le monde, dans la vie* (1906).

else nuns, because they were too timid to leave their convent schools. Many of them looked forward to marriage as an Eden full of delirious joys, or at least something that gave them greater freedom. But observation of the world as it was showed that women who were loved for their appearance had a very fragile happiness; that being married involved hard work running a home and carrying out numerous duties; that being able to afford beautiful clothes was a pleasure ruined by competition to outdo one's neighbours, which was why hats were piled higher and higher with plumes, ribbons and flowers; that friends were difficult to come by, and one had to accept any that offered themselves, particularly when they came from a class above one's own and flattered one's vanity; when one became a parent, one might well be abandoned by one's children; and when one grew old, the young generation would treat one in an odious and cruel way, pushing and insulting old women though always ready to help a pretty girl. Madame d'Alq was rather uncertain about what her readers ought to do. She herself had dealt with a 'reversal of fortune' by taking up writing, and her motto was 'work is the key to independence', but she had obviously found it a tough life producing her thirty volumes and she warned women against competing in a man's world. 'I make so bold as to affirm', she wrote, 'that a woman who has a sensitive husband has nothing further to ask in the way of happiness in this world.' Happiness could never be perfect, but a good husband would at least diminish the clouds which were inevitable. A woman should preserve her influence over him by her virtues, her sacrifices and her weakness, so that he would always see that her happiness was dependent on him. This might seem, she agreed, a rather humdrum prospect compared to the bright lights and applause that girls dreamed of, but even an ordinary husband who loved you was preferable to the trials of a personal ambition; and if his passion for you waned, at least you could do your best to keep his esteem. Madame d'Alq urged women to find esteem, indeed, wherever they could: they should go to church even if they were not believers, since it might raise them in the opinion of others; they should bear with men who smoked and even pretend to like the smell of tobacco, be willing to talk about stocks and shares and sport, so as to be attractive to the opposite sex. They should put

aside all thoughts of changing the world: 'let us criticise nothing; let us simply conform to the customs of the country we live
in.' Women should take great care whom they spoke to, for
every town was divided into coteries, and if one associated with
an inferior one, one would be rejected by the others. It was
true that modern society was supposed to be equal, and everybody could think they were as good as everybody else. But this
egalitarianism was riddled with jealousies, vanity and envy;
everybody wanted to be *distingué* and they claimed that talent
was an adequate substitute for wealth; but Madame d'Alq had
been forced to agree that the right though difficult course was
to know one's place and to accept that a hierarchy did exist.
The solution was to keep one's distance, and to do so in one's
family also. Familiarity was undesirable either between men
and women or between husband and wife. The sexual barrier
must preserve modesty on one side and respect on the other;
demonstrations of affection between father and daughter were
wrong. Women were allowed to make friends among themselves, but their rivalry and passion for malicious gossip made
their company difficult also. One can see now why politeness
was so highly prized. It alone made social relations possible; it
enabled people to please each other, to win affection or respect,
and it was something which one could learn.[1]

Fear of suffering remained stronger than the desire for pleasure among many conservatives right to the end of this period.
A provincial guide to good behaviour published in 1936 started
off by saying that young women were totally different from
what they were thirty years before, but it nevertheless repeated
the most restrictive traditional advice to them: 'Good taste
consists in remaining unnoticed, not in drawing attention to
oneself.' Fashion in clothes should be followed so as not to
appear eccentric, but all its exaggerations should be avoided.
This book had a section on careers for girls, but it still warned
about the dangers of shaking hands too readily with young men,
of excessive liberty in dancing, of seeing pornographic plays or

[1] Armand Bourgeois, *Conférence sur Madame Louise d'Alq et ses œuvres* (1901);
Madame Louise d'Alq, *Le Nouveau Savoir-vivre universel*: 3 volumes (i) *Le Savoir-
vivre en toutes les circonstances de la vie*, (ii) *La Science du monde*, (iii) *Les Usages et
coutumes de chaque profession* (1881, new edition); id., *Essais pour l'éducation du sens
moral. La Science de la vie. La vie intime* (n.d., about 1895); *Les Causeries familières*
(1880–95); *Paris charmant: Journal illustré des modes parisiennes* (1878–93).

films.[1] Another guide published in 1942, and reaching its fifth edition in 1954, was all about duty, about how to behave respectfully towards one's superiors, and firmly towards one's inferiors, for 'equality is rare'. One should make friends only with those whose families are honest, with the same education and the same beliefs.[2] The Association for Christian Marriage laid it down that once a person got married, his pleasures should be family, not individual, ones; but it did not hold out the prospect of much happiness, for it saw marriage as a way of 'suffering together'.[3]

A moral guide written for policemen, by a policeman, took the same view, but it went into rather more interesting detail on the particular torments and pleasures of this profession. In all times, it said, policemen have been ridiculed, and there was no policeman who did not dream of seeing his sons reach a social status higher than his own. The way to save oneself from mockery was to have good manners, and the way to advance one's children's careers was to give them a good education. 'Happiness, therefore, is to be found in the simple, quiet and regular life of the family home.' The first step to it was to keep clean: the Romans used to have daily baths but 'in France people bathe much less': to wash one's face every morning, to shave at least every time one went on duty, was recommended. One should spit 'as little as possible and then discreetly into one's handkerchief'; one should not scratch one's head or pick one's nose. Meal times should be the hour for relaxation and good humour, and gaiety assisted the digestion, but this gaiety should not degenerate into misplaced or malicious jokes; good food and good wine predisposed one to tell saucy stories, 'which might overstep the limits allowed by good education, if one does not take care'. One should not be so vulgar as to wear one's napkin tucked into one's collar, though in a restaurant one was permitted to use it to wipe one's plate if one suspected the plate was dirty; but nowhere should one throw bits of food one had not eaten under the table. Policemen were not in a position to lead a social life, to visit people outside their profession, so they should

    [1] Germaine Charpentier, *La Jeune Fille moderne. Guide de convenances et de politesse* (Strasbourg, 1936).

    [2] M. M. Laloyaux, *Savoir-vivre. Politesse, éducation* (1942, 5th edition 1954), 50–1, 119.

    [3] André Bragade, *Le Bonheur en famille, pourquoi pas?* (1934).

concentrate on being on good terms with their colleagues. A
good education made this easier; but to live on good terms with
one's colleagues did not mean being on intimate terms with
them. 'I will go further: experience has shown that the most
serious discord occurs between families which have been most
friendly. Avoid competitive vanity—a piece of advice for wives
in particular.' A policeman must take especial care not to expose
himself to ridicule, or to a loss of dignity. Good manners forbade
him 'to show his joy by loud laughter or noisy clapping of
hands'. He must avoid using slang or obscene language, particularly with his superiors; he must answer the telephone not
with 'What is the matter? What are you saying?' but 'To whom
have I the honour of speaking? Yes sir, no sir'. It was not laid
down how he ought to treat his inferiors, but at any rate as far
as superiors were concerned—and his world was very much a
hierarchical one—he should not presume to try to shake hands
with a person occupying a rank in society higher than his own.[1]
Happiness thus involved balancing self-esteem and resignation,
obtaining pleasure from behaving in a way one thought distinguished, and possibly giving vent to the emotions that
remained only by actions which would not damage one's public
reputation. Respectability was of course maintained only with
the support of hypocrisy. As has been shown, marital bliss was
closely associated with prostitution, and likewise prudery depended on an enormous pornographic industry. The least-
chronicled aspect of the Third Republic's granting complete
freedom to the press was its unleashing of a vast number of
pornographic publications.[2] Happiness through respectability
could ally equally well with religious morals or lay ideologies;
it reconciled the satisfactions of self-control with the stimulus of
limited ambition. Its weakness, of course, was that it could not
appeal for very long to those who had no real chance of ever
obtaining its rewards.

There were more pictures than books about happiness. Pictures were also concerned with the respectable and the proper,
but by their very nature they commented on a finite moment
of human experience, while books were freer to make qualifications and reservations. Novels were much more often about the

---

[1] Col. N. . ., *Conseils d'un ancien à un jeune gendarme* (10th edition, 1949).
[2] See my *Ambition and Love*, 303–14.

conflict and the difficulties of life, even if they had happy endings, so one probably gets a more direct appreciation of how people enjoyed themselves by looking at them doing so in paintings. The simple pleasures and beauty of children, dancing, couples in love, satisfaction in work well done, relaxing in the sun, looking at flowers and pretty scenery—these were ever-popular subjects for paintings.[1] By contrast the country's great authors had little to say to it about happiness. The members of the French Academy and similar celebrities who were questioned on the subject in 1898 gave gloomy replies. Melchior de Vogüé answered briefly that he had no experience of happiness, never having discovered its secret, and so could not advise anybody. Barthélemy Saint-Hilaire read out the preface he had written forty years ago to his edition of Aristotle's *Morals*, saying that men should not seek happiness, but only duty, though happiness might follow from that. The comte d'Haussonville, a specialist on social problems, was uncertain whether happiness increased or diminished with the standard of living, but he was inclined to believe it was something we dreamt about, or imagined had once existed or would exist some day, but which one never actually reached. Édouard Drumont, the panegyrist of nationalism, thought happiness was very rare: 'as soon as you get to know people intimately, you are astonished to see the sadness that is at the bottom of most lives'. Several people, including Alexandre Dumas, quoted Tolstoy's *Cruel Pleasures* as embodying their opinions. Victor Cherbuliez, the playwright, said happiness was a gift of the gods: so what was needed was books not on how to be happy, but how to do without happiness. This was the view also of the scientist Berthelot, who claimed that happiness 'depends upon our physiological constitution more than on our will'; the search for it was therefore futile.[2]

The tired old men, however, gave only part of the message of literature and learning. There were always talented writers to offer, if not a key to happiness, at least a guide to the conduct of life, and the inspiration of their ideas, even when these bordered on pessimism, gave meaning and sometimes purpose

---

[1] *Les Peinture. témoins de leurs temps*, volume iv: *Le Bonheur*. Exhibition at the Musée Galliera, March–May 1955 (B.N. 8°.V. 61463(4)).

[2] Victorin Vidal, *L'Art d'être heureux*. *Études morales* (1898), 338–66.

to many people's lives.[1] But the discussion of happiness itself was seldom to be found in them, at least in any direct way. It was left to secondary writers to put their teaching and the conventional wisdom of the age into simple formulae. A vast and increasing number of books were published on the subject of how to be happy. The masses who bought them must have believed, despite the warnings of their leaders, that the elusive prize could be captured. And they were encouraged in this belief by the teaching of the schools. This was one way in which the lay republic and the Church did differ. The state's schools promised rewards in this life for good behaviour. Jules Payot, one of their leading educational theorists and administrators, who ended up as a university rector, wrote a particularly interesting summary of their hopes, entitled *The Conquest of Happiness*. He believed that the application of intelligence to life could lead to happiness, with all the certainty that scientific method guaranteed. Ignorance was the cause of unhappiness. He agreed that there was a great deal of evil, but for 'reasons of mental hygiene' it was best not to think about it, and to rise above it by the contemplation of beauty. Péguy said that at the age of forty he discovered the terrible truth that no one was happy; but Payot replied that one should repress such thoughts, which might disturb the serenity one should aim for. Men had lost the consolations of religion, but in compensation they had been freed from the fear of evil spirits. Death should no longer be taken into consideration in planning one's life; it should be regarded simply as the rest, like sleep, which came at the end— a desirable end, since death allowed constant renewal. Modern man was emerging from centuries of violence and was at last recognising the value of co-operation and spiritual values: he was on the point of emerging from a barbaric childhood, and the reward would be happiness.

There were nine conditions, said Payot, that were required for this. The first was good health, and that ruled out debauchery. Most people thought pleasure meant 'having a good time', which meant stupid, vulgar, exhausting amusement, but these left only sadness and emptiness behind them. 'The miserable literature of anaemic townsmen' encouraged this, but it was the open-air life that was best. Happiness in one's work was the

[1] See chapter 12 and my *Anxiety and Hypocrisy*, ch. 2.

second condition. Most people in factories hated their work; intellectuals encouraged them in this hate, partly to win leadership of political movements, but also quite sincerely, because for intellectuals physical labour was hell itself. But even the humblest could find creative satisfaction in their work: that is what should be encouraged, and it would need better education to show people how. Understanding was the key to the third condition also, the enjoyment of moral liberty, because that meant understanding oneself and one's desires. Good sense could help people tackle the fourth problem, which was loneliness, 'the supreme unhappiness', but an active social life, which was how most people countered this, was only a source of new servitudes: better be content with a few good friends. Money was not very important, its only value being to reduce insecurity. Power was demoralising; Payot was scathing about politicians, as ambitious parasites, but he was rather vague about who should take their place, beyond saying that politicians should be those who were 'naturally gifted' for government: this was the doctrine of each man to the task he was fit for. Payot was more interested in the family as a source of bliss. The only escape from boredom was to discover the poetry of daily life. One should get rid of domestic servants, because running a home was a pleasure to be enjoyed. Love of nature was the final consolation. And to put all this into practice, one needed to cultivate the mind, for happiness was ultimately a question of good sense and clear thinking. Though Payot favoured greater social justice, he thought happiness could be won by the mind triumphing over material adversities; and the poor peasant could be as happy as any man, enjoying the beauty of the fields, loving his wife and children, reading fine books; wealth was indeed more an obstacle to than an aid to happiness. Happiness should not be judged by appearances, and it was not true that only the wicked succeeded, for one could not be happy except with a clear conscience.[1] Payot, for all his criticism of intellectuals, represented the view of those whose main assets were education and will-power, a view that hovered between a desire to improve the world and an inclination to avoid contact with it. There was always an element of bitterness in this view, despite its apparent complacency. But it was a

[1] Jules Payot, *La Conquête du bonheur* (1921) and *La Morale à l'école* (1907), 242-3.

natural view for those for whom the acquisition of knowledge had been a constantly thrilling and rewarding experience; it was a view held not only by teachers and educated men, but also by the autodidacts and all those who regretted not having had a better education. Faith in knowledge as the key to happiness may not have been universal among some cynical writers, but it was extremely widespread in the middle and lower ranks of the literate.

The effect of social change upon this, and upon traditional views of happiness, often produced uncertain and confused behaviour. Thus aristocratic politeness got a new lease of life in some quarters, precisely because birth and wealth became such unstable criteria of respectability after 1914–18. Since one's origins or background mattered less, one's behaviour counted for more and etiquette books by the aristocracy were both sneered at and much read. Some aristocrats, for their part, attempted to modernise their doctrines. The duc de Lévis Mirepoix and the comte Félix de Vogüé, for example, offered aristocratic politeness in 1937 as 'the armour' that Frenchmen could use in their search for 'distinction' and social success. They argued that distinction manifested itself above all in conversation, which they held up as an 'intellectual dance'.[1] Others, by contrast, found a new pleasure in *Sweeping Out Old Customs*, which was the title of a rival book. According to it, it was now (1930) increasingly fashionable for people to reveal themselves to each other in the nude; there was nothing wrong with husband and wife carrying out their ablutions together, after having done their Swedish exercises. 'If I had a son, I would be proud if he took walks with a volume of Kant or Bergson in his pocket, but also if he carried a contraceptive in his wallet.' The relations between the sexes had changed and conjugal subjection could not be expected. Nevertheless the author advises girls to pretend to be silly and submissive, because that made life easier. There is a repeated emphasis here on pretence as a valid modern principle. People should pretend to treat workers as equals, because that would ensure the workers did their job more efficiently; a handshake would go down better than a tip, which might now be considered offensive; though with lazy workers

[1] Duc de Lévis Mirepoix and comte Félix de Vogüé, *La Politesse, son rôle, ses usages* (1937).

only an authoritarian tone was any use. He advised against wearing monocles, which made one look cold, but was in favour of gloves, which could give men an air of elegance; and for all his modernity, he still wore a cotton bonnet at night, to protect himself from draughts. The combination of freeing oneself from some traditional restraints and clinging to others, was a very common feature.[1]

An aristocrat suggested in 1948 that it was probably the workers and peasants who now had the strictest codes of behaviour.[2] This might have much truth in it, though it is, as always, difficult to generalise too broadly about them. Certainly in the middle classes there remained a strong phalanx among the older generation who made a virtue of deploring all change.[3] Catholics continued to be worried by pleasure, though to different degrees in different parts of the country;[4] but in the 1930s, and still more after the Second World War, some Catholic intellectuals attempted to reconcile happiness with Christianity— through the medium, above all, of sport, the open-air life and healthy living.[5] However, one of the commonest attitudes to happiness was possibly that which was dominated by superstition, as is shown in the advice given by Marcelle Auclair, editor of the supposedly very modern women's magazine *Marie-Claire* (founded 1937). She was a Catholic (though a divorced one) but her attitude to life was a mishmash of faith in God, astrology, fate, intuition and will-power. Her very successful guide to happiness was full of quotations from Christian authors and the life of St. Thérèse, but also of anecdotes about coincidences in her own life, which, she argued, confirmed her philosophy. It is a most interesting book, because it seems to reproduce so accurately the conversations that millions of people must have had. It illustrates how new ideas were simply added on to old ones, without bothering about contradictions. Marcelle Auclair once obtained five kilogrammes of coffee during the war, when it was scarce; she over-generously gave it all away to friends.

---

[1] Paul Reboux, *Pour balayer les vieux usages. Le Nouveau Savoir-vivre* (1930, reprinted with almost no alterations in 1948).

[2] Marc de Saligny, *Précis de nouveaux usages* (1948), 11.

[3] Giselle d'Assailly and Jean Baudry, *Savoir vivre tous les jours* (Maine, 1951).

[4] Theodore Zeldin, *Conflicts in French Society* (1971), chapter on Confession, sin and pleasure.

[5] René Rémond, *Oui au bonheur*. Semaine des intellectuels catholiques (1970).

Then, out of the blue, a reader of her magazine, who knew nothing about this, sent her a present of exactly that amount of coffee. 'From that moment I had an unshakeable faith in the great principles which govern the world and which we know so inadequately.' She escaped injury in the war because she had a presentiment that a certain place was dangerous and lo! it was bombed. Her advice was to adapt oneself to conditions around one—'revolt is a very bad mental attitude'—and to avoid letting misfortune depress one: there is always an angel, a friendly hand or one's intuition to help one out.[1]

Péguy wrote that a happy man is a guilty man. All the forms of happiness that have been discussed so far have involved compromise or repression, and an awareness of guilt was an inseparable part of them. The attempts to get rid of guilt were not successful. Those who came nearest to achieving this were those who sought to simplify life by forgetting about its ultimate purpose and concentrating on the diminution of discomfort. The accumulation of wealth and of material goods was, in many people's minds, equated with happiness. To those who had very little experience of wealth, it opened up new worlds of enjoyment, as well as new worlds of desire. Zola's *Au bonheur des Dames* (1883), describing the temptations created by the new department stores, revealed the disturbing effects of this change; and the historian Rolande Trempé has shown, in her study of the miners of Carmaux, how the chain effect was created, of greater expectations and greater desire for material goods developing as their standard of living rose. The most profound change in the factors involved in happiness that took place in this period was without doubt the increasing prosperity of the country, or at least the decline of destitution, which meant that more people were raised above the starvation level, and became capable of having priorities and choosing between alternatives. As both government and science claimed to be able to do more, so more was expected of them: Freud argued from this that the sum total of unhappiness had therefore increased, because men felt more frustrated when they saw science carry out such marvels in the physical world while it was seemingly incapable of making equally rapid progress in the spiritual and emotional spheres.

[1] Marcelle Auclair, *La Pratique du bonheur* (1956) and *Le Bonheur est en vous* (n.d.)

Certainly ill health may well have become more intolerable when there was more prospect of its being cured.

At any rate, in 1949 an international opinion poll revealed that one-third of Frenchmen considered themselves 'not very happy', which was the highest proportion in any country: the next highest was only 12 per cent in the Netherlands. France had the largest proportion of people who said they had difficulty in sleeping; only one-tenth admitted to being 'very happy', compared with half of all Australians and a quarter of Britons.[1] These statistics, for what they are worth, do not support the theory that industrialisation or prosperity produce unhappiness. Dissatisfaction with the social order does not necessarily imply unhappiness, as the magazine *Express* showed in 1969, when it asked people aged between fifteen and twenty-five whether they were happy: 35 per cent said very, 54 per cent said quite, and only 9 per cent said not.[2] It is impossible to be certain about the relationship between these replies and the events of May 1968, or indeed about the value of these answers in general. But it has been plausibly argued—with reference to France in the 1970s—that the majority of French people are happy but that they dare not admit it. Happiness has not become—as it may be in Australia, for example—a condition that it is considered proper to flaunt. In France, it has been claimed, the only kind of pleasure one is allowed to talk about is food, just as the English confine themselves to talking about the weather or gardening.[3] France's religious, social and literary traditions may well have kept happiness under the cloud of guilt; and before 1945 that cloud was doubtless larger. Perhaps that is why the French were, in that earlier period, associated more with pleasure than with happiness—with gay times rather than with deep satisfaction with life. This may well be a condition that favours the flowering of literature and art, and militates against devotion to economic expansion.[4]

[1] G. Rotvand, *L'Imprévisible Monsieur Durand* (1956), 95.

[2] Christiane Collange, *Madame et le bonheur* (1972), 27.

[3] Ibid. 90.

[4] Abbé Raoul Pradal, *Le Bonheur, fin dernière de l'homme. Étude historique et critique.* Thèse de doctorat en philosophie presentée à la faculté catholique de Lyon (Montpellier, 1908); François Mauriac, *Souffrances et bonheur du chrétien* (1931); André Maurois, *Cours de bonheur conjugal* (1951); Victor Hugo, *L'Art d'être grand-père*, in *Œuvres complètes* (1914), 8. 621 ff.

Sport

It has been shown in another chapter how complex people's attitude to comfort was, and how relatively limited the increases in it were. But comfort and prosperity at any rate provided politicians with an easy method of measuring happiness. Increases not only in wage rates but also in productivity and trade came to constitute a new barometer. Economic science could thus claim to hold the key to the fulfilment of man's desires.

At the same time, however, the search for happiness seemed to involve turning away from work, to sport. Rousseau had observed that one of the effects of the civilisation of his time was that it transformed the happy child into 'a severe and irritable man'. Sport was one of the ways that perpetuated childhood, though it showed in the process that childhood was not as carefree as Rousseau imagined. Sport was also a result of a new relationship between work and leisure. It is sometimes argued that sport developed when people came to have more leisure, with the reduction in working hours and the invention of the weekend; but sport in fact developed before the laws reducing working hours; and the working classes were in any case the last to participate in the modern organised sports. People may well have had as much leisure in the middle ages as they do now; there were once nearly a hundred holy and feast days a year; free Saturdays are new, but previously workers used to take Mondays off, to recover from their Sunday orgies. The unique feature of the nineteenth century was that the adoption of factory methods made employers demand long hours from their workers, so that machines should never be idle; people probably worked harder in the early phase of industrialisation than they had ever done before, and certainly more regularly. One should see the growth of sport for the masses not as the cult of more free time but as a reaction against the lack of it; if they could no longer play when they pleased, they had to organise it after work. Sport, though it brought new rituals with it, was also a reaction against older rituals: the traditional village and religious festivals provided similar scope for relaxation, but they were governed by rules and everybody had to participate; the new sports enabled people to assert the individuality of their taste and their aptitudes. They brought about a new distinction between work and play. Sport institutionalised play into an apparently separate activity, and work was therefore looked at as more of a chore. This created a false dichotomy. In reality work and play were and continued to be intermingled. Peasants and workers had learnt to alleviate the severity of their toil by developing the social aspects of it into a form of play, and by compensating for routine with camaraderie; it was probably only in the early phases of industrialisation that workers failed to extract enjoyment from their factories, however dreary these were. But the more sport and leisure were distinguished as being dedicated to happiness, the more were the demands on satisfaction from work increased. It was professional people, and the clerks of the growing tertiary sector, who complained most about boredom, as they did about overwork, and they therefore played an especially active role in the growth of sport. Sport was thus much more than a way of filling in time: it represented both a continuation of the tradition of festivity and a search for liberation from it.[1]

A great deal was written about sports in this period, nearly all of it with a moral purpose. Many organisers of sport certainly believed that sport was a way of stimulating national prowess, improving health, taming violence and disciplining youth. These ideals did not preoccupy most of those who actually played games. A history in terms of these ideals would largely overlook the element of totally disinterested enjoyment that motivated most participants. Sports clubs had two sides to them. Their leaders included many who liked power, who were fond of organising, who wanted to receive recognition and decorations from the state for their public service, and who believed sport was a public service. The mass of members, however, were there to amuse themselves, to make use of the social amenities they offered, to drink and talk as much as to do physical exercises.

Sports seem to play a larger role in society in this century because improvements in communication meant that regional, national and international competitions were developed, and because sports were now organised in societies and federations;

[1] Alasdair Clayre, *Work and Play* (1974); M. R. Marrus, *The Rise of Leisure in Industrial Society* (Forums in History pamphlet, 1974), and his forthcoming book on 'The Emergence of Leisure in France'.

the whole appeared much larger than its parts. But many sports
continued on traditional lines, and despite the centralisation of
the country, most sports continued to be concentrated in certain
regions only. Cock-fighting, for example, was a speciality of the
department of the Nord. It had existed there for many centuries;
it had been prohibited as cruel (and also, no doubt, as encouraging dangerous meetings) in 1852; but the growth of the cities
led to its expansion none the less. In the first decade of the
twentieth century, several new cockpits were built in Lille and
Roubaix and in a single week in February 1904, 300 cocks were
killed in that region. Roubaix in 1892 had twenty-five cock-
fighting clubs; and in 1907 ninety-six societies, watched by
10,000 spectators, competed for several days. The municipality
of Douai even subsidised cock-fighting, which attracted people
from all classes. Gambling on the cocks was a widespread
passion; breeding cocks was a form of luxury, like horse-
breeding, which gave prestige to middle-class businessmen with
money to spare. The north continued with this violent sport
oblivious of the changes in the rest of France.[1]

The south, for its part, remained faithful to bullfighting. This
again was an old French sport, though the French version did
not involve killing the bull, but rather performing acrobatic
feats around it. In the mid-nineteenth century, however, the
Spanish *corrida* was introduced, and in the 1890s arenas were
built in several southern towns. This sport again was prohibited
by law (at least killing the bulls was illegal), but in 1896
prosecutions, claiming that 376 bulls had been killed in that
year, showed that the law was easily defied. Fifty-five newspapers devoted to bullfighting were published in France between 1887 and 1914. But this sport failed to become a major
interest despite all the efforts of commercial entertainment
organisers, because it was made too expensive. It had been
popular as a sideshow at local festivals when it had still been
informal; but the builders of arenas recouped their expenses by
charging admission fees too high for the masses. The one arena
in Paris, opened in 1889, collapsed because it charged 6 francs
for admission.

By contrast hunting, which was an expensive sport, prospered

[1] Richard Holt, 'Sports in France 1871–1914' (unpublished Oxford D.Phil.
thesis, 1977).

precisely for that reason. It was run by noblemen and as one of them said, maintaining it was 'like rebuilding the Bastille'. Families gave themselves up to it with passion, like the four generations of the du Joncherays, the third of whom (who died in 1927) claimed to have killed 1,373 stags. Baron Jacques de Vezins, who kept sixteen horses and 120 dogs in the 1880s, was particularly famous for his record-breaking feats, but he was only one of many similar aristocrats. There were then seventy-three major hunts with over forty hounds each, plus several hundred small ones. In 1912 it was estimated that about 70 million francs were spent annually on this sport, even though it was largely confined to the west and to the Île de France, and had to combat a great deal of litigation from protesting small peasant proprietors. It brought social prestige and constantly attracted recruits from the *nouveaux riches*. Napoleon III revived it as a court pastime and President Fallières took it up also, showing that republicanism was not incompatible with enjoyment of *ancien régime* pleasures.

Shooting was another traditional sport that grew enormously in this period. In 1844 there were about 10,000 shooting permits, in 1854 76,000; in 1899 430,000; in 1922 one million and in 1924 one and a half million.[1] These are official figures, which may however indicate that the repression of unlicensed shooting was gradually more successful. But now clubs and syndicates proliferated to enable townsmen to participate: they could charge over 2,000 francs for a season, though fees of as little as 300 francs (with very doubtful supply of game) did exist. It may be, however, that fishing was the most popular of this kind of sport. In Annecy in the 1960s it was found that 26 per cent of the population engaged in fishing (when only 13 per cent engaged in team sports).[2] This was a good example of rural pursuits surviving urbanisation.

Sport, at the end of the nineteenth century, was made out to be something peculiarly English, but France in fact had a sporting tradition which was just as remarkable, even if the townsmen had forgotten it.[3] Sir Robert Dallington, visiting

---

[1] J. J. Verzier, *La Chasse. Son organisation technique, juridique, économique et sociale* (Lyon thesis, 1926), 14; Comte de Chabot, *La Chasse à travers les âges* (1898).

[2] J. Dumazedier and A. Ripert, *Le Loisir et la ville* (1966), 1011.

[3] J. J. Jusserand, *Les Sports et les jeux d'exercice dans l'ancienne France* (1901).

France under Henri IV, was astonished to find that the *jeu de paume*, which later developed into tennis (etym. *tenez*), was played more in France than in the whole of the rest of Christendom; 'the players are more numerous here', he wrote, 'than the drunkards are in England.' France exported tennis to England in the fourteenth century, and reimported it as an English game in the 1890s. *Hoquet*, likewise, was an old Breton game, played with great violence, but when it was reintroduced as an English game and modified into hockey, by the schoolboys of Paris in 1898, it attracted a totally new kind of player; and the Bretons did not recognise it, though it became popular in Anjou. In fencing, the French had developed a national style of elegance, agility and silence, and had specialised in the foil, but in the second half of the nineteenth century this gave way to a greater popularity of sword fencing; there was however still great rivalry between the sword, foil and sabre, as the fencing federation (formed in 1906) discovered. *Boules*, which in 1945 had over 5,000 associations and 150,000 officially licensed players, had ancient origins, but seems to have become popular only in recent times. The *boule de fort* variety played in the west, very similar to English bowls, and requiring a carefully prepared pitch, started only around 1850; the southern variety *pétanque* and the Lyonnais *boules* seem to have become important only after 1919, and to have spread very rapidly; they were essentially an alternative to immobile drinking in cafés, and often continued to be played near cafés. In the 1960s, 25 per cent of the population of Annecy said they played it.

Rugby, again, was related to *la soule*, *choule barette* and *mellé* which were played all over northern and western France from the twelfth century onwards, with a ball usually twice the size of the modern one, of wood or leather, filled with hay, moss, bran or air. It used to be played in the fields between two parishes, each of which tried to keep the ball in its own camp. Victory went to the side that could get it to their church door. Teams could be of any size, from ten to as many as a thousand; the games could last half a day; and all forms of violence were allowed. '*La soule*', wrote Souvestre describing it in Brittany in the early nineteenth century, 'is not an ordinary amusement but a heated and dramatic game in which the players fight, strangle each other and smash each other's heads . . . a game that allows one to kill an enemy without losing one's right to Easter communion, provided one takes care to strike as though by accident. . . . Blood flows . . . a sort of frenetic drunkenness seizes the players, the instincts of wild beasts seem to be aroused in the hearts of men, the thirst for murder seizes their throats, drives them on and blinds them.' (Compared to it, American football was child's play.) Edicts forbidding it had been issued in the eighteenth century; one showed that women participated, sometimes with the married challenging the unmarried. *Soule* had fallen into decay when rugby was introduced into France. This was a game with much stricter rules, but it attracted the same kind of parish loyalties, except that now it was larger towns that played it. Rugby was introduced into France by the English— by the Havre Athletic Club of English residents in 1872—and the first Anglo-French match was played in the Bois de Boulogne in 1877. An English schoolboy introduced it into the Lycée Montaigne in Bordeaux, and a pupil of that school who moved to the Lycée of Bayonne introduced it there. Clubs grew up in the small towns of the south-west in the first decade of the twentieth century. The Scottish player Alfred Russell, who later became captain of the Glasgow Academicals, came to Bayonne to learn French and translated E. G. Nicholls's book *The Modern Rugby Game* into French. A player of Bayonne went to study business in Wales and in 1910 brought back the Penarth Football Club to play in Bayonne. One of their players, H. O. Roe, decided to settle there and under his influence the Bayonne club developed the Welsh style, with much more hand-passing.[1] In the regional competitions, the success of this team, which now claimed that its style was 'Basque', as opposed to the 'Catalan' style of its rivals in Perpignan, was associated with a passionate fervour for Basque traditions, the Basque beret and red-striped clothes. The Paris team meanwhile was captained by the Scotsman Jack Muir, but though in 1914 crowds of up to 30,000 gathered to watch rugby games in the Parc des Princes, the sport was most popular in the south-west. In 1921 Béziers's ground was invaded by enthusiasts six hours before the national final was due to be held there. In 1924 there were 891 clubs. But there was little progress beyond that; rugby

[1] Claude Duhan, *Histoire de l'aviron bayonnais. Tome 1. L'Époque héroïque 1904–14* (Bayonne, 1968), 44–95.

remained a regional interest; and was overtaken by association football.[1]

In 1914 the Anglo-French football matches at Gentilly drew only 800 spectators but in 1919 the Football Federation was founded and Henri Jooris, a rich businessman of Lille, who was president of the Olympique Lillois and the Lions de Flandres, provided the financial backing. The small town of Sète established the best team in the country by an astute policy of buying and selling players. Professionalism raised standards and increased interest. In 1931 France beat both Germany and England. By 1943 there were 7,000 clubs and about 300,000 registered players, of whom about 300 were professionals.[2] This is a small enough figure, but it is treble that of 1939 and about eight times that of 1935. The great growth of football, as of so many other sports, took place above all under the Vichy government, which gave them encouragement as the Third Republic had never done. The unique feature of French sport was that it developed very largely outside the schools, or at any rate schoolboys who were interested had to form or join private clubs to participate. Sport was an alternative to school, except in the few progressive establishments, like the Collège de Normandie, which existed to copy English methods. That was perhaps why regionalism showed itself so strongly. The Anglomania which was at the origin of much upper-class sport affected only small groups in the senior classes of the best schools. Sport was still something that the rationalist school system could not comprehend. It was the Catholics who were keenest to develop sport among young people, because they laid so much stress on 'moral' qualities, and particularly after 1905 they saw in sport a way of attracting young people into their leisure organisations. The state abstained from allocating any credits to sporting clubs, so it was the national union of students which autonomously took on the federation of school and university sport: the teachers kept largely clear of it, partly because they considered it beneath them, partly because they feared responsibility for accidents, and partly because they were reluctant to run activities over which they did not have full hierarchical control.

[1] Georges Pastre, *Histoire générale du rugby* (Toulouse, 1968), 1. 208; id., *Rugby, capital Béziers* (1972).

[2] Gaston Bénac, *Champions dans la coulisse* (Toulouse, 1944).

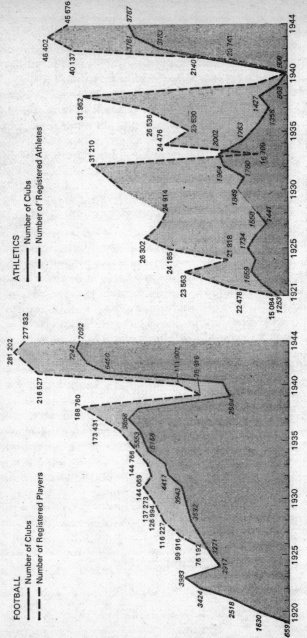

FOOTBALL
— Number of Clubs
--- Number of Registered Players

ATHLETICS
— Number of Clubs
--- Number of Registered Athletes

Graph. Football and Athletics (1919–44). Based on *Encyclopédie générale des sports* (1946), 33, 398.

What the state did approve of was gymnastics, because this had a clear didactic purpose. Gymnastics was made an optional subject in primary schools in 1850 and a compulsory one in 1869, and a part of the secondary syllabus in 1853, but this was purely on paper. Local authorities found the idea baffling: the general council of the Nièvre warned that children would lose their respect for teachers who 'engaged in exercises where the dignity of man can suffer cruel failures'. However, the defeat of 1870 transformed gymnastics into a patriotic duty and in 1880 four and a half hours a week of it were prescribed in every school. Numerous gymnastics societies were formed and by 1914 these had over half a million members. The idea was that the nation would be trained to beat the Germans with their own methods. These societies were noisily jingoist, their organisation military, their aim to teach discipline and movements in unison on the German model, rather than the individual agility that the Swedish school advocated. Membership was limited to French citizens. Both traditional sports and athletics were frowned on here, because these lost sight of the main purpose. But in practice the gymnastics societies were largely taken over by lower-middle-class people—shop workers, clerks and artisans —who used them for social purposes, and who spent most of their funds on dinners and excursions. The most military thing they liked doing was marching through the streets on festivals, dressed up and playing music, but there was probably more traditionalism than nationalism in this revelry. These clubs got official subsidies, and were one more way of milking the state. The proportion of non-practising members was soon far higher than those who actually did gymnastics: 'L'Ancienne Lorraine', in Paris, had only 91 active members out of 479. However, the shooting clubs which were often associated with this gymnastic movement were popular and led to successful national competitions, in a different town every year, from 1886; there were 3,500 such clubs in 1945.

Probably the most popular sport in France was cycling. No doubt the fact that bicycles were utilitarian as well as amusing made them popular, but in no other country has cycling as a competitive sport continued to attract so much public interest, even after the advent of the motor car. There are several factors that explain this. Cycling was the first sport that had a manufacturing industry behind it, and the cycle manufacturers showed great enterprise in stimulating racing and providing the finance to make this into a major national sport. Secondly, a specialised press developed which was exceptionally skilful at arousing interest, thanks to a number of remarkable journalists, notably Henri Desgranges, editor of *l'Auto* (combining car and cycle racing). As has been seen, he started the Tour de France to promote its sales, and made this into a national institution in the summer months. The press joined in to make heroes of the cycling champions, who should be compared to the stars of the music hall: men of humble origin who made good, like Edmond Jacquelin, the baker from Ménilmontant, champion of France in 1896, whose success made him so rich that he travelled around in a carriage with top hat and white gloves and had a box at the Comédie-Française, but who, like so many music-hall artists, died poor (1929) after a retirement spent in vain speculations: his invention of a street-cleaning tricycle was unsuccessful and his cycle-racing track became valuable—it was expropriated for a quarter of a million francs—too late, after his death. Just how much money could be made out of cycling was shown by Charles Terront (b. 1857) the son of a railway worker who had started life as a messenger boy for the Agence Havas, and who turned professional in the late 1870s. In 1895 he earned 6,000 francs by riding in sixty-five races, of which he won fifty-five. He retired in due course to become a cycle retailer and manufacturer. Another popular hero was Georges Paillard (b. 1904) champion of France six times 1928–34, who reached a speed of 137 k.p.h. Behind them were a new race of trainers and managers, like Paul Ruinart, who started in this profession in 1900 and claimed to have trained a hundred champions and to have made fifteen of them millionaires. Many cycle-shop owners and café keepers started up clubs to increase their custom. In 1898 there were twenty-two firms hiring bicycles in Bordeaux alone. Cycle racing was thus an industry as well as a sport, but it had the advantage that it was associated with cheap travel, easy movement, tourism, the discovery of the countryside and a new kind of holiday. By the time the car had become a more widespread means of transport, cycling had established an impregnable tradition.

Horse-racing started, like cycling, as a rich man's sport, but

in its case, popularisation came from its success in opening up
quite exceptional new opportunities for gambling. The state
used to organise lotteries during the *ancien régime*, with great
success. In 1789 it employed about a thousand people on this task
but it made about 12 million *livres* out of it, at a time when the
national budget was only three times that amount. However,
because the system was full of abuses, it was abolished by the
Revolution, but it was soon re-established, simply to bring more
money in. During the Restoration some 50 million francs were
staked annually, but in 1836 the state lottery was once again
abolished, this time on the ground that it was immoral.[1] Though
many lotteries were subsequently organised for specific purposes,
as for the benefit of the singers of the Opéra (1859) and all sorts
of other good causes, it was not till 1933 that the national
lottery was re-established, to become an indispensable institution.[2] Horse-racing appealed to gambling instincts, but its
attractions were more sophisticated, and it could be indulged
with varying degrees of participation. The state had looked upon
it with favour, because the improvement of breeding seemed
to be a national and military interest; and it had fixed the rules
and organised its beginnings. Already before the Revolution
racing had been attacked for 'bringing confusion to fortunes
and making the workers desert their workshops' but Napoleon I
nevertheless revived it in 1805 and Louis-Philippe established
the French Stud Book in 1833. In 1866 Napoleon III gave up
control of racing (as he gave up control of the Artists' Salons)
to the three leading societies then in existence, which specialised
in flat racing, steeplechasing and trotting respectively. The
aristocracy and the financial and industrial magnates put a lot
of money into horse-racing, which they continued to dominate.
The Jockey Club (founded in 1833) was probably the most
exclusive club in Paris.[3] By 1845 there were over fifty provincial
societies organising races and by the 1950s about 400, so horse-
racing became not a weekly, but a daily event. In 1973 it
was said that there were altogether 2,500 racehorse owners in
France.[4]

[1] Jean Lénnet, *Les Loteries d'état en France au 18ᵉ et 19ᵉ siècles* (1963).

[2] Marcel Charpaux, *La Loterie créatrice* (1943).

[3] J. A. Roy, *Histoire du Jockey Club de Paris* (1958).

[4] Guy de la Brosse, *La France au galop* (1973), 74; cf. R. Longrigg, *The History of Horse Racing* (1972).

Under the Second Empire, gambling was organised by some 200 bookmakers shouting their prices at the Paris courses, on the English model. A favourite method was *poules*, drawing a horse's name out of a hat, so that it was pure chance whether one won. The courts repeatedly forbade all this, and in 1887 Goblet, the minister of the interior, enforced the prohibition, declaring that betting was 'a principle of demoralisation'. Takings at the racecourses fell dramatically and it looked as though the sport would collapse. It was at last realised that betting was an indispensable part of its attraction. So in 1891 a law established the Pari-Mutuel, which collected all the money staked and distributed it to those choosing the winning horse, with a small amount being retained as a subsidy for the societies organising the races and for various charitable works.[1] Bookmakers were officially abolished in 1905 but survived all the same. However, the horse-racing societies leased their rights to two firms, Oller and Chauvin, who ran the new system. In 1930 the Pari-Mutuel Urbain was established to organise betting off the courses, with agents all over the country. The stakes rose as follows:

1892	169 million francs staked			
1913	395	,,	,,	,,
1920	1,324	,,	,,	,,
1930	1,844	,,	,,	,,
1938	2,567	,,	,,	,,

The betting habit was unevenly distributed. In 1950 Paris led the field with 11·24 francs staked per annum per head of population, while rural departments like the Cantal, Aveyron, Lozère and Creuse staked nothing at all. By 1965 the Alpes-Maritimes were in the lead, with 208 francs staked per annum, followed by the Bouches-du-Rhône and Paris third: the north and south of France (including Corsica) were keenest, while the Creuse still showed least interest, with only 13 francs a head. Between 1951 and 1970 the amount staked on horses rose fourteenfold. It was the press that turned this (like cycling) into a national pastime.[2]

[1] At first the subsidy was for the assistance publique, then for hospital building (2 per cent), for supplying towns with drinkable water (1903, 1 per cent), for repairing war-devastation (1919, 1 per cent).

[2] E. G. Sabatier, *Chevaux, courses et jeu. Histoire des courses et du pari-mutuel* (1972); L. F. Gabolde, *Les Sociétés de courses* (1937); G. de Contades, *Les Courses de chevaux en France 1651–1890* (1892).

In 1925 Jean Prévost wrote, of *The Pleasures of Sport*, that 'The Greeks trained to adapt themselves to their civilisation. We train to withstand ours.'[1] This was only partly true, or at any rate it betrayed a peculiarly narrow definition of civilisation that intellectuals favoured. Intellectuals considered their function to be the classification of values, to show what the priorities among different activities should be, and they not surprisingly always placed contemplation and thought as the 'purest'. There was therefore a breach between the intellectualism the schools tried to instil and the physical pleasures sport cultivated. Jingoist gymnastics did not bridge this gulf. Sport was the object of much derisory contempt. The educational system allowed intellectually gifted children to reach the very top without playing games of any kind. However, the intellectual whose main physical movement was to smoke cigarettes was only one type among several. In its early days the cycling and motoring paper *L'Auto* used to have articles by Clemenceau, Tristan Bernard and Franc Nohain. The development by the sporting press of its own popular style soon cut it off from the intellectuals, but there were many writers and academics who nevertheless continued to have a foot in both camps. The development of sport in France in fact owed a great deal to university students and senior schoolboys, acting in rebellion against the routine of their curricula. The nationalist movement of the end of the nineteenth century and the conservative reaction of the pre-1914 generation brought a new emphasis on physical prowess. Thus the science-fiction writer J. H. Rosny, one of the founders of the Association of Sporting Writers, and long-jump champion of the world in his youth, did morning exercises throughout his long life, saying physical fitness gave him a greater sense of security, which affected even his intellectual work: he wrote that the bicycle was one of the greatest inventions in history, comparable to fire, writing and printing. Thibaudet pointed out that novelists had been so absorbed by the passionate and voluptuous side of the human body that they had forgotten the other aspects of physical energy, and sport was producing an ethic of its own as

[1] Quoted in Eugen Weber, 'Gymnastics and Sports in Fin de Siècle France', *American Historical Review* (Feb. 1971), 70–98, an important article by the first professional historian to study the subject in France. See also his forthcoming work on the Tour de France.

worthy as that of eroticism. Paul Adam wrote a book on *The Morals of Sport* to attempt to spell this out. Marcel Berger, the dramatist, who was an *agrégé des lettres*, had been a school discus-throwing champion, and published an explanation of what some still considered an eccentricity: *Why I am a Sportsman*. The poet Tristan Bernard became Director of the Vélodrome de la Seine. Raymond Boisset, another *agrégé des lettres* and 400-metre record holder, wrote on the *Spirit of Sport* giving an inside view of the Olympic Games. Henri Chabrol, one of France's most famous football centre forwards, and author of *Youth of the World*, was another *agrégé*, as too was Georges Magnane, a leading sprinter, who also boxed, did judo and studied at Oxford: his novel *Bête à concours* was an attack on 'degenerate students' who simply worked for examinations, while his *Les Hommes forts* praised the new kind of all-rounder. Joseph Jolinon, author of *Le Joueur de balle*, which became a classic of sporting literature, had the manuscript rejected by five publishers before it was accepted: he had been responsible for introducing football into the Catholic University of Lille in 1908. Pierre MacOrlan, in *La Clique du Café Brébis* (1919), described the failure of a schoolboy to receive approval from his parents for his successes on the sports field; he suggested that during their games children vaguely realised that they were at least temporarily no longer under the control of their parents, that girls preferred men 'who knew how to win a liberty that they did not desire for themselves', and that the emotions that sports aroused would produce a new way of writing books and of reading them. Paul Valéry was a keen cyclist, swimmer and rowing man who regretted that his generation had underestimated sport, which required the same qualities of effort, discipline, style, simplicity, that intellectual work did. Jean Giraudoux attacked the view that strong men were necessarily stupid and criticised the professors who praised the Greek hero of the open air only in theory, refusing to copy him in practice. Sport, he said, was 'the art by which man liberates himself from himself', that is, from the burden of an unwieldy, neglected body. 'Every human with a dull, bent or obese body is in some sense a beggar.' The sportsman, contrary to his reputation, was not dominated by his body, but knew its capacities, and so was capable of being more honest with himself.[1] Louis

[1] J. Giraudoux, *Sans pouvoirs* (1946); *Le Sport* (1928).

Hémon's *Battling Malone* (1925) defended boxing against puritans, who, he said, tried to ignore that life involved constant battles. The Prix Goncourt was awarded in 1939 to Philippe Henriat for his novel praising sport, *Les Enfants gâtés*. The conservative novelist Georges Duhamel, who attacked spectator sports, particularly as they had developed in America, took care to add that he was not hostile to sport itself: 'I have walked across half of Europe with a haversack on my back. I can, like any reasonable man, swim, ride a bicycle, drive a car, wield a racket and even row. I have for years used fencing as an exercise. I do not disdain physical exercise: I love it, I recommend it, I often long for it as part of a studious retirement.'[1] Pierre Loti was devoted to gymnastics, which he saw, like love, travel and books, as one defence against death that terrified him.[2]

Sport brought out the interest in physical pleasures which had always been important but which moralists had either neglected or attacked. There was a close link between these pleasures and the erotic joys that most novelists concentrated on; but it was a link that was barely realised in this period, and on the whole the advocates of happiness in its physical aspects divided themselves into two hostile camps, who condemned each other for, respectively, brutality and degeneracy. The sexual changes of the post-1945 period could take place only when that antagonism was resolved; and already some people had seen that it could be. But organised sport still played too small a role in French life for it to be possible for it to be understood outside its own circles. In 1946, a government official estimated that barely 10 per cent of young people between fourteen and twenty were involved in the sporting organisations then existing, and that street life, the cinema, dancing, and the café were more popular interests among them.[3] The importance of sport in the liberation of women—physically, sartorially and morally—has often been stressed, but it had not affected more than a small minority of women in this period. In 1893 only about 1 per cent

[1] G. Duhamel, *Scènes de la vie future* (1930).

[2] Cf. M. Maeterlinck, *L'Intelligence des fleurs* (1907); Raymond Pouilliart and J. Willens, *Le Sport et les lettres. Le Sport dans la littérature française 1919–25* (Louvain, 1953) and G. Pronteau, *Anthologie des textes sportifs de la littérature* (1948).

[3] Georges Denis (ed.), *Encyclopédie générale des sports et sociétés sportives en France* (1946), 22–3. This massive work is the best source for statistics on every kind of sport.

of cyclists were women: they were so noticeable precisely because they were so rare. The male sports associations were
originally hostile to female sports; and the women who played
football or rugby, and even those who cycled, were attacked by
the press as pursuing excessively violent activities. Women held
their first athletics championships in 1915, and challenged the
women of England in football in 1920, but it was only during
the Second World War that women's sports obtained anything
like widespread participation.[1] In the 1960s roughly one-half of
the French population took no part in sport and had no interest
in it.[2]

Humour

What made people happy, and what made them laugh, was not
necessarily the same thing.

The idea of happiness implied a particular way of looking at
the world; and it is clear that not everyone was searching for it,
at least not with the deliberation it required. Happiness, as it
was understood by the people who gave advice about it, normally involved on the one hand thrift and on the other hierarchy.
It had to be accumulated gradually, saving up immediate enjoyment for the future, exactly like money. Some forms of pleasure
were regarded as better than others, in the same way as the
society of this time was composed of classes of unequal merit.
The affinity between happiness and capitalism was especially
striking in the views of those who held that happiness consisted
in doing one's duty, for there the criterion of efficiency was
decisive. Janet, professor at the Sorbonne, one of the leading
popularisers of this moral view, defined happiness as 'the harmonious and durable deployment of all our faculties in the order
of their excellence'; happiness was therefore not pleasure, nor
primarily a matter of feeling—let alone sensuality—but a problem of organisation.[3] Its attractions were most evident to those
people who were interested in rising in the social scale; it was
one form of ambition. It is clear, however, that many people

[1] M. T. Eyquem, *La Femme et le sport* (1944). For sport during the Vichy regime,
see André Frahier, *Sport et vie rurale* (1943); but for the inadequacy of facilities for
sport see M. Joffet, *Les Études et les réalisations sportives de la ville de Paris* (1943).

[2] Richard Holt, 'Sports in France 1871–1914' (Oxford unpublished D.Phil.
thesis, 1977) is the fullest general historical study.

[3] Pierre Janet, *Philosophie du bonheur* (9th edition, 1898), 20.

either did not think in this way or did so only intermittently. If one looks at this question from the perspective of those who were too poor or too miserable to entertain such hopes, and who were not primarily concerned with what other people thought about them, one sees that temporary relief from pain was the limit of their aspirations. Side by side with the long-term search for happiness, there was the more casual approach to life, aiming not at permanent contentment, but at momentary fun, not at married bliss, but at sexual gratification, and accepting even fleeting pleasure as a good in itself. This can be seen in the history of laughing, of eating and of drinking.

The creation of an American nation is said to have produced a people all of whom could laugh at the same joke. France had not reached that stage in this period. Laughter was not always approved of, nor as universal as might be assumed. It was impossible to conceive Christ laughing, wrote the author of a treatise on laughter, and in a perfect world laughter would be forbidden. There were both aesthetic and moral objections to it. On the first count, it was ugly, as proved by the general practice of covering one's mouth when one laughed; it was aesthetically undesirable also because it turned attention to the imperfect aspects of life, to what was ridiculous, instead of to the beautiful; and there was inevitably something inferior in an act for which no training was required. Morally, laughter contained too many elements of malice, rivalry and envy. Besides, 'the right to laughter does not belong to inferiors vis-à-vis their superiors'; laughter was dangerous as well as silly; it encouraged superficiality, and often obscenity too.[1] So laughter was repressed in the same way as sex was, and it is not accidental that people laughed about sex as much as about anything else. And yet France claimed to be a gay nation, the land of *gauloiserie*, of Rabelais and Molière, mistress of all the frivolous arts. These apparent contradictions need to be disentangled.

The barriers of propriety and of social pretension meant that there were at least three different forms of laughter—popular, middle-class and intellectual—in which Frenchmen shared in varying degrees. The poor did not have a totally different sense of humour from the rich, for the rich might enjoy jokes which

[1] Louis Philibert (avocat à la cour d'appel de Paris), *Le Rire: Essai littéraire, moral et psychologique* (1883), 450. 455.

pleased the poor; but there certainly were class and cultural conditions on what made people laugh. Thus the peasantry of the mid-nineteenth century had a ritualistic humour, which centred around two particular institutions. The *veillée* was the evening meeting of villagers, at which they pursued their indoor tasks, the women spinning or sewing, the men making or mending tools, while at the same time stories were told and, on special occasions, games played and celebratory meals eaten. What amused people most at these *veillées* was the repetition of stories and folk-tales that everybody knew but nevertheless enjoyed hearing over and over again. Repartee consisted not in verbal fireworks but in recognising the appropriate proverb for different situations. The most popular jokes were practical ones, and brutality was not always absent from them. In party games, dressing up was a particular favourite, with the sexes swopping clothes or the poor pretending to be rich, or putting on soldiers' uniform or that of different trades; and disguised in this way, people would go round the village visiting; but the arrival of the 60-watt electric bulb helped to put an end to this, by making it too obvious. Mimes were another entertainment, particularly of weddings, with grotesque mothers-in-law as a principal source of laughter. Singing and card-playing (especially tarots) were popular, but dancing had to be controlled, so as not to frighten the animals. Until the end of the nineteenth century, these *veillées* were essentially village institutions, often attended by twenty or even forty people, and it was only in the twentieth century that they became meetings confined to family and friends, meetings that is in the realm of leisure, as opposed to the combination of work and pleasure that they used to be; but *veillées* held in stables were still to be found as late as 1940.[1]

These home-made amusements were supplemented by another institution, that of travelling entertainers, whose visits broke up the working day. There were troupes of actors, who put on historical or sentimental playlets, or pantomimes; there were magicians, clowns, acrobats and fortune-tellers; and later magic lanterns and travelling cinemas arrived. To this should be added the visits of the snake hunter, the frog catcher, the song merchant, the seller of holy statues, and on an even more practical

[1] Suzanne Tardieu, *La Vie domestique dans le mâconnais rural préindustriel* (1964), 140 ff.; Émile Violet, *Les Joies et les peines des gens de la terre* (Mâcon, 1946).

level, those of artisans of every kind of trade like glaziers, knife sharpeners, cobblers and grocers, and not least the smugglers—the most important being the match-sellers (who sold contraband matches, much cheaper than the state monopoly ones). Visiting tradesmen would very often be asked to stay to a meal. The variety would not be diminished by the fact that all the transactions were totally predictable, or even that the villagers would sometimes know the plays put on for them by heart, from having seen them so often. Novelty was not always a requirement of entertainment. On the contrary, much peasant fun simply involved finding opportunities for the uttering of old saws, which were a regular signal for laughter: more often than not, this meant spotting faults in one's neighbours or deviations from normality, like a man being cuckolded by his wife, or having his fly-buttons undone ('It is Saturday, his shop is open').

With time, the café took on an increasing role in social life. By the turn of the century Paris had 27,000 of them and France as a whole 413,000. This period marked the apogee of their importance, for their numbers have progressively declined since: in 1960 Paris was down to only 11,000. The cafés were to the late nineteenth century what the *salons* had been to the eighteenth, but a democratisation of them. The peculiar brand of sociability they encouraged lasted till the age of broadcasting, which provided a less personal entertainment and made it easier for people to stay at home.

The café concert was one of the inventions of the nineteenth century which added most to the gaiety and sociability of Paris. Dances and open-air concerts, which were increasingly numerous in the first half of the century, were only occasional events, but the café concert was an institution which made entertainment much more regularly, and casually, available. In 1865 the government restriction on the use of theatrical costume outside the few licensed theatres was removed, and the humble performers at the café concerts, who had hitherto been compelled to appear only in ordinary clothes, were henceforth given free rein for their talents. The casual approach was nevertheless preserved: what distinguished the café concert from the theatre was that there was no formality involved; one came when one pleased, in shirt sleeves or overalls if one liked; one ate and drank as one watched the show; one shouted applause, abuse and comments freely; one was always incited to join in the singing. Originally, ordinary cafés simply put on a little show in a corner, sometimes by professionals working for paltry fees, but as often by local amateurs. Maurice Chevalier, who later became France's leading music-hall singer, started his career in the very humble café concerts of the Parisian suburb where he grew up; it was because he admired the performers at the Palais du Travail, a small café in the rue de Belleville to which his mother (the widow of a drunken housepainter) took him every Sunday as a boy, that he chose the profession he did. His first performances were at the Café des Trois Lions and the Concert du Commerce, where workers, prostitutes and idle *déclassés* on tiny incomes went for their relaxation.[1] What they got had no pretensions to art, but it made sense to them. The songs were above all about landlords and concierges, mothers-in-law, creditors, bureaucrats, love, drink and duped spouses; dirty jokes were an essential ingredient, while references to recent political events or crimes were also much appreciated. The performers had to make themselves heard over the din of drinking and conversation, the cries of the flower sellers and the pedlars of sweets and other trifles; and they had to put up with smoking, which was allowed here (as it was not in the theatres).[2] Such was the popularity of these entertainments that speculators came in to expand and profit from them, so that they gradually turned into music halls, before finally ending up as cinemas. The entertainment industry remained small scale, however, seldom going beyond family firms, so the variety remained, and every pocket continued to be catered for.

At the top end of the scale was the Eldorado, which had the same importance in the history of French entertainment as Canterbury Hall had in that of London. Built in 1858 in the Boulevard de Strasbourg, aiming at something of the grandeur and solemnity of the theatres, embellished in due course with electric lights, it was the palace of variety, where the most famous performers were to be seen. Across the road, its rival the Scala, stinking of dirty lavatories and the violent perfumes of the performers, was frequented by a much lower class of person, and it was much noisier, though in the twentieth century it outdid

[1] Maurice Chevalier, *Ma route et mes chansons* (1946), 29.
[2] André Chadourne, *Les Cafés-Concerts* (3rd edition, 1889), 13, 163.

the Eldorado and was considered by far the superior of the two.
The Moulin Rouge, immortalised by Toulouse Lautrec, was
built in 1889, a large ballroom with tables in the gallery where
one could drink while watching the show; and there was a large
garden with fine trees outside where one could take the air in
summer, watching the girls show off their black-stockinged legs
and their petticoats, as they took rides on the donkeys. The
owner, Joseph Oller (1839–1922), was a remarkable impresario,
who also founded Le Nouveau Cirque, Le Jardin de Paris, Les
Fantaisies Oller, Les Montagnes russes, L'Olympia, two horse-
racing courses and the Rochechouart swimming pool: he was an
inventive entertainer, but one who always got bored with every
enterprise he brought to fruition. The Folies Bergère was originally the Café du Sommier élastique founded in 1869 to produce
vaudevilles and concerts; when this went bankrupt in 1889, it
was bought up by the Allemand family, owners of the Scala,
who put the husband of their niece, Édouard Marchand, in
charge of it. It was he who raised it to European fame, travelling
all over the continent to recruit artists for his shows. On his death
in 1901 it was taken over by the Isola brothers, who showed how
the ambitions of these impresarios were growing. The Isolas
made a fortune out of the Folies Bergère but then left it to take
over the Opéra-Comique, where they proceeded to lose their
money in their search for culture. But individual singers and
comics also set up on their own. The best-known was perhaps
Mayol, a smooth, charming, romantic singer, who was very
popular even though the fact that he was a homosexual was
said to have limited his audience: his Concerts Mayol became
a major and long-lasting music hall. The Chat Noir in Montmartre has been written about more frequently, because poets
and painters frequented it, but it quickly lost its genuine character and became a night spot for the bourgeoisie. The landlord,
Rodolphe Salis, used to put on a masquerade of politeness, treating every client as a prince and addressing everyone by a title.
Aristide Bruant (1851–1925), who was one of the performers
there, moved out to set up his own establishment Le Mirliton,
which used a gimmick of exactly the opposite kind: he insulted
every client who entered, and served every drink with abuse:
the delighted audience was taught the routine of greeting every
woman who came in with a chorus of cries: 'O how pale she is'.

In 1900 there were perhaps 150 café concerts in Paris, but since their history has not been investigated, it is impossible to make more than a guess at the precise importance of their role in the life of the city, in the same way, for example, as it is possible to give statistics about the music-hall takings in New York. (There, in 1911, 700,000 people, that is 16 per cent of the total population, each week attended some forty 'low price' theatres whose takings were 315,000 dollars, compared to only 190,000 dollars a week earned by the theatres proper.)[1]

Inevitably, what survives of these café concerts is only a few photographs and drawings of the acrobats, magicians, comedians and musicians who performed in them. The only written records are of the songs. It is through them that one can try to get an idea of the sense of humour that prevailed in these audiences; one is helped also by the memories of the entertainers who sang the songs. The picture is blurred by the fact that a song-writing industry sprang up to cater for this market. This was concentrated in a little street between the Faubourg Saint-Martin and the Faubourg Saint-Denis (the centre of the café-concert world), the passage de l'Industrie, now renamed the rue Gustave Groublier, after one of the most successful of these writers. Aristide Bruant's songs give only an imperfect, or partial, idea of what was popular. He is famous because he was also an author and publisher, and that is a major reason why his songs survive and are easy to find. He ran a magazine, *Le Mirliton*, in which he printed his songs. Bruant shows how a song writer deliberately sought out themes to appeal to his audience. He was by birth a bourgeois but his father's death forced him to earn a living, as a jeweller, and then as a clerk in the Northern Railway. In his spare time he learnt music and frequented the cafés. At first he was horrified by the triviality and grossness of working-class slang, but in time he came to savour its richness and humour. He collected popular jokes and turned them into songs. He got part-time engagements in small cafés as his talents became known. He was probably more amusing and light-hearted in these early days: later, he specialised in laments on the sad lives of the down-and-outs of the slums, and biting satires on those 'who can eat and drink when

[1] Albert F. McLean, *American Vaudeville as Ritual* (University of Kentucky Press, 1965), 46.

they wish'. He became more and more of a showman; in his own café he always wore the boots and red shirt which were his trade-mark. He made a lot of money out of his singing and at fifty bought a farm in his native province, where he retired to write novels, journalism and a dictionary of slang. A gramophone record of his singing was made in 1924 when, at the age of seventy-three, he staged a come-back at the Empire theatre in the avenue de Wagram. From it and from his published songs, one can savour some of his boisterous pugnacity, which places him in the line of Pierre Dupont and Béranger, whose tunes were hummed as widely in the mid-nineteenth century. Though Bruant composed his songs from elements he found in the working-class and *déclassé* circles he frequented, there was a considerable element of art and artificiality in the finished product.[1]

The taste for dirty songs and dirty jokes, though much more difficult to document, can be illustrated from the life of Joseph Pujol (1857–1945) who is also quite revealing about the sort of people who were successful entertainers in this period. Pujol's speciality was farting. His performance at the Moulin Rouge produced, as Yvette Guilbert the popular singer recorded in her memoirs, 'the longest spasms of laughter, the most hysterical attacks of hilarity' ever seen in Paris. Nurses had to be employed to carry away the women in the audience whose laughter split their corsets and reduced them to agony or collapse. 'Le Pétomane', richly dressed in red and black silk, with a William II haircut and moustache, explained to the audience in a sober and serious way that he was endowed with unusual anal gifts, and that he would give imitations of a young girl, a mother-in-law, and a bride before her wedding night and on the morning after; culminating in the fart of the dressmaker, which lasted ten seconds and imitated the tearing of cloth. He inserted a hose into his anus and puffed at a cigarette attached to the end, and then played the flute with it. So popular was he that he built a theatre of his own, the Pompadour (1895), where he added imitations of birds and animals to his show, as well as a performance of black magic by his sister. So when Sarah Bernhardt was taking 8,000 francs at the box office, and Lucien Guitry 6,500, the Pétomane reached as much as 20,000 on a Sunday. He went

---

[1] A. Zévaès, *Aristide Bruant* (1943); *Le Mirliton* (1885–94); A. Bruant, *Dans la rue* (1889–95).

on tours abroad, being a particular success in Cairo, but he was
forbidden to perform in Madrid and had to change to a clown-
ing act at the last moment. He was the son of a stonemason
who was also something of a sculptor, whose works are exhibited
in the Museum of Marseille. He himself started life as a baker,
but his family moved into show business; one brother became
a peripatetic actor, ran a little theatre in Paris and also a lottery,
but worked as a baker in bad times; his sister was a regular
café-concert performer. He had ten children, who became either
singers, comedians and jazz musicians or else bakers, potato-
chips sellers or wine merchants. After the Great War, Pujol
returned to baking and set up a biscuit and slimming-bread
factory in Toulon which still survives in the hands of his
descendants.[1] The cohesion of the entertainment world can be
seen from the subsequent history of this family. One of Pujol's
sons was apprenticed as a mechanic, but alternated between
that trade and show business; his son, Marcel Pujol, was the
famous Marseille cycling champion.

The stars of this comedy world were generally of humble
origin, and they owed their success to their ability to perfect
some trait in working-class life. 'Thérèsa' (born in 1837 as
Emma Valadon) was one of the first of these stars. Originally
a dressmaker, she became famous as the chief singer of the
newly opened Eldorado. She earned the unprecedentedly large
fee of 200 francs a month. The Alcazar then offered her 300
francs a month, provided she changed to comic songs; and
eventually her salary rose to 233 francs a day. Her earnings
were not the least amazing thing about her; connoisseurs
doubted her talent, but she grew from a thin stripling to a large
and heavily jowled matron, and crowned her achievement by
publishing her memoirs, just as she fell out of favour.[2] She was
perhaps more than anything a symbol of the myth of success,
an example of how a humble girl could suddenly rise to riches,
and she became someone with whom the poor could identify,
in wishful thought. It is true she soon alienated them by her
brashness and arrogance: that was one reason why stars rose

---

[1] Jean Nohain and F. Caradex, *Le Pétomane 1857–1945. Sa vie, son œuvre* (1967).
[2] Emma Valadon, dit Thérèsa, *Mémoires de Thérèsa de l'Alcazar, écrits par elle-
même* (1865, reprinted six times); Albéric Menetière, *Les Étoiles du café concert*
(1870).

and waned so fast. A more talented performer was Paulus (Paul Habans), who was the inventor of the practice of dancing while one sang: he won his fame for romping jollity with his song *Les Pompiers de Nanterre*, which he performed surrounded by actors dressed up as sailors and dancing a quadrille around him. In 1878 he moved from the Eldorado to the Scala, where he earned 150 francs a day; he later appeared at several shows in different parts of Paris in the same evening, travelling in his own carriage. He made a display of his prosperity, changed clothes for every song, bought a magnificent house in Neuilly, toured throughout Europe and the U.S.A., became the owner of the Eldorado of Nice, the Alhambra of Marseille, the Bataclan of Paris and a vineyard, the Clos Paulus, in his native Bordelais. His haircut 'à la Titus' was imitated by every aspiring actor. But he was eventually overwhelmed by his speculations and broken by his divorce: in 1906 a charity performance was given to raise money for him and he died a ruined man two years later. Paulus used to sing his songs in a stentorian voice. Inevitably the next star did the opposite: Polin sang his in a whisper, waving a handkerchief before his face as though to conceal his embarrassment at the dirty jokes he made. He was for long the leading male star of the Scala and the Ambassadeurs, and had his own magazine, *Paris qui chante*. Another star of the Scala was Fragson (real name Pot) who specialised in songs about the English, accompanying himself at the piano. He had worked in London as a boy; his command of two languages made him one of the early international performers; his inseparable attachment to his father, who accompanied him everywhere, was one of the oddities which won him indulgent affection; his death in 1913 —shot by his father, who became jealous when Fragson showed too much interest in a mistress—was a contribution to the aura of legend and gossip that was already surrounding these popular heroes. Dranem, who was made an officer of the Legion of Honour, was not only a great sad-comic, in enormous shoes, ill-fitting clothes and an American sailor's hat on his bald head —singing with his eyes shut, without a gesture—but also a hard worker in the cause of the growing number of unemployed and ruined entertainers; and his many marriages provided plenty of gossip to publicise him. There were a whole variety of genres: Sulbac (born 1860) specialised in peasant roles; he appeared dressed as one, uttering farming monologues in pseudo-patois and singing songs explaining what was happening in his village. Baldy played the debauched beau; Moricey was a sort of epileptic clown.[1]

Nakedness on the stage came early, though it is not certain exactly when. By the 1890s, however, there were already thirty strip-tease shows in Paris. The critic Francisque Sarcey described Mademoiselle Cavelli, the star of the Alcazar d'Été, 'doffing her hat, her dress, her petticoats, her corset, her pretty white and pink underwear, with a decent interval between each stage of her undressing to allow the spectators to recover their sang-froid'. Hugo, who was for twenty years *maître d'hôtel* at Maxim's restaurant, recalled that this did not take place only on the stage: at a dinner given by a newspaper magnate in his restaurant, with fifty guests, a pretty young blonde, completely naked, was brought in and sat in the middle of the table; after it was over, she got up and went round to collect her tips from the guests. The Concert Mayol began putting on strip shows only in 1934. In the following year a fan dancer, Joan Warner, was prosecuted, at the instigation of the National Alliance against Depopulation, and fined fifty francs, after a three-week trial, but another court ruled that advertisements of naked girls outside strip clubs were not an outrage to morals, provided the pubic hair was concealed. It was only after the Second World War that, under the management of Alain Bernardin, who considered himself an apostle of 'visual education', stripping laid claim to being an art and that Rita Renoir, one of its most famous practitioners, defended it as a valuable ritual ceremony.[2] But photographs of music halls in the interwar period show a large proportion of the girls naked from the waist up, and the clothes of female singers were always provocative, far ahead of current fashions.

Popular entertainment of this kind made people laugh for several different reasons. On the one hand it lyricised, romanticised daily life, taking the small talk of ordinary people and giving it brilliance by skilful mimicry and presentation. The

[1] Jacques Charles, *Cent ans de music hall* (Geneva and Paris, 1956); id., *Caf'Conc* (1966).

[2] Jean Charvil, *Histoire et sociologie du strip-tease* (1969); Denys Chevalier, *Métaphysique du strip-tease* (1960).

performers who came from the same background as the audience, and who neither talked down nor preached at them, concentrated on pleasing without pretension or tension. But there was also another kind of laughter which was to be found here, created by the reversal of roles and situations, and by the public flouting of decency. These café concerts were places where the respectable values of family life could be momentarily mocked. This is why the history of humour is such an important adjunct to every other kind of history. It shows the reverse side of respectable institutions, and shows that the burdens these institutions imposed were borne only because they were not always taken seriously, or at least because outlets were available where relief from their weight could be found. The endless jokes about mothers-in-law were one of the essential pillars of this society. Here, the battle between Vulgarity and Distinction, as one commentator put it, was regularly won by the former, for the crowds nearly always came down on the side of 'trivial jesting and coarse farce' rather than of beautiful singing.[1]

Between the wars, the French music hall was dominated by Maurice Chevalier and Mistinguett. The contrasting approaches of these two stars—who were for ten years the symbol of the romantic couple until they separated, estranged by their intellectual and temperamental differences—illustrate the complexities concealed behind the happy masks. Chevalier and Mistinguett were both great successes because of their charm— he was the handsome, dandy, relaxed young man, who never seemed to take either himself or life too seriously, who sang catchy songs as though simply to please himself, and who always tried to exude gaiety and good humour; she never claimed to have a pretty face, but she made herself attractive by her exuberance, vitality and impishness, and by the skill with which she moved and showed off her body (she insured her legs for half a million francs). Both of them came from very humble backgrounds, and knew how to flirt with the public even when they became very rich. Chevalier, however, had a passion for learning, he was always trying to improve his style, move with the times, expand his horizons. He came to embody many of the petty bourgeois ambitions of his countrymen; his songs were mildly philosophical and moralistic, subtly mixing old saws with

[1] Menetière, op. cit. 35.

a surface optimism, designed to forget rather than to deny sorrow. In old age he became an author and wrote his memoirs in nine volumes. He needed the consolations of philosophy, because he always feared, and exaggerated, the jealousy he aroused among his fellow entertainers; and despite all the invitations he received to dine with the most celebrated people of his age—kings, ministers, industrialists and men of letters—he was never at ease except with members of his own profession and with the working class from which he came. His mother and his job were his two anchors of security. He could not get on with Mistinguett because he found her too capricious, and a challenge to his independence. She said that he loved playing the role of gentleman, while she liked being the urchin, but that was misleading. Mistinguett said of herself that she was a practical woman. 'God created us to be happy . . . I insist on being happy', but 'speeding along the boulevards in big American cars at all hours of the night, dancing until dawn—that was my idea of living'. She bought du Barry's château in Bougival and had a lavish villa in Antibes. She had the reputation of being selfish, mean and a hard worker. She lived for the moment. 'Chevalier's presence', she said of their ten years together, 'never brought me very much, but his absence has dominated the rest of my life. . . . I loved him too much to want to understand him.' The performances and the private lives of these two popular heroes were more than just distractions for their countrymen: they expressed widespread aspirations and equally widespread frustrations.[1]

Popular humour can be studied more precisely in the theatre, both because the texts survive and because more elaborate jokes, appealing to a wider range of sensibilities, were offered here. The dramatic classics always had to fight against shallow, humorous entertainments which were put on by theatres seeking quick commercial rewards. Voltaire used to complain that 'the masses are not happy if one offers them jokes which appeal only to the intelligence: they want to laugh loudly'; he grumbled

¹ Maurice Chevalier, *Ma route et mes chansons* (1946), 216; id., *Londres, Hollywood, Paris* (1946), 15; id., *Temps gris* (1948), 17, 130–2, 157, 196, 204; id., *Par çi, par là* (1950), 9, 25; *Y a tant d'amour* (1952), 7–11; id., *Artisan de France* (1957); André Rivollet, *Maurice Chevalier, De Ménilmontant au Casino de Paris* (1927), 239, 247; Mistinguett, Memoirs, translated as *Mistinguett, Queen of the Paris Night* (1954), 135, 143, 163.

that the farces of Dancourt and Legrand had accustomed them
to low and scurrilous comedy 'so that gradually the public has
developed the prejudice that one-act plays must be farces full
of dirt, and not noble comedies in which morals are respected'.[1]
In the early seventeenth century there had been little difference
in theatrical taste between the masses and the court, neither of
them noted for sophistication or refinement, but from 1630 a
new theatre audience developed, which was to be the counterpart of the *salons*, and which demanded higher forms of art. The
Parisian populace, however, with time showed an interest in
these plays also, and their presence in the pit—standing room
only before the nineteenth century—was an important influence
on dramatists. Voltaire used to hire a claque to make them clap
and laugh; their approval was indispensable for the success of
a play. The distinction between serious and popular drama was
therefore not complete, and this meant that a play attracted
wide attention, beyond the limits of a single class. When in 1791
the liberty of the theatre was established, forty-five new theatres
sprang up in Paris: Napoleon ended this liberty in 1806 and
allowed only eight theatres in the capital; but when liberty was
restored in 1864, they multiplied once again and there were
fifty-eight by 1875. Each tended to specialise in a particular
genre. The Palais-Royal put on gay humour (and the plays of
Labiche); the Gymnase went in for vaudevilles, Scribe and then
realist plays—it was fashionable and literary; the Vaudeville
was bourgeois, while Les Variétés and Les Funambules were
more working class. A play put on at the Comédie-Française for
thirty performances would be seen by 25,000 people. At the end
of the eighteenth century, this major theatre had an annual
audience of 170,000. The theatre was therefore an indication of
popular taste, and an element in life as important as newspapers
or novels.

Humorous plays had always been popular and the traditions
of the medieval travelling players, variously called the Joyful
Companies, the Fools, the Idiots, and the Scholars—whose
favourite character was the naïve man getting into scrapes—
were continued. The early modern comedies were never worried
by fears of repeating themselves: stock types like the libidinous

[1] John Lough, *Paris Theatre Audiences in the Seventeenth and Eighteenth Centuries*
(Oxford, 1957), 190.

old man and the naughty servant constantly reappeared, and always to receive their due chastisement or reward at the end. Humour was not taken seriously until Molière raised it to unprecedented heights and defended it as a dignified art, with a moral purpose; but because he introduced far greater depth and art into it, comedy for two centuries after his death was dominated by him and, with few exceptions, mediocre imitations of his genius became the rule: the public contented itself with noting how well the laws of drama were observed. But then, as a reaction against the five-act play, the *vaudeville* and the *revue* developed. The vaudeville was originally a happy song, and it then became a light comedy play, based around an amusing intrigue, with singing to some well-known tune. It developed into 'comic opera', and vaudeville became the branch of it without music. The revue paid less attention to plot and more to topicality: never aiming to last more than thirty or forty shows at most, it was, from about 1830 onwards, a popular form of satire. The Coignard brothers used to produce one every year under Louis-Philippe, at the Théâtre de la Porte Saint-Martin, one of the most successful being *1841 and 1941*, which made fun of all new inventions and the railways in particular; their *Îles Marquises* about a machine into which whole live sheep are inserted, to emerge at the other end transformed into ready-made overcoats and cutlets, was found so amusing that it was revived for the Exhibition of 1867. During the Second Republic there were a large number of reviews about politics, like *The Members of Parliament on Holiday* and *Property is Theft*; under Napoleon III, politics was forbidden, so writers turned their sarcasm on to every other aspect of life. *La Revue des Deux Mondes*, by Clairville and Abraham Dreyfus (1875), made fun of the press and the literary world, in a style that foreshadowed the tendency of authors and comics to talk increasingly about their own worlds, with jokes that outsiders could barely understand; but this revue had an amusing idea as its base: a provincial *pâtissier* bequeathed a sum to the *Revue des Deux Mondes* to award a prize for the best literary work of the year: the editor, accompanied by a woman reporter, go on a tour of the opera and theatres, which gave opportunities for a whole series of parodies of the shows and actors of the day. The decisive factor in the success of the revues was the skill of the performers; few of the texts were published. The vaudeville is therefore easier for posterity to appreciate, though it has barely been investigated. Jules Janin, writing in 1832, claimed there were 168 vaudevillists in his day. But the author who dominated this genre was Scribe (1791–1861). He specialised in perfect plots, where everything worked out in the end, with an unexpected explanation. He is important as the incarnation of anti-romanticism; he had a wild success and earned several million francs by attacking romanticism, just when romanticism was most fashionable: his play *La Camaraderie* (1836) mocked the mutual praise that the romantics gave each other.[1] Under the Third Republic Victorien Sardou (1831–1908) continued Scribe's methods, with the stress above all on intrigue; so that human characterisation was largely forgotten. Feydeau (1862–1921) represented the farcical culmination of this entertainment. He raised vaudeville to the level of higher mathematics, taking logic to its limits and fantasy to absurdity. His farces were, in effect, alternatives to detective stories, or to crossword puzzles, but with the clock-work inevitability of the action made ridiculous by merciless exaggeration. This kind of play was performed at a fast rhythm, with a liberal use of stereotyped gestures, so that it bordered on pantomime, and indeed it is said that some of Feydeau's farces produced so much laughter that the final scenes were played as pantomimes, because the actors could not make themselves heard above the din. Feydeau, who descended from an *ancien régime* marquis, was the son of the author of *Fanny*, condemned by the Archbishop of Paris for impropriety. He said he became a writer from laziness; he started writing plays at the age of seven, producing such pride in his parents that he was let off homework; his first play was put on when he was twenty-one. He then gambled his considerable royalties on the stock exchange, losing several million francs, and had to go on writing in order to pay his debts. He was reduced to living in a single room at the Hôtel Terminus St Lazare, and to drinking Vittel cassis at the café Napolitain, his favourite haunt. Despite the industrialisation of entertainment, the insecurity of the theatre somehow survived.[2]

[1] Maurice Descotes, *Le Public de théâtre et son histoire* (1964), 287–90.

[2] Marcel Achard *et al.*, 'La Question Feydeau', *Cahiers Renaud-Barrault* (Dec. 1960), no. 32, special issue. Cf. Henri Beaulieu, *Les Théâtres du Boulevard du Crime 1752–1862* (1905); Jacques de Plunkett, *160 ans de théâtre. Fantômes et souvenirs de la Porte Saint Martin* (1946).

Feydeau's farces were capable of repetition because they were based on absurd situations, with no realism to go out of date; and they provided great opportunities for actors. Labiche (1815–88) was more richly amusing but he wrote for his time, and his favourite subject, the problem of arranging marriages, of passionate interest to men on the make during the Second Empire, was presented in too simple a way to survive. Labiche had no desire to do more than make people laugh; he was extremely modest about his work, and consented only reluctantly to the publication of his collected plays. He wrote about 175 in all; in 1856 he had as many as eight performed: after 1860 he was, with Offenbach, the acknowledged master of the humorous theatre. But in 1877 he stopped writing, having invested his earnings in a 900 hectare farm, and preferring to devote his time to his new role as village mayor. His history is a success story dreamt of by many young men about town. He was the son of a syrup manufacturer; he wrote funny plays because he liked laughing and because he had no serious ambitions. He mocked the bourgeoisie, and they flocked to see themselves mocked; Labiche was a mild satirist, whose humour was like a vaccination, which ultimately reinforced the complacency of his audience.[1] But the passages in his plays which, according to contemporary accounts, drew the loudest laughter, now often seem insignificant, because the gestures and style of the performers were all important. Labiche was fortunate in having the amiable Geoffroy as one of his main actors, whose interpretations ensured that the plays came across not as satires on the audience, but as jokes at the expense of their neighbours. Labiche's characters, particularly his female ones, were unremarkable when they were not dull: it was the scrapes they got into that were amusing. Labiche catered therefore for a public which had developed certain habits of laughter; certain kinds of jokes were always successful. The joke which dominated all others was the ridiculousness of the bourgeoisie—an essential counterpart to the rule of the bourgeoisie that is supposed to have been established in this period. That is another reason why his humour appears either dated or formalistic. It is important to bear in mind that side by side with the liberal and progressive

---

[1] Philippe Soupault, *Eugène Labiche* (1964). See in particular his *Perrichon* and *Le Chapeau de paille d'Italie*.

developments of this century, which tend to monopolise the attention of history, there was also a vast body of third-rate plays and farces, which produced endless laughter by repeating jokes about things like *avant-garde* painting, Wagner, and the equality of the sexes.[1]

A more biting and sadder kind of humour was presented in the plays of Courteline.[2] Here humour consisted in the expression of the dreams and animosities of the petty bourgeoisie, but from the point of view of those of them who had not succeeded in life, and had little hope of doing so. What Courteline wrote about was the reverse side of ambition. He made laziness and failure tolerable. Courteline, again, came from modest stock and from a family of entertainers: his grandfather had a tobacco shop; his father was a banker's clerk who wrote many successful comic operas, libretti for Offenbach and amusing accounts of criminal trials for the *Gazette des tribunaux*. It was a family that was steadily rising into the lower middle class, but Courteline found the pressures to continue this rise unbearable. He was sent to a good school, which only filled him with a lasting horror of education and of the repressive, monotonous methods of schools. He looked back on his childhood with pain, saying schools 'brand children, like a red-hot iron, with a melancholy which time can never heal'. He was put into business (as a clerk in the firm of Bouillons Duval) but he lasted only a few weeks. Military service roused bitter resentment at the severity of the discipline, the constant punishments and the futile tasks: he got himself certified ill and spent six months convalescing from the ordeal. Finally his father set him up as a junior civil servant, at 100 francs a month, in the ministry of religions: this was a secure job, even if the wage was no more than a labourer's. Courteline could not bear it. He hated work. He much preferred sitting in cafés, watching the world go by, at most playing cards. To his father's fury, he had no desire to make a success of life; he used to absent himself from his office for extraordinarily long periods, but with impunity, because his boss liked to patronise the arts and also valued having a journalist on his staff, who could protect him against attacks in the press (this was the period when the ministry of religions was in the thick of its

[1] Cf. Félix Gaiffe, *Le Rire et la scène française* (1931).
[2] Real name Georges Moinaux (1858–1929).

battle against the Church; the boss was none other than Dumay, one of the main architects of the disestablishment of the Church). Finally, Courteline gave half his salary to an unemployed friend, who went to the office to do his work for him, carefully forging his signature. He was free now to devote himself to journalism and playwriting, which he had taken up at a young age to supplement his meagre salary, but also to fulfil his deeper ambition to be a travelling actor. He toured France with the Tournet Baret, a repertory company founded in 1889 by Charles Baret, a pharmacist's son (another social misfit).[1] He gave little talks before the performance of his plays, and he took parts in them; he wanted to be a complete man of the theatre. He alternated between a quiet sedentary life, centring round his café—'it is less difficult to change one's religion than one's café' he said—and restless travel: he went on tours of Belgium and Holland, accompanied by Zipette, the pornographic photographer. He lived with an actress by whom he had children, but he could not bear children and sent them away to their grandparents. He was both obsessed by women and despised them, treating them as 'instruments of pleasure'. He visited brothels and slept with many of the actresses who appeared in his plays, but he was always dissatisfied with sex: though he constantly wrote about this, he entitled a chapter in his *Philosophy* (a collection of maxims he published in old age)[2] 'Things of little importance: love, women etc.'. He quarrelled endlessly with all his women, but he eventually married his mistress on her death-bed, and then indeed married another. Quarrelling was an essential part of life for him: he loved making scenes in his café when he got the wrong change; he was violently angry when he was contradicted and always insisted on having the last word: he had a passion for practical jokes but was furious when he was a victim of one. He was a mass of contradictions and clarity of thought was never his strong point: he was anticlerical, but he solemnly took off his hat when a religious procession passed; he mocked medicine but was always consulting doctors; he called himself 'a bohemian whose bourgeois background

---

[1] The Tournet Baret has survived to the present day, being continued under the management of Janvier, the son of one of the principal performers of Courteline's plays.

[2] *La Philosophie de Georges Courteline* (1917).

bothers him and makes him go to bed too early'. He was made miserable by an inferiority complex, which the enormous success of his plays never diminished. He declared that he had no imaginative gifts: he was only 'a sculptor of umbrella handles'. This was probably what lay at the bottom of his horror of work. At forty-seven, just when he was reaching the apogee of his fame, he stopped writing, saying he hated working and he could afford to stop. He spent the rest of his life in provincial retirement, going daily to his café, playing bridge, gossiping with his cronies. The world, he said, was divided into two classes of people, with totally distinct mentalities: those who went to cafés and those who did not.[1]

The humour of Courteline's plays made game of all these dissatisfactions. It was humour for a definite class of people—nearly all his characters were from the middle and lower bourgeoisie—and it made fun of their plight by showing up the contradictions they had to cope with, and the absurd situations from which they could not escape. The plays were about civil servants, soldiers, lawyers, journalists, actors, cab-drivers and bus conductors faced by the problems of the big world and by the frustrations of their own inadequacies; they were a tirade against stupidity, selfishness, laziness, pride, irritability and dishonesty, but they pointed no moral. Courteline had no solutions. He held out no hopes, because in his own life he had found the business of growing up infinitely painful. His constant refrain was a lament for his lost youth and a curse on advancing age. 'I loved my youth madly,' he said. 'I loved it with passion, like a mistress for whom one would kill oneself.' The motto he asked to be put on his tombstone was: 'I was born to remain young'. He denied that every age had its pleasure, saying youth alone had any. So his life was dedicated to s'en foutre, as he said, to mock and forget. The characters in his plays were overwhelmingly unsympathetic: only sixteen out of 275 male ones, it has been calculated, and only two out of the 65 female ones could be said to be likeable.[2] Courteline felt deeply insecure about the loyalties around him: he never tired of 're-reading the letters from mistresses who have deceived me and friends who have

[1] Pierre Bornecque, 'La Vie de Georges Courteline' (unpublished doctoral thesis, Montpellier, 1968).
[2] Pierre Bornecque, Le Théâtre de Georges Courteline (1969), 453–4.

betrayed me'. He wrote a great deal about betrayal, and about
the problems of gratitude and obligation. Monsieur Badin 'the
clerk who did not want to go to his office', but who lived in
terror of losing his job, was presented as a funny character, but
only because his dilemma was so real to both Courteline and his
audience. Courteline was not a revolutionary, but his humour
fits into the broad category of humour that is protest if not
revolution, and is an armchair substitute for real insurrection.

The manufacturing of humour by professional entertainers
increased enormously in this period, and nowhere was the increase more pronounced than in humorous journalism. The
growth of printed humour was on a hitherto unprecedented
scale. It could perhaps be argued that this humour was an
answer to the greater stresses and complexities of life, and that
sharpened sensibilities, which laid people more open to frustration, also included a developing appreciation of the ridiculous;
but, in the present state of knowledge, such a view could not be
easily substantiated. The humorous press, rather oddly, is one
of the least studied aspects of literature and art. Most of the
caricaturists of this period are little more than names, and the
ideas behind their activities are difficult to discover. It was
in 1830 that journals devoted entirely to caricature first made
their appearance. Of course there had previously been a considerable production of humorous prints, which continued, but
the publication of humorous journals greatly widened the scope
and the impact of caricature. Charles Philipon (1800–62) was
the organiser of this development.[1] He was interested first in
making money, and secondly in attacking the government in
a new way. La Caricature (1830) and Le Charivari (1832) were
above all republican papers, ridiculing King Louis-Philippe, and
Philipon was sent to prison for his famous caricature turning the
king into a pear; but at the same time ridicule was poured on
a vast variety of subjects—the latest hairstyles, plays, inventions,
fashions, as well as soldiers, barristers, prostitutes and the inevitable 'bourgeois'. Philipon's achievement was to bring together
some twenty artists and to give them a regular supply of ideas.
After 1835 Le Charivari became, for a time, a daily and it
was for this paper that Daumier created Robert Macaire, the

incarnation of the modern speculator, and that Grandville produced his fantastic transformations of humans into animals, and
his enormously detailed studies of political demonstrations.
Caricature became such an important political weapon that
every party came to have its own funny paper: the monarchists
had *Le Triboulet* (1878–93), the Bonapartists *Le Droit du peuple*
(1885–6), the Boulangists *La Diane*, the republicans *La Lune*
(1865–8) and *L'Éclipse* (1868–1919). It does not seem that everybody found the same things funny, for almost every occupation
and every interest came to have a humorous paper, both with jokes
which appealed to it and as an instrument of attack against its
enemies. Soldiers had *La Vie militaire* (1883), sportsmen had *Le
Centaure* (1866); tenants had *L'Anti-Concierge* (1881–2); the beer
industry had *Le Bon Bock* (1865) to denigrate the Germans;
advertisers had *Le Comique-Annonces* (1885); bankers had *L'Éclat
du rire* (1877) and *La Vie de la Bourse* (1882). Parisians of Provençal origin had *Le Tartarin* (1884). The most famous paper to
combine both political satire and jokes which only the initiated
could understand was *Le Canard enchaîné* (founded 1915); it has
made itself into something of a national institution, incarnating
the resistance of the small man to authority and conformity,
while clinging tenaciously to such prejudices as anti-militarism,
anticlericalism, respect for education: the *instituteur* was always
sacred to it.[1]

During the Second Empire political journalism was restricted,
and so a great deal of energy was switched instead to newspapers
that would entertain. *La Vie parisienne*, founded in 1863 and
lasting till 1949, had as its original sub-title 'the elegant life,
topics of the day, fantasies, travel, theatre, music, fine arts, sport
and fashion'; it attempted to provide mild relaxation for those
with too much leisure: it won a firm foothold by being very well
informed on women's fashions and on Paris gossip in general,
but it attracted male readers by dealing with these subjects in
a titillating way. Its most successful issues were reprinted as mild
pornography, but just mild enough to escape prosecution. When
in 1890 a rival paper was brought to trial, its defence lawyer
complained that the supposedly respectable *Vie parisienne*, catering for well-to-do society, was no better: its speciality, he said,

[1] F. Batailler *et al.*, *Analyses de presse* (1963), section on 'L'Idéologie du *Canard
enchaîné*', 91–176.

was to show how women put on their stockings, 'in which all positions are shown, with plenty of indiscreet glimpses and it is not always the garter which marks the boundary limiting the sight offered to the spectator'. It would have a page of cartoons on 'how women take their baths, in baths which seem to be made of crystal; a page on how to put on a blouse, which arouses no preoccupation other than the desire to remove it from them'. There were infinite and subtle gradations in the scatological press. One of the papers that often got into trouble with the law, but which was also one of the most distinguished artistically (with Willette, Forain and Louis Legrand drawing for it), was *Le Courrier français* (1884–1913). It was read because its staff seemed to be 'at once boldly *avant-garde* and worryingly and scandalously paradoxical'. It was backed financially by the Geraudel pharmaceutical firm, and advised its readers to buy the pastilles of that name before they opened the paper. *L'Événement parisien* (1880–2), which was perhaps one of the most pornographic, was also one of the most successful; its highly profitable sale of 150,000 copies made the fines and convictions easy to bear.[1]

Professional humorists were very often bitter satirists, but it would be wrong to deduce that, generally speaking, French humour was always acid. Superficially, it is possible to argue that, in so far as there was such a thing as specifically French humour, it was more often than not biting and an instrument of attack. This would fit in with Coleridge's criticism of the humour of Voltaire, as being devoid of the pathos that gives humour its magic charm, and Carlyle's comment that Voltaire's laughter represented gaiety of the head, not of the heart, showing contempt but not sympathy; it would suggest that, because of a more turbulent political and social development, France did not experience the same transformation of humour that occurred in England at the turn of the eighteenth and nineteenth centuries, when the satirical tradition of the Restoration gave way to a more amiable sense of fun, in which eccentrics were presented as objects of delight and love, and the picturesque and the incongruous were portrayed with affection, not with

---

[1] Philippe Jones, 'La Presse satirique illustrée entre 1860 et 1890', *Études de presse* (1956), vol. 8, no. 14, 7–116. Cf. 'Les Journaux pornographiques', anonymous article in *Annuaire de la presse française* (1881), 91–119.

irony.[1] This argument would have it that England's complacency and stability in the nineteenth century were reflected in its humour, though after 1918, when that social background vanished, a more tough-minded style returned. But the bitterness of professional French humorists, such as it was, perhaps reflected the different social status of the artist and writer in France. Humour and caricature were low genres, which seldom led to honours or official recognition, and those who earned their living in this way were professional nonconformists. The angry humorists have attracted more attention from posterity, partly because they had more to say and said it with greater force; but this should not lead one to neglect the not inconsiderable number of happy humorists. Side by side with the gay paintings of the Impressionists, for example, there were successful caricaturists like Linder, Morlon, Numa, Guirard and Vernier who specialised in showing the joys of existence and the exuberance to be found in ordinary life. There is no bitterness and much ingenious fun in the cartoons of Albert Robida (1848–1926). He was an artist of great modesty, who lived quietly in Le Vésinet with his seven children; the son of a carpenter, his father had tried to make a notary's clerk of him, but Robida's inventive imagination turned instead to science fiction and to fantasy, which was always innocent.[2] Alphonse Allais (1855–1905) was his counterpart in prose. The son of a pharmacist, trained as a pharmacist, he gave up his career just before his final examinations and took up the café life, spending his time moving from one to another, and doing all his writing on their little tables, with endless drinks to help him along. He made fun of everything, pushing every situation to absurdity, using his scientific knowledge to imagine extraordinary inventions to cure common troubles. He proposed, for example, the nationalisation of the umbrella-making industry, so that umbrellas could be made in different sizes, with a view to diminishing the frequency with which they collided in the street; he stood for parliament with a programme advocating the abolition of the tax on bicycles, the re-establishment of licence in the streets so as to increase France's dwindling population, and the

[1] S. M. Tave, *The Amiable Humorist. A Study in the Comic Theory and Criticism of the Eighteenth and early Nineteenth Centuries* (Chicago, 1960).

[2] A. Robida, *La Vie éléctrique* (1895); id., *Le XIXᵉ siècle* (1888).

suppression of bureaucracy and the School of Fine Arts. He called his humour literature for the commercial traveller. It enabled him to earn 20,000 francs a year, buy his furniture in England and have a magnificent bathroom with constant hot water. It is true his gaiety was ambiguous, tarnished by a marriage to a pretty girl much younger than himself and ending in near-bankruptcy. Not everyone thought he was funny, even though he laughed so much. Madame Waldeck-Rousseau refused to use her influence to get him decorated, saying she found him stupid.[1]

Matthew Arnold claimed that what was attractive about French frivolity was that it took as its base 'the average sensual man', accepting the wishes of the flesh as part of life and so producing a much more relaxed kind of fun than the Englishman's doubts and repressions allowed. That France was a Catholic country and that puritanism had never won complete supremacy in it were certainly important factors, and perhaps comparisons with Irish humour would be more useful than with that of England or the U.S.A.[2] The vitality of the Rabelaisian tradition of gross humour was certainly emphasised by the extraordinary success of Gabriel Chevalier's *Clochemerle* (1936), a story about a urinal. There was no malice here but only laughter at what people had in common. The book has no individual characters, but only types, who give pleasure because everyone can recognise them as true. This was the laughter of sociability overcoming shyness and prudery.[3]

However, it is true that there was often great sadness behind much humour. The transformation of gaiety into gloom by the intellectual can be seen rather strikingly in the history of pantomime. Pierrot and Harlequin were originally happy characters, in a simple way, but the romantics turned them into philosophical commentators on the tragedy of life. The intellectuals discovered pantomime in the 1830s, when J. G. Deburau who used to play Pierrot at the working-class Théâtre des Funambules was turned into a fashionable hero by Charles Nodier and

---

[1] Anatole Jakovsky, *Alphonse Allais* (1955); *Tout Allais* (1964), a reprint of his works, in ten volumes.

[2] Francis Halkett, 'The Frivolous French', *The Atlantic Monthly* (Boston, June 1926), 726–33.

[3] Gabriel Chevalier, *Clochemerle* (1936); Marcel Tetel, *Étude sur le comique de Rabelais* (Florence, 1964).

Jules Janin. Deburau was a great change from the stock situations and stock types of the theatre of the time; he became a symbol of the pure working class, and was seen as the creator of fantasies that could distract one from the ugly realities of life. Formerly the heroes of pantomime were Harlequin and Columbine, young lovers who eventually triumphed over all obstacles. Now Pierrot, who was always the victim, deceived and punished, took on the central role, and as Deburau became more famous, he made Pierrot vicious also, hitting back and getting his way too. In the 1880s, the macabre side of the clown was greatly accentuated, to the point that he sometimes wore black.[1]

Daumier was one of those who portrayed these clowns as sad, because he saw behind them the insecure, despised, wandering artist, with whom he sympathised and identified. It is, however, very difficult to characterise Daumier's work as a whole by any simple formula, for though (at the last count) no less than 340 books and articles have been written about him, Daumier left very few explicit indications of his aims or ideas. In the early part of his career he was given his subject-matter by Philipon, who also provided the legends to go under the cartoons, or employed witty young men to write them for a small fee. Daumier was a republican, but he also nourished frustrated ambitions to be a painter; he was a caricaturist mainly to earn his living and was always hoping he could concentrate on grander forms of art. He was the son of a glazier, and like his father he was an artisan who produced for the market. He was not verbally fluent, but a quiet, contemplative and steady worker, whose interest was probably above all in visual observation and the expressive recording of life around him. His most revealing remark—one of the few he made—was 'It is necessary to be a man of one's time'. His contemporary, Champfleury, who knew him well, argued that caricature was 'the expression of the intimate sentiments of the people'; it was cruel, because it reflected the feelings of revolt of a people in a state of revolt; and it was significant only in periods of revolution. A great deal of Daumier's work was a satire on the bourgeoisie, but it was not

[1] V. J. Rubin, 'Clowns in Nineteenth Century French Literature: Buffoons, Pierrots and Saltimbanques' (unpublished Ph.D. thesis, Berkeley, California, 1970); F. Haskell, 'The Sad Clown: some notes on a nineteenth century myth', in U. Finke, *French Nineteenth Century Painting and Literature* (Manchester, 1972), 2–16.

always angry, for his good nature and his interest in character and physiognomy for its own sake survived his political commitment. He saw laughter as one answer to the problems of life, by which 'good humour and mental serenity' could be preserved.[1]

Forain was another caricaturist who was inspired by irritation with injustice and pity for its victims: 'on top', he said, 'there is neurosis; at the bottom, there is hunger.' But with him, again, the pictorial interest was uppermost: he drew his men and women first, gave them expressions 'and it is only when they are there, in front of me, that I ask what they have got to say —I question them and they reply'.[2] He showed that caricature need not be funny. Willette, whose art appeared to breathe disillusionment and regret, insisted however that people attributed excessively complex intentions to him. He was fond of drawing Pierrot, but that was not symbolic: 'it is above all by his clothes that Pierrot attracted me. I needed a personage sufficiently general to express all human passions through his movements. I did not want to put him into ordinary clothes: Pierrot's were the clothes of the poet.'[3]

There are definite limitations to what one can deduce from caricature.[4] Not that caricature in prose is much simpler. Alphonse Daudet's *Tartarin*, for example, has survived as a portrayal of the joviality of the Provençals. Daudet himself described his book as a *galéjade*—the Provençal word for a burst of mocking laughter. Tartarin was however a self-portrait, giving expression to Daudet's hesitation between heroic ambitions and cowardly fears, inflated to comic proportions. His book raises the question of whether there was more laughter in the south than the north: certainly their laughter was not entirely of the same kind.[5]

[1] Champfleury [J. F. F. Husson], *Histoire de la caricature moderne* (2nd edition, 1865), x, 170, 175; K. E. Maison, *Honoré Daumier, Catalogue raisonné* (1968); Oliver W. Larkin, *Daumier, Man of his Time* (1967); Arsène Alexandre, *Honoré Daumier* (1888), 199; and for a clever and well-argued political interpretation, T. J. Clark, *The Absolute Bourgeois* (1973), 99–123. On the ambiguity of the ridiculing of the bourgeoisie see Edith Melcher, *The Life and Times of Henry Monnier 1799–1827* (Cambridge, Mass., 1950).

[2] Adolphe Brisson, *Nos humoristes* (1900), 44.

[3] Ibid. 152; and Paul Gaultier, *Le Rire et la caricature* (1906), ch. 3.

[4] Jacques Lethève, *La Caricature et la presse sous la troisième république* (1961); J. Grand Carteret, *Les Mœurs et la caricature en France* (n.d.); and Raoul Deberdt, *La Caricature et l'humour français au 19ᵉ siècle* (n.d.) are valuable starting-points.

[5] Murray Sachs, *The Career of Alphonse Daudet* (Cambridge, Mass., 1965).

The most famous analyst of laughter in this period, Bergson, rightly stressed that laughter was a social art, involving complicity with others who laughed also: the larger the audience, the more laughter there was. He argued that the person who was laughed at was essentially unsociable: he was funny because he failed to adapt to circumstances around him, or because he acted automatically (as in absent-mindedness) without taking others into account; laughter was therefore above all a penalty meted out by society to those who took liberties against it, who were nonconformists or failures. It was designed to humiliate; it was a form of vengeance and was incompatible with compassion or emotion. He concluded therefore that comic situations were essentially creations of the intelligence.[1] There was always a strong element of this kind of humour in France, which reinforced the critical and combative characteristics of the society. But that is not the most significant function that humour performed. In other hands, humour was an instrument of detachment from the world, not a reinforcement of ties; it was therefore an emotional even more than an intellectual reaction. One can see this in Proust, for example, who certainly uses humour with fiercely satirical purpose on a large variety of subjects, but his humour is so universal, including even death, love and the author himself in its scope, that it emerges as a method by which Proust can take up a detached view of himself. 'Gaiety', wrote Proust, 'is a fundamental element in all things.' He showed how every action, every statement, however serious in appearance, could be shown to be funny, if only two people—in this case the author and his reader—conspired to declare it to be so: and he showed this by simply reporting such statements with a serious face.[2] Paul Valéry, who said 'anxiety is my real profession', was a southerner with a great admiration for gaiety and vivacity, who made humour the logical outcome of Descartes's universal doubt; he saved himself from madness by treating life not only as a drama but also as a game, making himself a spectator as well as an actor.[3]

The balance of this society was probably preserved by these

[1] H. Bergson, *Le Rire. Essai sur la signification du comique* (1900).

[2] Maya Slater, 'The Humour in the Works of Marcel Proust' (unpublished Oxford D.Phil. thesis, 1970).

[3] Paul Gifford, 'L'Humour chez Paul Valéry' (unpublished doctoral thesis, Toulouse-Mirail, 1971).

different kinds of humour, and not least by the fact that there were such a variety of them. Every serious political proclamation, every achievement of science and industry, needs to be seen also from the point of view of the jokes that were made about it. It is unfortunate that the jokes were recorded so much less frequently, and that they have been studied so much less by historians. The search for humour should not be regarded, however, simply as an evasion of, or escape from, the realities of life; it was also a positive attempt to create joy and pleasure around everyday events, as well as a rebellion against the restrictions of morality and prudence. As such, it deserves to have its achievements recorded quite as much as the more long-term efforts of the legislators and educators, whose success was perhaps not as great.

7. Eating and Drinking

EATING and drinking loomed large in the Frenchman's idea of the good life. No study of his sense of values can be complete without explaining the high priority he accorded both to the pleasures of the table and to discussion of those pleasures. But France's international renown as the home of good food was acquired only at the beginning of the nineteenth century, and what was understood by French cooking then was not the same as what it came to mean in the twentieth century. French food has a history which in some ways parallels that of the country's political development. There were the great cooks, and the philosophers of gastronomy, who created the ideals and theorised about the restaurant, originally representing a democratic advance but soon revealed as surrounded by privilege and profiteering. There was the clash of Jacobin centralisation—the efforts to create a French national style of cooking—and regional individuality. And there were the sordid realities which were allowed to survive while the leaders of fashion set the pace, like the adulteration of ingredients, the near-starvation of the poor, and the ever-rising toll of alcoholism.

In the nineteenth century, the vast majority of Frenchmen ate food which was very different from what the gastronomes were concocting in Paris. Peasant cooking was dominated first of all by the method of heating. The cauldron hanging from a hook in the fireplace was almost universal until the mid-nineteenth century. Inventories of furniture and effects, drawn up in connection with the distribution of property after death, show that the break in heating methods came at this time. In the Mâconnais, cauldrons disappear between 1850 and 1870, but they survived much longer in other parts of France, and in Normandy —though it was supposedly open to the influence of Paris—they were still to be found after the Second World War. Food used to be eaten with pocket knives, which each man brought with him, and spoons: there are few references to cutlery sets in poor households till the very end of the century. This meant that peasant cooking involved, above all, slow boiling. The basic dish was soup, made generally of vegetables, given bulk by the addition of chunks of old bread. Among the very poor, this soup would contain mainly salted water, and not all that much salt either, since it took a long time for people to get over the habits acquired under the *ancien régime*, when salt was taxed and expensive. The addition of pork fat transformed the soup into a luxury. In order to save fuel, enough soup would often be cooked for several meals; very little would be thrown away, and very confused tastes would develop as new ingredients were constantly added. The other basic food was porridge (*bouillie*), obtained by boiling grain or flour—often maize or buckwheat—in water or milk: this survived until the end of the nineteenth century, and much longer as a dish for evening meals and for children. As soon as one emerged from absolute poverty, one tried to keep a pig: the peasants usually killed one or two a year. Its main function was to produce fat, which immediately raised the level of cooking, but it was also eaten with spinach, potatoes and chestnuts; sausages were made from the entrails and the blood. Butcher's meat was the next step up: the principal way of cooking it was again boiling or stewing, or else *en daube*, i.e. in a pot called a *daubière*, placed between two layers of embers. But it is impossible to talk about peasant cooking once one has risen to this level of prosperity, for its essential characteristic was that it relied on local produce and local traditions. Thus in the Mâconnais, of which a particularly detailed study has been made, rabbits did not enter the peasant cook's repertoire till the end of the nineteenth century, whereas they were much used in other regions. The isolation of regions from each other meant that some villages would rely a great deal on fish, while others hardly knew this food; chickens were much eaten in the south-west, but only for feasts in the Mâconnais, and that only after 1870, for most of them were sold off to raise cash. The fact that a region produced a certain food did not mean that the peasants necessarily ate it, at least not until they had reached some prosperity. The Mâconnais had lots of mushrooms, but they began to be eaten only around 1900, and even today a certain dislike of them persists. Though chestnuts were much valued and eaten, other nuts were kept for making oil.

It is generally believed that the south of France has traditionally used olive oil for its cooking and the north butter, but this is a recent development. Quite apart from the fact that the basis of most cooking, first of all, was water and not oil, there was far more variety in the kinds of oil used than this simple division suggests, depending both on the province and on the social hierarchy within it. Thus the Morbihan was a major producer of butter, but until the twentieth century it exported it all. Nut-oil was widely used all over France until 1900, and in Touraine until 1920; it was valued for lighting as well as cooking. In the Vosges, pork fat was long used instead of butter, to spread on bread. This was connected with the way milk was treated: it was seldom drunk, except by the sick, but more often turned into soft cheese, whey and buttermilk, because of the difficulty of preserving it. In the west, butter was preserved by salting, but in many other regions by melting it—in which form it was treated as precious and used with parsimony. The peasants tended to eat fresh cheese themselves, to which spices or garlic might be added, but to set aside more elaborate cheeses for sale to the towns: even goat's cheese, when fermented in vine leaves, was treated as an export. In the Mâconnais, to use butter in cooking was a sign of one's rise in the social scale: colza-oil, nut-oil and pork fat were more common. Fresh fruit and vegetables were not a particular feature of peasant food. One reason was that peasants tended to eat only what they grew themselves; the habit of buying vegetables developed slowly and variety in salads, for example, came late. Another reason was that these foods tended to be kept for preserving. Dried vegetables, like beans and lentils, were popular; fruit was seldom eaten raw, more usually being turned into compotes and jams. Because sugar was expensive, beetroot was often used instead; but honey was an alternative: the *arrondissement* of Clamecy, it was recorded in 1832, had 2,540 beehives.

However, all this was a supplement to the single most important food—bread. In the Nivernais, peasants spent between one-third and one-half of their budgets on it, but this varied from region to region, as did the composition of the bread. Apart from the complication that most flour was severely adulterated, sometimes with noxious substances, so that not everyone knew what he was eating, some regions, like the Nivernais, mixed their flour—from equal parts of wheat, barley and rye—while others, like the Morvan, ate only rye bread. Townsmen were

not complimentary about the skill of peasants' baking, and
noted that their bread was kept for long periods, degenerating
into an almost solid lump. In Nevers in 1860 the best-quality
bread comprised only one-tenth of the total sold; by 1900 it was
one-third; there were many gradations in the bread available.
The quality of flour improved only gradually, from around
1880; bakers were notorious for their frauds and short weight
and made large profits. Peasant bread, as it is now esteemed,
is a recent invention, not a traditional food; the old bread was
seldom wholesome or pure. It tasted different also because there
has been a great change in the amount of salt added to bread:
in the eighteenth century hardly any salt was used; in the nineteenth, there was a great increase, to 3 per cent, the highest
proportion in Europe; since the Second World War, the proportion has fallen to 1·2 to 1·5 per cent, though in rainy years it is
raised to as much as 2·5 per cent, depending on the condition
of the wheat.[1]

In so far as peasants' cooking was influenced by ideas from
outside, in the nineteenth century it conformed to the medieval
school of thought. This had as its principle to mix many ingredients, without much attention to quantities—which medieval
recipe books seldom specified—and to add spices as liberally as
possible. Spices were esteemed, first, because they were a way
of preserving food, secondly because they were considered to
have medicinal properties, and lastly as a way of showing off
one's wealth, because they were expensive. Many different spices
were not often found in French peasant kitchens before 1900, but
individual spices—and herbs—were used liberally when they
were available. The medieval gastronome used to show his
knowledge by guessing correctly what a dish was made of, and
this guessing used to be a favourite entertainment at meals. So
the peasants were not encouraged either by culinary science, or
by their poverty, to depart from the rather indiscriminate mixture of ingredients and flavours. Peasant cooking, said a recipe
book produced in 1867 under the auspices of the ministry of
agriculture, was either insipid or too spiced: it was primitive,
traditional and monotonous.[2] Just how different peasant and

[1] J. J. Hemardinquer, *Pour une histoire de l'alimentation* (1970); Suzanne Tardieu,
La Vie domestique dans le Mâconnais rural pré-industriel (1964), 92–138.
[2] Madame Marceline Michaux, *La Cuisine de la ferme* (1867).

Parisian cooking could be may be seen by comparing the recipe for cabbage soup given by Madame Michaux, the author of this book, with that in *Le Cuisinier impérial* by one of the new generation of master cooks, Viard. In the peasant version, a cabbage was simply boiled with a leek and a clove of garlic, and a drop of butter was put in at the end. In Viard's version for the rich, two cabbages were boiled, then carefully dried and finally allowed to cook over slices of veal covered with bacon fat, together with carrots, onions and mushrooms. This required both time and money, but peasants had little leisure for elaborate preparations and observers of their methods commented on their adherence to recipes requiring the minimum of effort. What created bourgeois cooking was the almost limitless application that came to be given to it and the lavish use of more varied ingredients. In the peasant cook-book, vegetable recipes occupied over one-third of the space; in Viard's manual, they were allocated less than 5 per cent, for much more impressive dishes could be created with meat, fish and fowl. Most peasant cooking was probably not even wholesome: there were numerous comments about their 'poisonous' and fetid soups. When it came to cooking potatoes, they seem often to have been guilty of overboiling, whereas Viard suggested a whole range of imaginative and ingenious recipes. He proposed ten different ways of cooking artichokes, whereas the peasant book records only five. Greater variety was the mark of the new style: Viard's book, first published in 1806, had doubled in size by the time it reached its thirty-first edition in 1873, its range of soups rising from 74 to 134 different recipes.[1]

The long survival of the peasant style was shown in an inquiry carried out in the 1950s. This revealed two distinct types of meal still coexisting in France. In traditional regions like the Morbihan, soup was eaten at all meals, and this was above all vegetable soup, involving slow boiling in water. Soup was the staple diet not only of peasants but of many workers who retained peasant traditions: in Saint-Étienne, for example, 49·6 per cent of households still had soup for breakfast in the early 1950s. Modernisation meant the abandonment of this soup—

---

[1] A. Viard, *Le Cuisinier impérial, ou l'art de faire la cuisine et la pâtisserie pour toutes les fortunes, avec différents recettes d'office et de fruits confits, et la manière de servir une table depuis 20 jusqu'à 60 couverts* (1806); 31st edition 1873 is *Le Cuisinier national*.

which in wealthier families used to be accompanied by eggs, cheese, *charcuterie*, and wine or cider—in favour of the small breakfast of coffee and rolls. Soup next began disappearing from the townsman's midday meal—only one-third of the poor of Marseille, for example, still ate soup for lunch in 1950. But soup has survived most tenaciously at supper, which as the major family meal, respected older traditions more. One of the most important changes in popular methods of cooking came largely after 1919, when instead of boiling meat and putting fats in their soup, the poor began to roast and grill meat, garnishing it with butter. The greater use of butcher's meat was another innovation of the towns—between two-thirds and 90 per cent of urban households ate more of it in 1950 than pork, fowl and rabbit, whereas only 50 per cent of peasants did so. Peasants in general consumed about 300 more calories than townsmen, but that was largely because they ate more bread; the fall in consumption of this once staple diet was the final indication of modernisation, but bread ceased to be the basis of the peasant's diet only in the twentieth century.[1]

The traditional generalisation that the rich ate more meat than the poor needs qualification. In 1850 Paris consumed 62 kilogrammes of butcher's meat per inhabitant per annum, Rennes 60, Bordeaux 53, Strasbourg 44, Toulouse 38, and Caen 28; and if pork is added, the figures go from 72 kilogrammes in Paris to 33 in Caen. This does not seem to have any direct correlation with the prosperity or social composition of these towns: thus the predominantly working-class town of Saint-Étienne consumed 49 kilogrammes of butcher's meat, while Dijon, with a large bourgeois element, ate only 42. The same variation existed in drinking habits. Bordeaux came top of the table, drinking 196 litres of wine per head per annum, Caen came bottom with only 12, while Paris was in the middle with 113. If cider, beer and other alcoholic drinks are added, Rennes came top with 440, Caen second with 245 and Brest bottom with 80. Dijon, a leading wine centre, consumed much more beer than wine.[2] The explanation of these variations lies in local

---

[1] J. Claudian and Y. Soville, 'Composition des repas et urbanisation' in J. J. Hemardinquer, op. cit. 174–87; Cf. R. Mandrou, *Introduction à la France moderne 1500–1640* (1961), which has some instructive pages on food in this period.

[2] Mandrou, op. cit.; and cf. Armand Husson, *Les Consommations de Paris* (1856).

and family traditions, which resisted the spread of uniformity very strongly.

Mademoiselle Léontine, a cook writing in 1856, lamented that most people were very unwilling to alter their eating habits and were generally satisfied simply when their stomachs were full. Most people had confused notions of what was wholesome and what was not: the result was that 'half the population is constantly ill'.[1] The digestive process was, by this date, understood by doctors, but the value of different foods was still largely a matter of guesswork. In so far as any rules about diet were accepted, the main one was that different temperaments required different foods. The problem for those who got beyond the level of satiating their hunger was how to reconcile the preservation of their health with the titillation of their palates. A traditional approach to this was to go from one extreme to another, and alternate between relative abstinence and over-eating.[2] Popular cook-books with pretensions to science tried to develop different habits: they warned those with sanguine temperaments to avoid strong flavours (e.g. lemon, tomato, onion) but to eat lots of vegetables. The lymphatic were urged to keep off sweet things, even fruit; the nervous to beware of tea. Sexual exhaustion should be remedied by concentrated broths, intellectual exhaustion by coffee. But delicate women would be damaged by coffee and indeed were in danger from a large number of foods. Apart from all the differences that age, sex, temperament, climate and profession imposed, there was the problem of what was 'digestible' and what was not—pork, for example, was considered less digestible than beef. As late as 1913, a doctor recorded that pre-scientific superstitions about diet flourished unabated. Babies were still being purged for every trouble, including bronchitis. Women were addicts of every kind of indigestion and constipation pill offered in the advertisement columns of the newspapers. A very frequent complaint was 'the dislocated stomach', and many quacks made a fortune 'resetting' stomachs. There were phobias about a whole variety of foods, from spinach and sorrel to chocolate. Obsession with digestion led some to take laxatives daily, or even daily

[1] Mademoiselle Léontine, *La Cuisine hygiénique, confortable et économique, à l'usage de toutes les classes de la société* (new edition, 1856).

[2] L. M. Lombard, *Le Cuisinier et le médecin . . . ou l'art de conserver ou de rétablir sa santé par une alimentation convenable* (1855).

enemas.[1] Some people claimed that the peasant had none of these troubles and was the model of good health, but others described his food as disgusting, on the verge of being poisonous, and far from nutritious: 'One should not be surprised by the slowness, the laziness and the inertia of these poor devils.'[2]

What is now known as the French style of cooking was created largely in the nineteenth century by the efforts of four different sets of people, who reinforced each other's ambitions by their discussions, comparisons and competition. These were the professional male cooks, the restaurant-keepers, the gastronomes and the female cooks employed in the domestic service of the bourgeoisie. The development of the profession of cook took on new proportions in the nineteenth century. Every history of cooks mentions Vatel, who committed suicide in 1602 because he could not face the humiliation of not having two roasts he had planned for a banquet ready in time; there were doubtless many skilled cooks before the nineteenth century, who produced magnificent meals. But their pride in their work was now given a new range under the leadership of Antoine Carême (1784–1833). Carême was a man of letters and an architect as well as a cook. He raised cooking to the level of a supreme art, claiming that it was 'the most ancient of the arts and the art which has rendered the most important services to civil life'. It should be a science too, embodying knowledge of agriculture, chemistry and pharmacy; but to have full scope it had to be treated as a form of showmanship and advertising. Carême worked for the Tsar of Russia and for Talleyrand but he was fully happy only when he finally became cook to Baron Rothschild in Paris. Here he was allowed to spend as much money as he wished, which he said was 'the only way to stimulate the genius of cooks jealous of their reputation, for what use is talent if it lacks the money necessary to procure provisions of the highest quality?' Carême developed, in these conditions, what might be called ideal cooking, unlimited by considerations of economy; but though his menus could be attempted only by princes and millionaires, his style was highly influential, because he carried out several fundamental changes in the methods of preparing food. First,

[1] Dr. A. Mollière, *Les Préjugés en diététique et dans les maladies des voies digestives* (1913).   [2] Lombard, op. cit. 114.

he greatly reduced the use of herbs and spices: 'modern cooking', he wrote, 'must know how to extract the nutritive juices from foods by rational cooking.' Secondly, he limited the mixture of different types of food: in grand dinners it used to be common to serve fish, for example, surrounded by sweetbreads, pigeons, cocks' crests and kidneys: Carême mixed like with like, surrounding fish only with other fish. Thirdly, he transformed the decoration of food, making great use of skewers to create elaborate mountains of food, harmonising with the complicated silver and crystal plates they were served on; and he developed new ways of garnishing principal dishes to heighten their effect. This reflected the grandiose ideas he expressed in his architecture, which was his hobby. Carême argued that once the value of cooking of this kind was appreciated, cooks would be recognised as men of great importance: they should not stay in the kitchen but come out to the dining-room to supervise the eating; they were in fact doctors, with far more influence on their employers' well-being than the charlatans who posed as doctors (though the dietetical textbook he relied on was a very old-fashioned work of 1709).[1] A cook, as Carême conceived him, was 'a god on earth'. There were no limits to Carême's arrogance or self-confidence: he despised Cambacérès, the archchancellor of Napoleon's Empire, because he insisted on leftovers being used and would not give Carême his best wines to cook with; he was sorry for Napoleon's cook, who had to serve him the very simple foods he demanded. He advised humbler people who could not reproduce his recipes not to attempt simplified versions of them, but to put all their money into creating one grand dish: 'better give two great dinners than four mediocre ones'. His literary masterpiece (and he warned readers that unless they read it in its entirety 'they will largely lose the benefit of this fruit of long meditations', this 'most laborious work that any expert on cooking has ever undertaken') contained 500 soup and 500 fish recipes. Though he was confident that French food was the best in the world, he did not disdain *potage de choux à la paysanne russe*, or *bortsch*, or English turtle soup, though he embellished them appropriately.[2]

[1] Lémery, *Dictionnaire des aliments* (1709).
[2] Antoine Carême, *L'Art de la cuisine française au 19ᵉ siècle. Traité élémentaire et pratique suivi de dissertations culinaires et gastronomiques utiles au progrès de cet art* (1833).

Carême was venerated as the greatest of French cooks, but aspects of his teaching had different results. His stress on sumptuousness made the French cooking that followed his lead notable above all for its richness, and particularly for its sauces: it became the style adopted almost universally by embassies and later by grand palace hotels, where ostentation was all-important. The *sauce espagnole*, which, despite its name, was the basis of this French style, required, to be made properly, bacon fat, ham, fowl, veal, hare and partridge: it was clearly beyond the means of the ordinary small family. Carême's style was ostentatious also in its presentation, and this side of him was considerably exaggerated during the Second Empire. Urbain Dubois, who was one of the most famous cooks of this period (chef to the king of Prussia for a time), published illustrated books showing the most elaborate and amazing architectural arrangements of food, differing from Carême in that many colourful uneatable objects were added as ornaments.[1] But this system, which aimed to produce 'magnificent spectacles' had the serious disadvantage that the food was usually cold when it came to be eaten, since it was the practice to put these monuments on the table well before they were consumed. *Service à la française* meant that a meal was divided, like a play, into three acts—the first consisted of *potages*, *relevés* and *entrées*, the second of *rôtis* and *entremets* and the third of *desserts*—and that the food was brought on to the table not individually, but in these three stages. The enormous menus of this period—which in a dinner given by Talleyrand once contained no less than forty-eight *entrées*—were an indication not of what everybody would eat, but of the choice from which the diners would select. Thus in a dinner for thirty people, Carême would serve only half a dozen birds: not everyone would get a piece; but there would be many alternatives placed on the table at the same time. *Hors d'œuvres*, in this system, were designed to fill in the gaps, for those who were unable to get enough of the main courses. The table would be cleared after the *entrées*, and the various roasts and *entremets* would then be brought in all together. The snag of this buffet-like method was not only that the food got cold, but also that it was difficult to

---

[1] Urbain Dubois and Émile Bernard, *La Cuisine classique. Études pratiques, raisonnées et démonstratives de l'école française appliquée au service à la russe* (1864); Urbain Dubois, *Cuisine artistique. Études de l'école moderne* (2nd edition, 1882).

share out equitably; and from the middle of the nineteenth
century therefore *service à la russe* was increasingly adopted,
which meant that the food was cut up in the kitchen and each
diner was offered a portion by the waiters. This led to a great
diminution of the number of dishes that had to be cooked, but
it was only around 1890 that this Russian method became more
or less universal. The old 'costly prodigality, more suited to
dazzle than to satisfy' was thus moderated. 'Extravagant super-
abundance', said Dubois, should be avoided and meals should
be 'rich and luxurious without excess'—though he made up for
this by fantastic arrangements of the fewer courses that were
served.

Escoffier, however, who was perhaps the most influential cook
of the Third Republic, altered the character of the meal once
again. Writing at the beginning of the twentieth century, he
said that Carême and Dubois, though great cooks, had catered
for an age that had passed, and what had suited the Second
Empire 'when life was easy and the future assured' was no longer
appropriate when people were in a hurry, and demanded, above
all else, rapid service. He discarded the plinths, skewers, tam-
pons and borders that had been used to build up dishes into
artistic constructions, as well as the complicated garnishings.
He invented new equipment and new methods for simplified
presentation; he removed most of the uneatable ornaments, and
he compensated by increasing the savour and nutritional value
of the food, making it lighter and 'more easily digestible by
weakened stomachs'. 'My success', he said, 'comes from the fact
that my best dishes were created for ladies.' It was only around
the turn of the century indeed that it became respectable or
fashionable for ladies to be taken to restaurants. But Escoffier's
recipes were also drawn up with unprecedented accuracy, every
ingredient being carefully measured. 'Cooking,' he said, 'without ceasing to be an art, will become a science', leaving nothing
to chance. He was not opposed to the tradition of grand meals,
which were 'both a ceremony and a feast' but he quoted
Carême's maxim that in cooking the only principle was to satisfy
the person one served. Modern taste no longer accepted the
sauce espagnole, 'whose richness amazes our parsimonious eye';
sauces had, in the last quarter of the nineteenth century, reached
a stage of exaggeration with the result that they drowned the

aroma of the foods they were served with, and everything came
to taste much the same. Escoffier was not deterred from devoting
sixty-seven pages of his book to sauces, but he also made much
more use of *fumets*, the lighter juices of the meat and fish he
served. He reproduced many of the old-fashioned ornate recipes,
and he was a skilled sculptor in sugar and ice: *pêche Melba*, which
he invented, was originally called *pêche au cygne*, because the
peaches and vanilla ice-cream came served between the wings
of a swan made of ice (representing the swan in *Lohengrin*, in
which Melba had been singing); it was only later that he added
raspberry *purée* to create the present *pêche Melba*. But Escoffier
was not only a chef: he was also an associate of César Ritz and
his collaborator in organising the enormous new hotels that now
sprang up all over Europe. These provided a new venue for the
international aristocracy and set up a new pattern in entertaining and eating. Escoffier spent much of his life at the Savoy and
Carlton Hotels in London, ruling over eighty cooks. He was an
apostle of efficiency and saw that cooking methods had to be
adapted to meet the changed demands placed upon them by
large and rich clienteles. He established principles of team-
work, so that whereas previously an order for 'deux œufs sur le
plat Meyerbeer' would take a cook fifteen minutes to prepare,
now the eggs were cooked by the *entremettier*, the kidney was
grilled by the *rôtisseur* and the truffle sauce prepared by the
saucier: the order could thus be fulfilled in a few minutes.
Escoffier's ideas were influential not only in his own or other
large hotels, but throughout the profession, for he wrote frequently in the press, notably in the periodical *L'Art culinaire*.
His ideas, however, did not always triumph. Thus he lamented
the rise of *hors d'œuvres* into a regular course, saying that these
were only a method of keeping a client waiting in a restaurant.
Hors d'œuvres, it is true, had greatly altered in the course of the
century. Originally they had been prepared by a special cook,
the *officier*, in a separate kitchen, which had also been in charge
of making sweets and decorating the table.[1] The kitchen obtained command over them only in the second half of the
nineteenth century, and that is partly why they became mainly
cold dishes. Soups likewise were transformed in the course of the

[1] Étienne, *officier* at the British Embassy in Paris in the mid-nineteenth century
was one of the most influential, and one of the last.

century, from very substantial dishes, which were almost a meal in themselves, to mere exciters of the appetite. The result of all these changes was that grand French cooking was substantially different in 1939 from what it had been in 1850.[1]

This is not to say, however, that French cooking was uniform in any one period, for the ideas of these famous chefs never obtained complete sway. Thus while Escoffier was preaching greater simplicity, others simultaneously continued and developed the complicated style. The recipe for *lièvre à la royale*, in a cook-book by one of his contemporaries, was ten pages long, with *foie gras*, truffles, cognac and many condiments added, so that the taste of the hare virtually vanished.[2] In the 1920s one of the most famous and expensive restaurants in Paris was Prosper Montagné's in the rue de l'Échelle, where the food served was based on worship of Carême, whose manuscript notes in the Talleyrand archives the chef studied in order to achieve perfection. The spiritual descendants of Napoleon III's cook Jules Gouffée (1807–77), who was later chef to the Jockey Club, and who carried decoration and ostentation to its limits, found refuge in the international hotels, where cooking had to be more French than it was in France: the rivalry of restaurants encouraged fantastic mixtures and, as one chef put it, 'a paroxysm of amalgams'.[3] On the other hand, simple and rapid cooking obviously did not start with Escoffier, the popularisation of whose work might lead one to forget that he was a master of *haute cuisine* none the less. The pressure for quickly prepared meals had a strong popular base. The great recipe books were far outnumbered by humbler ones of limited pretensions which stressed economy above all: the most successful of these continued to be reprinted in disregard of changing fashion.[4] The

[1] A. Escoffier, avec la collaboration de Philéas Gilbert et Émile Fetu, *Le Guide culinaire* (1912, 3rd edition, containing over 5,000 recipes, and dedicated to Urbain Dubois and Émile Bernard); E. Herbodeau and P. Thalamas, *Georges Auguste Escoffier* (1955).

[2] *Gastronomie pratique d'Ali Bab* (1907). Ali Bab was the pseudonym of an engineer Babinski, brother of the famous psychiatrist.

[3] E. Darenne, secretary-general of the Academy of Cuisine, *La Cuisine française et étrangère* (26 May 1883); Mourier, thesis on 'La Cuisine naturelle et la cuisine composée', ibid. 63.

[4] The most popular recipe book of the early nineteenth century was said to be L. E. Audot, *La Cuisinière de la campagne et de la ville* (1818, 10th edition 1832, 41 reprints 1833–1900). The author was a publisher, not a cook. Other long-lasting books were *Le Cuisinier gascon*, first published 1740, and reaching its 29th edition

introduction of gas, which was a great aid to all forms of cooking, also encouraged fast cooking, particularly since the gas
companies organised lessons and issued recipes stressing this
advantage. The mass restaurant trade simplified dishes not on
principle, but to increase profits:[1] one *restaurateur*'s encyclopedia
abbreviated its 3,250 recipes into one or two lines each, so that
all its wisdom could be carried in the pocket.[2] In 1930 a book
of 'Ten-minute Recipes' claimed that there was a great demand
for these from students, working girls, shop assistants, artists,
scholars, poets, men of action and lazy people; Napoleon himself had after all prided himself on the speed with which he got
through his food. It recommended making soups out of pow-
dered extracts, some of which were terrible but others, it said,
excellent.[3] Tinned food, in the use of which the army were
pioneers, was welcomed by the official organ of professional
cooks as the solution to the problem of cheap catering for the
masses: the peasants of course had long experience of preserving
food. When in 1878 tinned beef was imported from the U.S.A.
for the first time, in a period of high meat prices, it was approved
because it was 40 per cent cheaper than European meat.[4] But
though France played a leading role in the discovery of methods
of preserving and refrigerating, the French canning industry did
not develop to take full advantage of this new knowledge.
Appert, who established a food-preserving factory at Massy,
outside Paris, in 1804, died in poverty. In 1847 Martin de
Lignac began manufacturing concentrated milk, and in 1854
desiccated beef. Charles Tellier founded a food-freezing factory
at Auteuil in 1874 and two years later built the first French
refrigerator-ship. But it was England which became master of
the meat-carrying trade from South America. At the turn of the
century, the French canning industry produced 120 million tins
a year, but of these, 80 million were of sardines, and the French

in 1896, and *La Cuisinière bourgeoise*, first published in 1746, 22nd edition 1866.
For the twentieth century, see in particular the works of Mademoiselle Rose,
published by Flammarion.

[1] *La Cuisine française et étrangère* (30 Nov. 1893), 155. In 1894 Paris had 140,000
gas cookers. Ibid., 25 Oct. 1894.

[2] P. Dagouret, *Petite Encyclopédie du restaurateur* (8th edition, 1923).

[3] Édouard de Pomiane, *La Cuisine en dix minutes. Ou l'adaptation au rythme
moderne* (1830), 14, 74.

[4] *La Cuisine française et étrangère* (25 Sept. 1893), 'Les Conserves alimentaires'.

themselves consumed only about 15 per cent of their sardine
tins, exporting the rest. The French canning industry was thus
about one-sixth the size of that of the U.S.A. In 1899 a commission was established to investigate the frequent cases of food-
poisoning occurring in the army—a principal consumer of tins
—which may suggest that hygiene was not a strong point. But
there is no evidence to support the view that the French did
not eat tinned food because they despised it as inferior; it may
well be that they would have got into the habit if there had
been more available, at reasonable prices. One may guess that
either food producers preferred to stick to traditional methods
of adulteration, which were well developed, in order to reduce
the cost of food, rather than embark on the expensive investment
that canning required, or else that profits in the retail grocery
trade were so high that there was little inducement to try new
methods; or finally that the preserving of food by the housewife
in the home was an established alternative. Escoffier was a great
believer in the value of tinned tomatoes, but it took him about
fifteen years to persuade French manufacturers to produce
them.[1]

France's reputation for good cooking owes a great deal to the
growth of its restaurants. The first Parisian restaurant with à la
carte menus was Beauvilliers's, in the galerie de Valois, founded
in 1782, but restaurants began to multiply and flourish above
all during the Revolution. There were less than fifty of them in
Paris in 1789, but nearly 3,000 by 1820. The chefs of the aristocracy, thrown out of work, set up public eating places, and it was
Chez Méot (formerly the prince de Condé's cook) that the leaders
of the Revolution drafted the constitution of 1793. Many luxury
artisans, such as goldsmiths and jewellers, whose businesses
collapsed, took up cooking also. In a period when food was
scarce and expensive, restaurants were the answer for those who
could afford high prices. Méot's had the reputation of always
being full of contractors and speculators newly enriched by
dubious methods, who now ate like kings. 'The Jacobins, who
abolished decorum and suspended politeness and courtesy, made
indulgence in good food fashionable', wrote Madame de Genlis.

[1] See the advice on the importance of stocking-up with tins of preserves in
Le Gourmet. Journal des intérêts gastronomiques (28 Feb. 1858), 2; Herbodeau and
Thalamas, Escoffier (1955), 101–3.

Whole streets of Paris filled up with restaurants of varying quality, and already in 1800 Paris seemed transformed by them. Les Trois Frères Provençaux, where Barras and Bonaparte used to dine, and which all the generals of the empire came to patronise, saw its takings rise to as much as 15,000 francs a day. Its fame, and that of other major restaurants of the time, became international and it was to them that the Russian officers who entered France in 1814 immediately hastened. Hunger during the Revolution, which has absorbed the attention of historians, went hand in hand with unequalled culinary abundance for the rich. Under the Restoration, the luxurious restaurants reached even greater heights of splendour and profitability. Lord Hertford was able to rent out the ground floor of his Paris house to a *restaurateur* for 12,000 francs a year. By 1848 restaurants were changing hands for as much as 320,000 francs. It was said during the Second Empire that it needed less than five years for a restaurant-keeper to recoup his investment and make a fortune sufficient to enable him to retire. The chef of the Café Anglais was then paid 25,000 francs a year; its owner was a member of a *conseil général*, living a leisured life on a country estate. The Café Riche was one of the most magnificent creations of Napoleon III's reign, a veritable palace, with a cellar worth 200,000 francs. In the 1870s, many of the famous old restaurants, like the Trois Frères Provençaux and Philippe's, disappeared, to make way for new ones which were to acquire equal celebrity, like Lapérouse. In parallel with the restaurants there grew up a large number of public caterers, who sold meals to take away, or served them in their clients' own homes. The most successful was Chevet, who used to supply roses to Marie Antoinette until arrested in the Revolution: he then took to making cakes and other foods which he and some of his seventeen children sold on the street: his became the best food shop in Paris. In 1869 the fourth Chevet succeeded to the headship of a firm which had an international clientele, supplying weddings in St. Petersburg and exporting to America. When Maxim's came to be founded in 1890, the restaurant trade was important enough for Lebaudy, the sugar manufacturer, to give it financial backing. These were places where the menu might well contain 200 different items; and where prices were purposely kept high to make them the exclusive preserve of the rich.

What distinguished Paris also, however, was the vast choice of restaurants for every pocket, as eating out became increasingly common. In the Latin quarter, it was possible to eat well for less than a franc at Flicoteaux, where the table-cloths were changed only once a week, or at Viot's, where 600 students ate daily, paying thirty centimes for meat dishes, fifteen centimes for vegetables and fifteen for wine—all the prices being standard.[1] In the rue Molière, Chez Dufour provided a five-course meal with wine and as much bread as you liked for 1 fr. 80. The artists and painters of the Second Empire used to go out to rural Montparnasse to eat wholesome, unpretentious food Chez la mère Saguet; an alternative outing would be to Jouanne's in Batignolles, which specialised in *tripes à la mode de Caen*. There were already innumerable *bistrots* serving meals of indifferent quality but in a gay and informal atmosphere, as well as more discreet ones to which ageing gentlemen could take their actress friends. In 1840–5 Les Bouillons hollandais toured the city in vans, offering cheap but wholesome soup, to cater for the very poor, who ate in the streets. In 1855 an improved version of this came with the establishment of the Bouillons Duval in the rue de la Monnaie, which within a decade had a dozen branches. Duval was a butcher, who originally served broth and beef only, of good quality, but he soon became famous for the new standards he introduced into mass catering. His restaurants had large rooms, clean marble tables, rapid service by well-dressed waitresses, but very low fixed prices for each item, and one paid the cashier as one left.[2] In 1860 two fashionable English restaurants were founded, Hill's in the Boulevard des Capucines and Peter's, off the rue Richelieu, to serve English food and beer; but the demand for this seems to have been limited, for in 1926 only three 'Anglo-American' restaurants were listed in a gastronomic guide of Paris, side by side with eleven Italian ones, eight Russian, four Jewish and one 'Hindu'.[3] Already during the Second Empire the business lunch was an established institution; and so of course was 'political gastronomy', by which

[1] See Jules P. Vatel, *Mémoires d'un garçon d'hôtel* (1892) for a description of a restaurant in the rue Monsieur le Prince frequented by Courbet and Vallès.

[2] See the biography of Pierre-Louis Duval (1811–70) in *Larousse du dix-neuvième siècle*.

[3] Edouard Dulac, *Le Tour de France gastronomique. Guide du touriste gourmand* (1926).

political meetings were held in the form of banquets. The fashion
spread, for banquets were popular with every kind of organisation, society, industry and corporation; publicity dinners to
launch new ventures, or theatrical plays, were very numerous
already in the 1840s.[1] Banqueting was carried to its absolute
extreme when in 1900 the President of the Republic gave one
for all the mayors of France and 22,695 of them attended: tables
7 kilometres long were laid out under tents in the Tuileries
gardens, and the manager of the famous catering firm of Potel
and Chabot drove around them in a car to supervise while his
maîtres d'hôtel did their duty on bicycles.[2] It should not be thought
that the food at these dinners, or at Parisian restaurants in
general, was always, or even usually, good. Complaints about
the tricks and frauds of restaurateurs arose from the very beginning: they were after all an extension of the food trade, which
was notorious for dishonest adulteration. A Manuel de gastronomie
in the 1890s already listed 927 restaurants with pretensions and
an author of that decade counted 1,400.[3] Good food was to be
found in a small minority of these. Already in 1858 Théodore
de Banville, in an article on restaurants, complained that the
poets, artists and authors of the capital 'have only one dream:
to eat something other than that eternal lamb cutlet and that
eternal uncooked beefsteak, to which they are condemned by
the cruelty of the Parisian restaurateur. . . . The basis of his
cooking is a brown sauce, mixed with flour, which, if one is to
judge by its execrable taste, must combine the most dangerous
ingredients and the most frightful poisons. Everybody is terrified
of this brown sauce, but the restaurateur spares no intrigue,
prayers or violence to force you to eat it', serving it with every
dish. Roast meat was seldom freshly cooked, and usually re-
heated from the day before; 'madeira sauce' had no connection
with that wine.[4] The esteem that French cooking enjoyed was
due to the masterpieces of an élite of cooks, and to the skill of a
fairly limited number of practitioners of the second class, in the
same way that French literature or art was far from being

[1] Eugène Briffault, Paris à table (1846), 75.

[2] André Castelot, L'Histoire à table (1972), 1. 82.

[3] Chatillon-Pléssis, La Vie à table à la fin du 19ᵉ siècle. Théorie pratique et historique
de gastronomie moderne (1894).

[4] Théodore de Banville, 'Les Restaurateurs', Le Gourmet. Journal des intérêts
gastronomiques (18 July 1858), 1–2.

universally, or even generally, of high quality. But what made France a paradise for gastronomes was the respect that good cooking, like good literature, received, the constant concern over standards and the excited discussions about recipes and quality.

The professional cooks of France were very interesting men, and it is surprising that their careers and ideas have not received attention. They were much concerned about their status in society, which was indeed ambiguous. 'Because of the art we practise,' wrote Philéas Gilbert, a famous cook who also managed to write for thirty-two different journals, 'we have a right to respect and consideration from all, because cooking can and must march hand in hand with the liberal arts. But it seems that cooks are, through prejudice, avoided and regarded as mercenaries.'[1] They demanded that they should be recognised as scientists; and they sought to develop their professional training so as to raise their status. The Academy of Cooking was founded in 1883. Membership involved the presentation of a 'thesis', which often embodied remarkable historical researches. Fondness for scholarship and writing was indeed a frequent characteristic of these cooks; they liked lecturing and attending each other's lectures; and they were exceptionally well travelled also. The propaganda they spread in favour of France was not negligible. They claimed that by 1900 there were about 10,000 of them distributed abroad throughout the world, mainly working for the ruling classes, so that they were in influential positions. The export of cooks perhaps came second only to the export of books. Cooks generally came from humble stock. Auguste Colombié, for example (born 1845), was apprenticed to a Toulouse *pâtissier* at the age of twelve. His reading of Carême's treatise on cake-making filled him with ambition to follow in the footsteps of the master, whose account of his early poverty showed that this was a career open to talent. Colombié spent his meagre savings buying books, and after doing his Tour de France, he founded a Society for the Study of Cooking, and a school of cooking in Paris, which lent books and organised lectures. Six hundred cooks attended his first lecture. He offered three levels of instruction: popular, bourgeois and grand cooking. He published a periodical to publicise his ideas. He became

---

[1] Philéas Gilbert in *L'Art culinaire: Revue bimenseulle, organe spécial de la société des cuisiniers français et de l'école professionnelle de cuisine* (1883), 23.

chef to the Prince of Hatzfeld-Wildenbourg, who gave him long vacations to allow him to write his books, of which he produced at least three. He was a brilliant lecturer, pouring out aphorisms, quotations and anecdotes in a colourful southern accent.[1] Cooks admired erudition and historical research; they often had a wide curiosity; they tended to move frequently from job to job, and sometimes from country to country, from Russia to America. Though proud of their native style of cooking, they had a surprisingly wide knowledge of foreign methods, and their journals were always publishing articles about culinary experiences all over the world, neglecting neither Colombia nor Korea. They generally worked their way up from an apprenticeship in a *pâtisserie* (skill in this field was considered, since Carême set the fashion, the first necessary accomplishment); the successful ones obtained jobs in the houses of the aristocracy and the rich, the best of them preferring financiers and foreign noblemen as employers; they would spend several seasons in large hotels, in Vichy, for example, or in London clubs; and they often ended their days reasonably well off as restaurant-owners, or as managers of food factories. Their families intermarried, so that the restaurants of Paris formed a community which was more than professional. They had a high opinion of their importance. One of them publicly complained in 1907 that doctors had developed a tendency to interfere in the cook's domain, giving complicated advice about what to eat and what not to eat. 'All this is nonsense.' Cooking was the 'patrimony of cooks. We have created and embellished it, we made it interesting and appetising and we therefore think we must defend it against encroachment.' Doctors should be consulted only by the sick: the hungry should turn to the cooks.[2] Escoffier wrote: 'Good cooking is the foundation of true happiness.' Unfortunately, it is by no means clear that they themselves always obtained this reward from the practice of their art. Their conditions of work were a subject of constant complaint: their health suffered from the badly ventilated kitchens they cooked in; many of them seem to have drunk more than they ate, partly to counteract perspiration, and alcoholism was frequent. Young cooks complained that they

---

[1] *La Cuisine française et étrangère* (25 July 1893), 95–8.
[2] *La Cuisine française et étrangère* (Jan. 1907), 2. This journal (1891–1927) contains numerous and very interesting biographies.

were seldom taught anything by the chefs, who demanded submissive obedience from their juniors; the chefs protested that their skills were not allowed full scope, owing to the thrift of the bourgeoisie and to the commercialisation of restaurants. Cooks were not well enough organised to obtain holidays, but they were frequently unemployed, seasonal engagements being common, and they were fleeced by the employment exchanges which charged exorbitant fees for finding them work (as high as 20 per cent of their wages).[1] The whole profession, moreover, rested on a foundation of appallingly exploited waiters and kitchen hands, whose tribulations were graphically recorded in George Orwell's *Down and Out in Paris and London* (1933).[2]

The cooks were backed up and encouraged by a new class of men, the gastronomes. Brillat-Savarin (1755–1826) is usually regarded as the first and greatest of these, but he was not in all ways their model and he received severe criticism from many cooks, which shows that gastronomy was no simple science. Brillat-Savarin's *Physiologie du goût* (1826) was important because it provided a justification of concern about food, but written with wit and style, so that it acquired the *cachet* of a literary masterpiece. It claimed that the discovery of a new dish gave more happiness to mankind than that of a new star; cooking was not just a branch of knowledge, but governed life itself; it should have an Academy, which would study subjects like the different species of thirst, the theory of frying, the influence of eating habits on sociability and conjugal harmony. Not everyone could be a gastronome—'a physical and organic predestination' was needed—but men of letters, doctors, the clergy and above all financiers were particularly gifted for the enjoyment of food. Englishmen could be seen in restaurants 'stuffing themselves with double helpings of meat, ordering the most expensive dishes, drinking the most famous wines and not always leaving without help': but that was not what eating was about. Carême criticised Brillat-Savarin for being a bore, witty only in his writings, and not fulfilling Carême's condition of being a host

[1] J. Barberet, 'Les Cuisiniers', in *Le Travail en France: monographies professionnels*, vol. 6 (1889), 15–285.

[2] For the waiters, see Union syndicale et mutuelle des restaurateurs et limonadiers du département de la Seine, fondée le 14 janvier 1876, *Annuaire de l'exercice 1890–91* (1892), which gives biographies, and describes their fight for the right to wear moustaches.

himself: he was a bachelor, in old-fashioned clothes, a mere theorist. Their contemporary Grimod de la Reynière, who published the *Almanach des gourmands*, provided an alternative approach: he was a very hearty eater, as though permanently suffering from tapeworm; his guests were required to drink a minimum of eighteen cups of coffee; he enjoyed not delicate refinement but food showing fantasy or burlesque and accompanied by macabre jokes.[1] This tradition was continued by people who had competitions as to who could eat most, and was symbolised by Balzac's comte de Montriveau who used to eat ten dozen oysters every day. Its survival could be seen during the Second Empire at Philippe's restaurant in the rue Montorgueil where on Saturdays eighteen diners were privileged to eat an enormous meal from six in the evening to midnight, followed by a second meal from midnight to six a.m., and a third one from six a.m. to midday on Sunday—each consisting of some ten courses and as many wines: they ate, that is to say, for a whole day.[2] Dr. Véron (1798–1867) was perhaps the last of the hosts who virtually kept an open table. He had made his fortune as the manufacturer of a cough mixture, the pâte Regnauld, as a newspaper owner and as director of the Opéra. His cook Sophie produced amazing meals, which went on almost like a permanent film-show, with people getting up from the table when they wished, and Véron himself often leaving first for the Opéra.[3]

One of the characteristics of gastronomy was that its followers nearly always lamented that taste was decaying and that good food was becoming increasingly rare. One of the very first journals devoted to it, *La Gastronomie* (1839), reported that people were already saying interest in food was no longer as great as during the First Empire, though it refuted this by showing that whereas in 1800 there were only three shops in Paris providing cooked food and delicacies, there were now forty, ten of which had very high reputations. This paper, which had a circulation of 2,000, organised tastings and excursions, and reported where specially remarkable ingredients could be found. It laid down that one should never talk politics at table:

[1] Maurice des Ombiaux, *La Physiologie du goût de Brillat-Savarin* (1937); Jean Armand-Laroche, *Brillat-Savarin et la médecine* (medical thesis, Paris, 1931).

[2] Jean Paul Aron, *Le Mangeur du 19ᵉ siècle* (1973), 83.

[3] Joseph d'Arcay, *La Salle à manger du Docteur Véron* (1858).

the conversation should always be light, so as not to distract from the main interest, which was the food: 'in a dinner of knowledgeable people, the arrival of the soup is followed by a silence'. What talk there was should be mainly about the food. 'If one eats eggs, one does not omit to recall that Louis XV liked them a lot and maintained that a well-cooked egg was the best of all foods.'[1] At the end of the century, another theoretician laid it down that 'until the third course, there should be no talk about anything except what one was eating, what one has eaten and what one will eat'. But 'after one has eaten well, one has a duty to make witty conversation'.[2] This kind of gastronomy was not in keeping with another tradition of sociability, for it was considered best, when one was eating seriously, to exclude women, so as not to be distracted by the needs of politeness. Perhaps that is why bachelors were the leaders of this cult; and they did turn out to be, as Brillat-Savarin anticipated, mainly authors or men on the fringes of the literary world, civil servants and doctors. Among the most famous were such men as Charles Monselet (1825–88) a club-footed bachelor, drama critic, author of vaudevilles and of *La Cuisinière pratique*, who was an advocate of experiment and novelty, attacking cooks for being slaves of routine: why were rats not eaten, he asked, while pigs were? (In fact the coopers of Bordeaux did not scorn them, treating them as delicacies, cut in half, grilled and seasoned with herbs.) Why were salads so limited, ignoring the vast possibilities of flowers? (Salads, wrote the Goncourt brothers, probably divided men more than politics.)[3] Baron Brisse (1813–76), another bachelor, was probably the first man to have a regular cookery column in a daily newspaper: his recipes became famous as *The 365 Menus*. But it was Curnonsky (1862–1956) who did more than anyone to broaden interest in gastronomy and to institutionalise it as a national pastime. Maurice Sailland (he adopted the pseudonym Cur-Non-Sky at the suggestion of the humorist Alphonse Allais) was an orphan bachelor journalist of enormous size and weight, who had originally moved on the fringes of the

[1] *La Gastronomie. Revue de l'art culinaire ancien et moderne* (6 Oct., 3 Nov. and 8 Dec. 1839, 6 Feb. 1840).

[2] Chatillon-Pléssis, *La Vie à table à la fin du 19ᵉ siècle* (1894), 12.

[3] Charles Monselet, *Lettres gourmandes. Manuel de l'homme à table* (1877). Cf. Léon de Fos, *Gastronomiana* (1870), also a bachelor, formerly in the Forests Administration.

music-hall world, as secretary of the Bataclan. In 1907 he
invented Bibendum for Michelin's motor-car tyre advertisements, and it was he who brought together the automobile,
tourist and catering industries for their common benefit. In that
same year *Les Lundis de Michelin* first appeared in *Le Journal*,
showing the pleasures to be derived from motoring. Curnonsky
toured France by car himself and wrote twenty-eight volumes
of *La France gastronomique* over a period of about as many years.
In 1933 he condensed this into a single volume, *Le Trésor gastronomique de France*. He spared no effort to track down a noteworthy cook, travelling all the way to Castelnaudary, for
example, to eat a perfect *cassoulet*, not hesitating to wait the
fourteen hours necessary for the dish to be prepared for him in
exactly the right way. In 1927 he was elected Prince of Gastronomes in a national ballot organised by a newspaper; he created
the Academy of Gastronomes, with forty members, to set the
standards. By now, good eating was being taken seriously by an
ever-growing body of people, who organised themselves into
clubs to cultivate the art. Dining clubs are to be found in the
early nineteenth century, but they now proliferated as never
before. They were particularly influential now because they
attracted many of the rich, articulate and powerful men from
industry, politics and the professions—those, that is to say, who
indulged in the new amusement of motoring, and who therefore
gave the provincial hotel and restaurant trade a vastly increased
clientele. The Academy of Gastronomes thus included the prime
minister André Tardieu, Fernand Payen, president of the corporation of barristers, the author Maurice Maeterlinck, the
mayor of Dijon, the secretary-general of the Opéra and a doctor
from the Institut Pasteur. The Club des Cents, founded in 1912,
admission to which was limited to those who had driven at least
4,000 kilometres by car, included the heads of the country's
major firms and leading civil servants. There were dining clubs
for barristers (Le Fin Palais, 1927), for singers, song writers and
publishers (Le Pot au Feu de la Chanson, 1930), for doctors
(Les Esculapes Gourmands, 1934), and for golfers (organised by
the periodical *Le Golf*, 1921).

Regional cooking took on a new importance as a result. The
impression the gastronomes spread was that there was a vast
variety of remarkable dishes to be found all over France like a

neglected treasure. There were indeed a number of provincial specialities which found new admirers, but quite as many were the creations of skilful cooks rather than genuinely traditional. The Parisian cooks had counterparts in the provinces, though these have not been so well recorded. Lyon certainly owed its high reputation to the efforts of its restaurants, established simultaneously with those of Paris (and dominated, rather exceptionally, by a number of celebrated women, like la Mère Guy, la Mère Fillioux and la Mère Brazier), as well as to its dining clubs, which flourished early in the nineteenth century, and to its prosperous bourgeoisie, who provided the patronage necessary for the rise of devoted local cooks.[1] In general, how-ever, popular provincial cook-books, though they used different ingredients, seldom made anything very elaborate out of these. *Le Cuisinier gascon*, for example, first published in 1740 and reaching its twenty-ninth edition in 1896, was an essentially simple book of recipes, with modest claims, not seeking to do more than teach peasant girls who went into domestic service rudimentary rules. Some of the originality of provincial cooking came from the return to simpler methods, to the long slow stewing peasants used to employ, but with rather better ingre-dients than peasants had generally been able to afford.[2] Southerners exiled in Paris did much to propagate the taste for the dishes of Provence: during the Second Empire Creste and Roudiel's food shop in the rue de Turbigo 'Aux Produits du Midi' kept them supplied with the necessary ingredients. How-ever, it was only towards the end of the nineteenth century that the tomato, for example, ceased to be a rarity in the northern half of the country.[3] It needed not only a revolution in transport, but also in market gardening, before the dishes of the provinces could be properly copied. The ministry of education distributed a cook-book, with recipes arranged by province, to schools in the first decade of the twentieth century: this, it was claimed,

[1] Mathieu Varille, *La Cuisine lyonnaise* (Lyon, 1928).

[2] Hugues Lapaire, *La Cuisine berrichonne* (1925), who however notes that interest in the cooking and dialect of Berry was, outside Berry, strongest in Germany: a German professor published a book on cake-making in Roman Gaul. Cf. Pierre Dupin, *Les Secrets de la cuisine comtoise* (1927); Maurice Beguin, *La Cuisine en Poitou* (Niort, 1932, by the Archivist of the Deux Sèvres).

[3] Cf. Marius Morard, *Les Secrets de la cuisine dévoilés* (Marseille, 1886) for southern cooking.

was the first book of its kind.[1] Madame Léon Daudet also wrote
a book drawing attention to regional specialities, which spread
the vogue. How exactly these new products and new methods
were used has not been the subject of much research, however:
the new history of the provinces of France, recently published in
many volumes, is, strangely, almost silent about cooking. The
exotic products probably came first and the re-creation of traditional recipes may well have been partly a romantic reaction
against their rather inexpert use. Already in 1854 Gravier's
grocery shop in Nevers was selling Roquefort, gruyère and
Dutch cheese, raisins, figs, almonds, dates, oranges, sardines and
anchovies. The incorporation of these luxuries into the national
diet required the advent of prosperity: the list stresses the great
difference between the food of the poor and the rich. On the
other hand, the *canuts* of Lyon were famous for the vast amount
of time and effort they spent on improving simple ingredients.
These ingredients, moreover, were once much more varied than
they have since become. Thus mid-nineteenth-century cook-
books often devoted much space to discussing the innumerable
varieties of fruit and vegetables. As production for the towns
became an increasing concern of the peasants, standardisation
made rapid strides and the fifty different types of pear once
available, for example, gave way to just two or three principal
varieties. Regional cooking thus had to be resurrected, like
regional dialects, when the economic basis for it had been partly
undermined.

Cooking had its parties, just like politics. Curnonsky once
produced an analysis of their programmes. The extreme right
were patrons of the grand, complicated learned style, requiring
a brilliant chef and first-class materials: theirs was 'diplomats'
food', though they often got only 'palace hotel food', which was
a parody of it. The right favoured traditional cooking on wood
fires and by slow methods, preferring the produce of their own
gardens and the style of their own cooks, who had been in the
family for thirty years; and they drew on cellars stocked with
pre-phylloxera wine. Then there was bourgeois or regionalised

---

[1] Edmond Richardin, *L'Art de bien manger* (n.d., about 1904); Curnonsky and
Austin de Croze, *Le Trésor gastronomique de France. Répertoire complet des spécialités
gourmandes des trente deux provinces françaises* (1933); Elizabeth David, *French
Provincial Cooking* (2nd edition, 1965).

cooking, occupying the middle ground; its adepts were willing to admit that one could dine well in a restaurant and they welcomed the development of good hotels. The left wing believed in simple and quick cooking, being satisfied with an omelette, a slice of ham, or an *entrecôte*; they did not object to tins and sometimes indeed argued that tinned beans were as good as fresh ones; they liked eating in little *bistrots*, and enjoyed the 'country style' and 'amusing' local wines. The extreme left, finally, were the innovators and the worried, the searchers for new sensations, for fantastic and exotic experiences; they liked colonial and foreign dishes; they had their saints and their martyrs.[1] All these parties have made contributions to what is known as French cooking. The temptation is to identify the national style with that of the middle group, the solid, careful bourgeois style, whose rules seem as well established as those of classical literary prose. There are arguments both in favour and against this. On the one hand the bourgeoisie did as much for the raising and maintenance of high standards as either the great cooks or the restaurants did. A description of achievements in cooking which limited itself to the public sector would be very incomplete. The best food in Paris, said a knowledgeable guide in 1846, is to be eaten in the homes of the well-to-do bourgeoisie. The grand restaurant cooks despised female cooks, but that was partly professional jealousy, for the humble but highly skilful women in private service 'whom tradition still designates by the name of cordons bleus' were often very remarkable in their own way. 'It is impossible to bring more care, more delicacy, more taste and more intelligence than they apply to the selection and the preparation of food. A good Paris *cuisinière*, to whom an appropriate liberty of action is left, has talents which can compete with those of the illustrious chefs, the only reservation being with regard to the great dishes of the table, the office and dessert.' They did not produce great architectural constructions; they were not allowed the luxury and extravagance of the masters; they avoided the 'monstrous foreign puddings', and they were slow to adopt new methods; but they laid great stress both on quality and on cleanliness. Bourgeois cooking involved co-operation between these cooks and the mistress of the household; and as one descended to lower levels of prosperity, even

[1] Curnonsky, *Souvenirs* (1958), 235.

more effort was applied, particularly in shopping. This guide of 1846 contrasts this kind of cooking with the 'outrageously simple' lunches served in canteens, the even worse food provided in factories and schools, and the hastily prepared and hastily eaten meals of small shopkeepers.[1] The cook-books used by the bourgeoisie certainly required ample leisure and full-time application; and those who ate the food prepared by their women cooks seem to have spent about two hours doing justice to each meal.[2] Good food was held to be one of the bases of the stable family life. When cooking came to be taught in schools from the 1880s, this was one subject where traditional virtues were significantly perpetuated. Thus one successful domestic science textbook pointed out the dangers of over-rich sauces, but insisted nevertheless that everybody should know how to prepare them and that no dinner was complete without them; the serving of appetising food, its artistic preparation and display were held up as one of the most important duties of every housewife.[3] It may be that lay schools stressed the scientific principles of nutrition rather more, and that Catholic ones were more traditionalist, more interested in encouraging food that was sensually enjoyable; but it is likely that bourgeois girls learnt more from their mothers, the schools being most influential on the poorer classes.[4] However, the attitude of the bourgeoisie to food was not uniform, as a study of the budgets of 547 bourgeois households, between 1873 and 1953, has revealed. The most important conclusion of this detailed investigation of income and expenditure is that the main characteristic of their behaviour was its astonishing diversity. This is what argues most strongly against the view that bourgeois cooking should be regarded as typically French. Only some of the bourgeoisie gave a high priority to eating. On average, throughout these years, the families studied spent between 21·5 and 25 per cent of their incomes on food; but the variations which produce these

[1] Eugène Briffault, *Paris à table* (1846), 53–64.
[2] Anon., *La Cuisinière bourgeoise* (1st edition 1746, 22nd edition 1866, published in Lyon, Avignon, Besançon, Montbéliard, etc.) is a good indication of this style.
[3] Madame M. Sage, *L'Enseignement ménager* (3rd edition, 1909), 268–77.
[4] Mesdames G. Rudler and A. Saint-Paul, *L'Enseignement ménager* (1910, 12th edition 1933), as an example of the scientific approach; for the private schools' approach see *Le Cordon bleu* (1897) and C. Driessens, *Alphabet de la ménagère* (1891, 2nd edition, 1900).

averages were very wide. Four-fifths of the families can be contained within the range of 14 and 34 per cent, but there were those who spent only 10 per cent on food. Engels's law that people spend a smaller proportion of their total income on food as they grow richer was not confirmed by this study. There was the case of one household, consisting of husband, wife and teenage daughter, who spent only 17·5 per cent of their income on food, but this turns out to be a very large sum indeed, for they were rich. A complicating factor is the proportion of the food budget spent on drink: this accounted, in most cases, for between one-tenth and one-third of the food budget, but a not inconsiderable proportion spent over a third and one even 49·6 per cent (though this was probably a case of a cellar being laid down). There is no link between how much was spent on wine and how much on food, except that expenditure on drink has fallen very considerably, from an average of 17·3 per cent of the food budget at the end of the nineteenth century to only 7 or 8 per cent in 1945–53, with expenditure over 10 per cent becoming very rare. There were equally wide variations in spending on different items of food: expenditure on bread varied between 3 and 16 per cent, meat between 17 and 40, cheese between 1 and 7; vegetables represented 6 to 8 per cent before 1914, and then went up to 10 to 12 per cent. It cannot be said that food was always an overriding preoccupation. Expenditure on clothes varied from 3 to 18 per cent, and in over one-third of these families, the men spent more on clothes than the women.[1] The bourgeoisie was certainly not representative of the country as a whole in what they ate. Baron Brisse's *365 Menus*, if they were an accurate reflection of their tastes in Paris during the Second Empire, show, for example, that they ate proportionately less pork and chicken than the peasants. Thus pork appeared in these menus only twenty-four times, mainly in the form of *charcuterie*, compared to 139 beef dishes and 102 mutton ones. Leg of mutton was the most frequent meat dish, occurring thirty-two times. Fish was eaten almost every day (363 times). More game (168) than fowl (139) was consumed, but chicken accounted for only half of the fowl. Vegetables were also eaten much less by the bourgeoisie than the peasantry, as the number of dishes using them shows: potatoes 62, beans 38, artichokes

[1] Marguerite Perrot, *Le Mode de vie des familles bourgeoises 1873–1953* (1961).

and asparagus 27, spinach 26, green peas 24, turnips 23, mushrooms 19, cauliflower 18, celery 17, sorrel 15, dried peas 14, lettuce and onions 13, tomato and cucumber 7, rice 75, Italian pasta 63. The potato invaded the bourgeois menu only in the years 1840–60, and cheese became a regular course only in the second half of the nineteenth century; fruit also used to be scarce, a pear in 1850 costing twice as much as a slice of Roquefort.[1] The services available to those wanting a good meal also changed. Thus whereas in 1851 Paris had one *pâtisserie* for every 2,640 inhabitants, by 1900 there was only one for every 9,000 (the number of shops falling from 402 to 294, while the population more than doubled). This was because about half of the city's 1,880 bakeries had taken to making cakes also: but it is likely that the standard of their cakes was not as high as that of the specialists, who moreover had produced not just sweet cakes but a whole variety of pastries.[2] There was thus, in the course of this century, a considerable change in the diet of the bourgeoisie. The number of people who could afford to eat what they liked increased only slowly and was never very large.

One of the great problems in the history of cooking is why England, which was a richer country than France and had a vastly richer aristocracy capable of spending without limit to obtain the best food, did not develop as sophisticated or as varied a style of cooking as France did. England's prosperity may in fact have been excessive: ample supplies of good meat may have made skilful preparation unnecessary—which was certainly what happened in the U.S.A. England also preferred to devote its attention more to the elaboration of sweet dishes; it consumed three times more sugar than France. The cooks of France complained that the French did not give large dinners and parties, and did not employ grand male cooks so much; but the English, precisely because they were rich enough to entertain at home, therefore ate out less, and there were far fewer restaurants in England as a result. The restaurant was an essential cause of France's competitiveness in cooking. But it would be wrong to contrast English and French cooking too

---

[1] J. P. Aron, *Essai sur la sensibilité alimentaire à Paris au 19ᵉ siècle* (1967), 85–117.

[2] A. Charabot, *La Pâtisserie à travers les âges. Résumé historique de la communauté des pâtissiers* (Meulan, S. & O., 1904); E. Darenne, *Histoire des métiers de l'alimentation* (Meulan, 1904), 162.

sharply in this period. The English were interested by good food, as the very large number of cook-books published shows.[1] French books were translated into English from as early as 1725;[2] and the English aristocracy employed a large number of French cooks. One must compare like with like: the best food in England was not inferior to the best in France. But when the English aristocracy lost their predominance, the grand style of life vanished with it. In France, by contrast, the tastes of the aristocracy were spread by their cooks who opened restaurants, and upper- rather than lower-class ideals became the most widespread in matters of food. The prosperous English worker kept his tastes even when he moved into the middle class; but the French peasant who ended up as a bourgeois sought to become, at least in his eating habits, a minor seigneur. The French have also put much more effort into propaganda about their food and they exported a very large number of cooks, whereas the English sent abroad more colonists, missionaries and administrators.

Another way that Frenchmen made themselves happy, or less unhappy, was by drinking. Wine, said Taine, is the people's philosopher. The part wine played in life was indeed as considerable and as complex as that of political or social ideas. Wine was held to be responsible for 'that part of the national character which was most admirable—cordiality, frankness in human relations, good humour, the gift for conversation and delicacy of taste'. Albert Lebrun, President of the Republic, declared in 1934 that 'wine does not only confer health and vigour. It also has soothing properties which both ensure the rational equilibrium of the organism and create a predisposition to harmony among men. In addition, it can, in difficult times, pour confidence and hope into our hesitating hearts.'[3] Wine, however, was drunk in very different ways in the course of this period, and the cult surrounding it went through interestingly changing fashions.[4]

[1] A. W. Oxford, *English Cookery Books to the Year 1850* (1913).

[2] Noel Chomel's *Dictionnaire oeconomique* translated 1725; *The French Family Cook* (1793); A. B. Beauvilliers, *The Art of French Cooking* (French edition 1814, English translation 1824); *La Cuisinière de la campagne et de la ville*, the French best-seller, translated as *French Domestic Cookery* (1846).

[3] M. L. Laval, *Le Vin dans l'histoire de France* (1935), ii, 87.

[4] For the economic history of wine production and the outlook of the wine-growers, see my *Ambition and Love*, 165–70.

The French were not always a nation of wine drinkers. Wine used to be a luxury, which only the well-to-do could afford; the peasants had to be content at most with *piquette*; and in the late eighteenth century the town worker still had relatively few bars where he could go to quench his thirst. The upper classes used to produce wine mainly for their own consumption. Tariff barriers between provinces, as well as problems of transport, made the exchange of wine between different regions rare or difficult, so that the very rich who wanted something special tended to drink imported wines from Spain or Portugal for preference. The wines of the Beaune region were an exception: they won a high reputation in Paris, but perhaps even more in the Netherlands. Bordeaux wines were better known in England than in Paris, until Louis XIV was converted to them on medical grounds, but it was not until the Second Empire that they received their present-day classification into graded *crus*. While they rose in esteem, the wines of the Île-de-France and of Orléans, on which Paris had hitherto relied, lost their reputation. The choices open to wine drinkers and the number of wine drinkers changed drastically in the eighteenth and nineteenth centuries. The rise of democracy was paralleled by a vast increase in the production of wine, so that people got the right to vote and to drink roughly simultaneously. This was due to the expansion of the production of *vin ordinaire*, mainly from the south. Between 1840 and 1875, the amount of wine produced in France roughly doubled. Then the phylloxera crisis, which led to the replanting of most vineyards with American plants, both changed the taste of wine and, by reducing supplies for a decade to less than their level in 1840, forced people who had acquired new tastes either to drink foreign wine or to take to other forms of alcohol: and it is in this period that spirit drinking made enormous gains. The building of the railways meant that cheap wine could be carried cheaply to every part of the country, but it meant also that wines could be mixed and blended in new ways, and turned effectively into an industrial product.

A guide to wine drinking published in 1865 recommended that sherry or dry madeira should be served after the soup; between the first and the second course madeira, cognac, rum or vermouth were suitable; bordeaux or burgundy could be served indifferently with any food, but the plainer varieties should be served first and the better ones later in the meal; champagne should come with the dessert.[1] The 'oenological education' of the country was only effected gradually. The 'wine connoisseur' is a modern creature. Originally, it was considered acceptable to drink red or white wine indiscriminately, and the best wines were drunk to the accompaniment of the vegetables. This was now condemned, by a new kind of author, as 'rudimentary and unmethodical'. Dogmatic rules developed as to what was proper, though there were disagreements. Thus in the 1920s, it was recommended, by Paul de Cassagnac, who was not only the leading Bonapartist journalist in France, but also an expert both on duelling and on drinking, that fish should be accompanied by sauterne, which could also be used at the end of the meal for dessert and cheese; bordeaux and burgundy should not be served at the same meal; bordeaux should be decanted but burgundy should not, though others declared that it should.[2] These rules were perhaps the necessary counterpart to the unprecedented variety of options that were now available. But it was difficult for them to have permanent validity, because the conditions of wine production changed so frequently. Thus burgundy which was once the supreme French wine was badly hit by the phylloxera crisis and never fully recovered: none of the new vintages, it was said, ever equalled the Musigny 1869 or the Chambertin 1865. Burgundy was one of the wine-producing regions where land ownership was most divided. Thus Chambertin wine was produced from only 27 hectares (67 acres) and these were divided between twenty-five owners; Clos Vougeot came from 50 hectares divided among thirty-eight owners. This meant that no owner could produce his own wine. The situation was completely different from that in the Bordeaux region, where the estates were large enough to allow independent vintages to be manufactured by individual owners: Château d'Yquem was an estate of 148 hectares, with 90 hectares of vine, yielding on average 125 casks (of nearly a thousand litres each); Château Margaux had 90 hectares of vine producing 275 casks of the best quality. The result was that in Burgundy, wine was made above all by wholesale merchants, and

[1] L. Maurial, *L'Art de boire, connaître et acheter le vin et toutes les boissons. Guide vinicole du producteur, du commerçant et du consommateur* (1865, 2nd edition).

[2] Paul de Cassagnac, *Les Vins de France* (1927), 45.

the reputations of different wines depended as much on their
names as on the regions they purported to come from. Now the
law on labels and trade-marks in the nineteenth century was
designed to protect the producer rather than the consumer, and
it was only in 1919 that a law was passed requiring that wine
had to come from the region specified on its label. The effect of
this was, paradoxically, disastrous. It meant that any wine produced, say, in the commune of Pommard, was allowed to call
itself that. However, Pommard originally was a high-class
wine; inferior grades were not marketed under that name. Now
they had a right to be; and the peasants exploited this new
situation by growing as much wine as they could, even on the
poorest soil which had never been used for this purpose, and
selling it, quite legally, with an expensive-sounding label. But
Pommard, as it was once known, had not been made exclusively
from vines of that village: Chassagne's wines, for instance, were
incorporated in it. Because some names had become famous,
neighbouring villages had sold their wine under these famous
labels: thus Morey wine, which was just as good as Chambertin,
used to be sold under the latter name: but this could no longer
be.[1] Bordeaux wine, for its part, had seldom contained only
locally produced wine; and it was considered that it was improved, that its bitterness was diminished, by the addition, for
example, of Ermitage or Roussillon wine. There were regions,
like the Gaillac in the Tarn, which produced wine almost solely
for the purpose of selling it to the Bordeaux producers, for
mixing.[2] The alcoholic content of some fine wines was too low
(little above eight degrees) for the taste of northern France, and
it needed to be reinforced. The quality of wine, besides, varied
each year, but the consumer demanded that it should always
taste the same: this required very skilled blending. A wine merchant writing in 1903 said that only 10 per cent of wines, at
most, were not mixtures.[3] Connoisseurship therefore had to
battle against these charges and these frauds, and it was in some
way an answer to the challenge thrown to the consumer. Some

[1] On the legislation, see Joseph Giraud, *La Vigne et le vin en Franche Comté.
Les Vignobles comtois devant le problème des appellations d'origine* (Besançon, 1939).

[2] J. L. Riol, *Le Vignoble de Gaillac depuis ses origines jusqu'à nos jours et l'emploi de
ses vins à Bordeaux* (1913), 262.

[3] P. Maigne, *Nouveau Manuel complet du sommelier et du marchand de vins.* New
edition by Raymond Brunet (1903), 400.

experts declared that one could only tell the difference between years, not between vineyards of the same type. Their battle with the producers was certainly an unequal one, particularly because of the way the wine trade developed, which placed further complications in the path of the consumer.

Most wine was of poor quality, and this was increasingly the case as mass production, aiming above all at quantity, spread in the south; improvements in techniques of manufacture failed to keep up with this. It used to be the practice for peasants to drink the worst wine themselves and sell only the best, which could fetch a decent price. Thus in the mid-nineteenth century there was a whole range of unknown wines, described as 'disagreeable' and 'bad', which were produced in considerable quantities but consumed locally. The most important development of this century was the rise of the wholesale wine merchant, who barely existed in the eighteenth century, and the enormous multiplication of retail wine merchants. In 1790 Paris had only 4,300 *cabarets*; but the Revolution allowed anyone to open one and their numbers quickly increased. Though restrictions were reimposed, the number of bars and shops selling wine rose as follows:

1830	282,000	1913	483,000
1865	351,000	1922	452,000[2]
1900	435,000[1]	1937	509,000
1901	464,000[1]	1953	439,000

This meant that France came to have in 1937 on average one bar for every 81 inhabitants, and in 1953 one for every 97 inhabitants. This compared with one for 225 in Italy, 273 in Germany, and 425 in England (1953).[3] The great jump in the number of bars came after 1880 when the decree of 1851, which had required the prefect's authorisation to open a bar, was rescinded: within a decade, the number of bars in Paris rose by 37 per cent. The general averages conceal great variations: thus in the Nord, there was one bar per 46 inhabitants already in 1890, which could mean, in some communes, two for every three adult men. The wine-producing regions had, for obvious reasons, far fewer—but even so the Gers still had one for every

---

[1] Paris is not included in the statistics until 1901.
[2] Alsace Lorraine included.
[3] S. Ledermann, *Alcool, Alcoolisme, alcoolisation* (1956), 78.

187 inhabitants at that same date (comparing with one for 580 in Boston). The result of this proliferation was impossible competition between the bars, and profits could only be made by adulterating and diluting the wine. There was a great difference therefore between the wine bought from the grower (which was seldom done now) and from the retailer. Adding water was perfectly legal, and until 1919, so was mixing wines. Wholesalers used to do the mixing—or some of it—in the presence of the retailers, usually so as to produce a wine with an alcohol content five degrees higher than that which it was proposed to sell to the consumer. The retailer could then add 20 per cent of water, and still serve wine above the legal minimum of 10°. However, since growers often also added water, before sending their wine to the wholesaler, the customer may sometimes have drunk as much water as wine. Adding water was harmless—indeed it was very common for people to dilute even good wines in the nineteenth century, the prohibition on this by the connoisseurs being quite recent. Gambetta defended this kind of dilution as 'honest fraud'. Wine from the south of France was often 15° strong, and when it arrived in Paris up to one-third of it was frequently water when it was sold in bars, at 10°. The bar-keepers almost had to do this, because it greatly reduced the taxes they paid, raising their profits by about 25 per cent. The customers used to joke about this 'baptism' to which wine was subject, with only the state being the loser. More serious, however, was the addition of alcohol, sugar, chalk, and a whole variety of chemicals and colorants, some of which had a defensible place in the making of wine, but some were positively noxious. It was no easy matter spotting the fraud, though many ingenious methods were tried by amateur analysts. When in 1880 the municipal laboratories of Paris tested 300 samples of wine bought at random in local bars, they found 225 of them to be seriously adulterated, fifty slightly so, and only twenty-five to be pure. It was ironical that bar-keepers, who tended to be radical or boulangist or advanced in politics, should have based their leadership on regular commercial fraud.[1]

High-class wine, with recognised *appellations*, formed only about one-tenth of the wine consumed. France consumed more

[1] Adrien Berget, *Les Vins de France . . . Manuel du consommateur* (1900); J. Barberet, *Les Débitants de boisson* (monographies professionnelles, vol. 7) (1890).

alcohol than any other country in the world. In 1950–4 France consumed 30 litres of pure alcohol per adult, which was accounted for by 200 litres of wine, 25 litres of beer and 3·8 litres of spirits (expressed in terms of litres of pure alcohol). This was double its nearest rival as the table shows.

Consumption of Alcohol per adult, 1950–4[1]

	Litres of pure alcohol	Consumed as		
		Litres of wine	Litres of beer	Litres of spirits (pure alcohol)
France	30	200	25	3·8
Italy	14·2	130	4·5	1·1
U.S.A.	8·8	5	100	3·3
Great Britain	8·5	1·5	137	0·8
West Germany	5·1	12	66	1·6
Sweden	5·1	2	36	3·6

The national average again concealed the fact that in Brittany the average annual consumption of pure alcohol per male adult was between 54 and 70 litres (but only 21 to 31 litres in Provence). The really hard drinkers constituted 7 per cent of the population—30 per cent in Brittany, and 3 to 4 per cent in Provence; they drank one-quarter of all the alcohol consumed in the country. By themselves, they would have been unable to resist legislation to stop them, but they were protected by one of the most powerful lobbies in the country, that of the *bouilleurs de cru*. These were the people who took advantage of the law that though alcohol sales were taxed, ordinary individuals who made spirits for their own use were exempt. Their numbers increased sixfold in the course of this period:

Bouilleurs de cru in 1877	490,000
1890	550,000
1900	930,000
1920	1,730,000
1925	2,640,000
1934	3,100,000
1951	3,100,000
1955	2,490,000

[1] Ledermann, op. cit. 68–9.

The result was that they became too united a force for the politicians to offend: in twenty-three departments, half the electors were *bouilleurs*, and in twenty-four others, one-third were.

Absinthe, which thus became a popular drink, was, of course, only one way of forgetting one's troubles. This century also developed rather more elaborate ways—if not to forget, then at least to cope—as people began analysing their troubles with a more minute curiosity. It is these troubles and worries that are examined in the sequel to this work, entitled *Anxiety* and *Hypocrisy*.

GUIDE TO FURTHER READING

THE subjects treated in this volume fall, on the whole, within the domain of the hobbyist and the amateur. Devoted collectors and intelligent laymen have contributed as much to our knowledge as university scholars, and it is likely that they will long continue to do so. There are still no professors of Humour or of Wine, even if a few Professors of Fashion and of Cinema have appeared. There are thus few academic experts to whom the reader must bow, and further reading must inevitably be less systematic than in other fields. There are (fortunately or unfortunately) few textbooks to provide guidance and repeat out-dated generalisations. Controversy rages here because myth and ignorance have free rein; the reader must, even more than usual, avoid believing what he is told. What I offer in this list is raw material from which he can draw his own conclusions, and which may perhaps provide the basis on which he can develop his own pet expertise.

Popular taste and beliefs may be approached through the remarkable works of A. van Gennep, *Le Folklore: croyances et coutumes populaires françaises* (1941) and above all his *Manuel de folklore français contemporain* (1943–58). Robert Mandrou, *De la culture populaire* (1964) is an analysis for the 17th and 18th centuries; P. J. Hélias, *The Horse of Pride* (Yale 1978) is a vivid autobiographical account of Breton folklore. The publishers Maisonneuve have brought out a large number of local studies of folklore; the Musée des Arts et Traditions Populaires on the outskirts of Paris is the place to visit for a visual introduction.

The way books tried to penetrate the world of inherited beliefs may be investigated through Julien Cain, *Le Livre français* (1972); Bernard Grasset, *La Chose littéraire* (1929); Robert Laffont, *Editeur* (1974); J. Mistler, *La Librairie Hachette* (1964); A. Retif, *Pierre Larousse* (1975); Marc Soriano, *Guide de la littérature enfantine* (1959); Regis Messac, *Le Detective novel* (1929), and F. Lacassin, *Mythologie du roman policier* (1974).

On newspapers, the fullest guide is C. Bellanger *et al.*, *Histoire générale de la presse française* (six volumes, 1969–   ); the fullest history of an individual newspaper is F. Amaury, *Le Petit Parisien* (1972); for the journalistic life see Henri Rochefort, *Les Aventures de ma vie* (5 volumes, 1896) or R. L. Williams, *Henri Rochefort* (1966), Pierre Lazareff, *Dernière édition* (n.d., about 1950), and the forth-

coming study of press agencies by Michael B. Palmer. There is of
course a vast amount to be found in the lives and letters of famous
literary figures: the fullest bibliography for them is H. Talvant and J.
Place, *Bibliographie des auteurs modernes de la langue française* (1928 ff. in
many volumes, still in progress).

Painting is the art on which most has been written, though seldom
in a totally satisfying form. Some of the major works are referred to
in the footnotes of chapter 3 above; in addition useful studies of
individual painters and writings by them include: Henri Perruchot,
La Vie de Manet (1959, English translation 1962); Anne Coffin
Hanson, *Manet and the Modern Tradition* (Yale, 1977); G. H. Hamil-
ton, *Manet and his Critics* (1954); Joel Isaacson, *Claude Monet* (Oxford,
1978); John House, 'Claude Monet, his aims and methods', Ph.D.
London thesis, unpublished, 1976; Theodore Reff, *Cézanne, The
Late Work* (1977); Emile Bernard, *Conversations avec Cézanne* (1978);
W. Feldman, 'The Life and Work of Jules Bastien-Lepage', N.Y.
University Ph.D. thesis, 1973, unpublished; T. Reff, *Degas: The
Artist's Mind* (1976); C. Pissarro, *Letters to his son Lucien* (1972);
Reminiscences of Rosa Bonheur, ed. T. Stanton (1910); G. Jean-Aubrey,
Eugène Boudin (1969); Marcel Guicheteau, *Paul Serusier* (1976);
Marc Roskill, *Van Gogh, Gauguin and the Impressionist Circle* (1970); B.
Welsh-Orcharov, *Van Gogh in Perspective* (1974); D. Cooper, *Toul-
ouse-Lautrec* (1950); P. L. Mathieu, *Gustave Moreau* (1977); W. A.
Camfield, *Francis Picabia* (Princeton, 1979); Wayne Anderson,
Gauguin's Paradise Lost (1972); Lilian Browse, *Forain* (1978); J. D.
Flam, *Matisse on Art* (1973); Isabelle Monod-Fontaine, *Matisse*
(1979); Christopher Green, *Léger and the Avant Garde* (Yale, 1976);
J. Milner, *Symbolists and Decadents* (1971); John Russell, *Edouard
Vuillard* (1971); Timothy Hilton, *Picasso* (1975); Françoise Gilot and
Carlton Lake, *Life with Picasso* (1965); P. Courthion, *Georges Rouault*
(1962); M. Sauvage, *Vlaminck* (1956); William S. Rubin, *Dada and
Surrealist Art* (1969); and M. Gieure, *Braque* (1956).

Less studied subjects may be approached through Aaran Scharf,
Art and Photography (1968); Pierre Sorlin *Sociologie du cinéma* (1977);
James Laver, *Taste and Fashion* (1945); Brigid Keenan, *Women we
wanted to look like* (1976); Georges Snyders, *Le Goût musical en France
au 17e et 18e siècles* (1968); Fritz Noske, *French Song from Berlioz to
Duparc* (N.Y., 1970); Lucien Roux, *Vingt ans de chansons de France*
(1966); Michel Dorigné, *Jazz, Culture et Societé* (1967); Jean Cazeneuve, *Sociologie de la radio et télévision* (1976); and visits to the Musée
Forney (for furniture) and the *Musée des Arts Décoratifs*.

To understand scientific speculation and discovery, start, if you
have the courage, with Auguste Comte, *Cours de philosophie positive*

(1830–42): It is indeed four volumes long, but it is one of the most impressive books of all time, even if it is largely misguided; it is as essential to the appreciation of French thought as Darwin is to English thought. See also C. Bernard, *La Science experimentale* (1878); R. Virtanen, *Claude Bernard* (1960) *Marcellin Berthelot* (1965); R. Vallery-Radot, *La Vie de Pasteur* (1900, English translation 1921); Robert Reid, *Marie Curie* (1974); E. Renan, *Souvenirs d'enfance et de jeunesse* (1959 edition); and H. Taine, *The French Philosophers of the 19th century* (English translation 1857). For technological history, start with Patrick Fridensen, *Histoire des usines Renault* (1972), and René Chambre, *Histoire de l'aviation* (2nd edition 1972).

Recreation is beginning to find its historians: Richard Holt, *Sport and Society in Modern France* (1980) is the best introduction. Books on humour are usually unfunny: but one can look at old caricatures (there is a useful guide: J. Lethève, *La caricature et la presse dans la troisième republique* (1961)), one can go to theatres, to the light opera, to the chansonniers, and to the night-clubs which maintain old traditions. Maurice Chevalier's memoirs (in 9 volumes, 1946 ff.) illustrate the world of entertainment quite interestingly. The best historian of food is J. P. Aron, *Le Mangeur de 19e siècle* (1973), to which one could add Curnonsky, *Souvenirs* (1958); one can keep up to date on new research into food history through Alan Davidson's periodical, *Petits Propos Culinaires*. On wine, Nicholas Faith, *The Winemasters* (1978) is a readable introduction on Bordeaux.

INDEX